JEWISH ENLIGHTENMENT IN AN ENGLISH KEY

JEWISH ENLIGHTENMENT IN AN ENGLISH KEY

ANGLO-JEWRY'S CONSTRUCTION
OF MODERN JEWISH THOUGHT

David B. Ruderman

PRINCETON UNIVERSITY PRESS   PRINCETON AND OXFORD

Copyright © 2000 by Princeton University Press
Published by Princeton University Press, 41 William Street,
Princeton, New Jersey 08540
In the United Kingdom: Princeton University Press,
3 Market Place, Woodstock, Oxfordshire OX20 1SY
All Rights Reserved

Library of Congress Cataloging-in-Publication Data

Ruderman, David B.
Jewish enlightenment in an English key: Anglo-Jewry's construction
of modern Jewish thought / David B. Ruderman.
   p. cm.
Includes bibliographical references and index.
ISBN 0-691-04883-5 (cl. : alk. paper)
1. Judaism—Great Britain—History—18th century.
2. Jews—Great Britain—Intellectual life—18th century.
BM292.R93 2000
296′.0942′09034—dc21   00-027869

This book has been composed in Sabon

The paper used in this publication meets the minimum
requirements of ANSI/NISO Z39.48-1992 (R1997)
(*Permanence of Paper*)

www.pup.princeton.edu

Printed in the United States of America

10 9 8 7 6 5 4 3 2 1

IN MEMORY OF

Milton S. Taylor (1909–1995) ⎯⎯⎯⎯⎯⎯⎯⎯⎯⎯⎯⎯⎯⎯

Contents

Illustrations

Preface and Acknowledgments _____

THIS IS a book I never imagined I would write. Having spent most of my scholarly career studying the intellectual and cultural history of Jews in early modern Europe, especially in Italy, Jewish thought in eighteenth-century England always appeared far out of my sights. Furthermore, there seemed to be a clear scholarly consensus that the subject of this book is not a subject at all, or, at least, a subject of little consequence for either English or Jewish history. With little encouragement from the histories I perused about my prospects for uncovering new materials or new perspectives on old materials, my most prudent course might have been to abandon the presumption that my plan was actually worth carrying out. Nevertheless, I persisted, stubbornly and perhaps foolhardily, and the modest results are now before the reader. Before proceeding, some words of explanation are in order on how I embarked on this intellectual journey and how I was able to complete it with the help of supportive and generous colleagues.

My initial encounter with Jewish thought on English soil was most fortuitous. In previously examining the intellectual impact of Padua's medical school on its Jewish graduates in the seventeenth and eighteenth centuries, I noted that one of the most illustrious of this group, David Nieto, decided to uproot himself from Italy to assume a new position, not as a physician, but as the rabbi of the sephardic Bevis Marks Synagogue in faraway London. Through an examination of Nieto's writings, I concluded that Nieto had sufficiently acclimated himself to English culture to take cognizance of the new merger between science and religion preached by some of the Latitudinarian clergy, especially through the widely publicized Boyle lectures of the early eighteenth century. I speculated that Nieto had learned of Samuel Clarke's creative use of Newtonian science to bolster the claims of Christianity and that he adapted Clarke's formulations in presenting his own defense of traditional Judaism. Nieto's creative articulation of the Jewish faith left little immediate impact on his own students and followers.[1] His most accomplished disciple, Jacob Sarmento, even left the synagogue and abandoned Judaism altogether.[2]

---

[1] D. Ruderman, *Jewish Thought and Scientific Discovery in Early Modern Europe* (New Haven and London, 1995), pp. 310–31. See also my discussion in chapter 5.

[2] On Sarmento and the impact of Newtonianism on his thinking, see now M. Goldish, "Newtonian, Converso, and Deist: The Lives of Jacob (Henrique) de Castro Sarmento," *Science in Context* 10 (1997): 651–75.

But Newtonianism, that cluster of scientific, religious, and political ideas that left its far-reaching impact on the culture of England as well as on the Continent, affected profoundly the thinking of several other Jewish figures in England some generations after Nieto, particularly Mordechai Schnaber Levison and Eliakim ben Abraham (Jacob) Hart.[3]

This preliminary exploration of Jewish Newtonians was thus my first entry point into the vibrant cultural space of eighteenth-century England. My second entry point was also unforeseen. Six years ago I assumed a new position as the director of the University of Pennsylvania's Center for Advanced Judaic Studies, the proud heir of the former Annenberg Research Institute and, before it, Dropsie College. The bulk of the center's vast library holdings in Judaica are from the original Dropsie collection assembled at the turn of the twentieth century, and based on the still older collection of Maimonides College, especially the private holdings of Isaac Leeser, the prolific and influential rabbi of nineteenth-century Philadelphia.[4] Scholarly agendas are often shaped by the libraries researchers most regularly frequent. My new encounter with the Leeser collection impressed on me the obvious fact that many Jewish works printed in England in the eighteenth and early nineteenth centuries, like so many Christian works, were almost instantaneously reprinted in Philadelphia and other American cities. Leeser himself was profoundly affected by Jewish thinking emanating from London and, to my pleasant surprise, he collected and probably read almost all the writings of its most published Jewish author and most prominent controversialist, David Levi. Through the guidance of an unpublished paper of Richard Popkin on Levi I had casually perused some years earlier, and which I subsequently encouraged him to publish,[5] I was launched in my quest to retrieve David Levi and his fascinating cultural world. Through the manifold riches of the Leeser library, the other holdings of the center collection, and the other impressive eighteenth-century collections of Philadelphia's outstanding libraries, I enlarged and intensified my initial probings. And before too long, I was becoming a regular visitor to London and its vast library resources as well.

[3] For a general overview of Newtonianism, see B. J. T. Dobbs and M. C. Jacob, *Newton and the Culture of Newtonianism* (Atlantic Highlands, N.J., 1995). I have treated Levison in *Jewish Thought and Scientific Discovery*, pp. 332–68, but see also my discussion in chapter 5 and the appendix. On Hart, see chapter 5.

[4] See R. Singermann, "Books Weeping for Someone to Visit and Admire Them: Jewish Library Culture in the United States, 1850–1910," *Studies in Bibliography and Booklore* 20 (1998): 111.

[5] R. Popkin, "David Levi, Anglo-Jewish Theologian," *Jewish Quarterly Review*, n.s., 87 (1996): 79–101.

One further obstacle remained, however, to deter this new pursuit. For more than a century, historians of Anglo-Jewry have generally maintained that English Jews in the modern period had little or no intellectual history, and whatever they did produce paled in significance to those of their German and eastern European counterparts. Take, for example, the unambiguous judgment of the English rabbi Simeon Singer (1848–1906), writing as early as 1896:

> The Mendelssohnian revival in Germany during the last quarter of the eighteenth century had no counterpart in England. The smallness of the Jewish population, their comparatively recent settlement in this country, the character of their pursuits, which ran almost exclusively in commercial channels, the low state of education, both secular and religious alike, within and outside the Jewish community, may help to explain the absence among them at that period of men, I will not say like Moses Mendelssohn himself—for genius is always an incalculable phenomenon in regard alike to time, place, and circumstances— but of men of the type of the *Meassephim* [the followers of Mendelssohn and promoters of the "Enlightenment" among Jews].[6]

The attitude of more recent Anglo-Jewish historiography, especially in the work of Todd Endelman, has not changed significantly since Singer's decisive verdict. It is all the more remarkable, therefore, that I sought and received so valuable and indispensable assistance and support for this project from Endelman himself and from the other major historian of Anglo-Jewry of this period, David S. Katz. Both scholars encouraged me to pursue my preliminary observations, even when they appeared to be at odds with their own published work, patiently led me to archives and specialized libraries, responded to each and every request I made of them, and eventually read every word of this manuscript, offering me their critical comments, which saved me from so many potential errors. David S. Katz's *The Jews in the History of England, 1485–1850* (Oxford, 1994) had been a virtual goldmine of information and insight to me, as my notes fully acknowledge. There was hardly a book or manuscript of which I made use that Katz had not already seen and for which he was eager to present to me his notecards for my benefit. My dialogue with Todd Endelman, who openly welcomed my criticism of his own position and then helped me refine and sharpen my insight even more, was most meaningful indeed. It is my great pleasure to thank both of these "gentlemen and scholars" for their personal kindness to me and for their critical sup-

---

[6] S. Singer, "Early Translations and Translators of the Jewish Liturgy in England," *Transactions of the Jewish Historical Society of England* 3 (1896–98): 58–59.

port of my endeavors. I could not have written this book without their constant guidance and encouragement.

I am also indebted to several other colleagues and friends who showed great interest in this book and offered their suggestions and insights at critical stages of its evolution. Arthur Kiron, Richard Cohen, and Richard Popkin read the entire manuscript and offered me their detailed comments and criticisms. I received additional encouragement and insight from Stuart Semmel, Moshe Idel, Anthony Grafton, Matt Goldish, Michael Heyd, Joanna Weinberg, and Margaret Jacob. I benefited immensely from five different invitations to address learned colleagues, who heard my initial thoughts on the subject and offered me valuable feedback. They include a conference sponsored by the Boston Colloquium on the History and Philosophy of Science in March 1996; a conference on "Two Nations: The Historical Experience of British and German Jews in Comparison," at Clare College, Cambridge University in September 1997, sponsored by the Leo Baeck Institute of London; a faculty seminar sponsored by the Institute for Jewish Studies of University College London in January 1998; a workshop on the Jewish contribution to Western civilization in honor of the late Isadore Twersky, sponsored by the Institute for Advanced Studies of the Hebrew University, Jerusalem, in June 1998; and a seminar in the research group on the *Haskalah* and the General Enlightenment held at the University of Pennsylvania's Center for Advanced Judaic Studies in January 1999. I also want to thank Brigitta van Rheinberg, my editor at Princeton University Press, for her wise counsel and helpful prodding in improving this work, and Brian R. MacDonald for his careful and judicious effort in copyediting the manuscript, and Alice Calaprice for her conscientious supervision of the entire process of producing the book.

I am most grateful to the supportive staffs of the libraries in which this work was accomplished. First and foremost, I am indebted to the staff of Penn's Center of Advanced Judaic Studies Library, especially Ms. Judith Leifer, for tracking down and finding almost every book and article I requested. I also want to acknowledge the support of the staffs of the University of Pennsylvania's Van Pelt Library, the Library Company of Philadelphia, the Rare Book Library of the Jewish Theological Seminary of America, the British Library, the Bodleian Library of Oxford University, the Jewish Studies Library of University College London, Jews' College Library, the Library of the United Grand Lodge of Freemasons in London, and the Hebrew University and National Library in Jerusalem. I am particularly grateful for the invitation of Professor Mark Geller of the Institute for Jewish Studies of University College London to spend a month as a visiting scholar at the institute, which enabled me to work in the wonderful libraries of London.

I wish to mention several preliminary versions of my work here that were published previously. I first published a succint overview of my subject as "Was There a *Haskalah* in England? Reconsidering an Old Question" (in Hebrew), *Zion* 62 (1997): 109–31. This was followed by "Was There an English Parallel to the German *Haskalah*?" in *Two Nations: The Historical Experience of British and German Jews in Comparative Perspective*, edited by M. Brenner, R. Liedtke, and D. Rechter and coordinated by W. E. Mosse (Tübingen, 1999), pp. 15–44, from which I draw throughout this book, especially in chapters 4 and the appendix. Finally, "On Defining a Jewish Stance Towards Newtonianism: The Case of Eliakim Ben Abraham Hart's *Wars of the Lord*," *Science in Context* 10 (1997): 677–92, is incorporated into chapter 5 of this work. My thanks to all of these publications for allowing me the use of this material in the expanded version of the book.

As in the past, my wife Phyllis has offered me her cheerful and unstinting support and encouragement as I struggled to find time to think about Anglo-Jewish thought in the midst of my heavy administrative duties. In dedicating this book to my uncle, the late Milton S. Taylor (1909–95), I acknowledge an inspiring and supportive mentor of my youth who conveyed to me his constant enthusiasm and deep commitment to Jewish books and to Jewish life.

JEWISH ENLIGHTENMENT IN AN ENGLISH KEY

Introduction _____

IN THE FIRST comprehensive effort to describe the emergence of Anglo-Jewish thought in the eighteenth and early nineteenth centuries, this book introduces the work of a dozen or so hitherto neglected Jewish thinkers who lived and worked in England during the era of the Enlightenment and who articulated their own Jewish identities through a lively encounter with English intellectual and religious currents of their day. As such, it offers a contribution to the history of Jewish culture in England and to Jewish thought during the Enlightenment.

By introducing this new portrait, however, this work aspires to do more: to reconsider the formative beginnings of modern European Jewish culture in general. It seeks to challenge the conventional ways of thinking about the first modern encounters between Jewish and European culture both on English soil and on the European continent as a whole. Its initial point of departure is the new emphasis among several historians who have recently questioned the long-standing assumption that the beginnings of modern Jewish consciousness are to be located exclusively in Germany within the circle of the Jewish philosopher Moses Mendelssohn and his disciples (generally called the *maskilim*).[1] Following this conventional approach, these German *maskilim* eventually inspired Jews elsewhere in the nineteenth century to follow their example by reformulating traditional Jewish thinking in the light of Enlightenment categories. By pointing to a stimulating intellectual encounter between Jewish and English thought manifestly unrelated and uninspired by the better known German experience, I hope to problematize the notion that Jewish strategies of coping with modernity originated exclusively under the aegis and in the pattern of the Berlin *maskilim*. At the same time, by demonstrating the existence of a dynamic intellectual life among English Jews, I simultaneously question the standard account of Anglo-Jewry in this era, which has decisively claimed that Anglo-Jewry had no meaningful intellectual life nor any substantial Jewish thinkers who attempted to reformulate their own religious identity in the light of their exposure to modern English culture.[2] I shall elaborate on both points.

---

[1] The new emphasis is especially evident among several of the contributors in J. Katz, ed., *Toward Modernity: The European Jewish Model* (New Brunswick, N.J., 1987), and even more clearly in P. Birnbaum and I. Katznelson, eds., *Paths of Emancipation: Jews, States and Citizenship* (Princeton, 1995). See also J. Frankel and S. Zipperstein, eds., *Assimilation and Community: The Jews in Nineteenth-Century Europe* (Cambridge, 1992).

[2] I mean especially T. Endelman, *The Jews of Georgian England, 1714–1830* (Philadelphia, 1979).

Almost from the beginnings of modern Jewish scholarship in nine-teenth-century Germany, German Jewry has been deemed the locus of modern Jewish origins, and the German *Haskalah*, the primary paradigm for understanding the transformation of traditional European Jewish soci-eties from the eighteenth century onward.[3] The major exponent of this position in more recent times has been the late Israeli historian Jacob Katz whose classic *Out of the Ghetto* (1973) traced the origins of enlighten-ment, emancipation, and cultural assimilation to German Jewry and ar-gued implicitly that the German model was the proper lens for viewing similar developments among other European Jewries.[4] In a volume of es-says, *Towards Modernity* (1987), meant to offer a more nuanced and refined understanding of Jewish modernity by comparing Jewish societies in Europe and North America, Jacob Katz, the editor, still revealed his own deep ambivalence regarding pluralistic models by upholding the cen-trality of the German one and inquiring how the German Jewish situation influenced what happened elsewhere.[5]

One of Katz's chief critics, both as a contributor to the aforementioned volume and as the author of several works on English Jewry, was Todd Endelman.[6] In his pioneering history of early modern Anglo-Jewry, *The Jews of Georgian England* (1977 and 1999), Endelman challenged Katz's view that modern Jewish history began in Berlin and that it should primar-ily be focused on intellectuals as agents of change. In Endelman's fascinat-ing portrait of a Jewish social world in England inhabited by assimilated aristocracy, middle-class businessmen, rag merchants, pickpockets, and pugilists, he left little room for Jewish intellectuals, either of the tradi-tional or secular bent. In fact, Endelman strongly maintained that his lack of emphasis on the role of intellectuals in shaping Jewish patterns of accul-turation reflected precisely the reality of the community he was studying. There were plainly no seminal figures in England—lay or rabbinic—who contributed to the development of modern Jewish thought or continued the scholarship of rabbinic Judaism. Moreover, those who left the Jewish fold rarely articulated their motives for doing so. Unlike their counter-

---

[3] Two good examples of this dominant view are M. Meyer, *The Origins of the Modern Jew: Jewish Identity and European Culture in Germany, 1749–1824* (Detroit, 1967); and G. Cohen, "German Jewry as Mirror of Modernity," *Leo Baeck Institute Year Book* 20 (1975): ix–xxxi.

[4] J. Katz, *Out of the Ghetto: The Social Background of Jewish Emancipation, 1770–1870* (Cambridge, Mass., 1973).

[5] Katz, *Toward Modernity*, introduction, pp. 1–12. This point is well developed by Pierre Birnbaum and Ira Katznelson in their opening essay, "Emancipation and the Liberal Offer," in Birnbaum and Katznelson, *Paths of Emancipation*, pp. 20–23.

[6] T. Endelman, "The Englishness of Jewish Modernity in England," in Katz, *Toward Modernity*, pp. 225–46.

parts in Germany and in eastern Europe, the Jewish elite of England never created an ideology to justify or promote the modernization of Jewish life: "Well-to-do Jews who embraced the English way of life felt no need to appeal to a set of ideas to justify their actions. They showed little interest in the intellectual reconciliation of English culture and Jewish tradition. . . . Their unarticulated ideal was that of upper class gentility."[7]

As Endelman later admitted, he was not merely offering an English alternative to the Germanocentric model. He was challenging Katz's conviction that ideologically articulated shifts in conscious thought are the landmarks of historical change. In Endelman's formulation, Katz had incorrectly privileged "self-reflective thought over unselfconscious behavior, intellectual life over social life, the educated and the wealthy over the humble and the unremarkable, and the exceptional over the unexceptional."[8] Not only was the German model irrelevant to England, Endelman claimed; it also distorted the German Jewish experience as well. For Endelman, a student of the new social history of the 1960s and 1970s, the modern transformation of the Jews was never exclusively a top-down process "initiated by an urban elite of publicists, reformers, educators, and magnates, who articulated a new vision of Judaism and then labored to convert less 'enlightened' Jews to their outlook."[9] Endelman particularly bridled at the assertion by Katz that intellectual articulation makes new behavior significant in historical terms and that nonreflective accommodation (as exemplified by the English experience) "does not count."[10] For Endelman, such a privileging of intellectual over social history, or of equating consciousness with reality, revealed Katz's ideological bias in German idealism and the shortcomings of his historical judgment.[11]

In this book, I attempt to stake out a position that concurs partially with both positions while arguing simultaneously with each of them. On the one hand, my claim for a Jewish Enlightenment among a small coterie of Anglo-Jews, the product of an intellectual style indigenous to England and independent of German developments, offers a new challenge to the

---

[7] Endelman, *The Jews of Georgian England*, p. 121.

[8] T. Endelman, *The Jews of Georgian England, 1714–1830*, Ann Arbor Paperbacks Edition (Ann Arbor, 1999), p. xi.

[9] Ibid., p. xiii.

[10] Ibid.

[11] Ibid., p. xiv. Katz's point is a bit more complex than Endelman allows. As Katz writes in his introduction to *Toward Modernity*, p. 3, it is not that nonreflective accommodation "does not count," rather that "Factual, nonreflective accomodation, as exemplified by the English experience, is by nature locale-bound. Studied and reasoned change is prone to be mobile." And later (p. 11), Katz adds: "Due to him [Mendelssohn], Jewish aspirations to have access to non-Jewish society were not simply displayed in practice, as in England, but carried out under the cover of intellectual vindication. . . . By virtue of intellectual articulation, the German-Jewish social experiment became mobile."

Germanocentric model. If my argument is correct, the *Haskalah* was not conceived unilaterally in Berlin and Königsberg and needs to be studied regionally and pluralistically, always taking into account the enormous impact of specific social, political, and intellectual stimulants on Jewish cultural formation. On the other hand, the evidence of Jewish intellectual life in England in dialogue with English thought and society complicates the overly simple portrait of nonreflective Jewish modernization and acculturation painted by Endelman. Without privileging intellectual over social history, and without claiming that Anglo-Jewish intellectuals were the primary agents of social change, it is sufficient to argue that Endelman's social emphasis may be, in the end, as misleading as Katz's intellectual one.[12] Jewish modernization in England was never inarticulate or nonreflective. And this insight obliges us once again to rethink the role of ideas and intellectuals in the social and cultural history of modern Jewry. It was neither a "top-down" or a "bottom-up" process, but both—a constant negotiation and reciprocity between persons of variegated economic, social, and intellectual standing.

I

What uniquely marks the intellectual life of Anglo-Jewry in the modern era is the process of translation into the English language and, accordingly, the issue is given prominence throughout the book. English Jews living in the eighteenth century, increasingly native-born, felt the acute need of approaching the literary sources of their culture in the only language they eventually could understand, in English. With the relative decline of Hebrew, Spanish, Portuguese, and even Yiddish as Jewish spoken and written languages, Anglo-Jews, to a degree unprecedented in the rest of Europe, became monolingual. It is, of course, well known that the signature of the Berlin *Haskalah* was Mendelssohn's bold project of translating the Torah into German, albeit with Hebrew characters, for the use of Jews who had mastered or wished to master the German language. But the conditions that motivated Mendelssohn and his colleagues to undertake their translation were hardly similar to those prevailing in eighteenth-century England. Despite the proliferation of Jewish writing in the German language by the end of the eighteenth century, the German *Haskalah* remained both a Hebraic and German cultural movement. For the educational reformers among the later *maskilim*, Hebraic literacy still remained a primary educational goal, albeit with a focus on those ele-

---

[12] See Endelman's own comments in this regard in the Ann Arbor preface to *The Jews of Georgian England*, pp. xviii–xix.

ments of Hebrew culture that were more compatible to the ideals of integration and cultural renewal advocated by this group. In the *Haskalah* of eastern Europe, Hebrew literacy played an even more critical role in the construction of a new curriculum of Jewish and secular studies and in the new emerging republic of letters.

In England, the situation was radically different. In a society that allowed its Jewish minority a relatively higher degree of social integration than anywhere else in Europe, where many professional, educational, and social barriers had practically disappeared by the end of the eighteenth century, despite the failure of the Jew Bill of 1753 and despite a residue of public hostility to both the Jewish upper and lower classes,[13] linguistic assimilation into the English language proceeded rapidly, in the course of one or two generations, across all classes of English Jewish society. The handful of Jewish educators attempting to offer their constituencies an essential textual knowledge of Judaism eventually succumbed for the most part to the weight of this pervasive diminution of Hebraic literacy. Their only recourse was to undertake a massive project of translating the primary sources of their tradition into the language Anglo-Jews could comprehend. Young Jewish students educated in the home, in the synagogue, and in Jewish schools were soon mastering their prayers, their Bible stories, their normative rules of Jewish conduct, and their smattering of rabbinic wisdom through English translations. By the end of the eighteenth century, most English Jews thought about their identity almost exclusively in non-Hebraic, English terms. And through the medium of English translation, their religious attitudes and behavior resembled to an unparalleled degree those of their English Protestant neighbors. Judaism as translated, modified, and glossed in English came to signify something quite different from that experienced by German or eastern European Jewries.

As Anglo-Jews sought to define their religious and cultural identity within a linguistic frame of reference, a kind of English playing field, so to speak, common to both Christians and Jews, the ultimate issues that concerned them, the way they reflected on themselves in relation to the other, and their social and religious aspirations were all thoroughly affected. In a society where the English Bible was central in defining the character of the nation as a whole, English Jews became indistinguishable from their Christian counterparts in learning to appreciate sacred scriptures through the agency of the official King James Version. But some

---

[13] On this, see F. Felsenstein, *Anti-Semtic Stereotypes: A Paradigm of Otherness in English Popular Culture, 1660–1830* (Baltimore and London, 1995), especially chap. 8, which takes issue with the earlier interpretion of T. W. Perry in *Public Opinion, Propaganda, and Politics in Eighteenth-Century England: A Study of the Jew Bill of 1753* (Cambridge, Mass., 1962). See Endelman's cautionary remarks about Felsenstein's approach in the Ann Arbor preface to *The Jews of Georgian England*, pp. xix–xxi.

soon discovered that the English Bible was not necessarily an authoritatively Jewish one, and that translation could often distort the original
meaning of a text, blurring the traditional boundaries that had separated
Jewish from Christian readers and believers. If the translation was inferior
or theologically spurious, how could a Jew who knew better sit silently
by without objecting to the obvious violation of the text and its originally
assigned meaning? At the very least, the official English translation had
previously been dependent on a traditionally Jewish Hebrew version, the
Masoretic text. In an age where Christian clerics were mastering the Hebrew language in an effort to translate anew the original in order to bring
it closer to its "authentic" Christian understanding, and when they even
questioned the reliability of the Masoretic version, the matter became
more complicated for Jewish rabbis and educators alike. Did Christians
actually have the audacity to claim that they could understand the Hebrew text better than Jews, the original guardians of the text? If the Hebrew Bible could be made accessible to Jews and Christians alike in English translation, which translation was to be used? And who had the
ultimate authority to determine the true meaning of the text in translation,
to interpret the authentic words of God?

In the new intellectual world of Christian scholars and clerics armed not
only with Hebraic knowledge but also with a new array of paleographical
and linguistic methods of reading the text, it became increasingly difficult
for the Jews of England, at least their most highly educated, to claim a
commanding position as the proper transmitters and interpreters of the
Holy Bible. In a Jewish community that had virtually translated itself into
an English religious and cultural entity, the challenge of a new Christian
ascendancy of master translators of the biblical text, along with their new
prerogatives claiming exclusive Christian ownership of the text, was felt
acutely and painfully by Jewish leaders and educators. German Jews were
to experience a similar encounter with the new Christian biblical scholarship and its alarming claims to undermine the traditional Jewish hegemony
over the Hebrew text. But English Jews encountered this threat more directly and more profoundly than others given their already considerable
stake in reading and studying the Bible in English translation.

II

Thus, English Jews living at the end of the eighteenth century confronted
educated Anglican and Dissenting clergy equipped with Hebrew knowledge and eager to engage in religious polemics and debate. At the same
time, however, they stood with their Christian counterparts in facing an
array of secularizing ideologies that threatened all religious orthodoxy:

atheism, deism, and Newtonianism, to name only the most obvious and persistent in Enlightenment England. By the time individual Jewish thinkers reflected on these formidable challenges to the foundations of Judaism, there had long developed an arsenal of arguments and strategies for refuting and taming their most lethal assaults within the Christian community. The Jewish response that eventually emerged drew heavily from these Christian arguments and adapted them creatively for Jewish usage. In other words, while similar challenges confronted Mendelssohn and his disciples in constructing a rational Jewish faith within the intellectual world they confronted, their Jewish counterparts in England faced freshly and directly the intellectual challenges of their environment without recourse to the German example and with minimal contact with German Jewish responses. English Jews read Locke, Newton, Stillingfleet, Cudworth, Bolingbroke, and even Voltaire (in English translation) in the original. They absorbed radical ideas about God, revelation, nature, and history from their firsthand engagement with books and conversations present in their own culture and society. Although Locke and the English deists and Newton and his varied interpreters eventually penetrated the German cultural world, German Jews such as Mendelssohn became aware of their impact only through the mediation of their German intellectual environment. For English Jews their contact with both the literature of the radical and religious Enlightenment in England was immediate and unmediated. Their formulation of Judaism against the backdrop of Locke and Newton offered a unique and original response to the secularizing forces of modernity in their own environment.

Along with the impact of new ideas was the formative encounter with novel social and political structures Jews had hardly encountered under absolutist regimes on the continent. With the relative diminution of rigid rules of social behavior isolating and alienating Jews from Christians, English Jews were offered unprecedented opportunities to forge new social relationships with their Christian neighbors. Initially an elite phenomenon involving primarily Jews of wealth, power, or intellect, it increasingly involved Jews of many social and economic levels. Scientific and intellectual societies of all types, Masonic lodges, taverns, and even activities within the home allowed individual English Jews the opportunity for new personal encounters that far surpassed similar opportunities on the continent. No doubt the "semineutral" spaces of German Christian and Jewish dialogue were repeated with greater regularity and with less self-consciousness and among more different kinds of social circles in an English context. And enhanced social contact often meant more intense intellectual contact and theological encounter as well, as the case of Jewish involvement in scientific societies and Freemasonry will make abundantly clear.

Furthermore, in a society whose democratic institutions of government represented a dramatic contrast to the absolutist regimes under which Jews lived in central and eastern Europe, the Jewish encounter with new theories of government, new attitudes about the authority of the state over its citizens, and the appropriateness of dissent and challenge to governmental policies was equally novel and unique. Jews had rarely had the opportunity to live under democratic regimes that treated them almost equally in practice if not in theory. Most English Jews instinctively supported unconditionally and sycophantly the royal family and prayed for its continued welfare. But in rare instances, Jews could also identify with their new form of government by dissenting against some of its policies and practices, a posture virtually impossible in a continental setting. And given the level of normalcy in which free speech was unfettered in the acrimonious public sphere of English culture, Jews could express themselves relatively openly about matters pertaining to Jewish rights and liabilities in a manner unlike that of any contemporary Jewish community throughout Europe.

Thus, under the unique circumstances of English life, a particular Jewish culture emerged shaped from specifically English ideas and English social and political organization, and especially from a culture that conversed and published almost exclusively in the English language. Ultimately, this rich blending of English elements with Jewish culture would create its special effect: the diminution of a separatist Jewish community and elite religious authority; the erosion of Jewish literacy and praxis to the lowest common denominator; the translation of Jewish belief into Protestant terms, with respect to both forms of worship and more personal expressions of religious faith. Those thinkers, publicists, and educators who were most aware of the opportunities and challenges of this new environment consciously responded to them with either enthusiasm or alarm or sometimes a mixture of both. Their response, unlike many of their less articulate coreligionists, was never unreflective or unconscious. Writing in Hebrew and in English, and publishing their work increasingly in the English language, they wrestled with the implications of their new surroundings for Jewish survival and renewal. It is their initial articulations of Jewish self-reflection in a modern English environment that this book sets out to document and analyze and to insert within the gamut of responses to modernity within European Jewish culture.

III

In light of the relative singularity of English Jewish thought in the era of the Enlightenment and its lack of connection with German Jewish culture, should it be labeled a *Haskalah*? Certainly Cecil Roth considered it such in a provocative article he penned as early as 1967 called "The Haskalah in England."[14] Roth was the first to argue that English Jews had a *Haskalah*, although he problematized his case from the outset by the ambiguous manner in which he used the term. He indicated, quite unclearly, that he did not mean the movement for spreading European culture among Jews in central and eastern Europe, only more generally "the movement for the revitalization and modernization of Hebrew culture." Roth admitted that in England as well as in Holland "the lines of this process were blurred" because of the presence of an influential sephardic element with strong interests in Hebrew and general culture long before the time of Mendelssohn.[15] Nevertheless, he felt justified in offering a survey of Jewish writers in England in the late eighteenth and early nineteenth centuries, almost all of them ashkenazic Jews, who wrote primarily in Hebrew and shared common cultural and pedagogic concerns with the Jewish enlightenment of central and eastern Europe. Offering little more than a biographical and bibliographical survey of a handful of Jewish intellectuals and their writings, and providing only scanty evidence regarding the points of substantial intellectual contact with the larger European *Haskalah*, Roth remained considerably vague about the nature of the so-called *Haskalah* in England and its relative significance either for Anglo-Jewry or for modern Jewish thought in general. He also remained imprecise about the genesis of this awakening he had identified. Had it developed indigenously or was it simply the result of cultural contact with Jews from the European continent?

Already in his 1979 book Todd Endelman mentioned Roth's article in passing and dismissed it out of hand.[16] He later elaborated on this conclusion by arguing that the individuals discussed in the article were not communal leaders, did not create institutions to modernize Judaism, and did not constitute a cohesive circle of intellectuals committed to the transformation of the fundamental structure of Judaism.[17] And even later he continued to maintain that Roth had "failed to show there was an ideological movement to modernize traditional Jewish life, which was the hallmark of Jewish enlightenment everywhere."[18]

Endelman was right in underscoring Roth's vague appropriation of the term *Haskalah* and in questioning its suitability for an English context.

---

[14] C. Roth, "The Haskalah in England," in *Essays Presented to Chief Rabbi Israel Brodie on the Occasion of His Seventieth Birthday*, eds. H. J. Zimmels, J. Rabinowitz, and I. Finestein (London, 1967), pp. 365–76.

[15] Ibid., p. 365.

[16] Endelman, *The Jews of Georgian England*, p. 149.

[17] Endelman, "The Englishness of Jewish Modernity," pp. 228–29.

[18] T. Endelman, "Writing English Jewish History," *Albion* 27 (1995): 625, n. 3.

If one adopts the language of some recent historians of the German *Haskalah*, the latter was distinctly "a socio-cultural movement powerful enough to effect a major shift of consciousness . . . more than a fleeting flare-up of ideas supported by a few isolated individuals."[19] It was also "a new ideology to shape a new community . . . a public social world informed with a new ideal of man."[20] By these definitions, an "English *Haskalah*" never came into being, and the implications of Roth's essay that an ideological movement of some kind actually existed are clearly misconstrued.

Yet the term *Haskalah* is more ambiguous than these definitions seem to imply. As Uzi Shavit has argued, the term first emerged among eastern European Jews in the late nineteenth century as an equivalent to the German *Aufklärung*.[21] It has generally been used to designate the specific cultural movement that emerged in Berlin and in Königsberg in the 1780s and 1790s, and later as the movement that took shape in eastern Europe in the 1820s. Despite this more limited usage, it has also been favored as a virtual equivalent for the process of modernization of European Jewry. Most recently, David Sorkin has argued that, more than an internal Jewish response to modernity, it was part of a larger development of religious enlightenment in western and eastern Europe—that is, part of a larger movement that employed enlightenment ideas in the service of revealed religion. By this latter definition, Mendelssohn's rational interpretation of Judaism became the quintessential example of the Jewish version of religious enlightenment.[22]

What is abundantly clear from all of these prior definitions of *Haskalah* from the nineteenth century through that of David Sorkin is their German provenance. Should one use the term only in reference to a paradigm of a cultural and pedagogic movement originating in Germany? Are there paradigms of the *Haskalah* other than the Mendelssohnian or that of its eastern European successors? By adopting the term and considering its applicability to England, are we not in danger of seeing the English case exclusively through the lens of the Germanocentric view of modern Jew-

[19] M. Graetz, "The Jewish Enlightenment," in *German-Jewish History in Modern Times*, vol. 1, *Tradition and Enlightenment, 1600–1780*, ed. M. A. Meyer (New York, 1996), p. 263.

[20] D. Sorkin, *The Transformation of German Jewry 1780–1840* (Oxford, 1987), p. 4.

[21] U. Shavit, "What Is the Haskalah?" (Hebrew), *Meḥkarei Yerushalayim be-Sifrut Ivrit* 12 (1990): 51–83.

[22] See D. Sorkin, "Enlightenment and Emancipation: German Jewry's Formative Age in Comparative Perspective," in *Comparing Jewish Societies*, ed. T. Endelman (Ann Arbor, 1997), pp. 89–112, where he also discusses the previous usages of the term; his "From Context to Comparison: The German Haskalah and Reform Catholicism," *Tel Aviver Jahrbuch für deutsch Geschichte* 22 (1991): 23–58; and his *Moses Mendelssohn and the Religious Enlightenment* (Berkeley and Los Angeles, 1996). See also note 24 below.

ish history that we are trying to overcome, rather than viewing it in its own terms?

The problem is complicated even more by the recent work of Shmuel Feiner on what he calls "An Early *Haskalah*" and on the tenuous relation between Mendelssohn and his maskilic disciples.[23] For Feiner, and also for Sorkin,[24] it is useful to divide the history of eighteenth-century Jewish culture into two distinct periods: a period roughly falling between 1720 and 1770 called the early *Haskalah* and the *Haskalah* proper of the 1770s and 1780s. Feiner and Sorkin, while stressing different aspects in their separate analyses,[25] both concur that this earlier period had primarily a religious and intellectual coloring, whereas the later period focused more on reforming Jewish society through an emphasis on social and political issues. In Feiner's characterization, the early *maskilim* were itinerant intellectuals, physicians, men of traditional Jewish learning primarily from Germany, Poland, and Lithuania, who devoted themselves to the construction of a rational view of Judaism grounded in humanism and an appreciation of the natural world. In their common agenda to expand the intellectual borders of Judaism without undermining traditional Jewish norms, they emerged as a new republic of letters, a secondary elite who, through the publication of their Hebrew works, contributed to the enlargement of Jewish cultural horizons and paved the way, while not being necessarily connected, to the later ideological movement of the 1770s and 1780s. Although Feiner includes in his analysis Jewish intellectuals from diverse origins including Holland, Italy, and eastern Europe—even Mordechai Schnaber Levison, whom I treat as a primarily English Jewish thinker—the focus of his remarks is still primarily Germanocentric. Even the key term of his analysis is borrowed from the German *Frühaufklärung*, as Feiner readily acknowledges.[26]

Even more perplexing is Feiner's perceptive analysis of the relationship between Moses Mendelssohn and his later so-called disciples. Feiner examines a field of some two hundred so-called *maskilim* who were active in Berlin, Königsberg, Frankfurt an der Oder, Breslau, Hamburg, Dessau, Hanover, Copenhagen, Prague, Vienna, Metz, Strasbourg, Shklov, and

---

[23] S. Feiner, "The Early Haskalah in Eighteenth-Century Judaism" (Hebrew), *Tarbiz* 67 (1997–98): 189–240, and his "Mendelssohn and 'Mendelssohn's Disciples': A Re-examination," *Leo Baeck Institute Year Book* 40 (1995): 133–67. See also his "The Dragon Attached to the Beehive: Y. L. Margaliot and the Paradox of the Early *Haskalah*" (Hebrew), *Zion* 63(1997–98): 39–74.

[24] David Sorkin "The Early Haskalah," in *The Berlin Haskalah and German Religious Thought: Orphans of Knowledge* (London and Portland, Or., 2000), pp. 38–62.

[25] Sorkin elucidates the differences in their approach in "Enlightenment and Emancipation," p. 109, n. 15.

[26] Feiner, "The Early Haskalah," p. 203.

even Vilna by the late eighteenth and early nineteenth centuries. He concludes that essentially two distinct groups loosely fit under the banner of the *Haskalah*: an assimilationist intelligentsia, writing in German for primarily non-Jewish audiences with radical and deistic beliefs that led them to abandon altogether Jewish particularism; and reformists who remained within the Jewish fold and wrote in Hebrew while hoping to renovate Jewish culture and society through new programs and institutions.[27] Although Mendelssohn represented a cultural hero to both groups, he had no interest or genuine involvement in the projects of the *maskilim* themselves. He was hardly a reformer but stood alone as a pessimistic philosopher considerably aloof from the enthusiasm of the reformist *maskilim*. Their active, enterprising sense of mission as ideological secular preachers seemed remarkably alien to his nature and his self-proclaimed task to demonstrate the reasonability of Judaism in the modern world. In other words, Mendelssohn himself was more a man of the Enlightenment than a true *maskil*. Men like Wessely, Euchel, Satanov, and the editors of the Hebrew journal *Ha-Me'asef* were the true founders of the *Haskalah*. They were responsible for promoting their own agenda through a Mendelssohnian myth of their construction, as distinct from the actual person.

Utilizing the clarifications of Feiner and Sorkin regarding an early *Haskalah* versus a *Haskalah* proper, and taking into consideration the nonreformist and intellectual persona of Mendelssohn in contrast to that of the later *maskilim*, one can reasonably draw a parallel between him and the English Jewish intellectuals. As men of letters interested in exploring Judaism's reasonability and in probing its relevance in relation to the simultaneous challenges of secularization and Christian assertiveness, the Anglo-Jewish group had much in common with such Jewish men of the Enlightenment as Mendelssohn himself, as well as Marcus Herz, Solomon Maimon, and other primarily intellectual figures who remained generally uninterested in the program of the *Haskalah*. We might conclude that the Anglo-Jewish thinkers considered here might be called "early *maskilim*," albeit with the proviso that they not be reduced to a mere subcategory or English analogue of the Berlin *Haskalah*. They still were different and distinct precisely because their thinking was shaped within an English and not a German environment. And, of course, English Jews did not produce in the end a cultural and pedagogic movement comparable with that of the German *maskilim*.

Whatever similarities can be discerned between the English and German contexts are far overshadowed, however, by the differences between

---

[27] He borrows the terms from Anthony D. Smith, *Theories of Nationalism* (London, 1971), pp. 133–38, as cited in Feiner, "Mendelssohn and 'Mendelssohn's Disciples,' " p. 149.

the two. Under what conditions did the German *Haskalah* emerge and to what extent were these lacking in an English setting? On the surface, it might appear ironic that English (or Dutch) Jews experienced no *Haskalah* proper since they certainly enjoyed greater freedom under the English constitutional regime than in Germany and thus appeared to be more open to their environment and more receptive to its modernizing influence.[28] If English Jews, at least their sephardic and ashkenazic elites, were more acculturated and more accepted socially than their German counterparts, why did they not produce an educational and cultural movement in some way equivalent or even more substantial than that of German Jewry, at least relative to their numbers? And, if Endelman is right, why was integration into English society primarily social and legal-political rather than cognitive?

At the conclusion of his well-known study of the transformation of modern German Jewry, David Sorkin argues that social integration alone was not the critical factor in the emergence of the *Haskalah*. More significant was a critical mass of Jews, especially those living under the norms of traditional Judaism with a concomitant Judaic literacy that could sustain a literary and ideological movement expressed in both Hebrew and German. The German Jewish community constituted 1 or 2 percent of the general population and the English Jewish one just .01 percent, despite its relatively large size as a Jewish community. Equally important were the German factors of incomplete emancipation and partial integration, the discrepancy between German Jewry's actual and idealized situation. Indeed, following this line of thought, Anglo-Jewry's most successful integration, its lack of confrontation with an absolutist government, elicited relatively little creative tension with its environment. Unlike English Jews, who gradually assumed they were English and entitled to the rights and privileges of this status, German Jews were obliged to assert themselves constantly in demanding a status that seemed to elude them and to define themselves and the community to which they belonged by the standards of the universal enlightened ideals of German society. Their ideological reflections and their cultural fermentation were thus a product of their incomplete integration, the gap between their real status and their social aspirations. Their form of *Haskalah* then could only emerge within a condition of political dissatisfaction and social inequality, on the one hand, and a cohesive and Jewishly literate community, on the other. In England, both of these conditions were relatively absent.[29]

---

[28] This is pointed out by Graetz, "The Jewish Enlightenment," p. 264.

[29] Sorkin, *The Transformation of German Jewry*, especially pp. 173–78. Compare also D. Biale, *Power and Powerlessness in Jewish History* (New York, 1986), p. 102: "What is striking about the *Haskalah* is that it emerged only in absolutist states and not in democratic countries such as England or France. Only in those lands where emancipation was delayed

More recently, Sorkin has refined this analysis by describing the particular communities where the German *Haskalah* emerged, specifically Berlin and Königsberg, as new northern towns where Jews were first permitted to settle after the Peace of Westphalia. In these settings, the central European states attempted to graft unnaturally a mercantilist, commercial policy onto a primarily agrarian society. Under such circumstances, the Jews lived with a series of overt contradictions that enhanced the cultural tension with their environment: wealthy Jews were given new economic opportunities but suffered restrictive legislation, while poor Jews were excluded altogether. The German *Haskalah* was thus the product of the tensions inherent in an agrarian society in transition between an older way of life and a newer emerging one. In sharp contrast was the relative absence of tension and explicit *Haskalah* ideology among port Jews, Sorkin's term for Jews living in the relatively open port cities of the Mediterranean, the Atlantic seaboard, and the New World—in, for example, Trieste, Bordeaux, London, Amsterdam, Surinam, and Recife.[30]

Sorkin's analysis makes a powerful case for the unique evolution of the *Haskalah* in Germany, and indirectly in eastern Europe as well, but does not provide a sufficient explanation of the English side of the comparison. Besides the obvious point of accepting too readily Endelman's strong conclusion that English Jews lacked a serious intellectual life, it fails to factor in the unique conditions of English culture that existed at the end of the eighteenth century (before one can consider whether English Jews had a *Haskalah*, one first needs to ascertain whether the English people had an "Enlightenment"), and it discounts too quickly the possibility that, despite the great strides in social integration Jews enjoyed in England, many still remained in creative tension with their environment. In an intellectual and political world still dominated by clerical leaders, as we shall soon see, the issues that traditionally separated Christians from Jews, specifically the right of Jews to preserve their own faith and practice their own religion with impunity, could still be called into question. Even in the relatively open climate of the early nineteenth century, some English Jews continued to feel both overt and covert forms of cultural and social rejection and sought ways to overcome it.

That Jews in England lacked a *Haskalah*, that is, an ideological movement for cultural and political reform, had more to do with the nature of

---

or incomplete, where the Jews were caught between the promise of individual freedom and the reality of continued group disabilities, did a specifically Jewish movement of enlightenment emerge."

[30] See Sorkin, "Enlightenment and Emancipation," pp. 104–6, and his "The Port Jew: Notes toward a Social Type," *Journal of Jewish Studies* 50 (1999): 87–97, which relies on the insight of L. Dubin, *The Port Jews of Habsburg Trieste: Absolutist Politics and Enlightenment Culture* (Stanford, Calif., 1999).

English intellectual life in general than to any Jewish internal factor per se. While the full-fledged movements of *Eclaircissement* and *Aufklärung* were under way and winning intellectual and political victories in France and Germany, an "Enlightenment" movement was unknown in England. Even the widely discussed cluster of ideas known as deism hardly constituted an organized school of thought.[31] Roy Porter's characterization of the Enlightenment in England, written in 1981,[32] comes as close as any in describing what is today a general consensus about England's unique cultural ambience at the end of the eighteenth-century.

Porter begins with the remarkable paradox that while England, through its freethinking, empiricism, and utilitarianism, "irrigated enlightenments everywhere,"[33] it really never had its own. In England, formal and systematic thinking was relatively rare. The world of the writer and his audience in Georgian England had little patience for synthetic philosophy. Ideas were produced in the marketplace, in Masonic lodges, in taverns and coffeehouses, and friendly societies for large public audiences. As coffee table philosophers, English thinkers tended to be concrete, practical, and entertaining. Because most English thinkers easily combined their reasonable Enlightenment goals with their Christian piety, they saw no need to overthrow religion. There were no pope, no inquisition, and no Jesuits. The typical English intellectual was "the scientific parson of the Anglican Church,"[34] who was as fond of Locke or Newton as any French *philosophe*. Citing E. P. Thompson's *The Poverty of Theory*, Porter underscores the lack of systematic thought in England: "Since few intellectuals were thrown into prominence in a conflict with authority, few felt the need to develop a systematic critique. They thought of themselves rather as exchanging specialized products in a market which was tolerably free and the sum of whose intellectual commodities made up the sum of knowledge."[35]

Taking this point one step further, Porter posits two typologies: the French and German philosophers, who painted the world in dualisms and contending opposites; and the English thinkers, who strove for comprehension and harmony in the cosmic and social orders. Porter enlists Locke as the quintessential English thinker exemplifying a shift from the ethic of a transcendental righteousness to "a selfhood which is psychological

---

[31] On this, see, for example, E. C. Mossner, "Deism," in *Encyclopedia of Philosophy* 2 (New York and London, 1967), 327, 331.

[32] R. Porter, "The Enlightenment in England," in *The Enlightenment in National Context*, ed. R. Porter and M. Teich (Cambridge, 1981), pp. 1–18.

[33] Ibid., p. 4.

[34] Ibid., p. 6, n. 46.

[35] Ibid., p. 6, n. 56, cites from E. P. Thompson, *The Poverty of Theory* (London, 1978),p. 59.

and personal."[36] Out of an emphasis on the individual comes a concern for sociability among rational gentlemen, or the "clubbableness"[37] of English cultural life. Despite the social ruptures of class conflicts, the burgeoning of Evangelicalism, and the turmoil of the French Revolution at the end of the century, the English style of enlightenment remained relatively intact, at least through the eighteenth century.

Porter's contrast of English intellectual life to that in France and Germany sounds remarkably similar to the comparison Sorkin has offered between German and English Jews. What Sorkin failed to stress in his comparison of Jewish creative tension with the larger environment in Germany and its relative absence in England was the simple fact that these two Jewish patterns essentially mirrored the larger societies as a whole. In the case of England, Jewish thinkers appear to have patterned their intellectual lives, whether consciously or unconsciously, in the mold of their Christian counterparts. They were clubbish (most belonged to Masonic lodges), individualistic, unsystematic, and eclectic in their interests, and they reflected on a variety of practical, moral, religious, and political issues from diverging points of view.

Yet English Jewish intellectuals deviated from the general pattern Porter describes in one fundamental way, a unique feature that obliges us to refine somewhat the stark lines of Sorkin's contrast between a German Jewish minority in creative tension with its majority culture and an English one where the tension appears not to exist at all. I return to Porter's evocative image of the "scientific parson of the Anglican Church." As B. W. Young has most recently pointed out, the English clergy formed the greater part of the university-trained elite—or, as he puts it, the eighteenth-century university was "as much a seminary as it ever was a finishing school for the political elite."[38] Young is just the latest of a long line of recent scholars, beginning with J.G.A. Pococke, who have argued that the English Enlightenment was decidedly clerical and intellectually conservative in nature. Reacting strongly to Peter Gay's Gallocentric and highly secularized reading of the Enlightenment ("A troupeau des philosophes and their crusade against Christianity"), these English historians have tended to reinstate the significant place of religion in the culture of the Enlightenment by demonstrating especially how religion and political life remained thor-

---

[36] Porter, "The Enlightenment in England," p. 14.

[37] Ibid., p. 15, borrowing the term from Samuel Johnson. On this feature of English life, see S. Shapin, *A Social History of Truth: Civility and Science in Seventeenth-Century England* (Chicago and London, 1994), and for the eighteenth-century and from differing perspectives, J. Brewer, *The Pleasures of the Imagination: English Culture in the Eighteenth Century* (New York, 1997).

[38] B. W. Young, *Religion and Enlightenment in Eighteenth-Century England: Theological Debate from Locke to Burke* (Oxford, 1998), p. 6.

oughly intertwined.[39] Young's focus on William Warburton, "the irascible English bishop" who commanded more attention in his age than David Hume, is as good an example as any of the recent historiographical emphasis on the religiosity of the Enlightenment in England.[40]

Such a historiographic sea change has important implications for studying Jewish intellectual life in England. If religiosity, especially questions of biblical translation and interpretation, were at the very heart of English intellectual life in the period of the Enlightenment; and if such groups as the Hutchinsonians, Methodists, and Unitarians, or such individuals as George Horne, John Wesley, or Theophilus Lindsey played a more central role in shaping the social and religious norms of English culture, it seems more likely that traditional theological passions between Christians and Jews would not dissipate so easily on English soil. They might even flare up in ways unanticipated in the past. Indeed, this is one of the main conclusions of this work: the persistence of medieval Jewish-Christian polemic in a modern guise. In eighteenth-century England, English Protestants debated each other on questions of biblical authority and exegesis. But in discovering in their midst a small Jewish minority as familiar with the English Bible as they were, they constantly drew them into their oft-heated discussions. In so doing, they challenged the viability of Jewish readings of the Bible and concomitantly the nature of Jewish belief in general. Jewish intellectuals, despite their reticence in being drawn into potentially dangerous theological discussions, found themselves obliged to defend the validity of the Masoretic text of the Bible and its interpretive traditions, and to demonstrate anew the legitimacy of their cultural and social position in English society. And in light of the intimate connections between religion and politics in English society, Jewish participation in Christian theological debates had political ramifications as well. In short, in view of the religious coloring of English culture and society in the late

---

[39] See, for example, J.G.A. Pococke, "Post-Puritan England and the Problem of the Enlightenment in England," in *Culture and Politics from Puritanism to the Enlightenment*, ed. P. Zagorin (Berkeley, 1980), pp. 91–111 (the phrase "troupeau des philosophes . . ." is found on p. 92), and "Clergy and Commerce: The Conservative Enlightenment in England," *L'età dei lumi: Studi storici sul settecento europeo in onore di Franco Venturi*, ed. R. Ajello, E. Contese, and V. Piano (Naples, 1985), pp. 523–62; J.C.D. Clark, *English Society, 1688– 1832: Ideology, Social Structure, and Political Practice during the Ancien Regime* (Cambridge, 1985); J. E. Bradley, *Religion, Revolution, and English Radicalism: Non-Conformity in Eighteenth-Century Politics and Society* (Cambridge, 1990); K. Haakonssen, ed., *Enlightenment and Religion in England: Rational Dissent in Eighteenth-Century England* (Cambridge, 1996), especially the introduction; R. Hole, *Pulpits, Politics, and Public Order in England, 1760–1832* (Cambridge, 1989); J. Gascoigne, *Cambridge in the Age of Enlightenment: Science, Religion, and Politics from the Restoration to the French Revolution* (Cambridge, 1989); and Young, *Religion and Enlightenment*.

[40] Young, *Religion and Enlightenment*, pp. 167–212.

eighteenth century, one should not assume the absence of creative tension between Jews and their environment. In consequence of the often contentious religious climate in which they lived as a still conspicuous minority, English Jewish intellectuals were challenged to define themselves against the "other" at many levels and in manifold circumstances.

IV

This book then seeks to reclaim a place for a small group of Jewish intellectuals in England who have been generally neglected in the study of both modern Jewish history and in the history of Anglo-Jewry. It argues for the uniqueness of the English political and social climate in shaping a particular Jewish cultural response to modernity, one, in many ways, unlike those emerging in Germany or in eastern Europe. Wishing to underscore its Englishness, I have tried to point to the parallels of Anglo-Jewish thought with that of the early *Haskalah* and even Mendelssohn himself, while simultaneously delineating the more important differences. Whether one chooses to call the emergence of Jewish self-reflection in modern England an English *Haskalah* or not, there is no question regarding its autochthonous character. One need not assume that English Jews required either the cultural image or the philosophical ideas of Moses Mendelssohn and his followers to precipitate their own ruminations on Judaism and general culture.

The book modestly attempts to correct a certain imbalance in privileging social over intellectual or cultural history in recent Anglo-Jewish historiography.[41] In highlighting the role of religious polemics and theology in both the internal and external intellectual world of Anglo-Jewry, it provides a unique vantage point to view the clerical nature of English cultural and political life in the period of the Enlightenment. In considering the radical nature of Jewish political thinking in England, it also explores an area of Jewish thinking hardly visible elsewhere in the same era, weighing especially how the image and the reality of the Jewish dissenter, as well as the rational and irrational dimensions of dissent in England, apparently converge. Finally, in stressing the role of the English language and the prominence of the English Bible in the shaping of Anglo-Jewish consciousness, it begins to chart a specific regional process—later to characterize not only Anglo-Jewry but American Jewry as well—of cultural develop-

---

[41] On the flowering of Anglo-Jewish social history in recent years, see Endelman, "Writing English Jewish History," pp. 634–35. For a listing of some of the key works, see p. 632, n. 16.

ment patently dissimilar from that of other Jewish communities of modern Europe.

The chapters that follow focus on these large themes by highlighting the careers and the literary output of several prominent figures in the Anglo-Jewish community in the second half of the eighteenth and early nineteenth centuries. David Levi and Abraham Tang appear and reappear throughout, given the prolific nature of their writing as well as the originality of their thinking. But the voices of other figures such as Abraham and Joshua Van Oven, Mordechai Schnaber Levison, Samuel Falk, Eliakim Hart, Raphael Baruh, Isaac Delgado, Solomon Bennett, Hyman Hurwitz, Isaac D'Israeli, Emanuel Mendes da Costa, and Ralph Schomberg are also given a hearing in the following pages. They represent a relatively heterogeneous configuration of individuals, ranging from traditionally conservative to religiously and politically radical, Jewishly observant to religiously assimilated, sephardic to ashkenazic, communal to isolated, immigrants to native-born, and older to younger. The one common denominator that unites them, beyond the fact that they thought and wrote, is their need to reflect in some way about their Jewish identity, whether it was the hundreds of manuscript pages of Tang or the few casual comments of da Costa and Schomberg.

The first two chapters of this work consider in depth one of the most formidable challenges some of these thinkers faced, already alluded to: the need to justify the traditional Hebrew text of the Bible as authentic in the face of a new community of Christian scholars who claimed that, through new "scientific" philological and paleographical methods, they could overcome their dependence on the Masoretic text and on traditional Jewish canons of scholarship. Benjamin Kennicott and the powerful bishop of London Robert Lowth brought with them formidable scholarly credentials in declaring they could reclaim the Old Testament as a Christian text. While Moses Mendelssohn and his colleagues quietly responded to this perceived Christian threat to the legitimacy of the Jewish Bible through their new German translation and commentary, a small group of English Jews found themselves even more entangled, forced to take public positions in the heated controversy over the Kennicott project and the "metrical" English translations of the Bible that emanated from the new Christian scholarship. Maneuvering between the Christian followers of Kennicott and Lowth and their religiously conservative opponents, the Hutchinsonians, they were obliged to insinuate themselves into the debate by defending the authenticity of the Masoretic consonants and points and the integrity of the Jewish tradition that rested on them. In this affair, David Levi was to assume the major role of presenting the Jewish position and upholding its authority.

Chapter 3 considers the role of deism in English Jewish thought, focusing especially on the large body of unpublished Hebrew writings of Abraham Tang. It considers the degree to which English thinking on God, nature, faith, and reason, particularly that saturated with Lockean empiricism, was absorbed by Jewish thinkers in England to a degree previously unknown or unappreciated. The radical nature of Anglo-Jewish thought was a result of the direct encounter with the English sources of Anglican and dissident thinking and appears to be totally independent of such expressions of radical Jewish thought in Germany or elsewhere.

Chapter 4 looks at the place of political radicalism in English Jewish thought. Despite the common assumption that Jews remained traditionally faithful to the monarchy and politically conservative as a vulnerable minority, this chapter considers a number of notable examples that challenge this assumption, including Abraham Tang's public support of John Wilkes, the conversion of Lord George Gordon to Judaism, and the bizarre cultural politics of the *Ba'al Shem* of London, Samuel Falk. Despite David Levi's ostensibly conservative instincts, it also considers his particular style as a form of political radicalism. The chapter both provides a rich example of the originality of English Jewish thinking and even suggests that the genesis of Jewish radical politics might in fact be situated in late eighteenth-century England.

Chapter 5 continues my previous work on the impact of Newtonianism and modern science on Jewish thought in considering, among others, the belated response of Eliakim Hart to Newton and his radical followers. It also considers the place of Judaism in the scientific writing of one of the most notable of scientific writers of the eighteenth century, Emanuel Mendes da Costa.

The final chapter shifts from the articulations of a few intellectuals to examine the more difficult question of the potential impact of these thinkers and their cultural agendas on a larger community and its existential concerns. In so doing, it treats broadly the question of translation—the reconfiguration and reformulation of Judaism in the English language. In returning to the question of the biblicism of English and English Jewish culture, it begins to assess how this critical component of Jewish intellectual life in England transformed both the medium and content of Jewish literacy in England and eventually throughout the English-speaking world.

I close with some brief observations about the legacy of Anglo-Jewish thinking in North America, followed by an appendix on the image of Mendelssohn in Anglo-Jewish culture, one initially of indifference and even disdain in the 1770s to one of adulation and lionization by the third decade of the nineteenth century. This appendix provides some further indication of the autonomy and independence of English Jewish self-reflection at least until the early part of the nineteenth century.

One

"The Scripture Correcting Maniae":[1] Benjamin Kennicott and His Hutchinsonian and Anglo-Jewish Detractors

IN 1775 a relatively obscure sephardic Jew, an immigrant from Leghorn, Italy, published his first and apparently only book in his newly adopted city of London. The author's name, as he wrote it in English, was Raphael Baruh and he entitled his work: *Critica Sacra Examined or an Attempt to show that a new Method may be found to reconcile the seemingly glaring Variations in Parallel Passages of Scripture and that such Variations, consequently, are no Proofs of Corruptions or Mistakes, of Transcribers.* Baruh, despite his obvious liabilities as both a Jew and a foreigner, boldly entered the arena of public debate over a highly contentious and polarized issue located at the very core of Christian self-identity in eighteenth-century England: Benjamin Kennicott's project to establish a novel and correct Hebrew text of the Old Testament.

Kennicott's ambitious attempt to collate all extant Hebrew manuscripts in order to reconstruct the original version of the Hebrew Bible has long been recognized as a milestone in biblical scholarship, ushering in a more systematic and comprehensive examination of the formation of the biblical text and canon by subsequent scholars.[2] That Kennicott's project evoked a not inconsiderable debate among English and continental Christian theologians and exegetes is also well known, though suprisingly less studied than one would imagine.[3] Additionally, a recent study has ex-

---

[1] The phrase in the chapter title is that of David Levi, *Dissertations on the Prophecies of the Old Testament*, vols. 1–3, 2nd ed. (London, 1817–1819), 1:266: "I cannot here forbear observing, that Bishop Lowth's note on this verse, is one of the most false, and wretched pieces of criticism ever penned; and appears to me, to be the consequence of an infatuate adherence to systems; one of which . . . may not unaptly be called the *Scripture Correcting Maniae*, with which, for some few years back, the Christian commentators, but more especially, the Authors of the *New*, and *Metrical translations* of the Prophetic writings, have been so miserably afflicted."

[2] On Kennicott and his project, see *Dictionary of National Biography* 31 (London, 1892): 10–12; W. McKain, "Benjamin Kennicott: An Eighteenth-Century Researcher," *Journal of Theological Studies* 28 (1977): 445–64.

[3] In addition to the works cited in the previous note, see D. S. Katz, "The Hutchinsonians and Hebraic Fundamentalism in Eighteenth-Century England," in *Sceptics, Millenarians,*

plored the stimulus of Kennicott's endeavor in understanding the evolution of Moses Mendelssohn's Bible translations and commentaries in Germany.[4] But the storm over Kennicott, at least in its initial stages, was essentially an English phenomenon engaging the energetic responses of a remarkably large number of clerics and other intellectuals, even including the king himself. And given the pretentious claims of those who heralded the new scholarship of Kennicott as a watershed in reclaiming the Hebrew text for Christians by liberating it from the previously unchallenged authority of the "rabbins," it could hardly go unnoticed by the small community of Jewish scholars living and working in London and Oxford in close proximity to where Kennicott had established his reputation and following.

Raphael Baruh's modest effort thus represents no less than the tip of a huge iceberg, signaling a stormy sea of controversy and mutual recriminations among Christians, which eventually involved Jews as well. A project merely seeking to establish the correct text of the Hebrew Bible by utilizing the latest methods of biblical criticism, the systemic collation of Hebrew manuscripts, and the comprehensive study of ancient translations soon became a cause célèbre in a war of passionate spokesmen, each claiming to determine which text to study, how to study it, and who was ultimately authorized to establish its true meaning. Despite the novelty of Kennicott's program, the issues he has raised were profoundly related to a longer continuum of efforts to define Christianity and its scriptural foundations against the older and competing claims of Jewish self-understanding and exegesis of the Bible. Ironically set against the backdrop of a highly secularized and sophisticated London society of politicians, book publishers, theatergoers, and merchants, a new and critical phase of the Jewish-Christian debate, the legacy of centuries of Catholic, Protestant, and Jewish self-reflections and interfaith rivalries, was unfolding with startling intensity and unbridled fervor. Baruh's modest reflections on the alleged "sacredness" of the new Christian critical study of the biblical text thus provide an appropriate opening into a significant chapter in the history of Christian self-understanding as well as Jewish-Christian debate and the intimate links between the two. That Jews like Baruh living in London, though small in number, participated in this debate, playing a critical role both publicly and behind the scenes, represents a curious circumstance virtually unnoticed by previous scholarship. By exploring this contemporaneous Jewish response to the Kennicott debate in its various

---

and Jews, ed. D. S. Katz and J. Israel (Leiden, 1990), pp. 237–55, and see my subsequent discussion.

[4] E. Breuer, *The Limits of Enlightenment: Jews, Germans, and the Eighteenth-Century Study of Scripture* (Cambridge, Mass., 1995).

manifestations, we can place it within the larger and multifaceted discussion among Christians that was unfurling with increasing tension from the time Kennicott first reported on his grandiose program for biblical reform at midcentury.

I

Who was Raphael Baruh; what prompted him to leave his native home for England; and what were the circumstances that led him to produce his book? The meager data about his life hardly allow us to answer any of these questions. One can initially point to the path of other Leghorn Jews of converso ancestry, who made their way, primarily for commercial reasons, to the dynamic economic centers of Amsterdam and London. Sephardic Jews settled in London throughout the seventeenth and eighteenth centuries, including the distinguished Italian Jew of sephardic ancestry, David Nieto, who came to serve as rabbi of the Bevis Marks Synagogue in the city of London at the beginning of the eighteenth century.[5] Coincidentally, the only other work written by Baruh is an extant Hebrew poem he composed to eulogize the death of Isaac Nieto, David's son and rabbinic successor, who died in the early 1770s.[6]

Baruh's birthplace was a significant entrepôt of commerce and Jewish cultural activity in the eighteenth century, attracting rabbinic scholars and

---

[5] For a brief overview of the history of Leghorn Jewry, see *Encyclopedia Judaica* 10 (Jerusalem, 1971): 1570–73. Its history until 1700 is treated by R. Toaff, *La Nazione ebrea à Livorno e à Pisa (1591–1700)* (Florence, 1990); F. A. Levi d'Ancona, in "The Sephardi Community of Leghorn (Livorno)," *The Sephardi Heritage*, ed. R. D. Barnett, vol. 2 (New York, 1971), pp. 180–202; R. Bonfil, "The History of the Spanish and Portuguese Jews in Italy," *Moreshet Sepharad: The Sephardic Legacy*, ed. H. Beinart, vol. 2 (Jerusalem, 1992), pp. 217–39. On the sephardic migration to England in general, see A. M. Hymanson, *The Sephardim of England: A History of the Spanish and Portuguese Community, 1492–1951* (London, 1970); V. D. Lipman, "Sephardi and other Jewish Immigrants in England in the 18th Century," in *Migration and Settlement: Procedings of the Anglo-American Jewish Historical Conference Held in London . . . , July, 1970* (London, 1971), pp. 37–62; R. D. Barnett, "Anglo-Jewry in the Eighteenth Century," in *Three Centuries of Anglo-Jewish History*, ed. V. D. Lipman (London, 1961), pp. 45–68. On Nieto, see Ruderman, *Jewish Thought and Scientific Discovery in Early Modern Europe* pp. 310–31, with references to earlier scholarship. The links between Leghorn and London deserve further study in light of their importance for such prominent figures of the nineteenth century as Moses Montefiore and Sabbatai Morais.

[6] See I. Solomons, "David Nieto and Some of His Contemporaries," *Transactions of the Jewish Historical Society of England* 12 (1931): 82–83. I should also mention the only other account of Baruh's response to Owen in S. Daiches, "The Beginnings of Anglo-Jewish Biblical Exegesis and Bible Translation," *Miscellanies of the Jewish Historical Society of England* 4 (1942): 20–24.

especially students of the kabbalah throughout Italy and the entire Mediterranean basin.[7] His brother, Jacob Baruch was a noteworthy Hebrew scholar who compiled a Hebrew anthology entitled *Shivḥei Yerushalayim* (The Praises of Jerusalem), containing the works of several authors on the holy sites of Jerusalem and the land of Israel. The work enjoyed great popularity and was republished some ten times after its initial appearance in 1785 in Leghorn. Some five years later Jacob edited a part of Yohanan Alemanno's fifteenth-century commentary on the Song of Songs, which he called *Sha'ar ha-Ḥeshek* (The portal of delight).[8] Alemanno, a complex thinker with strong philosophical, kabbalistic, and magical interests, had written this previously unpublished work at the behest of Pico della Mirandola in Florence.[9] Jacob's desire to save this work from oblivion is most interesting in the light of his own syncretistic interests. It might be favorably compared with the almost simultaneous republication of part of the kabbalistic works of Joseph Delmedigo, a seventeenth-century Italian kabbalist who might even be considered a kind of disciple of Alemanno, by Eliakim ben Abraham Hart, a probable acquaintance of Jacob's brother Raphael in London.[10] Judging from Baruch's approbation of Alemanno's work and his strong scientific interests, as suggested by his introductory remarks, Jacob too appears to be a complex thinker with an amalgam of kabbalistic and other intellectual concerns.[11]

Raphael's intellectual profile is relatively unknown except for a few tantalizing references to him and his limited literary output. His more prolific contemporary Mordecai Gumpel Schnaber Levison refers to his English work favorably and acknowledges him as a friend in the introduction to his Hebrew commentary on *Kohelet*.[12] The same reference is copied rather awkwardly by Jacob in his introduction to Alemanno's work, who noticed the publicity Raphael received through Levison's notice and obviously took great pride in the accomplishment of his brother.[13] In addi-

---

[7] In addition to the references cited in note 5, see G. Scholem, *Sabbatai Sevi: The Mystical Messiah* (Princeton, 1973), index, s.v. "Leghorn"; G. Scholem, *Meḥkarei Shabta'ut*, ed. Y. Liebes (Tel Aviv, 1991), pp. 489–567.

[8] On Jacob Baruch and his writings, see *Encyclopedia Judaica* 4 (Jerusalem, 1971): 274 and the references cited.

[9] On Alemanno and his work, see, for example, M. Idel, "The Magical and Neoplatonic Interpretations of the Kabbalah in the Renaissance," *Jewish Thought in the Sixteenth Century*, ed. B. Cooperman (Cambridge, Mass., 1983), pp. 186–242.

[10] Hart's work is entitled *Ẓof Novelot* and was published in London in 1799. On Hart, see chapter 5.

[11] He clearly deserves further study. I have consulted the reprint of *Sha'ar ha-Ḥeshek* (Halberstadt, 1862). The introduction is found on pp. 2b–5a.

[12] Mordechai Gumpel Schnaber Levison, *Tokhaḥat Megillah* (Hamburg, 1784), p. 2b. See my appendix.

[13] Jacob Barukh, *Sha'ar ha-Ḥeshek* (Halberstadt, 1862), p. 5a.

tion to the aforementioned connection Raphael had with Isaac Nieto, we can also point to the interesting fact that the copy of the *Critica Sacra Examined* in the original Mocatta collection, presently housed in the library of University College London, was owned by Abraham Van Oven, another physician and prominent member of London's Jewish intellectual elite.[14] Both Van Oven and Levison were ashkenazim who obviously appreciated their sephardic colleague's intellectual achievement.

Although the general thrust of Baruh's work is directed to the Kennicott enterprise, it was clearly written as a direct response to another small work composed by Henry Owen (1716–95) entitled *Critica Sacra or, A Short Introduction to Hebrew Criticism* published in London in the previous year. Owen was both a physician and ordained clergyman who held the rectory of St. Olave, Hart St., in London while serving as chaplain to Dr. Shute Barrington, the bishop of Llandaff.[15] Owen's reputation as a scholar and theologian was considerable; he even served as Boyle lecturer between 1769 and 1771. Among his numerous publications, his study of the Septuagint and Samaritan versions of the Old Testament in relation to the Hebrew stand out. He was obviously a scholar who was capable of and committed to defending Kennicott and his accomplishments. His book, a kind of introduction and strong endorsement of Kennicott's project, was published without the name of its author, leaving the mistaken impression that Kennicott himself might have penned the work. In the light of Baruh's reply to the book, however, Owen was obliged to reveal his identity in a *Supplement to Critica Sacra in which the Principles of that Treatise are Fully Confirmed and the Objections of Mr. Raphael Baruh Clearly Answered*, published in 1775.[16]

To the reader of Kennicott's earlier and more weighty publications, Owen's arguments rehearse already articulated positions of his Oxford mentor.[17] Owen argued like Kennicott that Scripture had not reached us "in a pure and perfect state"; on the contrary, "Many great and grievous corruptions, occasioned by the ignorance or negligence of transcribers," had been introduced over the centuries.[18] It was the purpose of the new critical method "to compare together, in the Hebrew text, the several cor-

[14] On Abraham Van Oven and his literary work, see my subsequent discussion.

[15] Isaac Delgado, Baruh's sephardic contemporary, dedicated his work on the Bible to Barrington some fourteen years later. He too was even encouraged by Owen. See chapter 6. On Barrington, see *Dictionary of National Biography* 1 (New York, 1909): 1214.

[16] On Owen, see *Dictionary of National Biography* 42 (New York, 1909): 412–13. The confusion regarding the authorship of *Critica Sacra* is reflected in the British Library's listing, which attributes the work to Kennicott himself.

[17] Kennicott's writing is treated later. See also note 5.

[18] Henry Owen, *Critica Sacra or, A Short Introduction to Hebrew Criticism* (London, 1774), p. 5.

respondent passages of Scripture; noting their differences; and then adopting those particular readings, which best agree with the tenour of the context, and the rules of grammar."[19] Upon noting the parallels within Scripture, it was further possible to consult ancient versions, especially the Samaritan version of the Pentateuch discovered in the previous century. Such a systematic and exhaustive study of the text and its versions could not help but yield positive results whereby "many corruptions may be discovered and the true readings restored."[20] In addition to offering his own numerous examples of this system, Owen referred his readers to Dr. Kennicott's own work, especially his comparison of the books of Samuel/Kings with Chronicles found in the first volume of his *State of the Printed Hebrew Text of the Old Testament Considered a Dissertation in Two Parts*, a study "well worthy of imitation."[21]

Baruh's reading of the Owen pamphlet prompted him to publish his own rejoinder. It is obvious that he had also carefully studied Kennicott's original publications and referred to the latter throughout his own exposition. His tone is restrained and polite throughout. He would not make extravagant claims for the inviolability of the Hebrew printed text: "It's not my intention . . . to maintain, by any means, that a continual miracle was performed in favor of Jewish transcribers, that no errors might be ever committed by them in their copies of the Old Testament; this being what the Jews themselves do not pretend to. . . . Nor do I pretend to hold, that the printed Hebrew text is absolutely free from any the least error; this would be preposterous and insupportable."[22] He proposes instead a cautious and self-imposed discipline in evaluating the alleged corruptions found in the Hebrew text. No passage should be deemed corrupted upon mere conjectures or on the authority of parallel passages alone. Only after "a great number of ancient copies of known and established character" have been examined and after "very mature deliberation" should any emendations be introduced at all. Baruh has no doubt about Dr. Kennicott's "integrity and candour," but he is concerned that some of Kennicott's readings are highly conjectural and too hastily offered.[23]

The approach Baruh advocates instead is indeed a traditionally Jewish one. The Masoretic text with its variant readings and list of corrections (*tikkun sofrim*) already acknowledges that its text is the best possible reading but hardly perfect. Furthermore, "it is unanimously allowed by

---

[19] Ibid., p. 6.

[20] Ibid., p. 24.

[21] Ibid. p. 25. Owen refers specifically to Benjamin Kennicott, *The State of the Printed Hebrew Text of the Old Testament Considered a Dissertation in Two Parts*, vol. 1 (Oxford, 1753), pp. 19–247 (hereafter cited as *Dissertations*).

[22] Raphael Baruh, *Critica Sacra Examined* (London, 1775) , p. i of the preface.

[23] Ibid., pp. ii–iii.

the Jews that even at the establishment of the canon of the Bible, in the time of Ezra, some various readings were found; and such were preferred and admitted in the text which were authorized by the greater number of the esteemed copies. . . . The same method was followed in after times, by Jewish criticks, who laboured hard in comparing and collating ancient copies, to render the text as pure and genuine as possible."[24] In this regard, Baruh refers to the critical readings of the printed texts by his fellow countrymen, the Italians Menaḥem de Lonzano (1550–c. 1624) and Yedidyah Solomon Norẓi (1560–1616), who offered corrections to the Masora upon the authority of ancient readings.[25] The implication is clear: the Kennicott initiative is not new nor is it radically different from what Jewish critics had been doing for years. Kennicott's "attempt merits the greatest commendation" since it represents "a very useful undertaking" but it should be seen as a continuation of an approach pursued by the Jews themselves up until the present.[26]

Nevertheless, there remains a significant gap between Kennicott's liberties with the standard text and the more modest emendations by the Jewish students of the Masora. The latter acted in a more restrained manner because they realized their limitations in reconstructing an authentic text solely on the basis of parallel passages and manuscripts that are often unreliable. In such a situation, "we should endeavor to reconcile or explain them [problematic passages], by studying with great attention, the genius of the Hebrew language."[27] Baruh explains that he had previously undertaken an exhaustive collation of the entire book of Chronicles. When the *Critica Sacra* "fell into his hands," he decided to draw from his larger work to offer a case study on how to deal with discrepancies be-

[24] Ibid., p. i.

[25] On the history of the Masoretic text and its critical study by Jews before the eighteenth century, see C. D. Ginsburg, *Introduction to the Massoretico-Critical Edition of the Hebrew Bible* (London, 1897; reprint, New York, 1966); E. Wüethwein, *The Text of the Old Testament* (Grand Rapids, Mich., 1995); M. Goshen-Gottstein, "The Rise of the Tiberian Bible Text," in *Biblical and Other Studies*, ed. A. Altmann (Cambridge, Mass., 1962), pp. 79–122; P. E. Kahle, "The Hebrew Text of the Compluensian Polyglot," *Homenaje a Millas-Vallicrosa* (Barcelona, 1954), 1: 741–51; S. Z. Leiman, ed., *The Canon and Masorah of the Hebrew Bible: An Introductory Reader* (New York, 1974); H. Orlinsky, "The Textual Criticism of the Old Testament," in *The Bible and the Ancient Near East*, ed. G. E. Wright (Garden City, N.Y., 1961), pp. 113–32; S. Talmon, "The Old Testament Text," *The Cambridge History of the Bible*, ed. P. R. Ackroyd, G.W.H. Lampe, and S. L. Greenslade, 3 vols. (Cambridge, 1963–70), 1:159–99; B. J. Roberts, *The Old Testament Texts and Versions: The Hebrew Text in Transmission and the History of the Ancient Versions* (Cardiff, 1951); E. Tov, *The Textual Criticism of the Bible* (Philadelphia, 1992); I. Yeivin, *Introduction to the Tiberian Massora*, trans. and ed. E. J. Revell (Missoula, Mont., 1980); Breuer, *The Limits of Enlightenment*, pp. 29–40.

[26] Baruh, *Critica Sacra Examined*, pp. iv–vii. The citation is from p. vi.

[27] Ibid., p. vi.

tween biblical passages, in this case between the narratives found in the books of Samuel and Kings and between those in Chronicles. His objective then is "to throw light on those passages which he [the Chronicler] purposely copied out of other books; and by altering, adding some phrases, meant only to explain such dark passages, or to resolve a difficulty which stared in the face of the Reader, in those very ancient accounts, as they stood recorded." In other words, Baruh elected to revisit the same texts treated in great detail by Kennicott in his extensive treatment of the historical narratives of the Bible in the first volume of his *Dissertations*. To Baruh's way of thinking, the variations between Chronicles and the earlier books were not the result of scribal mistakes and omissions. Rather, they were purposeful, introduced by the Chronicler himself who simply chose "to record some facts, to restore some deficiency or even to introduce a different account of some circumstance in history, as he found it registered in some other authentick record, not quite agreeing with that recorded in those ancient books. . . . This inspired man chose rather this method of repeating with some variation what had been so recorded, than to take upon himself to alter the Originals."[28]

In the next 250 pages Baruh then offers a close reading of selected passages in Samuel/Kings and in Chronicles that appear to contradict each other in an effort to offer a rational explanation for each discrepancy. So, for example, Baruh considers the differences between the lists of David's mighty men presented in 2 Samuel 22 and 1 Chronicles 11. It is obvious, claims Baruh, that the lists are distinct and separate, "intended to serve for the history of two different periods of David's reign, and consequently cannot be collated together for the purpose of correcting the supposed errors in either of them."[29] This example leads Baruh to a general formulation of his understanding of the role of the Chronicler:

> Upon the whole, the history in Chronicles is to be looked upon as additional, or explanatory, to that in Samuel, only repeating those things, which he thought required an elucidation; and indeed it seems evident, that the book of Chronicles was wrote to serve as an appendix, or illustration to other parts of Scripture. On this Supposition, I flatter myself, the studious Reader will be able to account with ease for most of the other variations between the corresponding passages, without rashly determining them to be corruptions or mistakes of transcribers.[30]

In still another explanation of the Chronicler's role, he plainly states that "his purpose was that of a commentator."[31]

---

[28] Ibid., pp. 7–8.
[29] Ibid., p. 31.
[30] Ibid., p. 42.
[31] Ibid., p. 83.

Whether the differences in the two versions were the result of sloppy transmission, as Kennicott had maintained, or of intentional editing and commentary, the view of Baruh, or both,[32] this Jewish exegete had, at the very least, raised some doubts about Kennicott's self-assured pronouncements. Owen could not remain silent for long.

Owen's *Supplement to Critica Sacra* appeared in the same year as Baruh's publication. Both the haste in which he prepared a response and the respect which he displays to "the learned examiner. Mr. Raphael Baruh"[33] testify to the serious impression Baruh's composition had made on him. His own rebuttal was less an examination of specific readings and more a general evaluation of Baruh's method. He picks up on Baruh's admission that the Jews themselves had acknowledged that the Masoretic text was far from perfect. And if they admit some mistakes, there are still others that they overlooked or neglected. Baruh's elaborate effort to reconcile the differences in the spellings of names of people and places between the two versions remains unconvincing. For Owen, it is more honorable to Scripture to "admit some slight mistakes than by running into those fanciful and groundless etymologies which Mr. Baruh recommends for the reconciliation of the passages."[34] In the final analysis, Baruh's stance is unworthy of further response since his religious affiliation pre-

---

[32] For a fine overview of earlier and contemporary views of the Book of Chronicles, see S. Japhet, *I and II Chronicles: A Commentary* (London, 1993), and her "The Historical Reliability of Chronicles: The History of the Problem and Its Place in Biblical Research," *Journal for the Study of the Old Testament* 33 (1985): 83–107. See also S. L. McKenzie, *The Chronicler's Use of the Deuteronomistic History*, Harvard Semitic Monographs, no. 33 (Atlanta, 1984); M. P. Graham, *The Utilization of 1 and 2 Chronicles in the Reconstruction of Israelite History in the Nineteenth Century* (Atlanta, 1990). As Japhet points out in the introduction to her commentary (pp. 31–32), Baruh's view of Chronicles as a commentary on Samuel/Kings was shared by several scholars of the nineteenth and twentieth centuries beginning with Leopold Zunz, who understood the book as the midrashic activity of "the men of the Great Assembly." See, for example, I. L. Seeligmann, "The Beginnings of Midrash in the Book of Chronicles" (Hebrew), *Tarbiẕ* 49 (1979–80): 14–32; P. R. Ackroyd, "The Chronicler as Exegete," *Journal for the Study of the Old Testament* 2 (1977): 2–32; T. Willi, *Die Chronik als Auslegung, Forschungen zur Religion und Literatur des Alten und Neuen Testaments*, vol. 106 (Gottingen, 1972); M. Fishbane, *Biblical Interpretation in Ancient Israel* (Oxford, 1983), pp. 385–403. Japhet (*Commentary*, p. 24) also points out how the comparison between the two versions of biblical history became a favorite in illustrating the general features of biblical transmission. By comparing Chronicles to its biblical sources, scholars could point out the many differences caused by either international editing or unintentional scribal errors. In other words, both the positions of Kennicott and Baruh have their support in subsequent scholarship on the subject, acknowledging both textual corruption in the standard text as well as conscious editing or a combination of both.

[33] Henry Owen, *Supplement to Critica Sacra in which the Principles of that Treatise are Fully Confirmed and the Objections of Mr. Raphael Baruh Clearly Answered* (London, 1775), p. 4.

[34] Ibid., p. 29.

cludes him from ever acknowledging the truth: "I must not however expect, that the prejudices of my opponent and those of his persuasion
should be so easily removed. But, nevertheless, I am not without hopes,
that when the Jews come to observe the vast multitude of various readings
which Dr. Kennicott has collected, chiefly from their own manuscripts,
their high preconceived opinion of the absolute integrity of the Hebrew
Scriptures will gradually subside."[35]

II

The relatively calm and dignified exchange between Owen and Baruh
took place some twenty-two years after Benjamin Kennicott had published the first of his famous *Dissertations* and years after a series of controversies had erupted in the Anglo-Christian community over the intellectual flaws and theological perils inherent in Kennicott's entire project.
It is clearly beyond the scope of this chapter to reconstruct fully the histories of these debates and their significance for Christian theology and exegesis. Rather, I would like to focus only on two stages of these debates
relevant to the Jewish involvement and response to the Kennicott phenomenon: the initial outburst of criticisms leveled at Kennicott immediately after the publication of his first volume in 1753 from one particular
school of theology, known generally as the Hutchinsonians, named after
their founder John Hutchinson (1674–1737);[36] and a new flare-up of denunciations emerging in the mid-1770s at the same time Owen and Baruh
were sparring. In the latter case, the detractors of Kennicott went far beyond the measured words of Mr. Baruh to undermine both the intellectual
and religious legitimacy of Kennicott's entire enterprise. Both waves of
public debate allow us not only to contextualize Baruh's own critique
but also to set the stage for the more ambitious and extensive assault on
Kennicott and his admirers by a more prominent member of the Anglo-
Jewish community, David Levi, the subject of the next chapter.

Kennicott's *The State of the Printed Hebrew Text of the Old Testament
Considered a Dissertation in Two Parts* was published in two stages in

---

[35] Ibid., p. 31.

[36] I am well aware of the coincidence of this debate over Kennicott in the same year as
the controversy over the so-called Jew Bill. On the latter, see Perry, *Public Opinion, Propaganda, and Politics in Eighteenth-Century England*; Felsenstein, *Anti-Semitic Stereotypes*,
pp. 187–214; and J. Shapiro, *Shakespeare and the Jews* (New York, 1996), pp. 195–224.
On the surface, I have not noticed any direct connection between the participants in this
conflict, especially the Hutchinsonians, with those who opposed the Jew Bill of the same
year. But the subject requires more study. At the very least, it should be stated that two
public debates about the standing of the Jews in English society were raging simultaneously,
whether or not they were at all connected in the public mind.

Oxford in 1753 and 1759. Kennicott stated his objective quite clearly in the opening pages of his first volume: "to compare Scripture with itself, to explain a difficult phrase or passage by a clear one, that bears some relation to it, to consider the natural force of the Original Words, the tendency of the Context, and the Design of the Writer; to compare the most ancient editions of the Original, with one another, and with the best copies of the most celebrated versions."[37] This dual approach of comparing parallel passages with the Bible while collating them with ancient manuscripts was clearly not new, as we have seen, because Jewish exegetes, including the Masorites themselves, had long been engaged in such activity. Furthermore, the earlier editions of the Hebrew Bible, the Complutensian Polyglot edited by Francisco Ximenes, the archbishop of Toledo, in 1514–17, as well as the rabbinic Bible of Jacob Ben Hayyim, printed by Daniel Bomberg in 1516, both published under Christian auspices, had relied extensively on ancient manuscripts in attempting to establish the authentic Hebrew text.[38] What was new about Kennicott's attempt was its ambitious scope and its dramatic claims that he could eventually recover the original text of the Bible. Thus, he believed, "the Honour of Revelation" would be vindicated "that so the Bible, the gracious gift of God to Man, may be universally receiv'd, unexceptionably admir'd and beyond all contradiction, appear to what it really is, worthy of God and worthy of all acceptation."[39]

Kennicott implies but does not state explicitly that his agressive search for new manuscripts, his assembling of a large staff of assistants and collators, and the extraordinary fund raising involved in sustaining his project are all motivated by a Christian purpose, to wrest the authority of determining the words of divine revelation from the Jews and to restore them to Christians. He is careful not to blame mistakes on the prejudices of Jewish transcribers, "since there are sufficient proofs, that the existence of mistakes has been, by the wiser part of them, in fact acknowlg'd in the Hebrew text."[40] The Jews did not willfully corrupt the Old Testament, he openly acknowledges at another point. But the Jews are not fully exonerated either: "And yet there can be no doubt but that the later Jews, where they have found copies reading differently in any passages relating to the Messiah, may have sometimes preferr'd that Reading which was the least favourable to the Christian Cause."[41]

---

[37] Kennicott, 1:12.

[38] On the Complutensian Polyglot, see Kahle, "The Hebrew Text"; on Jacob Ben Hayyim, see J. Penkower, "Jacob Ben Hayyim and the Rise of the *Biblia Rabbinica*" (Hebrew) (Ph.D. dissertation, Hebrew University, Jerusalem, 1982).

[39] Levi, *Dissertations*, 1:223.

[40] Ibid., 1:235.

[41] Ibid., 1:175.

In *The Ten Annual Accounts of the Collation of Hebrew Mss. of the Old Testament Begun in 1760, and Completed in 1769*, Kennicott published in 1770 a composite of ten years of annual reports of his project primarily directed to his subscribers. By this time, Kennicott had been forced to respond to his critics on several key issues, including the quality of his own collations and the level of Hebraic literacy of his staff. He strongly affirms that his assistants were highly trained in reading Hebrew manuscripts and that, through a disciplined system of supervision, their work was surely as reliable as possible. He describes his hunt for Hebrew manuscripts throughout Europe, the Middle East, even America and China. Despite the Christian coloring of his endeavor, he still waxes eloquently about the general English pride generated by his project: "Reader! What a sum is here! Let foreign Nations read, with astonishment, this story of Britons and their King . . . voluntarily contributing, for ten years . . . a work sacred to the Glory of God and the Good of Mankind."[42] And elsewhere he underscores the support he has received from non-Christians: "Learned Men of very different Persuasions in Religion: who have united in their Opinions of the Tendency of this Work to Promote . . . the Honour of Revelation."[43] In fact, among a long list of subscribers, three sephardic Jewish names appear.[44]

Kennicott's ardent critics wasted no time in casting aspersions on Kennicott's books and on the viability of his entire project. The primary protagonists in this campaign of vilification were the followers of John Hutchinson. Hutchinson and his chief disciples, Robert Spearman and Julius Bate, had argued vigorously that Christians should confront the Hebrew Bible directly as the continuing revelation of God, unmediated by Jewish interpretations of Scripture, and divested of the vowel points invented by modern Jews to mislead Christians in understanding their own sacred scriptures. Through a bizarre and highly unsystematic study of Hebrew roots, whereby all the possible permutations of a single Hebrew root could be related to each other with utter disregard for rules of grammar and pronunciation, the Hutchinsonians claimed to unravel the authentic and Christian meaning of Scripture.[45]

[42] Benjamin Kennicott, *The Ten Annual Accounts of the Collation of Hebrew Mss. of the Old Testament Begun in 1760, and Completed in 1769* (London, 1770), p. 171.

[43] Ibid., p. 46.

[44] Baron Aguilar, Solomon da Costa [Athias], who had donated a large Hebraic collection owned by Charles II to the British Museum in 1759, and Daniel de Castro. Cf. R. Loewe, "Jewish Scholarship in England," in *Three Centuries of Anglo-Jewish History*, ed. V. D. Lipman (London, 1961), p. 142.

[45] On the Hutchinsonians, see *Dictionary of National Biography* 28 (London, 1892): 342–43; and Katz, "The Hutchinsonians" and the additional references he offers primarily on their views of natural philosophy and geology. See also D. S. Katz, " 'Moses's Principia':

We shall return to this method of reading and David Levi's encounter with it in the next chapter. What is relevant here is their powerful motivation for opposing Kennicott. Given their biblical literalism, they excoriated him for tampering with the consonants of the Hebrew Bible by offering his myriad of emendations and alternate readings. By destabilizing the text, Kennicott had undermined the force of their unique exegesis that rested on the assumption that the Hebrew text was fixed and standardized. They also abused him for relying on the vowel points in collating manuscripts and in ultimately determining his preferred readings of the text. In the same year that Kennicott's first volume had appeared, one of the Hutchinsonians, Fowler Comings, already produced *An Answer to Mr. Kennicott's "Dissertation."* Many similar works followed, laced by an interesting combination of rational criticism, on the one hand, and religious fanaticism, on the other.

Julius Bate's *The Integrity of the Hebrew Text and Many Passages of Scripture Vindicated From the Objections and Misconstructions of Mr. Kennicott*, published in London in 1754, is a fine example of the Hutchinsonian approach to Kennicott's project. Julius Bate (1711–71) was on intimate terms with Hutchinson before his death and collaborated with Spearman in the publication of Hutchinson's works. Bate published on his own several works in defense of the Hutchinsonian methods of reading Scripture, including *Critica Hebraea or a Hebrew-English Dictionary without Points* which appeared in 1767.[46]

Bate opens his pamphlet against Kennicott by railing against his temerity of correcting the sacred pages of Scripture with the same "vague and licentious spirit of criticism" that has plagued the new readers of Shakespeare and Pope.[47] Bate primarily opposes Kennicott in his notion that private manuscripts can overrule the authority of a time-honored text, publicly acknowledged as such over the centuries. But Bate must deal with a conundrum in defending the integrity of the printed text against the specious authority of Kennicott's manuscripts. To defend the former against the latter meant to acknowledge the reliability and authority of those Jewish caretakers of the text who were primarily responsible for its present condition. Bate, accordingly, walks gingerly in formulating his position. It is true that Jewish scribes were capable of making mistakes in determining the Masoretic text, "yet we may suppose that they would revise, read, and compare, perhaps over and over again, what they had

---

Hutchinsonianism and Newton's Critics," in *The Books of Nature and Scripture*, ed. J. E. Force and R. H. Popkin (Dordrecht, 1994), pp. 201–11; Clark, *English Society, 1688–1832*, pp. 218–19; Young, *Religion and Enlightenment*, pp. 136–51.

[46] On Bate, see *Dictionary of National Biography* 3 (London, 1892): 391.

[47] Julius Bate, *The Integrity of the Hebrew Text* (London, 1554), p. vi.

transcribed; which if they did, no great mistakes could be made. . . . This being the case, it is hoped that without vesting the rabbies with the prophetic furor, we shall not find so many very material mistakes, and corruptions in our present text as Mr. Kennicott seems so confident he has discovered in it."[48] Bate's obvious discomfort in defending the Masoretic text and the integrity of Jewish transcribers is mollified by the sheer pretensions of the "The English Ezra," as he calls Kennicott, and his obsessive penchant for tampering with the text: "He is pleased no doubt, when he comes to a mistake, triumphs upon it, and treats with too much levity, as well as affected superiority, those great men, who have laboured in vindicating these supposed errors in our Bible, though he is often mistaken himself. . . . It is an easy way to get rid of Difficulties by correcting the Words, and would lesson the labour of the Commentator were it a genuine way of explaining Scripture."[49]

In his study of the Hutchinsonians, David S. Katz, has emphasized the anti-Jewish nature of their biblical probings, their emphatic rejection of Jewish interpretations of Scripture, their denunciation of the Jewish invention of the nefarious vowel points, and even their diabolical plots to Judaize the Christian world and to spread their own lies and those of Islam. Their academic fraternization with Christians since the Reformation has left the Christian world overrun with the scourge of rabbinism, as they saw it. Until the Hutchinsonians had reclaimed the study of Hebrew as their own, to be mastered through their own sacred methods, it was essentially a Jewish discipline, left to the rabbis by Christians who had abdicated their own sacred responsibilities.[50] Indeed, Bate can be downright abusive in venting his contempt for the Jews when describing their vowel point system: "But away with everything that is the Invention of the Synagogue of Satan, for there is no reason to call them Inaccuracies of the Transcribers . . . but away with them . . . away with the Points. . . . pointing is the Ultimatum of the Devil, and changes the whole Scripture from the Work of God into that of the Worst of Men."[51]

Bate, in the end, is incapable of reconciling his appreciation for the honesty and reliability of Jewish scribes of the consonantal text with his utter contempt for Jewish inventors of the vowel system. Notwithstanding his animus toward the Jews for polluting the sacred world of Christian text study, he still requires their authority in challenging the greater danger of "the English Ezra." Bate had not vested "the rabbies with prophetic furor," as he proclaims, but they emerge, paradoxically, as rather unlikely

[48] Ibid., pp. 8–9.
[49] Ibid., pp. 9–11.
[50] Katz, "The Hutchinsonians," especially pp. 252–55.
[51] Bate, *The Integrity of the Hebrew Text*, p. 19.

and precarious allies in his campaign to besmirch Kennicott and his effort to reconstruct the biblical text.

One other rich example of the outpouring of criticism over Kennicott in the years immediately following the publication of his *Dissertations* is the anonymous pamphlet entitled *A Dialogue between Doctor Cunningham and Sir Charles Freeman, Bart. Concerning Mr. Kennicott's Method of Correcting the Printed Hebrew Text*, published in London in 1760. In this instance, it is not clear if the author was a Hutchinsonian although it is obvious, by the end, that the author remains skeptical and critical of Kennicott's entire work. The setting is a conversation in the home of the fictional Sir Charles after he receives a visitor named Dr. Cunningham intent on selling him a subscription to Kennicott's collation project. After a short encomium for Kennicott offered by Cunningham, Freeman bluntly proclaims:

> Mr. Kennicott seems too fond of using the incision knife, and often cuts away sound flesh, for no other reason, as far as I can see, but to shew his skill in surgery. . . . He seems to make corruptions his game, and hunts for them with the eagerness of a poacher rather than a fair sportsman. . . . When he alters and corrects out of his own head he peremptorily presumes to give us what Moses and the prophets wrote, and no otherwise; which is to appoint what is Scripture, and what is not. Collating of mss. and collecting various readings is one thing, altering the text is another, especially when Self is the sole judge.[52]

This severe indictment of Kennicott is followed by another charge: the accusation that Kennicott changes the text of the Old Testament merely to have it conform with the theological doctrine of the New. The supposed "scientific" objectivity of the project is blatantly called into question: "But why must the authority of the New be established upon the corruption of the Old? May not the enemies of revelation say, that we altered the text of the Old, to make it agree with the rest of the New?"[53]

Cunningham responds by attempting to demonstrate how the printed edition of Scripture actually distorts the true meaning, undermining a cardinal principle of the Christian faith. He refers to the supposed Masoretic reading of Psalm 16:10, a text discussed by Kennicott in the first volume of his *Dissertations* and highly promoted by him as an example of how his correcting methods came to the aid of Christian faith. Kennicott had charged that the Masoretic text adds an additional *yud* in the word *ḥasidekha*, meaning "your faithful ones" in the plural, rather than the singular "your faithful one." The import of this deliberate Masoretic

---

[52] *A Dialogue between Doctor Cunningham and Sir Charles Freeman* (London, 1760), pp. 3–5.

[53] Ibid., p. 7.

alteration was supposedly intended to obscure a clear reference to the resurrection of Jesus. In reality, there was no substance to the charge since the Bomberg Bible pointed the word in the singular and a Masoretic note in the margin indicated clearly that the extra *yud* was superfluous. This did not seem to bother Kennicott, however, who raged on incessantly about how the Masorites had undermined the true testimony of the Apostles and had severely vitiated the authentic Christian message of David's words.[54] As we shall see, the example was often cited by both the detractors and followers of Kennicott well into the next decade.

Kennicott's discussion of this line is ironic for two reasons. In the first place, he had stated quite candidly at the beginning of his work that the multiple corrections he was offering had no bearing whatsoever on matters of theology; this example appeared to be in direct violation of that claim.[55] In the second place, he continued to hold up this verse as a shining example of how he had rescued the Christian understanding of the text when in reality his accusation was absurd. Sir Charles too would not be taken in by Kennicott's alleged "salvaging of the text." In a lesson to Dr. Cunningham on how the Apostles Peter and Paul inconsistently cite the Psalms, one time in the singular and another in the plural, Sir Charles insists that Kennicott should have left well enough alone. By introducing an emendation only in this one instance, he wrought more confusion rather than clarity. Because the Apostles were inconsistent in the first place, no one would regard them as false witnesses regarding this one verse based on whether it appeared in the plural or singular.[56]

Cunningham finally resorts to an ad hominem attack on Kennicott's opponents, naming, in particular, Comings and Bate, whom he labels "a couple of madmen, enthusiasts, followers of Hutchinson, who possessed with the low dull method of picking mysteries out of letters, have been only able to extract the crude nonsense of the Cabbala to I can't tell what kind of quintessence."[57] Cunningham's implication that the Hutchinsonians studied the biblical text like Kabbalists is truly ironic in light of David S. Katz's observation that the Hutchinsonian school marked the end of the influence of the Jewish kabbalah on Christians.[58] Be that as it may, Sir Charles appeared unflappable in calmly answering his interlocutor. Instead of personal attacks, let Kennicott respond to them with appropriate evidence, he remarked. In truth, Kennicott never fully addressed their criticisms; he merely dismissed them as unintelligible. The pamphlet con-

---

[54] Ibid., p. 9. Kennicott's discussion appears in *The State of the Printed Hebrew Text*, pp. 496–99. Compare also the remarks of McLain, "Benjamin Kennicott," p. 462.

[55] See Kennicott, *Dissertations*, 1:11.

[56] *A Dialogue*, pp. 10–12.

[57] Ibid., p. 13.

[58] Katz, "The Hutchinsonians," p. 252.

cludes with Sir Charles's refusing to support the project and advising the humbled Cunningham to postpone the entire affair "till Mr. Kennicott gives a better account of himself and his scheme, than he has yet done."[59]

In actuality, Sir Charles's plea for a reasoned response from Kennicott had gone unheeded. Kennicott had attempted to respond to the Hutchinsonians some four years earlier when he apparently published a pamphlet (although he thinly veiled his true identity) directed to members of this circle who had exerted considerable influence in their public preaching at the very center of Kennicott's textual activity in Oxford. The work was entitled *A Word to the Hutchinsonians or Remarks on Three Extraordinary Sermons Lately Preached Before the University of Oxford by the Reverend Dr. Patten, the Reverend Mr. Wetherall and the Reverend Mr. Horne by a Member of the University* and was published in London. We shall return to the last of the three and his substantial criticism of Kennicott. Kennicott, like the fictional Dr. Cunningham, has little to say in response to the specific criticisms of his opponents. He rather restricts himself to disparaging Hutchinson and his followers, to poking fun at their credentials as true scholars and Christians, and in lamenting the fact that "a little learning is a dangerous thing."[60] He objects especially to their equating human learning, reason, and the light of nature with "the religion of the Devil." And he alerts the community of Oxford to be wary of such men who "make Words signify what they please, turn the plainest History into sublime Prophecy and compel Sentences as to be oracular, in various ways, with all such meanings as were never meant."[61]

Kennicott's effort to isolate the Hutchinsonians as a lunatic fringe by deeming them unworthy of a serious response may not have been the best way of handling their pointed and effective criticisms of his endeavor. They continued to attract followers in the decades to follow. Moreover, their serious reservations about Kennicott's project would be echoed by a new group of critics, including the Jews themselves, throughout Kennicott's career. As we have already seen, when the Hutchinsonians temporarily abandoned their own exegetical idiosyncrasies to focus exclusively on the dangers and unfulfilled claims of Kennicott's program, they could hardly be dismissed nor could their cogent arguments be ignored.

III

The second wave of public criticisms of Kennicott emerged in the 1770s at about the same time Baruh and Owen exchanged their opinions on

---

[59] *A Dialogue*, p. 31.

[60] Benjamin Kennicott, *A Word to the Hutchinsonians* (London, 1756), p. 5.

[61] Ibid., pp. 41–42.

the Oxford divine. Before turning to this even more rancorous debate, I consider one unusual figure who suprisingly attempts to situate himself in the middle of the two contending sides, between the followers of Kennicott and their opponents—namely Anselm Bayly (d. 1794).

Bayly once wrote under the pseudonym of Anti-Socinus when he publicly attacked David Levi in the wake of his famous debate with Dr. Joseph Priestley.[62] Bayly's highly emotional remarks written in defense of Priestley took the form of a threat to Levi and to his *Lingua Sacra*, a three-volume Hebrew grammar and dictionary, which Levi angrily cited in his own response to him: "Had you not used audaciousness and contempt towards my Lord and Master[Priestley], whom and whose cause I regard more than property, honours, and life itself. I hope you will ask his pardon, or at least, evermore be silent before him—on these conditions only, I remain your friend, firmer than ever: but if you offer again to touch his Name, Word, and Character, with profane lips and profane hands, I will tear you to pieces, you and your *Sacra Lingua*."[63] In response, Levi first pokes fun at Bayly for reversing the order of the names of his book, adding that his passion probably "almost choaked him" or perhaps, "like the witches [he made the mistake], who say their prayers backwards." Then later, he again paraphrases Bayly in mocking fashion: "You, you wicked brat [meaning Levi], and Dr. Priestley, that serpent of old, that first drew you to make scholastic distinctions of the second person in the Trinity [implying that Levi had been influenced by Priestley], shall be served, as Calvin caused Michael Servetus to be served . . . in plain English, ye shalt all be burnt."[64]

Such a vituperative outburst and mocking parody in so coarse a language seem astonishing in the still rare public forums in which Christians and Jews felt free to verbally assault each other and their faith in the eighteenth century. It is also surprising to see Bayly in a totally different light some fifteen years earlier when he published *A Plain and Complete Grammar of the Hebrew Language With and Without Points* in London in 1773. Bayly, who held church positions of some distinction as minor canon of St. Paul and of Westminster, as well as subdean of the Chapel Royal, had obviously befriended Levi at an earlier time, as his own remarks make clear, and was obviously familiar with Levi's comprehensive study of the Hebrew language. His own effort to compose a Hebrew

---

[62] On Bayly, see *Dictionary of National Biography* 3 (London, 1892): 448. On his criticism of Levi, see chapter 4.

[63] David Levi, "A Letter to Anti-Socinus, alias Anselm Bayly Occasioned by his Remarks to Mr. David Levi's Answer to Dr. Priestley's First Letters to the Jews," in David Levi, *Letters to Dr. Priestley in Answer to His Letters to the Jews Part II. . . . Also Letters to Dr. Cooper etc.* (London, 1789), pp. 154–55.

[64] Ibid., pp. 155, 157.

grammar reveals as well considerable erudition and a rational and tolerant spirit.

Dedicating his grammar to Robert Lowth, the then bishop of Oxford
and the major supporter of Benjamin Kennicott, Bayly focuses in the introduction to his grammar on one issue alone: the value of the vowel
points inserted by the Masorites into the Old Testament to allow a consistent and relatively correct pronunciation of the Hebrew text. He notes
the two contending sides: those Jews and some Christians who consider
the points "absolutely necessary" and some other Christians, by which he
primarily means the Hutchinsonians, who maintain that they are totally
useless. He calls for an open and frank discussion of the issue, a balanced
presentation of the pros and cons of the system by someone "conversant
in the Rabbinical writings," and even the creation of a coalition of members of both parties who could lay aside their prejudices to reach common
agreement. Certainly, given the chaotic state of affairs, any call for a new
English translation is premature and even dangerous in his opinion.[65]

What is immediately striking about Bayly's comments is his intimate
awareness of Jewish students of the Hebrew language and his genuine
appreciation of their knowledge, which he deems far superior to that of
Christians. In preparation for his own grammar, he had consulted a long
list of Jewish and Christian grammarians. It is clearly the former who
deserve his adulation because to them it was never a dead language: "It
is alive to this day in the mouths and understanding of the wise and
learned Jews, who all over the world can converse with each other, and
write in the biblical as well as in the Rabbinical Hebrew." In a footnote
to this remark, he adds:

> This is a fact affirmed by every Jew of knowledge, that I have conversed with
> and whom I have experienced to be men of understanding, candor, and integ-
> rity, particularly the following, who bear the title of *ḥakhamim*, which answers
> to our Doctor: Moses Choen D'Azivedo,[66] Isaac Netto,[67] Isaac Mendes Belisa-
> rio,[68] and Gumperz Levi.[69] Of the last person I beg leave to say, that he merits

[65] Anselm Bayly, *A Plain and Complete Grammar of the Hebrew Language With and
Without Points* (London, 1773), pp. ii–iv.

[66] On Moses Cohen de Azevedo, see his sermons preached in the sephardic synagogue of
London listed in C. Roth, *Magna Bibliotheca Anglo-Judaica* (London, 1937), pp. 312, 324,
325. See also M. Gaster *History of the Ancient Synagogue of the Spanish and Portuguese
Jews* (London, 1901), pp. 131–41.

[67] The son of David Nieto. His liturgical and homiletical publications are listed in Roth,
Magna Bibliotheca, pp. 271, 303, 304, 323. See also, Solomons, "David Nieto and some of
His Contemporaries," pp. 1–101.

[68] On Isaac Mendes Belisario, see his sermon listed in Roth, *Magna Bibliotheca*, p. 324.
He is also mentioned in a letter of Emanuel Mendes da Costa discussed in chapter 5.

[69] This is Mordechai Gumpel Schnaber Levison discussed in Ruderman, *Jewish Thought
and Scientific Discovery*, pp. 332–68. Also see chapter 5 and the appendix.

particular notice from his own people, and such Christians would wish to be
instructed critically and rationality [*sic*] in the Hebrew language by one who is
thoroughly acquainted with it, and very conversant not only in Rabbinical writings but in the Sciences and modern philosophy, upon which he has written a
very curious book in Hebrew, mentioned at the end of the grammar.[70]

And indeed, Bayly inserts an advertisement at the end of his grammar
for Gumperz's [Mordecai Schnaber Levison] Hebrew book *Ma'amar Ha-
Torah ve-ha-Ḥokhmah* and for Hebrew lessons his Jewish friend is willing
to give to Christian students for a price.

This remarkable passage is fascinating for what it reveals about the
close interaction between Christian clerics and Jewish scholars, especially
in the field of Hebrew and biblical studies. In his own writing the same
Levison praises Robert Lowth, the then bishop of London as his friend
and for his tremendous learning in the Hebrew language.[71] Bayly's own
education in Hebrew was undoubtedly facilitated through his Jewish
teachers, and it would be quite reasonable to assume that such contacts,
not only in the social or economic spheres but in the field of Hebrew
studies, were a commonplace in eighteenth-century England. At the very
least, Kennicott and Lowth required these contacts in order to further
their ambitious plans of collation and translation.

That Jews have preserved a living language which they both read and
spoke is the most telling proof that the Jews were in the best position to
know its pronunciation. Because Elia Levita had demonstrated several
centuries earlier that the points were inserted into the biblical text at a
relatively late time,[72] their antiquity is not really the issue at hand, contends Bayly. Rather, "every wise man of the Present Jews" only pleads for
"their necessity and usefulness, for a uniformity of pronunciation to enable the Master and Pupils to understand each other in their Schools, and
the People their priest in the Synagogue; this plea is just and proper for
them; but the case is widely different among Christians, who may be allowed to understand the Hebrew without any exactness in pronunciation."[73] Nevertheless, adds Bayly, Christians should be "curious and calculated to preserve, without changing the letters of the text, a traditional
and uniform pronunciation, and in general, may be made use of for a
ready but not infallible interpretation."[74]

---

[70] Bayly, *A Plain and Complete Grammar*, p. xiii.

[71] See note 12.

[72] For the most recent assessment of Levita and his position on the points, see J. Penkower, "New Considerations on *Sefer Massoret ha-Massoret* of Elijah Levita" (Hebrew),
Italia 8 (1989): 7–73.

[73] Bayly, *A Plain and Complete Grammar*, p. xvii.

[74] Ibid.

Bayly's appreciative attitude toward the points stands in sharp contrast to the other Christian scholars we have already encountered: certainly the Hutchinsonians and Kennicott, although the latter retained their usage in his own version of the Old Testament. Bayly's view is shaped by his contact with living Jewish scholars—with a community, albeit minuscule, where "living" Hebrew is still taught and where pronunciation counts, and which is totally different from the coterie of Christian savants who approach the biblical language as a language distant in time and space.

Bayly concludes his introduction with a review of the history of Hebraic studies from the medieval Hebrew grammarians until his day. He even describes John Hutchinson in sympathetic terms and attributes to him the revival of Hebrew studies in the preceding century: "He opposed the points with greater warmth than Capellus[75] and stood up for the correctness of the Hebrew writings, with more zeal than even Buxtorf. . . . [He] proposed to open a wider path to the Hebrew; he professed to enter into the language more profoundly than any that preceded him, with a eye to philosophy as well as divinity."[76] Coming from a non-Hutchinsonian, Bayly's observation offers a more balanced view of Hutchinson's importance to Hebrew studies in England than that of Kennicott and his other fierce opponents. It is hard to concede that the Hutchinsonians had anything but contempt and anti-Judaic animus for the "wicked" points. Nevertheless, Bayly, despite his different theological orientation, preferred to regard the Hutchinsonians as potential allies in the cause of Hebraic learning; and, additionally, he was seeking peace between the contending parties.

His conclusion is thus not unexpected: "It is one thing to correct the mistakes or abuses of points, and another indiscriminately to reject their use." Those who first learned Hebrew with points and now vilify them "seem to manifest the kind of ingratitude, and the same excess of passion and prejudice as modern unbelievers, who receiving knowledge from Divine Revelation through the means of education, reject and write against Revelation under a deception, that their knowledge is their own, and that they shine with unborrowed light."[77] Bayly's telling analogy seeks to make a point that could only have emerged through his warm and respectful relations with the Jewish intellectual community of London. Just as atheists should not be so self-assured that their opinions are unrelated and independent of their Christian upbringing, so too Christians should not pronounce so cavalierly their liberation from centuries of faithful Jewish

---

[75] Louis Capellus (1585–1658). See P. G. Schnedermann, *Die Controverse des Ludovicus Cappellus mit den Buxtorfen über das Alter der Hebräischen Punctation* (Leipzig, 1879).
[76] Bayly, *A Plain and Complete Grammar*, p. xxiii.
[77] Ibid., p. xxiv.

preservation and cultivation of a language and text sacred to both traditions. By analogy, we can assume that Bayly's appreciation for the value of the points extended to the consonantal text as well. He could not have countenanced the kind of textual criticisms the Kennicott school was promoting with increasing and with often careless regularity.

At the end of Bayly's work he appends a brief appendix announcing the appearance of a work published in France by an anonymous author consisting of five letters addressed to Dr. Kennicott. Consistent with his neutrality in avoiding to take sides in the debates over the biblical text, he refrains from commenting on the substance of the letters. Instead, he comments on several grammatical points without offering his readers any real sense of what this recent work is about. Nevertheless, two of his comments in total agreement with the author of the French work are worthy of notice. In the first instance, he praises the "penetrating sight" of the author's understanding of the Hebrew language, an author who fully appreciates "that in it no letters or syllables are useless or insignificant" and that this insight "can't be conveyed in translation." Second, in commenting on the differences between the narratives in Kings and Chronicles, the particular concern of both Kennicott and Baruh, Bayly appears to agree with the latter over the former: "The best interpreter of Scripture is Scripture; and the books of Chronicles, if read in this view, will be found not only a most excellent abridgment, but also in many instances a very valuable commentary and supplement."[78]

IV

Bayly's appendix on the French text was a clear indication that it had been fully noticed by the English intellectual community surrounding Kennicott and that it could hardly be taken lightly by a community still passionately divided over the value of Kennicott's project. The text to which Bayly referred was first published in 1771 as *Lettres de M. l'Abbé de * * * ex professeur en Hébreu en l'université de * * * au Sr Kennicott*, purporting to be published in Rome but sold in Paris. Only a year later it was translated into English by William Stevens and published in Paris as *Letters of Mr. the Abbot of * * * Ex Professor of the Hebrew Language in the University of * * * to Mr. Kennicott*. The translation was republished the following year.

The volume offers no clue regarding the identity of its author other than the sense that it was composed by knowledgeable clerics apparently located in Paris. From its opening, it attacks Kennicott and his program

---

[78] Ibid., appendix.

with contempt and cynicism, exposing his most vulnerable claims that his manuscripts can produce a better text than that found in the printed Bible. The authors are particularly appreciative of the Jewish role in carefully preserving and transmitting the text:

> Are you not sensible that we have the Bible through the channel of the Jews? That this book has been spread forth among the nations by their means? That they have always had for the same the most profound veneration, and by an effect of Providence they have never dared to diminish from it, or add a single word to it? And you will have them to have wantonly contributed to the corruption of it, by furnishing imperfect manuscripts to print it: this is diametrically opposite to common sense. Whatever the Jews have done, and which is a consequence of their ignorance, is to convert into strange objects the passages which were too conspicuously applied against them, or in favor of Jesus Christ: and they have rather been inclined to excommunicate him, who would calculate Daniel's weeks, than touching the text where their condemnation is so plainly pronounced.[79]

The argument lacks the sympathetic regard of Bayly toward the Jewish editors of the text but it at least credits them with relatively high marks for preserving the text even when it might have been in their best interest to emend it. But whatever the degree of their faithfulness to the text in the past, Kennicott's project is flawed from the start on the basis of simple logic: "If the printed text is corrupted, because manuscripts have been made use of that were furnished by the Jews, what confidence can you expect from your present corrections, since all the ancient copies, on which you flatter yourself to improve our text, are of their own hand? And I defy you to produce in this matter any such manuscript whatsoever, that has not been written by a Jew." And what follows is the obvious question: "By what chance should the Jews of the fifteenth century [those responsible for the edition of Cardinal Ximenes] have furnished bad copies to print the Bible? And how could the libraries produce some excellent ones three hundred years after to improve it?" Or by the same token, in commenting sarcastically about Kennicott's search for manuscripts in far-off America, "why should the Jews of America be more honest than those of Spain?"[80] Kennicott was simply fooling himself in believing that he could recover an authentic Hebrew text that had not been previously written, preserved, and transmitted by Jews. Since the printed text had been collated as faithfully as possible centuries earlier, how was it possible to

---

[79] *Letters of Mr. the Abbot of * * * Ex Professor of the Hebrew Language in the University of * * * to Mr. Kennicott,* trans. William Stevens (Paris, 1772), pp. 9–10.
[80] Ibid., pp. 10–11, 17.

now discover better texts and better readings than had been previously known?

The author then attacks Kennicott for his useless, imaginary corrections, "follies, ignorant productions, omissions, or some addition, which only deserve contempt and derision." In the final analysis, Kennicott's competence in the Hebrew language is called into question: "Before anybody takes upon himself the task of correcting a text, and especially one so precious as that of the Holy Scriptures; he must understand perfectly the language in which it is wrote, know radically the genius of it, have always the principles before his eyes, make the most exact application of them and especially not cause the word to disappear where they are found contrary to the sense he had a mind to present."[81] The accusation is coupled with the insinuation that Kennicott's "scientific" enterprise really masks a theological agenda. If, indeed, one is to take Kennicott at his word that his corrections do not affect the Christian faith, then why bother: "What utility, nay what profit does it accrue to the Christian of knowing that in certain places *Ya'akov* is written with a *vav* and in others . . . without a *vav*; that before the captivity *David* was wrote without a *yud* and after . . . with a *yud*." But Kennicott wishes to have it both ways, as his useless emendation of Psalm 16:10 suggests. Rather than bolster the Christian faith, such irresponsible tampering with the text waters the ground of Pyrrhonism particularly in the present age of materialism and disbelief.[82]

One of the author's last arguments against Kennicott deserves special mention. He strenuously objects to Kennicott's claim that he had the full support of the leading Jews of England. The author appears to have specific information on this matter since he points out that until 1767, some seven years after the project had begun, "there was not a Jew of any country whatsoever, that wrought under his direction." Furthermore, the undertaking had always been criticized by the Jews: "For the whole nation must be enflamed to be accused of having maliciously corrupted the Bible, i.e. the only book that contains their faith and religion, for which they have always had the most profound veneration." He again reiterates in the strongest terms Jewish disapproval of his project: "No Doctor, you will not find a single Jew who applauds your undertaking; all in general blame it and condemn it."[83] The emphasis on what the Jews think about the project, their distancing themselves from it, and the lack of Jewish assistance is curious if indeed the work was penned by French clerics. Why should they have cared about Jewish sensibilities and why would

[81] Ibid., p. 147.
[82] Ibid., pp. 154–58. The quotation is from p. 154.
[83] Ibid., pp. 198–200.

they have seen the lack of Jewish assistance as a flaw in judging the quality of Kennicott's undertaking? Would it have not been more understandable that such an outburst might have been penned by a Jew?

Before addressing the last question directly, we might first consider the response the French book generated almost immediately after its publication on the part of Kennicott and his followers. Already in the same year as the English translation of the French work was published, a short pamphlet appeared, conceivably stemming from the hand of Kennicott himself, entitled *A Letter to a Friend Occasioned by a French Pamphlet Lately Published Against Doctor Kennicott and His Collation of the Hebrew Mss*, published in Oxford in 1772. The pamphlet summarizes the book's contents on the basis of the French original and then proceeds to identify its authors. They are supposedly affiliated with the society of Capuchins in the convent of St. Honoré at Paris. They established a *Societas Clementina ad linguae sacrae* and they go by the names Louis de Poix, Jerome d'Artois, and Sepaphin de Paris.[84]

The pamphlet offers a very full summary of the contents of the letters noting their special affection for the Jews: "They offer a eulogy upon the Jews; as men of such principle, that not a single letter of the Bible would they alter, under any consideration." It also acknowledges their argument that Kennicott's project in underscoring the obscurity of the Sacred Writings, further weakens Christian faith by "furnishing Infidelity with a buckler, which will be proof against the most piercing weapons of reason, faith, and religion."[85]

The response to this battery of criticism is rather lame. The author of the pamphlet can do nothing more than reassert that the "non-integrity of the present printed text is a palpable matter of fact demonstrated and undeniable." He also claims that Kennicott's competency in reading rabbinic characters in Hebrew manuscripts is beyond question, although it is true that some of his assistants may be less qualified. Beyond this retort, there is no serious engagement with the French criticism. The ultimate impact of this response seems to be negligible other than to offer a convenient synopsis of the arguments of Kennicott's detractors.[86]

Three years passed before another response was published by the Kennicott camp. It was written by George Sheldon, the vicar of Edwardston, Suffolk, and formally of Trinity College, Cambridge, entitled *Remarks Upon the Critical Parts of a Pamphlet Later Published in Titled Letters to the Rev. Dr. Benjamin Kennicott by Mr. l'Abbé * * * Hebrew Professor*

---

[84] *A Letter to a Friend Occasioned by a French Pamphlet Lately Published Against Doctor Kennicott* (Oxford, 1772), p. 3.

[85] Ibid., pp. 17, 26.

[86] Ibid., pp. 27–33. The quotation is from p. 27.

in the University of * * * published in 1775 in London. Sheldon does not summarize the contents of the French work but rather responds generally that the printed versions of the Masorites are indeed corrupt and that Kennicott's project "will surely be of some service to Religion" to furnish the learned the materials to enable them to produce a more correct and intelligible English version of the Bible. He pauses to consider Kennicott's already famous emendation of Psalm 16:10. Acknowledging that the Masorites did indicate the singular reading of "your faithful ones" rather than the plural, he nevertheless contends "that out of a superstitious regard for the sacredness of it [the text] they left untouched all those blunders committed by careless transcribers." They noted them in the margins but essentially left the text uncorrected "without presuming to remove out of it those words or letters they thought faultily written or to insert as they judged to be wanting." Their "superstitious scrupulosity," as he calls it, accounts for the plural reading of "our faithful ones" in the present printed text.[87]

Sheldon offers little more of a rebuttal other than to note sadly the spirit "of spleen, envy, and ill nature [that] runs through the whole of these letters . . . that does no harm to the writer."[88] Given the seriousness of the charges against Kennicott articulated in the French publication, it is quite astonishing that the Kennicottians were unable to muster enough energy and rhetorical power to defend themselves adequately. We should recall that Kennicott hardly presented a serious counterargument to the barrage of charges leveled at him by the Hutchinsonians some twenty years earlier. He had simply dismissed them by stigmatizing them as religious fanatics. By identifying his new enemies as Capuchin monks, he was certainly belittling them before his Protestant supporters. But here again he walked away from any substantive encounter regarding the pitfalls of his undertaking. Perhaps because he enjoyed the solid backing of the king and the ecclesiastical establishment, he could afford to ignore these critics, or perhaps their arguments were sufficiently effective as to raise doubts even among his most enthusiastic supporters.[89] In any case, his relative silence in the face of his critics is indeed enigmatic.

Yet one more piece of evidence sheds considerable light on Kennicott's project and the nature of the alliance of interests posed against him. In the Bodleian library, Oxford, I discovered a manuscript entitled "Observations on Dr. Kennicott's Manner of Collating Hebrew Manuscripts of the

---

[87] George Sheldon, *Remarks Upon the Critical Parts of a Pamphlet Later Published in Titled Letters to the Rev. Dr. Benjamin Kennicott* (London, 1775), pp. 3, 68–69.

[88] Ibid., p. 72.

[89] Kennicott did respond to J. D. Michaelis, his chief German critic, first in 1777 in a long Latin epistle and again in 1782. See *Dictionary of National Biography* 3 (London, 1892): 12.

Old Testament wherein the Inaccuracy and Inutility of that Work Under his Direction are clearly proved and confirmed by many Examples." The author signs his name as Ignatius Adophus Dumay, late chief collator then four years past under Dr. Kennicott at Oxford. The manuscript is dated on the front page as 1770 but it was apparently written in 1765 as indicated later in the text. The document consists of two parts: a preface directed "To the Publick," in which the author explains his personal circumstances and his grievances against Dr. Kennicott that motivated him to pen this composition; and a second and longer section offering his observations about the manner in which Kennicott had collated Hebrew manuscripts. The second section bears an uncanny resemblance to the French text of 1771. We shall return to this resemblance in due course.[90]

From the very opening of his preface, Dumay states his complaint against Kennicott, "who has treated me with great inhumanity." He relates how he had approached Professor Thomas Hunt (1696–1774), Kennicott's teacher at Oxford and a major supporter of the collation project, informing him of the manner he had been treated and offering him his low opinion of the entire undertaking. Hunt was obviously irritated by the charges and accused Dumay of being a "treacherous man" who had left France after betraying his army and country. Dumay was obliged to defend his honor and explain in detail the circumstances that brought him to England.[91]

He then relates how, upon the recommendation of Hunt, he secured employment as Dr. Kennicott's assistant in collating Hebrew and Samaritan manuscripts. He soon realized that this project "which like many other things of small account, has made so great a noise in the world," was not worthy of his effort. He particularly was "not pleased with Dr. Kennicott's undertaking, perceiving very plainly, by the many faulty miserable manuscripts which had already passed under my hands, and that air of authority with which the Doctor obliged me to register all their blunders, that this work would never be of much service to the Christian world."[92] By 1763 (he apparently began his employment in 1761), he had had enough and submitted his resignation. Kennicott refused to accept it and threatened to defame his character. Having subsequently married, Dumay received an assurance from Kennicott that he would also employ his wife, so he stayed on the job.[93]

---

[90] MS Oxford Bod. Kennicott e. 43, Bodleian Library. It is listed in M. Clapinson and T. D. Rodgers, *Summary Catalogue of Post-Medieval Western Manuscripts in the Bodleian Library Oxford* (Oxford, 1991), vol. 2, as no. 47782.

[91] "Observations on Dr. Kennicott's Manner of Collating Hebrew Manuscripts of the Old Testament," "To the Publick," fols. 1–9.

[92] Ibid., fols. 9–11.

[93] Ibid., fols. 11–15.

Dumay had no illusion about the nature of their relationship and about his employer's character: "Dr. Kennicott, who has always shewn himself impatient of contradiction, and insolent in his language towards all those who have differed from him, will endeavor all he can to prejudice people against me."[94] Kennicott had even called him a "Hutchinsonian," a label he did not understand, although he had heard at Oxford that they held a low opinion of the project. Kennicott's opinion notwithstanding, Dumay had a high regard for himself, at least with respect to his competency to evaluate the value of Kennicott's achievements: "I must have some good grounds for my opinion, having seen many collations of manuscripts and performed at least three times as much of this work with my own hands and eyes, as the Doctor himself, with all his assistants."[95]

Dumay begins the second part of his composition by acknowledging that a more correct version of the Hebrew Bible "would be a great and valuable treasure, but only if the materials are of the best sort" and benefit from "a degree of caution and fidelity of the workman."[96] But, of course, on both counts, Kennicott's project is lacking: he neither has useful manuscripts nor does he have competent assistants to carry out his work, other than Mr. Dumay himself.

He also is quick to point out the contradictory nature of Kennicott's claims in a manner similar to that of the French critics. Kennicott professes, on the one hand, that his manuscripts have no bearing on matters of faith, thus rendering them useless to the Christian community, while, on the other hand, he appears as a champion of the Christian faith through his alleged correction of the Masoretic text of Psalm 16:10. "He would make us believe," continues Dumay, "that the Massora has established what it has certainly corrected." For this alleged correction, he claims to have protected a cardinal principle of faith "though the error he exhibits in so pompous a manner, be in strictness no error at all."[97]

Also, in a manner similar to the French critics, he pokes fun at the notion that Kennicott can produce better manuscripts than those of Cardinal Ximenes some 150 years earlier, or that his recent manuscript discoveries are any less Jewish in their origin than those that were utilized for the printed text. He is prepared to challenge the Doctor "to produce any one ancient Hebrew manuscript which has not been written by a Jew."[98]

He again returns to the matter of the assistants' qualifications and to the quality of the manuscripts procured, in each case adding rich detail

[94] Ibid., fol. 17.
[95] Ibid., fols. 19, 21–22. The quotation is from fol. 19.
[96] Ibid., fol. 25.
[97] Ibid., fols. 28–32.
[98] Ibid., fols. 38–42.

to his accusations. He relates that one of the present assistants is a sailor whose only qualification for the job is that he is a son of a converted Jew. He describes the manuscripts he has inspected in Cambridge, Paris, and the British Museum and concludes that all of them are unreliable, corrupt, and useless. Finally, he also argues that the project is ultimately deleterious to the Christian faith in leading "to confusion, scepticism, and profaneness." He concludes with a dire warning: "But time . . . will shew that I have spoken the words of truth and soberness; and I wish they may be attended to, before the evil is become too inveterate to admit of a remedy."[99]

Mr. Dumay's testimony is of a different sort than those of any of his other critics. He had personally worked for Kennicott for four years and had witnessed as an "insider" both the manner in which his employer had conducted the project and its final results. But who was this character and how reliable was his testimony in the first place? Furthermore, how are we to account for the obvious parallels between his handwritten comments and those of the French monks described earlier?

We are fortunate to have a full answer from another eyewitness who was in a position to know firsthand Kennicott and his rebellious assistant. The report comes from William Jones of Nayland (1726–1800), the life-long friend of George Horne, a cleric we have already encountered as a member of the Hutchinsonian camp. When Horne became bishop of Norwich, he appointed Jones his chaplain. Another close associate of Jones was William Stevens who collected Jones's writings in twelve volumes and penned a short "Life" of the author. It is this same Stevens who translated the aforementioned critique of Kennicott from French to English. Jones, in turn, was highly devoted to his own mentor, George Horne, publishing in London in 1795 *The Memoirs of the Life, Studies, and Writings of the Right Reverend George Horne, D.D., Late Lord Bishop of Norwich*. It is this latter book that offers us a portrait of Mr. Dumay and his relationship with Dr. Kennicott.[100]

Jones discusses Dumay in the context of a highly informative portrait of Horne's relation to both the Hutchinsonians and Kennicott. Horne as a high churchman was an important advocate of Hutchinsonianism and was an especially important defender of its views during his long tenure at Oxford. When Kennicott published his disparaging remarks in *A Word*

---

[99] Ibid., fols. 47–68. The final quotation is from fol. 72.

[100] On William Jones, see *Dictionary of National Biography* 30 (London, 1892): 177–78. For George Horne, see *Dictionary of National Biography* 27 (London, 1892): 356–57; N. Aston, "Horne and Heterodoxy: The Defence of Anglican Beliefs in the Late Enlightenment," *English Historical Review* 108 (1991): 895–919. See also, on both figures, Clark, *English Society, 1688–1832*, pp. 218–22, 230–32, 247–49, 273–74; Young, *Religion and Enlightenment*, pp. 136–47.

to the Hutchinsonians, Horne immediately responded in *An Apology for Certain Gentlemen in the University of Oxford, aspersed in a late anonymous Pamphlet*, published in 1756. Four years later, he addressed the Kennicott project directly in *A View of Mr. Kennicott's Method of Correcting the Hebrew Text*. Despite this public assault on Kennicott's project, Horne and Kennicott remained good friends for many years. Nevertheless, "he thought it would be of disservice to turn the minds of the learned more toward the letter of the Bible, when they were already too much turned away from the spirit of it."[101]

Jones provides a useful summary of Horne's specific reservations and those of his circle about Kennicott. They consisted of six key issues:

1. The translation project was deemed dangerous since several suspect persons like the Socinians had previously recommended a new translation.

2. "It hurt and alarmed them, to see a learned gentleman plead and argue, as if he had a victory to obtain by proving the corruption of the Hebrew text, and [as if] it were the game he was hunting after; for this did not look as if the glory of God was the object in view, but rather his own emolument as a collator."

3. They considered the project superfluous "because the exactness of the Masoretical Jews had guarded and secured the text of their Bible in such a manner, that no other book in the world had ever been so guarded and secured."

4. Since Cardinal Ximenes and his associates had carefully collated the Hebrew text with manuscripts several centuries before, in as perfect a manner as possible, Kennicott could not expect to do it better.

5. The argument in defense of the integrity of the printed text had long ago been stated by Dr. Carpzov in his work against William Whiston and translated into English by Moses Marcus, a converted Jew.[102]

6. "As the work of confounding the text by unfound criticism would be carried on with the sanction of public authority, and the Bible left open to the experiments of evil-minded critics and cavillers," the project would have a negative effect on unbelievers, skeptics and heretics.[103]

---

[101] William Jones, *Memoirs of the Life, Studies, and Writings of the Right Reverend George Horne* (London, 1795), p. 108.

[102] He refers to *Defence of the Hebrew Bible, in answer to the charge of corruption brought against it by Mr. Whiston, in his essay towards restoring the true text of the Old Testament, etc. Wherein Mr. Whiston's pretences are . . . confuted, by . . . Dr. Carpzov . . . Translated from the Latin, with additional notes by Moses Marcus* (London, 1729). On Gottlob Carpzov (1679–1767), see R. Smend, "Spätorthodoxe Antikritik: Zum Wek des Johann Gottlob Carpzov," in *Historische Kritik und biblischer Kanon in der deutschen Aufklärung*, ed. H. G. Reventlow, W. Sparn, J. Woodbridge, Wolfenbütteler Forschungen 41 (Wiesbaden, 1988), pp. 127–37.

[103] *Memoirs of the Life*, pp. 97–100.

Jones adds one more argument voiced against Kennicott by Horne's circle. Kennicott had criticized Cardinal Ximenes for relying too heavily on Jews and their manuscripts to compile his edition. But whereas the cardinal had used converted Jews, Kennicott had hired unconverted ones as his agents, who "were still in their unbelief, except one."[104] This information appears to contradict the explicit statement in the French pamphlet that all the English Jews were hostile to Kennicott's project. It did state that at least until 1767, no Jews were employed by him, implying that they were in his employ after that date. Thus the two testimonies might be reconciled.

Be that as it may, it is the converted Jew that Jones feels compelled to describe to his readers, an extraordinary character called Dumay. Here is part of Jones's long description of him:

> [He was] a person, who having been encouraged upon benevolent motives in the beginning, proved in the issue to be not much better than the Dumas [an Irish highway robber Jones had mentioned earlier in his narrative] , who had been attended in the Castle at Oxford; and of whom it is still uncertain, whether he did not come to the same untimely end. . . . And it is doubtful to me whether anybody is better acquainted with his character and history than myself. He was a French Jew, born upon the borders of Lorrain, and had received such an education as enabled him to understand Hebrew, and to write it with consummate excellence. . . . He had the ingratiating address of a Frenchman, with an appearance of sincerity; but with the unprincipled mind of a Jew; so that there was no depending upon him. Before he was twenty years of age, he appeared at Oxford as a petty Jewish merchant, whose whole stock consisted of a few seals, pencils, and other trinkets. . . . [Jones relates that he initially hired him and that he became friends with Horne, but then he returned to France where he became a Christian] and received baptism from a priest of the Church of Rome, under the name of Ignatius. Then he went into the army of the King of France, promoted desertion among his comrades, quarreled with his officer, and ran him through the body but without killing him."[105]

Jones continues to relate how during an engagement with the army of Prince Ferdinand, Dumay was taken captive. He eventually secured a passport to return to England upon the recommendation of a Mr. De Reiche, the Hanoverian secretary at St. James. In 1761 he presented himself to Horne in Oxford who assisted him in gaining employment with Kennicott. Dumay soon argued with his new employer and complained bitterly to Jones "that I might be a witness with him to the futility of the undertaking." Jones advised him to make peace with Kennicott and re-

[104] Ibid., p. 101.
[105] Ibid., pp. 101–3.

turn to work, but the situation worsened and Kennicott was obliged to dismiss him.[106]

He concludes with the following bizarre twist to the story:

> [He] formed a plan for forging Hebrew mss, with all the appearances of antiquity, and putting them off for genuine, to shew how the world might be imposed upon. . . . He had a wife and child to maintain, he was seldom far from beggary. . . . He could justify himself to his own conscience in any act of perfidy, against the best of his benefactors. . . . [So he] went to Paris, introduced himself to a society of Hebrew Scholars among the Capuchin Friars at St. Honoré; and amongst them all they fabricated a work in the French language which came over into England under the title of *Lettres de M. l'Abbé de* . . . , sold in Paris, 1771. . . . [Although] the pamphlet is severe . . . and yet some of its assertions are but to the same effect with those of Mr. Horne in his View. . . . [The work was translated into English] and a small anonymous pamphlet was published soon after its appearance, apologizing for the silence of Dr. Kennicott and alleging that he had no time to answer it.[107]

Jones finally adds that he consulted a Mr. Asseline, a professor of Hebrew studies at the Sorbonne, who acknowledged that the Capuchins were suspected of having compiled and edited the volume. Jones closes his account of Dumay with the apparent satisfaction that he had surely entertained his reader: "Now the reader has heard my story, let him consider, whether he can recollect a more extraordinary character, than that of this Jew, Christian, Papist, Protestant, Soldier, Scrivener, French, Englishman!"[108] And Mr. Dumay had apparently succeeded in settling his score with the poor Dr. Kennicott!

Dumay's manuscript and Jones's corroborative testimony offer us remarkable evidence about Kennicott, the unfulfilled claims and real limitations of his project, and the opposition he engendered from a variety of dissenters. Despite Dumay's unsavory character, his own account of himself and his dealings with Kennicott generally conforms with the report of Jones. Jones offers a more balanced picture of Kennicott's handling of his problematic assistant. Nevertheless, on the critical issues regarding the viability of the project, the quality of the manuscripts consulted, and the work of the assistants, a remarkable consensus emerges. Even Dumay's depiction of Kennicott's arrogance and his difficulty in accepting the criticisms of his detractors seems to be confirmed not only by Jones but by the long history of Kennicott's skirmishes with those who disapproved of his ambitious undertaking. Furthermore, Jones's contention that Dumay

---

[106] Ibid., pp. 103–4.
[107] Ibid., pp. 104–6.
[108] Ibid., p. 106.

was the catalyst and even the coauthor of the French criticism of Kennicott appears to be substantiated by the close parallels between Dumay's own manuscript of 1765 and the French publication of 1771. Dumay had apparently engineered a campaign of vilification of Kennicott as a means of "paying him back" for the personal indignities he claims to have suffered at the hands of his former employer. But his criticisms went beyond the matter of his personal situation. He articulated positions that paralleled and reinforced those reservations of both Horne and the Hutchinsonians as well as the Capuchin Hebraists of Paris. Jones, while harshly criticizing his moral scruples, was obliged to admit that Dumay's accusations against Kennicott were in general agreement with those of Horne. And because this knowledgeable assistant had the personal experience and linguistic expertise to evaluate Kennicott's project as no other critic could, he proved to be a valuable agent in a collusion of interests between Protestants, Catholics, and Jews to damage Kennicott's reputation and undermine his well-publicized undertaking.

We have thus come full circle in reconstructing a part of a complex history of the Kennicott project and its reception in England and Paris during the author's lifetime—a story that begins with a Jew and ends with another, albeit a converted one. The public debate over Kennicott's initiative is primarily situated in a Christian scholarly world, pitting two communities of churchman against each other. Nevertheless, several prominent English Jews had a vital stake in this debate as well. In the complex and shifting alliances between Hutchinsonians, Kennicottians, and Catholics, Jews were not insignificant players in the drama that unfolded from the 1750s through the 1770s, as learned defenders of the Masoretic text who were not timid to express their views in print, as teachers and interlocutors with churchmen who relied on their Hebraic expertise, as collectors and collators of Hebrew manuscripts, and even, in the case of the colorful Mr. Dumay, as operators manipulating public opinion to advance their own personal needs. That they were noticed for the variety of roles they performed by Kennicott, the Hutchinsonians, Anselm Bayly, Henry Owen, and others, has been amply demonstrated. Kennicott had presented them with a rigorous challenge to the authenticity of their faith and its scriptural foundations. They responded as Jews had responded in previous centuries to Christian provocations, but, in this instance, their manifold engagements with the Christian world reflected their unique social and cultural status in mid-eighteenth-century England. They were small in number but confident and secure enough to defend publicly the integrity of Judaism while aligning themselves with powerful members of the Christian community who would espouse their interests even more.

Yet, despite Kennicott's vociferous opposition, he numbered among his supporters some of the most formidable and well-connected leaders of the Church of England, especially the illustrious bishop of Oxford and then London, Robert Lowth. Kennicott could afford to remain silent against his critics' stinging barbs, because he could count on his powerful friends to continue to offer him sufficient moral and financial support. Furthermore, by winning over Lowth and several of his colleagues to his cause, he could enjoy the firstfruits of his exhaustive effort of collation with the appearance of new English translations of various books of the Old Testament based on his "sacred criticism" and suggested methods of emendation. With the appearance of Lowth's impressive new translation of the book of Isaiah based explicitly on Kennicott's methods of determining the Hebrew text, a new stage of Kennicott's influence was set and an even more alarming object of Jewish consternation and anxiety became evident. A systematic and comprehensive Jewish evaluation of the practical results of Kennicott's system was thus urgently called for, a task that David Levi, Anglo-Jewry's most effective defender, assigned himself.

Two

The New and "Metrical" English Bible: Robert Lowth and His Jewish Critic, David Levi

DAVID LEVI (1742–1801) was clearly the most prominent figure among the small coterie of learned Jews in London in the late eighteenth century. Although raised in humble surroundings and obliged to earn a modest livelihood as first a shoemaker and then a hatmaker, Levi was a remarkably articulate spokesman of Judaism. Both an accomplished Hebraist and vociferous reader of Christian scholarship on the Bible and ancient history, he was in a particularly strong position to digest and evaluate the new Christian scholarship, particularly as it presented Judaism and its scriptural foundations. A man of seemingly unlimited physical stamina and unbounded ambition, Levi assigned himself the formidable tasks of becoming Anglo-Jewry's primary educator as well as its principal apologist and defender against the verbal assaults of Christian theologians, biblical critics, Evangelicals, deists, and atheists. He was a one man Jewish antidefamation league and his list of publications constituted a virtual Judaic library in their own right. Significantly, Levi wrote exclusively in English. Despite his considerable knowledge of the Bible and the Jewish exegetical tradition, and despite the fact that he published Hebrew books by other contemporary authors, he made a conscious decision from the very beginning of his career to publish exclusively in the language of his homeland (Fig.1).[1]

Already in his first publication in 1782, *A Succinct Account of the Duties, Rites, and Ceremonies of the Jews*, Levi assumed the dual functions of educator and apologist-polemicist by addressing Jews and Christians simultaneously. Subsequently, as an educator, he singlehandledly published translations of the prayer books for both ashkenazic and sephardic Jews, supervised a translation of the Bible into English, produced a three-volume Hebrew grammar and glossary of key Hebrew terms, and attempted to present the essentials of Jewish faith and practice in a way

---

[1] The most recent study of David Levi is by Popkin, "David Levi, Anglo-Jewish Theologian," pp. 79–101, which lists earlier studies. Levi's relation to Eliakim ben Abraham Hart and his Hebrew books is discussed in chapter 5. Levi's relation to radical dissent in England is treated in chapter 4 and his role as a translator in chapter 6.

1. Portrait of David Levi.

accessible to the most assimilated Jew. As an apologist-polemicist, he ex-coriated every Christian author he had read who misrepresented Judaism and placed the Jews in a bad light from the historian Humphrey Prideaux to the Evangelicals Richard Brothers and James Bicheno to the Anglican bishops Newton and Lowth to the Unitarian minister and scientist Joseph Priestley to the atheists Voltaire and Paine.[2] There was simply no other Jew like him in all of eighteenth-century Europe with the audacity and

---

[2] These are all mentioned in Popkin (ibid.). Prideaux's misunderstanding of the Pharisees and Sadducees on resurrection partially motivated Levi to compose *A Succinct Account of the Duties, Rites, and Ceremonies of the Jews* (London, 1782). In his *Letters to Dr. Priestley* (London, 1793), pp. 7–8, Levi declares defiantly how he will refute Priestley as he had previously done in the cases of Prideaux and Hutchinson: "To which I answer in the lan-guage of the little champion [David], 'thy servant slew both the Lion [Dr. Prideaux] and the Bear [Hutchinson]; and this uncircumcized Philistine [Priestley] shall be as one of them,' for 'he cometh against me with a sword [elegance of diction], and with a spear [criticism], and

perseverance to take anyone on who dared to denigrate his faith and community. There was also no Jew comparable with him who so brilliantly succeeded in utilizing the printing press to present his own ideological messages to friends and foes alike. In addition, he was unique in appraising the new reality for Jewish life for what it was and for adjusting his educational and apologetic strategies accordingly. Judaism could survive in England only in translation, only if its eternal message could be converted into a language accessible to non-Jews and to Jews whose primary tongue was English. Levi never attained the same stature of Moses Mendelssohn, Berlin's Jewish philosopher. Unlike Mendelssohn, he was not a profound or original thinker and his decision to write only in English severely circumscribed his readership to England and North America alone. Nevertheless, he rightfully deserves to be considered one of the earliest, if not the first, major "public Jewish intellectual" in modern Europe who saw the larger community of Jewish and Christian readers as his primary target and essential constituency.

Levi's multifaceted career and his relations with his Christian friends like Henry Lemoine and his adversaries like Priestley and Paine have been adequately summarized by Richard Popkin and other scholars.[3] This chapter considers only one aspect, albeit a central one, of Levi's literary career and presentation of Judaism: his response to the contemporaneous Christian study of the Bible by both the Hutchinsonians and Kennicottians.

Levi became aware of the Hutchinsonians and their reading of the Bible when preparing his *Lingua Sacra*, his Hebrew grammar and dictionary, and chose to respond to them in a relatively long entry in his dictionary. While he had originally intended to write a complete response to Benjamin Kennicott and his Bible project,[4] Levi's massive *Dissertations on the Prophecies of the Old Testament* in three volumes, completed between 1793 and 1800, drained his energies and never allowed him to compose such a work as that of Raphael Baruh. Nevertheless, by the time Levi composed this most mature and sustained work in the 1790s, he was then

---

with a shield [sophistry], but I come in the name of the Lord of Hosts [simple truth].' " I have transposed Levi's own words in the notes to my bracketed passages.

[3] In addition to the account in Popkin, "David Levi, Anglo-Jewish Theologian," see the new material on Lemoine and Levi in I. McCalman, "New Jerusalems: Prophecy, Dissent, and Radical Culture in England 1786–1830," in Haakonson, *Enlightenment and Religion*, pp. 317–19. See also the chapters that follow.

[4] Levi, *Dissertations*, 1:263–64, in discussing Robert Lowth's commentary on Isaiah, writes: "In this Note, he has committed, a far greater blunder; and which clearly evinces his Ignorance of the Prophetic language, and his slavish adherence to a wretched system, of correcting the printed text by manuscripts, &c. . . . and of which, I mean to take notice in a future publication, dedicated entirely to that subject, and Kennicott's foolish, and ridiculous scheme."

forced to confront Kennicott and his agenda of collation, emendation, and translation in a new and more tangible way. Kennicott's dream of offering a new English and Christian translation of the Old Testament was in the process of being fulfilled. Robert Lowth's new translation of the book of Isaiah constituted a major literary event in London when it appeared at the culmination of the distinguished bishop's career in 1778. Lowth's artistic translation rested not only on his novel understandings of biblical poetics but also on the assumptions and results of Kennicott's scholarship.[5] Benjamin Blayney's new translations of Jeremiah and Lamentations as well as William Newcome's version of the Minor Prophets and Ezekiel followed soon after, offering the English reader an entire new set of translations of all the Old Testament prophecies, based on the model Lowth had established and informed by the principles of textual criticism Kennicott had advocated.

Given the relatively large space Levi reserved for his reactions to all three translations, especially to that of Lowth, we might correctly assume that Levi's magnum opus was written primarily with these works in mind. There were certainly other translators and other Christian misreadings to contend with in these volumes; and his polemics with the deists and atheists also engaged his attention throughout this work. Nevertheless, this trilogy of new English translations of the prophecies especially offered Levi a formidable intellectual and literary challenge and an opportunity to demonstrate his mastery of the original Hebrew text on which these translations were based. Although Levi's assaults on Thomas Paine and Joseph Priestley involved considerable daring on his part, he could at least take comfort in the fact that he was writing to a Christian reading public who generally despised Paine for his radical views and found Priestley suspect for his anti-Trinitarian positions.[6] Taking on Lowth and his part-

---

[5] For a general introduction to Lowth, see B. Hepworth, *Robert Lowth* (Boston, 1978); *Dictionary of National Biography* 34 (London, 1892): 214–16. On his theory of biblical poetics, see J. Kugel, *The Idea of Biblical Poetry: Parallelism and Its History* (New Haven, 1981), pp. 274–86; M. Roston, *Prophet and Poet: The Bible and the Growth of Romanticism* (Evanston, Ill., 1965); and S. Prickett, "Poetry and Prophecy: Bishop Lowth and the Hebrew Scriptures in Eighteenth-Century England," in *Images of Belief in Literature*, ed. D. Jaspers (London, 1984), pp. 81–103; *Words and the Word: Language, Poetics, and Biblical Interpretation* (Cambridge, 1986), pp. 105–23; and *Reading the Text: Biblical Criticism and Literary Theory* (Oxford, 1991), pp. 182–224.

[6] See, for example, Jacob Barnet, *Remarks upon Dr. Priestley's Letters to the Jews upon his Discourse on the Resurrection of Jesus and upon his Letters to the Members of the New Jerusalem* (London, 1792), pp. 7–8: "You may fall into a species of idolatry, by looking up to Dr. Priestley, exalted into a saint of superior order, power, and beatitudes, for converting you according to his own description. . . . [But] it is best, perhaps, for you [the Jews] to invite Dr. Priestley to come over to you, and be circumcised, or remain as you are, in humble

ners in translation was another matter. Lowth was in every respect a central figure of London's political and religious establishment. For a Jew to
attack him and his cohorts publicly, even after Lowth had died in 1787,
represented an act of audacity and self-assurance, well surpassing any of
Levi's earlier missiles, and with higher stakes than even Levi's unpleasant
exchanges with Joseph Priestley and his ardent supporters. Compare, for
example, the polite and timid demeanor in which Raphael Baruh offered
his suggestions on Kennicott's project to Henry Owen; or the lavish praise
of the "saintly" Bishop Lowth's Hebraic knowledge by Mordecai Gumpel
Schnaber Levison;[7] or even the measured tone of Levi's earlier comments
on the Hutchinsonians (to be considered later), with his hostile and blis-
tering disparagement of Lowth's, Blayney's, and Newcome's accomplishments. Despite its importance as a significant chapter in Jewish-Christians
relations in the modern era and in the long contest of Jewish and Christian
readings of the Bible, Levi's work and his animadversions on the new
English "sacred criticism" have been virtually ignored. What follows is
an effort to explore this subject for the first time.

I

As we have seen in the previous chapter, the Hutchinsonians' preoccupation with reading the Hebrew text of the Old Testament in the original
and extracting from their peculiar readings the Christian "meaning" of
the text was colored throughout by an anti-Jewish animus and a deep
resentment of Christian dependence on a Hebrew text shaped and preserved through the centuries by the Jews themselves. As in the case of
Kennicott, their new commitment to recovering the Hebrew text was ultimately related to their obsession to liberate the Hebrew Scriptures from
the clutches of Jewish domination and influence. Nevertheless, as we have
also seen, this compulsion could be considerably mitigated and deflected
by their still inherent need to rely on the Masoretic consonantal text, if
not its vowel points, in their attempts to undermine Benjamin Kennicott
and the credibility of his editing project. No matter how deeply they re-
sented Jewish preeminence in determining the text of the Hebrew Bible,
they hated even more the presumption of mere human critics to tamper
with what they still considered to be an accurate testimony of divine revelation. So, ironically, they were forced to defend the integrity and reliabil-

---

expectation, till it shall please God to call you in his own appointed time, and convince you
of the truth, as it is in Jesus!" On Barnet, see also chapter 4.

  [7] For both these examples, see chapter 1.

ity of Jewish scribes and to share a common front with Jews in challenging Kennicott and his following.

One wonders how Jews felt about these strange advocates of Hebraic literacy who vigorously promoted the constancy of the printed Hebrew text while casting aspersions on the vowel points and its other vestiges of "rabbinic" influence. David Levi seems to be the only contemporary Jew to have responded to them in print.[8] His careful attempt at formulating an appropriate answer is probably indicative of his difficulty in understanding the mixed signals they were sending out regarding the study of the Hebrew Bible. His lengthy response certainly offers an interesting contrast to his later unambiguous reaction to the new Christian critics and translators.

What precipitated Levi's reflections was a major conflagration among Christian exegetes that broke out at midcentury over one of John Hutchinson's most convoluted but rhetorically powerful interpretations of a

---

[8] Abraham Tang, one of Levi's Jewish contemporaries, to be considered more fully in chapter 3, may have had in mind the Hutchinsonians in the following: after commenting on the biblical phrase, "sons of God," and its mistranslation by Christians, he adds, "And were I to have the happiness of translating the *Panteteuch* in particular, I would very obviously point out this great secret [regarding the unity of God], which is latent under the various terms of *Elohim* and Jehovah, and more particularly so in the first chapter of Genesis, treating concerning the Creation: you shall not find the name of Jehovah mentioned, until the creation of man. And I do aver that the *Panteteuch* in its present Translation, is nothing but a confused chaos, with regard to the Glory of Creation; nay, it even is not systematically: but were the same rendered to the public with truth, according to the original, it would reflect honor on the work, and with the greatest ease clear these thorny bushes, which now infest and puzzle the brains of the Oxonian Divine: And let me tell them all, that though they were to comment to Eternity, they will neither do themselves nor others any real service, to encrease the understand of the scriptures; unless a true, fair, and honest translation is made from the original; and the translator must with operosity observe the sense of the Ebrew: In truth, neither flattering the Jews nor calumnizing the Nazarines. Why such a work is not accomplished in a country abounding in learned men, and several Universities, is best known to themselves . . . they cannot effect it, from want of a thorough knowledge in the Ebrew." The quotation is from *The Sentences and Proverbs of the Ancient Fathers in Six Chapters called Abouth . . . and now Translated into the English Language . . . by a Primitive Ebrew* (London, 1772), pp. xxxvi–xl. Tang's call for a more accurate translation of the Hebrew Bible does not seem related to a similar plea of Benjamin Kennicott, whose project emerged from his dissatisfaction with the condition of the original Hebrew text. Tang, in contrast, is unconcerned with the Hebrew original but rather with the mistranslations of the present English Bible and the theological suppositions upon which these inaccuracies are based. S. Leperer, in his "The First Publication of *Pirkei Avot* in to English," *L'Eylah: A Journal of Judaism* 26 (1988): 46, n. 57, identifies the "Oxonian Divine" with Kennicott but this seems inappropriate given "the thorny bushes" of misinterpretations and faulty translations to which Tang is alluding. It may be more likely he had in mind one of the Hutchinsonian divines in Oxford like George Horne, William Jones, or others.

Hebrew term. Hutchinson had argued that the word *elohim*, one of the primary ways God is designated in Scripture, is based on the three letter root *alah*, meaning either to swear or to take an oath or, simultaneously, to curse or to denounce a curse. In 1751, a long essay was published on this interpretation as well as on Hutchinson's understanding of the word *berit* (covenant)[9] entitled *Two Dissertations Concerning the Etymology and Scripture-Meaning of the Hebrew Words Elohim and Berith Occasioned by Some Notions Lately Advanced in Relation to Them* by Thomas Sharp. The essay soon provoked a torrent of criticism from Hutchinson's staunch followers—Catcott, Bate, and others, including a former Jew named David Aboab. Sharp, too, had his defenders who quickly lined up in support of his scholarly skepticism. The issue was hardly over a grammatical point alone; it revolved around the more weighty issue of how a knowledge of Hebrew grammar, especially a faulty and idiosyncratic one, could and should be mobilized to support a fundamental position of Christian theology. Levi was drawn into the controversy when a friend, "a member of the Church of England" shared with him the tracts of Hutchinson, Catcott, and Bate along with the refutation of Mr. Sharp. Levi had no alternative but to study these new Christian specimens of Hebraic learning and to judge them both with respect to their grammatical and theological underpinnings.

Before considering Levi's appraisal, let us reconstruct something of the substance and the flavor of Sharp's dissertation and those of his opponents. Thomas Sharp (1693–1758), archdeacon of Northumberland and prebendary of Durham,[10] addressed his work to Robert Spearman, Hutchinson's primary associate, as a result of several conversations they had had about the late John Hutchinson's "new rules for constructing the Hebrew language and interpreting the Scriptures." He was also responding to Mr. Catcott's own exegesis on "Elahim" informed by Hutchinson's principles. Sharp acknowledged the "uncommon derivation and construction of certain words in the Hebrew tongue" proposed by Hutchinson, but what irked him the most was the emphatic certainty in which they were proposed:

If presented as conjectures, I would not object but Mr. Hutchinson's Etymologies and Interpretations of several words, which occur almost in every page of Scripture, have been delivered to the world in another style, and under another character, viz., as certain truths, not only happily discovered after being long

---

[9] While all of the authors in this controversy also address Hutchinson's understanding of "berit," I have ignored this part of their discussions since Levi only focused on the root "alah" and the word *elohim*.

[10] On Sharp, see *Dictionary of National Biography* 51 (London, 1892): 416.

concealed and disguised by apostate Jews, but as now proved beyond contradiction. And this not without intermixing some pre-mature reflections on the weakness of interpreters in general, and the ignorance of our translators of the Bible in particular.[11]

Sharp also indicated that the case for Hutchinson's exegesis has been strenuously argued both from the pulpit and in the press, Mr. Catcott's sermon being a prime example.[12]

To derive *elohim* from the root *alah* is only a probable conjecture carrying no more weight than other learned conjectures, contends Sharp. He summarizes Hutchinson's opinion that *elohim* thus signifies the persons of the Diety engaged in an oath to perform a covenant or, in Catcott's words, "Persons who have sworn to a covenant have laid themselves under a conditional execration." Despite the homiletic power of such a derivation, "it is doubtful and questionable," Sharp concludes, "whether this word doth ever signify to swear, as a verb; or simply an oath, as a noun." Such a reading also seems inappropriate "since the Divine Persons themselves could want no assurances from each other." Rather it seems more plausible to argue that the name of God has no root at all. Because "Christ and his Apostles" were themselves "totally silent on this very interesting interpretation of "Elahim," it is best to conclude that we "cannot with any certainty make out the derivation or original import of this word, we must be content with our ignorance."[13]

Sharp's scholarly caution seemed reasonable enough. He had not ruled out Hutchinson's interpretation, arguing that it could not be taken as certain truth but only as conjecture. The Hutchinsonians took it more personally; it struck at the very heart of their hermeneutic enterprise. Julius Bate, the indefatigable defender of Hutchinsonian interests, fiercely replied to Sharp in two works printed over a four year span. In his *The Scripture Meaning of Aleim and Berith Justified Against the Exceptions of Dr. Sharpe in his Two Dissertations Concerning Elohim and Berith* published in 1751, months after Sharp's publication had appeared, Bate made it clear that the issue was hardly one where scholarly indifference should prevail. Sharp's doubts about Hutchinson's inspired interpretation "gives great apprehension of mischief to follow."[14] The heart of the matter is actually "the rules of Grammar and Construction laid down by the apostate Race [the Jews], to whom the Book of God has been sealed, ever

[11] Thomas Sharp, *Two Dissertations Concerning the Etymology and Scripture-Meaning of the Hebrew Words Elohim and Berith* (London, 1751), pp. ix, viii, xix.

[12] Ibid., p. xv.

[13] Ibid., pp. 5–6, 37, 42, , 60, 72, 81.

[14] Julius Bate, *The Scripture Meaning of Aleim and Berith Justified Against the Exceptions of Dr. Sharpe* (London, 1751), p. 11.

since they sealed the Prophecies with the Blood of the Messiah; and which became sealed among them, from their diabolical Attempts to seal it from Christians. Mr. H[utchinso]n has laid this open at large." Bate concludes: "Many have doubted about these and other Points, and will for ever doubt about these, and open a Door to doubt about everything else in Scripture, as long as that execrable Rabble called the Rabbins, are suffered to teach or influence us in the Construction of Scripture."[15]

In the course of the same year, three other works appeared responding to Dr. Sharp, two critical of him and one supportive. Benjamin Holloway, rector of Middleton-Stone in Oxfordshire, published from Oxford his *Remarks on Dr. Sharp's Pieces on the Words Elohim and Berith*. He had read Mr. Bate's rejoinder to Mr. Sharp and clearly agreed with him. He could not understand how Sharp as a "Divine" could fail to acknowledge the truth that a covenant actually took place "betwixt the Divine Persons, long before, even before the World was."[16]

A more substantial defense of the Hutchinsonian reading followed from a rather surprising source. David Aboab, who called himself professor and teacher of Hebrew, Chaldee, Italian, Spanish, and Portuguese, and was obviously a member of the famous Aboab family,[17] published in London his *Remarks upon Dr. Sharp's Two Dissertations Concerning the Etymology and Scripture-Meaning of the Hebrew Words Elohim and Berith*. Aboab had already published two English works before joining the anti-Sharp forces. His testimony of "coming out," so to speak, in converting from Judaism to Christianity was published in 1748 as *Sefer Ḥesed ve-Emet, The Mercy and Truth, or A Brief Account of the Dealings of God with David Aboab, a Native of Venice, Born and Educated a Jew, but now converted from the Darkness and Blindness of Judaism to the glorious Light of the Gospel of Christ*. Aboab's fascinating account of his peregrinations from the ghetto of Venice to London and the West Indies, his miraculous deliverances from constant disasters, and his baptism in London under the influence of various English divines need not detain us here. What is more relevant in the context of his purported expertise as a scholar of the Hebrew language is his observations regarding the low level of Hebraic literacy among the Jews of his day: "For we see among a hundred Jews, there is not five of them that understands the Old Testament in its original Hebrew." Despite their public institutions of learning,

---

[15] Ibid., pp. 12, 88.

[16] Benjamin Holloway, *Remarks on Dr. Sharp's Pieces on the Words Elohim and Berith* (Oxford, 1751), p. 6.

[17] On this family, see *Encyclopedia Judaica* 2 (Jerusalem, 1971): 89. In this article, Cecil Roth, the author, mentions David Aboab and suggests he is possibly identical with the David, born in Italy, who was excommunicated in Curaçao in 1746 after a bitter controversy with the rabbinate.

Jewish children study from masters "who are insufficient, ignorant men, who attempt little more than to bring them to the Pronunciation and the reading of it. . . . They spend a great deal of time to learn the musical marks of singing that are invented upon the Bible, as if it was some essential thing belonging to it." At the end of his treatise, Aboab announces he is publishing his own Hebrew-English dictionary to study the Bible in the original.[18]

Two years later, Aboab published *A Short, Plain, and Well-Grounded Introduction to Christianity with the Fundamental Maxims of Jesus Christ and the Confessions of a Christian.* He claims he was translating a text first written in Arabic and Italian by a Jesuit who eventually became a Protestant. In the preface to this work, he adopts a position that could have been embraced by any ardent Hutchinsonian:

> I lament the Imperfectness of all the Translations of the Scriptures, especially of the Old Testament; proceeding from the corrupt Constructions introduced by the Masorets, and other Rabbies of various denominations. . . . About 700 years ago they began to introduce the use of Points, thereby fixing the Pronunciation of the Hebrew Words, and, as they pretend, taking away all Ambiguity in the Reading and Meaning of Them: But by this means they altered the Sense of the great many Passages, which, according to their original and real meaning required by the Context, plainly described the Messiah as one coming in an humble station, and as one who was to bear on a Tree the Curse due to the sons of Adam, for the Transgression of their first Parents.[19]

Aboab, at one point, even identifies the Hebrew *Eloha* [God] in Job 4:17 as a participle passive from the root *alah*, meaning both a curse and a tree, rendering the meaning: "fallen and miserable man shall be justified by him [*Eloha*] who upon a tree shall bear the curse [of the law]."[20] Aboab had surely demonstrated that he was as able as any Hutchinsonian to confront the scholarly Dr. Sharp.

Aboab's remarks on Sharp's work begin where the Reverend Bate had left off. He is upset about Sharp's scholarly indifference about the meaning of Hebrew terms: "It is a kind of Opiate to lull men's Inquiries, telling us, 'We must be content with our Ignorance in Points concerning the Hebrew Language, which may or may not be that of Paradise, or pure and unmixed.' We are not sure it be the Mother of all Tongues, or only of the Oriental Languages; or whether it be, like the rest of them, no more than

---

[18] David Aboab, *Sefer Ḥesed ve-Emet, the Mercy and Truth, or A Brief Account of the Dealings of God with David Aboab* (London, 1748), pp. 31, 45.

[19] David Aboab, *A Short, Plain, and Well-Grounded Introduction to Christianity* (London, 1750), pp. viii–x.

[20] Ibid., p. xii.

a plank of the Shipweck at Babel."[21] Aboab is unwilling to accept so stoic
a response. Instead he offers "with great zeal" his own confirmation of
the Hutchinsonian position based on a knowledge of Hebrew grammar
far exceeding that of Holloway or Bate. In the end, he recommends that
Sharp not be misguided by "rabbinical positions" regarding pointing of
the final letter of the word *alah*. Sharp's distinction between the mutable
hey or immutable *hey* of the Jewish grammarians should be ignored. Because the points have no authority, in his view, Hutchinson's position can
be vindicated. He announces that in a separate treatise he will offer a
full critique of the points "wherein will be shewn many wrong and false
constructions of the Masorites and Rabins introduced by their points, in
matters of great consequence, to impose upon the World, especially upon
Christianity."[22]

Having dispensed with the points, Aboab can now proclaim: "Blessed
be God! We now study our Bible with better Light and upon better Foundation than the Translators and Lexicographers did, whose Foundation
and Light was only the Masorites' Notes and the Expositions of the Rabins."[23] By a simple empirical method of looking at all instances of how
a word is used in the Bible, it is legitimate to conclude, claims Aboab,
that *elohim* is derived from *alah* and that the action of swearing or taking
an oath, though not the leading sense of the word, fits the meaning in
this instance. Furthermore, "how applicable [it is] to Jehovah who had
interposed or put himself against Satan in behalf of Man."[24]

Aboab's treatise evoked the response of a George Kalmar in his *Censurer Censured or a Defense of Dr. Sharp's Two Dissertations on the
Hebrew Words Elohim and Berith Being a Reply to Mr. Aboab's Remarks*. Kalmar could do little but defend the integrity of rabbinical punctuation as more than a mere invention and "still of some use and importance." Sharp's distinction between the two types of *hey* endings was also
legitimate in his estimation. Kalmar also mentions in a postscript how he
had read Aboab's introduction to Christianity, which, he claimed, was
strewn with false translations and unjustifiable malice directed against the
rabbis.[25]

It remained for Julius Bate to have the last derisive word in attacking
Dr. Sharp a second time. In his *Reply to Dr. Sharp's Review and Defense
of his Dissertations on the Scripture Meaning of Aleim and Berith*, pub-

---

[21] Aboab, *Remarks upon Dr. Sharp's Two Dissertations*, p. 5.

[22] Ibid., pp. 11–12.

[23] Ibid., p. 14.

[24] Ibid., pp. 38–40.

[25] George E. Kalmar, *Censurer Censured or a Defence of Dr. Sharp's Two Dissertations*
(London, 1751). While Julius Bate mentions that Kalmar published three treatises, I was
only able to locate this one.

lished in London in 1755, Bate replied to a rebuttal of Sharp to his first treatise and also dismissed three treatises Kalmar had published in Sharp's defense as poorly written in a foreigner's English and as ill-mannered. That Bate was insinuating that Kalmar was a Jew or a former one from this remark seems possible. But Bate's primary target was not Kalmar but Sharp. He opens with the following formula: "Human authority is a treacherous and inadequate guide to a searcher after truth." Sharp can quibble all he wants about the grammatical problems inherent in the Hutchinsonian interpretation. But in so doing he misses entirely the proper role of the Christian interpreter of Scripture:

> For if the sense can't be made to comport, and the etymology to speak the great truths of Christianity, we need not trouble ourselves about objections found on grammatical terms and on the other side, if these titles fairly appear to point out that relation God and man stand in to each other by the Covenant of Grace; and the surprising Condescension of one of those ever-blessed Persons in becoming our Surety, and bearing the Weight of divine Justice for us, then we shall come with less biased minds to inquire into the grammar difficulties which were raised by the enemies of the Cross, and owe their bulk and size, to the mist of rabbinical evasions.[26]

Rabbinic grammar does not matter since the points do not matter: "The prophets never wrote nor spoke in points. And the letters is all they have left us to understand their meaning by. They that are so fetter'd with the Rabbinical shackles as not to care to stir a foot till gored on by the pricks, may perhaps not readily acknowledge the truth of what I say."[27] But educated Christians, Bate contends, can determine the context and the grammatical usage as well as the "apostate Rabble" did. And they can also look forward to the assistance of the Holy Spirit, "which has forsaken those wicked men, and turned to the Gentiles."[28]

Bate adds that his reading of "Aleim" rather than *elohim* conforms with its derivation from the root *alah* and corrects the pronunciation falsely introduced by the rabbis. These "execrable wretches who hatched the accursed thing of pointing . . . have [also] renounced the Trinity and a suffering Messiah, and have been ever since busy in forging evasions of the evidence of those important doctrines in the Old Testament." Thus "Aleim" asserts the coequality of all three persons of the Trinity and their sacred contract before creation. Thus "it is easy now to see the source of the opposition Mr. Hutchinson has met with on this head. Jews, Arians,

---

[26] Julius Bate, *A Reply to Dr. Sharp's Review and Defense of his Dissertations on the Scripture Meaning of Aleim and Berith* (London, 1755), pp. 5, 90.

[27] Ibid., p. 113.

[28] Ibid.

and Socinians, deny a Trinity, the Divinity of Christ and his Satisfaction, with the Sanctification and Assistance of the Holy Ghost."[29] It was patently clear that neither Sharp nor his camp could possibly respond rationally to such an assault. By arguing a grammatical point and calling for a healthy skepticism in reading the Hebrew Bible, Sharp found himself branded a heretical Christian and an agent of the diabolical Jews whose authoritative readings had disallowed the true Christological meaning of the text to emerge. Sharp continued to publish works on the antiquity of the Hebrew language and even penned a critique to Hutchinson's understanding of the Cherubim, but on this point he appeared to be silenced. He died in Durham in 1758.

II

Bate's vitriolic barbs on the Jews and rabbinic Judaism are considerably different than his characterization of them in his critique of Kennicott. In the latter Jews almost appear as a kind of silent partner in his polemic against the Oxford divine. When his cherished mentor's biblical exegesis was questioned, however, he abandoned altogether his tolerance and slight appreciation of Jewish transcribers and grammarians for an outright condemnation of them and those who made use of their grammatical rules and standardized text. It was this latter profile of Jews and Judaism that Levi encountered when studying the treatises surrounding Thomas Sharp's critique of Hutchinson. How was he to respond?

Levi treats the controversy in his Hebrew dictionary under the entry "Eloeha, God" (fig. 2). He begins with a succinct and neutral statement on the relationship between the verb *alah* and *elohim*: "Under this root the generality of lexicographers have arranged *elohim*, and which, as some say, it is a plural noun. To this, many of the commentators, both Jews and Christians agree, though in different senses. But others go much farther and place it under the root *alah*, 'to curse, or denounce a curse', and that *elohim* signifies 'those that have denounced a curse.'" He adds that the Jewish exegete Isaac Abravanel claims it has no root and Levi concurs.[30]

Levi then introduces the controversy between the Hutchinsonians and Sharp. He presents in a scholarly fashion the various positions with citations from Hutchinson, Catcott, Bate, and Sharp. He is, of course, most sympathetic to Sharp's objections. He imagines that Sharp's objection

---

[29] Ibid., p. 161.

[30] David Levi, *Lingua Sacra in Three Parts* (London, 1785–87), part II, vol. 1, entry "Eloeha, God" (no pagination).

אלה Eloeha, GOD.

Under this root the generality of lexicographers have arranged אלהים, *Elocheem*; and which, as fome fay, is a *plural* noun. To this, many of the commentators, both Jews and Chriftians agree, though in different fenfes. But others go much farther, and place it under the root אלה *Alah*, (a verb) " To curfe, or denounce a curfe;" and that, אלהים *Elocheem* fignifies, " thofe that have denounced a curfe." But the learned *Abarbanal* is of opinion that it hath no root, but is a compound word. To this laft I heartily agree; and fhall therefore produce my reafons for embracing that opinion; and which I fubmit to the candour of a liberal public; who, I hope, will view them with an impartial and candid eye.

But, before I proceed, I muft take the liberty to mention, that fome time before I propofed publifhing this dictionary, I fpent much time in inveftigating this point, which took its rife from the following caufe:—A worthy friend of mine, (a member of the church of England) in confequence of a converfation between us concerning the etymology and fcripture meaning of the noun אלהים *Elocheem*, put into my hand feveral tracts written on the fubject, by Mr. *Hutchinfon*, Mr. *Catcott*, and Mr. *Bate*, who had embraced the opinion of the derivation of אלהים from אלה; and archdeacon *Sharp*, who hath endeavoured to confute it. The fruit of which inveftigation I now propofe laying before my readers: and that they may the better be enabled to judge of the force of my obfervations, I fhall lay before them as much of the controverfy as is neceffary for the purpofe.

Mr. *John Hutchinfon* was of opinion, that, אלהים being derived from אלה *to take an oath*, fignified *the Perfons of the Deity*, engaged *in an oath to perform a covenant*. See Mofes

2. A page from David Levi's *Lingua Sacra*, vol. 1 (London, 1785), which contains the opening of his discussion of the Hebrew root *alah* and the bizarre interpretation of the Hutchinsonians, who are mentioned by name.

"proceeded from the great difficulty he experienced in fixing on a root able to convey so forcible and comprehensive a signification, as to be adequate to the true meaning of the noun *elohim*." After citing him, he pauses to announce he will not follow the whole argument because

> my design being only to state the different opinions of each party as the means of giving birth to the above-mentioned investigation. For when I, with the greatest attention, fully weighted and considered the arguments on both sides, pro and con, it chanced to me as to the prophet Daniel. . . . I was astonished for one hour, and my thoughts troubled me; when I began to reflect, how it was possible that men, who make profession of paying adoration to the supreme Being, should thus degrade him by advancing such doctrines . . . [referring to Him as] persons who have sworn to a covenant. . . . This I presume, at once, annihilates his Omnipotence . . . by being obliged to lay a part of himself under a conditional execration, is to circumscribe his power; consequently, he cannot be that Omnipotent Almighty Being he is described to be.[31]

Sharp had previously alluded to the theological problem of limiting the Divinity through an obligatory covenant but Levi makes it explicit: "If he had not thus bound himself to the performance of this covenant, he might have been tempted not to have fulfilled it. How could a supreme being become execrated? Unless we subject him to mutability." It is not the plurality of persons of the Diety that is problematic to Levi, only their binding contract, a notion whose dreadful consequences offer "a clear demonstration to what length man's passions will hurry him in the maintenance of a favorite point." Even this theological error does not prompt him to condemn the Hutchinsonians for "he will not read their hearts." Instead, he calmly offers to rescue them from the error of misrepresenting the Diety: "However, whether they foresaw the evil tendency of their proposition or not; I was determined, after mature deliberations, and due reflection on their pernicious hypothesis, to endeavor, if possible, to apply an antidote to their poison, by shewing the true etymology of the noun Eloheem, and thereby vindicate the honour and glory, omnipotence and immutability, of the Lord Jehovah. . . . This I shall endeavor to perform with candour, impartiality, and justice to all parties."[32]

What follows is a comprehensive digest of Christian and Jewish exegetes on the etymology of *elohim*. Among the English clerics, he includes Dr. Mathew Henry (1662–1714), author of the six-volume *Exposition of the Old and New Testaments*, who proposes the usual Christian interpretation of *elohim* as alluding to the Trinity. Levi is remarkably tolerant of this reading, even praising this divine for "for his great and intrepid spirit,

[31] Ibid.
[32] Ibid.

in braving all dangers, and boldly plunging into the ocean of theology."
However, he adds, "I must freely confess my astonishment at his temerity,
in thus building the doctrine of the Trinity upon so slight a foundation. . . . what proof hath he produced, that that plurality implies the
Trinity, and no more."[33] He similarly treats John Gill (1697–1771),[34] Bap-
tist minister and student of rabbinics, on his exegesis on Genesis 1: "I am
utterly unable to conceive, how so learned a man as Dr. Gill is represented
to be, and withal so zealous for the Christian religion, should endeavor
to establish the Trinity (and which I opine to be the very corner stone of
Christianity), upon so slight and tottering a foundation as the passage
alluded to in Psalms [Gill referred to Psalm 32:6]."[35]

I shall mention only one more of the Christian clergymen Levi cites,
primarily because it is quite unusual Levi would have referred to him in
the first place. This is William Dodd (1729–77), cleric, popular writer,
Freemason, and instigator of various charities, known as "the Macaroni
Parson," who was hanged for forging the signature of his patron on a
bond.[36] Long before his debacle, Dodd had published a commentary on
the Bible from manuscripts attributed to Locke, which appeared in
monthly installments between 1765 and 1770 and then was published in
its entirety. Dodd presents the interpretations of the Hutchinsonians and
Sharp with full impartiality, adding as well Locke's own note on the meaning of *elohim* that included Calvin's dismissal of the connection between
the Trinity and *elohim* as "a strained gloss." Levi apparently appreciated
this citation from Calvin who expressed his own view precisely and made
light of the eisegesis of commentators such as Henry and Gill. This apparently allowed him to ignore the dubious source of his quotation: a cleric
whose immoral character had led him to his ruinous end.[37]

Having surveyed a sampling of Christian commentators on *elohim*,
Levi then turns to the "Hebrew" ones. They include the standard medieval luminaries: Maimonides, Ibn Ezra, Kimḥi, and especially Abravanel.
In his effort to be evenhanded, he does not refrain from criticizing some
of their views as well. He comes finally to his own position that the noun

[33] On Henry, see *Dictionary of National Biography* 9 (London, 1908): 574–75.

[34] On John Gill, see *Dictionary of National Biography* 7 (London, 1908): 1234. M.A.G.
Haykin, ed., *The Life and Thought of John Gill (1697–1771)*, Studies in the History of
Christian Thought, vol. 77 (Leiden, 1997). Gill also wrote *The Antiquity of the Hebrew
Language, Letters, Vowel Points, and Accents* (London, 1767), which Levi cited favorably.

[35] Levi, *Lingua Sacra*, II, 1, entry "Eloeha, God."

[36] On William Dodd, see *Dictionary of National Biography* 5 (London, 1908): 1060–62;
J. Money, "The Masonic Moment; Or, Ritual, Replica, and Credit: John Wilkes, the Macaroni Parson, and the Making of the Middle-Class Mind," *Journal of British Studies* 32
(1993): 358–95; G. Howson, *The Macaroni Parson, a Life of the Unfortunate Dr. Dodd*
(London, 1973).

[37] Levi, *Lingua Sacra*, II, 1, entry "Eloeha, God."

elohim is a compound word, singular, and has no root in the Hebrew language. He acknowledges that it is not his view alone but is based primarily on that of the "learned Abravanel" who "is to be equalled by few, but surpassed by none." Furthermore, Abravanel presents his opinion, so Levi claims, "as the joint opinion of all the learned men of the Jewish nation, in Spain and Portugal who were contemporary with him. For, being of noble birth, and possessed of a princely fortune, he spent it in the most noble and unbounded hospitality imaginable. . . . This being the case, I resume his opinion ought to have great weight." But beyond Abravanel's status as a Jewish "high churchman" is his "eminent learning, integrity, and candour; never delivering his opinion, without a full investigation of the subject, founded on the most clear and undeniable proofs."[38]

Of course, Abravanel's qualifications are transparently those by which Levi himself would like to be judged. In a similar vein, he writes elsewhere about his own scholarly presentation: "I have been thus particular, that the learned Reader may be enabled to judge of the truth and impartiality of my criticism by comparing what I have quoted with the original. For I abhor the idea of partial or mutilated quotations; and I think those highly criminal who make use of such mean arts, as they, by that means, make an Author say what he never intended . . . for it is a maxim with me, never to assert, what I cannot clearly prove. This is the criterion I wish to be judged by; and from which, I hope the public will never have cause to say, that I have in the least deviated." It is with this sense of academic responsibility that Levi proceeds to offer his argument, the details of which need not concern us here. It includes a full explanation of the two principal names of God that point to his essence and influence and eloquently describe " the supreme being" who "is perfection himself."[39]

Levi thus avoided a direct confrontation with the Hutchinsonians by presenting his opinion in as evenhanded and balanced manner as possible. He had apparently not examined all of their works written in the heat of the controversy over Sharp. He cites specifically a section of Hutchinson's collected writings, Catcott's sermon of 1735, and Bate's *Critica Hebraea*, his Hebrew-English dictionary "without points," published in 1767, and not the two pamphlets Bate had addressed to Sharp himself. But even if he had consulted only these works, they were sufficient to enlighten him on the methods and highly provocative views of the Hutchinsonians on interpreting the Hebrew Bible and on the Jewish traditions of textual criticism and interpretation. In sharp contrast to his relentless battering of Lowth and his colleagues, which we shall shortly examine, he remains restrained throughout, preferring a strategy of seeming academic even-

[38] Ibid.
[39] Ibid.

handedness and fairness to open polemic and fierce rebuttal. This approach no doubt still allows him to point out the flimsy grounds on which *elohim* is supposed to represent the Trinity or the theological shortcoming of binding the will of the persons of the Trinity in a fixed covenant. Nevertheless, this muted criticism is couched in polite and measured comments; he enlists the support of other Christian exegetes to reinforce his point, and he even disagrees with some Jewish commentators, all presented with an air of dispassion and impartiality. Perhaps, we might reasonably conclude, that in this case, Levi calculated that picking a fight with the likes of Bate and Catcott could never be effective. Given the irrational but absolute certitude in which they presented their claims, a studied neutrality ignoring their inflamed and crude anti-Jewish remarks seemed the only pragmatic way to respond to them.

III

Although Levi never mentioned Kennicott by name and Lowth only once in his *Lingua Sacra*, he was already sufficiently aware of the Christian assault on the Masoretic tradition and, specifically, the system of vowel points. In the preface to this three-volume work, he contends with this position by conveniently rebutting his own coreligionist, Elia Levita. For Levi, this fifteenth-century scholar had argued that the points were a late invention of the Jews of Tiberias "contrary to the sentiments and persuasion of the whole nation." "This is a mere assertion without proof," continues Levi, "and that, by a person who lived near a thousand years after the supposed transaction. It is really very strange, that he only should be in the secret; that no history, Jewish or Christian, should make mention of it for such a course of years."[40]

However unfounded Levita's opinion was, it soon gained adherents both with the Protestant and "Papist" communities. Levi notes sarcastically the "politics" of the Catholics who encouraged the Protestants to question the antiquity of the points. The latter

> were not aware of the snare laid for them, nor the aim of the Papists, who hoped in the issue to avail themselves of their credulity; since it would appear from hence, that the sense of Scripture the Protestants had given to, depended on the invention of men; even of some Jews, long since the time of Christianity. This being the case, they might hope that, on this account, they would at length be

[40] Ibid., I, p. 20. On Levita, see Penkower, "New Considerations of *Sefer Massoret ha-Massoret* of Elia Levita," 8:7–73.

induced to neglect the points; and then, as words would undoubtedly be subject to various senses without them, and some contrary to each other, they would at last be convinced of the necessity of one infallible interpreter of Scripture.[41]

Levi also parries the argument that since Jews easily read rabbinic works without vowel points, they are similarly unnecessary when reading Scripture. It is true that rabbinic texts can be readily mastered by someone who is well versed in biblical Hebrew, "but as the learned Buxtorf and others have observed, there is a wide difference between the Bible and Rabbinical books, in style, in manner, and means of learning and reading them." Moreover, the sacred scriptures "contain mysteries, things sublime, and more remote from the capacities of men." When the ancient Greek translators of the Bible—"The Septuagint interpreters, Aquila, Theodotio, and Symmachus"—neglected the points and translated without them, they made gross and even blasphemous mistakes, as Dr. Gill points out in his *Dissertation Concerning the Antiquity of the Hebrew Language*, which Levi amply cites. Even Robert Lowth is enlisted in support of Levi's position regarding the inadequacy of the ancient translations, citing his *Praelectiones de Sacra Poesi Hebraeorum* published in 1753 but not his commentary on Isaiah, published twenty-five years later.[42]

Levi concludes his impassioned defense of the vowel points by offering a large inventory of rabbinic, Karaite, and Christian writers who support his opinion. Even the argument that the scroll of the Torah in Jewish synagogues is unpointed cannot go unchallenged by Levi, who contends that accompanying the unpointed text is a long oral tradition of points and accents. So Levi concludes: "For all which reasons, I am clearly of the opinion that the vowel points, as well as the letters, were given by God himself."[43]

---

[41] *Lingua Sacra*, I, p. 22.

[42] Ibid., pp. 26–27.

[43] Ibid., pp. 28–36. The last citation is from p. 33. Levi's position on the letters and vowel points of the Hebrew Bible was shared by his Jewish contemporary Israel Lyons, the elder (d. 1770). In his *Observations Relating to Various Parts of Scripture History* (Cambridge, 1768), pp. 27–39, he argues for the antiquity of the letters and for its traditional pronunciation. In his *The Scholar's Instructor: A Hebrew Grammar with Points* (Cambridge, 1735) (I have used the 4th edition, Glasgow, 1823, p. 4), he cites Louis Capellus's argument in favor of retaining the points of the Masoretes and disapproves strongly of teaching Hebrew without the vowel points. On Lyons, the elder, see *Dictionary of National Biography* 12 (London, 1908): 357. In contrast, Mordecai Schnaber Levison, in his commentary on *Kohelet, Tokhaḥat Megillah*, 1a, differs with Mendelssohn about the authority of the vowel points. Unlike him, he is willing to accept certain modest emendations in the texts since he knows the vowel and cantillation marks were later inventions. As already indicated, he also has high praise for Robert Lowth for his knowledge of Hebrew. He calls him his friend, the

Levi had apparently been too preoccupied in the preparation of his grammar and dictionary to take serious note of Robert Lowth's most mature work, his new translation of the Book of Isaiah, when it first appeared in 1778. Blayney's translation of Jeremiah in 1784, followed immediately by Newcome's version of the Minor Prophets (1785) and his rendering of Ezekiel (1788), obliged him not only to pay considerable attention to Lowth and his imitators but to reflect seriously and painfully on how best to respond to their formidable initiative. The result, his *Dissertations on the Prophecies of the Old Testament*, was long in coming—the final volume of his trilogy was not published until 1800—but it finally addressed directly the challenge Lowth had so effectively posed some twenty years earlier in his powerful statement introducing the Isaiah translation.

Lowth already established the full significance of his project from the first page of his handsome volume, dedicated to the king of England, as a part of "Sacred Criticism, which to the honour of this Nation, and to the universal benefit of the Christian Church, hath been set forward, and is now greatly advanced, under your Majesty's distinguished Patronage" (fig. 3.)[44] Wrapped in the aura of both national patriotism and Christian piety, the bishop's crusade on behalf of a new Christian text of the Old Testament, both artistically and religiously superior to the older version taken from the Jews, was no small matter to be taken lightly. Lowth's "declaration of independence" accompanied by the weight of the full Christian political and religious establishment, was meant to undermine Jewish claims of being the sole arbiters of the text. And in the new environment of Christian Hebraism, the notion that a Christian, especially one with the credentials of the erudite Lowth, could understand the Hebrew text and translate it more effectively and more poetically than any contemporary Jew was surely a painful pill for so proud a Jew as Levi to swallow. Lowth's contribution to the notion of prophecy as poetry and his penetrating insights into the mechanism of parallelism as the key to understanding biblical poetics was greeted universally as a major watershed in biblical studies. For Lowth himself to provide the example of how to translate a biblical text correctly, armed with his own literary insights developed in print years earlier and with the assistance of the Kennicott project already nearly thirty years old, was indeed a major event in the English literary and religious world.[45]

---

noble saint (p. 8b). Levison's position stands in sharp contrast to all his Jewish contemporaries, especially Levi. See also the appendix.

[44] Robert Lowth, *Isaiah: A New Translation with a Preliminary Dissertation and Notes Critical, Philological, and Explanatory* (London, 1778), dedication to the king.

[45] On Lowth and his scholarly and political standing, see the works listed in note 5.

I S A I A H.

A NEW TRANSLATION:

WITH

A PRELIMINARY DISSERTATION,

AND

N O T E S

CRITICAL, PHILOLOGICAL, AND EXPLANATORY.

By ROBERT LOWTH, D. D.

F. R. SS. LOND. AND GOETTING.

LORD BISHOP OF LONDON.

L O N D O N:

Printed by J. NICHOLS;

For J. DODSLEY in Pall-mall, and T. CADELL in the Strand.

M DCC LXX VIII.

3. Title page of Robert Lowth's *Isaiah, A New Translation with a Preliminary Dissertation and Notes Critical, Philological, and Explanatory* (London, 1778).

From the opening of his "Preliminary Dissertation" Lowth is emphatic
in his declaration to free himself from the authority of the Masoretic text,
especially its vowel points:

> We know nothing of the quantity of the syllables, in Hebrew, and of the number
> of them in many words, and of the accent, [it] will hardly be denied by any
> man: but if any shall still maintain the authority of the Masoretical Punctuation
> . . . , yet it must be allowed that no one, according to that System, hath been
> able to reduce the Hebrew Poems to any sort of harmony. And indeed, it is not
> to be wondered, that rules of Pronunciation, formed, as it is now generally
> admitted, about a thousand years after the language ceased to be spoken, should
> fail of giving us the true found of Hebrew verse. But it was impossible for the
> Masoretes, assisted in some measure by a traditionary pronunciation, delivered
> down from their ancestors, to attain to a true expression of the founds of the
> language."[46]

No doubt Lowth is honest enough to admit that the contemporary
critic "so much further removed from the only source of knowledge" can
ever hope to provide a better system. He is also prepared to acknowledge
"the scrupulous exactness and subtle refinement of the Masoretes" that
occasionally allowed them "some insight" in mastering the poetical and
rhetorical harmony of the biblical verse, even at the expense of their
"complicated System of Grammatical Punctuation, more embarrassing
than useful." He is even more complementary to the Italian Jewish scholar
Azariah de' Rossi of the sixteenth century, whose profound insights regarding the versification of the biblical text long preceded his own and
are required reading for any study of biblical poetics. And he also is fully
aware that his own method of distributing the sentences of the text into
stanzas and verses, based on the assumption that all the prophetical writings are poetical, rests on a high degree of probability.[47]

Nevertheless, none of these concessions can disavow his firm conviction
regarding the questionable authority of the Jews as the sole interpreters
and conservators of the text: "The Masoretic Punctuation, by which the
punctuation of the language is given, the forms of the several parts of
speech, the construction of the words, the distribution and limits of the
sentences, and the connection of the several members, are fixed, is in effect
an Interpretation of the Hebrew Text made by the Jews of late ages, probably not earlier than the Eighth Century; and may be considered as their
Translation of the Old Testament." If indeed the Hebrew printed Bible is
no more than a Jewish interpretation, then the Protestant translations,

---

[46] Lowth, *Isaiah: A New Translation*, p. ix.

[47] Ibid., pp. xxv, xli (he subsequently translates the chapter of the *Me'or Einayim* dealing
with Hebrew versification).

based on the latter "are in reality only versions of second-hand Translations of the Jewish Interpretation of the Old Testament." Again Lowth is
willing to acknowledge that this version still has some enduring value:
"We do not deny the usefulness of this interpretation . . . ; it has probably
the great advantage of having been formed upon a traditionary explanation of the Text, and of being generally agreeable to that sense of Scripture, which passed current, and was commonly received by the Jewish
nation in antient times; and it has certainly been of great service to the
moderns in leading them into the knowledge of the Hebrew tongue." But
this version should only be an "assistant" to contemporary students of
the Bible, "not an infallible guide." The status of the Masoretic text, adds
Lowth, is analogous to the ancient translation of the Vulgate; both are
interpretations of an authentic text unretrievable in our present day.[48]

Lowth reserves his sharpest criticisms for the Jewish scribes who introduced numerous mistakes in transmitting and preserving the text. It is
for this reason that Dr. Kennicott's accomplishment deserves the highest
praise, "a Work the greatest and most important that has been undertaken
and accomplished since the Revival of letters." Lowth acknowledges his
use of the manuscript readings of Kennicott and his assistant Mr. Bruns,
which he still must use selectively until the final results of their project
are published. He also counters the argument that his critical methods
undermine the authority of the Bible: "If it be objected, that a concession,
so large as this is, tends to invalidate the authority of Scripture; that it
gives up in effect the certainty and authenticity of the doctrines contained
in it, and exposes our religion naked and defenceless to the assaults of its
enemies; this I think, is a vain and groundless apprehension. Casual errors
may blemish parts, but do not destroy, or much alter, the whole." He
finally offers the analogy of how critical methods of reading classical
Greek literature enhance rather than diminish the proper understanding
of the original text.[49]

IV

At least seventeen references to Lowth's Isaiah translation, many of them
quite detailed and extensive, appear in Levi's *Dissertations*.[50] In offering
his critical evaluations, Levi had consulted both the original text of Lowth

[48] Ibid., pp. liv–lvi.

[49] Ibid., pp. lix–lxvii.

[50] While the following may not be an absolutely complete list, it certainly covers the
majority of the cases where Lowth's edition of Isaiah is cited and discussed. Levi, *Dissertations*, 1:60, 128–29, 142–43, 148–50, 160–61, 170–73, 204, 207, 237–39, 241, 263–64,
266, 280, 293–94; 2:27–28, 30, 53–57.

as well as *A New Translation of Isaiah. with Supplementary Notes, by a Layman* by Michael Dodson (1732–99) published in 1790.[51] His approach is to comment on specific translations and interpretations of Lowth in his notes. On several occasions, he pauses to question the general value of the entire translation and the severe limitations of the translator. He consistently objects to the facile use of variant readings taken from manuscripts that misconstrue the authentic meaning of the verse. He also is quick to point out how Lowth never possesses an intimate knowledge of ancient Jewish ritual and practice or a deep sense of the Hebrew language available to only a person reared in the language from childhood.

A good example of Levi's frustration with Lowth's Hebraic knowledge revolves around the latter's translation of Isaiah 41:27:

> This sentence, I find, has greatly perplexed the generality of Christian commentators; who not being able to enter into the true spirit of the language, its idioms, and phraseology; have totally mistaken the sense of the passage: for it is not the reading of Hebrew superficially, or collating of incorrect and faulty manuscripts, how numerous soever, that forms the true Hebraist, and enables him to understand perfectly, the prophetic language, so as to know for a certainty, where an ellipsis, emendation, or transposition is necessary: No: these will not effect it: on the contrary, it requires a profound knowledge in the language, which is scarcely attainable, but by many years intense study, and application; especially, an early acquaintance with it in one's youth, so as to become habituated to it, as to a mother tongue. It therefore, is no wonder, that inferior judges, often imagine that to be obscure, which had they been thoroughly acquainted with the language (so different in the boldness of its style: but above all, in the sudden transition of person, time, and place) would have appeared exceedingly clear. Of this we have an instance . . . for Dr. Lowth, late Bishop of London . . . observes . . .[52]

Levi's attitude toward Lowth's translation of Isaiah 18:3 is equally dismissive. After questioning his understanding of the words "standard and trumpet" in the verse, Levi writes:

> This indeed, is the real state of the matter, and that not of this verse only, but of the whole chapter: for the great part of his translation, and the whole of the comment on this prophecy, is wild, distorted, unconnected, and disjointed, on account of its supposed obscurity; at the same time that the sense of the pure Hebrew is wrested (to accommodate it to his system) to the Chaldee and Syriac; so that a real Hebraist, perfectly acquainted with the idiom and phraseology of

---

[51] On Dodson, see *Dictionary of National Biography* 5 (London, 1908): 1081.

[52] Levi, *Dissertations*, 1:237–38.

the prophetic language, who is able to enter into the true spirit of the prophecy, can scarcely forbear smiling, to see what pains hath been taken, to render them unintelligible, that in itself is not so.[53]

The Christian misrepresentation of Jewish beliefs and rituals is particularly unbefitting such a scholar as the bishop. Levi had long been dismayed by the false Christian claim that the Jews had no notion of resurrection and that it first had been conceived by the disciples of Jesus. In his first publication of 1782, *A Succinct Account of the Duties, Rites, and Ceremonies of the Jews*, Levi had attacked Humphrey Prideaux's "notorious falsehood" of claiming that the Pharisees lacked a true belief in resurrection but only a Pythagorean idea of transmigration from one body to another.[54] In the *Dissertations*, he accuses Lowth of falsifying the meaning of Isaiah's prophecy in chapter 26 by arbitrarily maintaining that it merely conjures up "images used to represent the deliverance of the people of Israel from a state of the lowest depression" instead of its obvious meaning of bodily resurrection. Lowth was obliged to offer this forced explanation, claimed Levi, because it would have been highly repugnant for him to admit "that the Jews were certainly well acquainted with the doctrine of the resurrection in the days of Isaiah, who lived almost eight hundred years before the incarnation."[55]

In his comment on Isaiah 49:16, Lowth had observed that the verse alludes to a Jewish practice of making marks on the hands and arms by puncturing the skin. This triggers the following reaction from Levi: "As it is not to be supposed, that he could be so ignorant of the Jewish Ritual, as not to know, that the making of marks by punctures on the skin in the manner he describes, was strictly forbidden them (Leviticus 19:28), how could he then suppose it to be a practice common among them at that time? What! because ignorant, zealous, bigotted, and superstitious pilgrims [read "Christians"], get themselves marked, at what they call the Holy Sepulcher, with some foolish signs, are the Jews therefore to be branded with a crime to which they were strangers?" It is also a blunder since Lowth is also "so little acquainted with their [the Jewish] customs and manners at this present time; for no such art is practiced by the travelling Jews all over the world . . . as I never knew, nor heard of any such in my life; notwithstanding a strict inquiry on this subject, in my correspondence with the learned Jews in several parts of the world as well as those in this kingdom." Levi naturally assumed that Lowth's knowledge of exotic

[53] Ibid., 1:142–43.
[54] Levi, *A Succinct Account*, pp. 252–76.
[55] Levi, *Dissertations*, 1:171–73.

cultures should also extend to the contemporary Jewish community, including that of England as well.[56]

Levi's most biting satire of the entire Christian enterprise of collation and translation is found in his extended comments on Isaiah 52:8. Despite its length, it deserves to be quoted in full as a remarkable parody of the activity of Lowth's circle, a caricature that Levi conceivably adapted from the kind of familiar stories or popular narrative perhaps making the rounds of the Jewish neighborhoods he frequented. After ridiculing Bishop Lowth for a pointless emendation, he continues:

> This is the case, with all those that form new translations: who as soon as they meet with anything, that they, through their want of a thorough knowledge in the sacred language, . . . cannot instantly comprehend, and adapt to their fastidious nicety of English metre; or that will not easily yield to their system, to pronounce it a mistake the assistance of manuscripts is called in, and the poor printed text is immediately discarded. This being to my mind a reflection that I have read somewhere and that I shall relate in the words of the Author, as far as my memory will permit:
>
> As there is not absolutely a great difference between "parot", kine and 'pahot', princes. Could there not have been some, who in those amazing manuscripts (made use of by Dr. Kennicott) might have imported the latter word? I know nothing of any such thing; but let us suppose it for a moment. I immediately represent myself as a copyist of the last century; or perhaps my contemporary, who does his utmost to be expeditious in framing on the printed text, a very respectable manuscript for its antiquity. As he has been taught to read, write, and understand Hebrew indifferently, he finds in Amos iv:1: "Hear this word 'parot ha-Bashan', Ye kine of Bashan." He stops, reflects, and instantly concludes, this cannot be: "Surely," says he to himself, "it is a fault; but 'pahot' denotes Princes. Let us write it: it is more noble to address the word to the Princes of Bashan than to the kine of that country." Thus "parot" is unregistered and "pahot" recorded, How many thousand variations are of this kind!
>
> I now follow the steps of this manuscript, and see it some few years after, take its flight towards some famous Library. It is received, and treated there with a respect due only to venerable old age. They have given it a date, and that is sufficient. At last, they entrust some of the curious with it, that they may extract some variations from it. Here it is where my imagination forms a singular scene, I think I see five or six waggish boys round their master, comparing, by cursing and swaring, some old ragged copies with the printed text. One of them having my manuscript before him, falls upon Amos, and finds in his copy "pahot", Princes: and going back to the printed text, he reads there "parot",

---

[56] Ibid., 1:264–65. Note Levi's comment about his correspondence with Jews around the world, which does not seem to be extant.

Kine. "Ah! master," he exclaimes, "what horror! the Hebrew text imports kine." The old pretended Hebraist runs to it, turns his spying glass, verifies by himself the two lessons, and applauds both the ignorance of his pupil, and that of the copyist. A variation of the utmost consequence! An acclamation of triumph; an excommunication of the printed text: a consecration without reserve of the manuscripts."

Is not this the dream of my author very pleasant, and highly deverting? I am sure it must be extremely edifying to the profound critics.[57]

V

At one point, Levi linked explicitly his criticism of Lowth with that of his two admirers and collaborators Benjamin Blayney and William Newcome. It is a good starting point to consider the latter two and Levi's misgivings about their biblical scholarship. In commenting on Lowth's understanding of Isaiah 59:18, Levi chastises the bishop

who not being able to enter into the true spirit of the Language, its idiom and phraseology, much less of the form and manner of the prophet, notwithstanding all the pompous language he has made use of, to make us believe that he was perfectly acquainted therewith . . . has miserably perverted the text . . . , together with the whole of his wretched system of correcting the present printed text by manuscripts; and to wish, Dr. Blayney in his new Translation of Jeremiah, and Dr. Newcome, Arch Bishop of Armagh in his Translation of Ezekiel, and the minor prophets, as will also Kennicott's foolish and ridiculous scheme: nay, I will not scuple to call it profane, as well as foolish, notwithstanding the high bombastical encomiums bestowed on it by the Authors of the New and metrical Translations.[58]

Levi was correct in noticing the linkage and in treating the other two men in the same breath as Lowth and Kennicott. Benjamin Blayney (1728–1891), the rector of Polshott in Wilts and fellow of Hertford College, Oxford,[59] and William Newcome (1729–1800), the bishop of Waterford and then archbishop of Armagh,[60] were not only the same age but also become good friends through their connection at Hertford College. Both had pursued seriously the study of the Hebrew Bible and both were inspired by the earlier achievements of Kennicott and Lowth, to whom

---

[57] *Dissertations*, 1:293–94.

[58] Ibid., 2:27–28.

[59] On Benjamin Blayney, see *Dictionary of National Biography* 2 (London, 1908): 670.

[60] On William Newcome, see *Dictionary of National Biography* 14 (London, 1908): 322–23.

they were much indebted for their own methods of understanding and translating the prophets. Blayney was the first of the two to publish his *Jeremiah and Lamentations: A New Translation* in 1784. Newcombe published in the following year *An Attempt Towards an Improved Version, a Metrical Arrangement and an Explanation of the Twelve Minor Prophets*, which was followed three years later by his *An Attempt Towards an Improved Version, a Metrical Arrangement, and an Explanation of the Prophet Ezekiel.*

Levi had also noticed "the high bombastical encomiums" bestowed on the methods of Kennicott and Lowth by these two men in the introductions to all three of these works. Blayney openly announces to his readers that he has followed the rules and principles "of sacred criticism so precisely laid down" by Lowth, and adds:

> As concerning the present defective state of the Hebrew text, the various kinds of mistakes that have found their way into it, and the ordinary sources of its corruption; the probability of rectifying many of those mistakes by the help of ancient versions and manuscripts; the history of those Versions and their absolute or comparative value . . . all these points have been so thoroughly examined, and represented with so much learning, skill, and precision, in the beforementioned Preliminary Dissertation of the Bishop of London, and in Dr. Kennicott's General Dissertation . . . that I have nothing new to offer concerning them.[61]

Blayney triumphantly calls for "a select assembly of the most learned and judicious Divines, commissioned by public authority to examine into the state of the Hebrew Text, to restore it as nearly as possible to its primitive purity, and to prepare from it a new Translation of the Scriptures in our own language for the public service." This new planned edition of Scripture will not become an incentive to disbelief and ridicule of the words of Scripture, as the Hutchinsonians had contended. On the contrary, a sound text and a correct translation will silence the enemies of revelation. Only a text that is understandable can protect "the vulgar and unlettered Christian" and promote "the honour of God and his true religion."[62]

Newcome's introduction to the minor prophets shares the almost identical sentiments. Newcome acknowledges that "the method of translating the prophetical books according to their supposed measure is adopted from the learned Bishop Lowth." Then he pays tribute to his mentor: "This truly learned and ingenious Prelate has contributed more than any

---

[61] Benjamin Blayney, *Jeremiah and Lamentations: A New Translation*, 2nd ed. (Edinburgh, 1810), pp. vi–vii.

[62] Ibid., pp. xiv–xvi.

writer of the age towards enabling us to understand the sense of the Hebrew Scriptures, to taste their beauties, and to restore their integrity by
the rules of sound criticism. His exposition of Isaiah is the best commentary extant on any part of the Old Testament. His translation represents
the meaning of the original with great judgment and learning." He is
equally gushing of praise for the collation of Hebrew manuscripts by "the
late learned indefatigable Doctor Kennicott, a fit instrument in the hands
of Providence";[63] and, in his opening to the book of Ezekiel, he again
praises Lowth "who, like Newton, Locke, and Clarke, raises the character
of commentator on the Scriptures to rank and dignity"[64]—encomiums
that Levi labeled as "high bombastical"!

Levi discusses Blayney's commentary some five times and Newcome's
some fifteen times.[65] I shall present only a small sampling of his reactions
to the quality of their work. Blayney's comments on Jeremiah 3:14 triggers a long response by Levi of some five pages on the subject of Jewish
converts to Christianity. Levi is incensed by Blayney's facile conclusion
that the call of the prophet in this verse refers to that of the Christian
church calling the Jews to approach the baptismal font. He remarks:
"This, may perhaps be what the authors of the *new* and *metrical* translations, may call *sound criticism*; but I am sure, it is not truth: it is not
dealing fairly by the word of God, thus to torture and wrest it from its
true sense and meaning, in order to support a certain system; and to
which, every thing is rendered subservient, without any regard as to its
relation to the subject; as is clearly the case at present." Levi proceeds to
discuss the actual reality of Jewish conversion. Throughout history and
into the present time, the church has failed to attract voluntary converts.
Jews embraced Christianity "only on account of the numberless massa-
cres, persecutions, and banishments, which the nation suffered" or they
were persuaded to relinquish their faith "by the power of gold. In the
latter case, the converts were usually insincere and reverted to their former
state "after they had pocketed the money." Levi even relates the experiences of several such insincere individuals who profited financially from
their feigned conversions. In the case of one such impostor, Levi himself
was almost implicated when it was rumored that he too was willing to
convert.[66]

---

[63] William Newcome, *An Attempt Towards an Improved Version . . . of the Twelve Minor Prophets* (Dublin, 1785), pp. iv, viii, xviii.

[64] William Newcome, *An Attempt Towards an Improved Version . . . of the Prophet Ezekiel* (Dublin, 1788), p. xvii.

[65] For Blayney, see Levi, *Dissertations*, 2:111–16, 144, 152–53, 157–8; 3:187. For Newcome, see ibid., 1:60–61; 2:214, 215, 248, 279–80, 286, 297–98, 300; 3:48, 56–57, 88, 105, 132, 221, 234.

[66] Ibid., 2:111–16.

Blayney's emendation of Jeremiah 31:15, eliminating the supposed re-
dundancy of the repetition of *al baneha* (for her children), is held up for
ridicule by Levi: "had he been fully acquainted with the sacred Language,
so different in idiom from all others; especially, the prophetic part; (into
the spirit of which, he was by no means able to enter) he would not have
decided so hastily on the word of God; contrary to all the Hebrew printed
Bibles; the Hebrew Commentators; the Chaldee Paraphrast, and the received reading." Levi also points out the embarrassing observation that
even Blayney's own teacher, the late archbishop Thomas Secker, whose
unpublished notes on the Old Testament were regularly consulted by the
entire Lowth circle, and published for Jeremiah as an appendix by
Blayney himself, had accepted the repetition.[67] Similarly, Blayney's arbitrary substitution of Moab for Edom in translating Jeremiah 49:22 is
dishonest and reprehensible to Levi who adds: "And what is still more
extraordinary, [He] has not given the least reason, in support of this *highly
valuable emendation*, as his admirers no doubt judge it to be."[68]

Levi takes to task Newcome's translation of *mikdash me'at* as "a sanc-
tuary for a short time" in Ezekiel 11:16. Levi cannot imagine why Newcome had perverted the meaning "unless it was, to expose as much as in
his power, the *corruptions* of the present printed text; and which seems
to be the sole aim of all the authors of the *new* and *metrical* translations."[69] He finds ludicrous the archbishop of Armagh's emendation of
"in the hand of Judah" to "in the hand of God" (where Judah is shortened
to the abbreviation of God's name) in Ezekiel 37:19. Levi first points out
that unlike rabbinical writings, the biblical text never uses abbreviations.
He also mockingly upbraids the commentator for his ignorance of biblical
history in suggesting Ezekiel's prophecy was fulfilled under Zerubbavel.
He writes: "But with all due deference to the Archbishop's great knowledge, in sacred and profane learning, I fain would ask him, where he
found that Zerubbabel ever reigned over Judah, Ephraim, and *all* the
house of Israel. . . . Now, . . . this promise surely, cannot be said to have
been fulfilled under Zerubbabel, who was nothing more, than the gover-
nor of Judea under Cyrus; and not the king under whom the whole nation
is to be united." He concludes with a touch of irony: "It however, is some
consolation to us poor Israelites, that in his great goodness the Archbishop has allowed us to hope that, 'it may be fulfiled hereafter, under a
great king of that tribe.' "[70] Finally, he objects to Newcome's replacing
tedah, "thou knowest," for *ta'ar*, "rise up," in Ezekiel 38:15, and points

[67] Ibid., 2:152–53.
[68] Ibid., 3:187.
[69] Ibid., 1:215.
[70] Ibid., 3:279–80.

out the incorrect grammatical form the bishop proposes. And in the course of this remark, he adds sarcastically: "All this, is very fine to be sure; and sounds pompously in the ears of a mere English reader; or the half taught Hebraist. But the true Hebraist, views such false criticism with pity; and smiles at the superficial tinsel; for unfortunately for these profound critics all this will not help them."[71]

"The true Hebraist," as Levi obviously considered himself to be, had spoken the last word in offering his verdict on the highly publicized volumes of Lowth and his circle. Levi had demonstrated in a convincing manner the limitations of these translations as scholarly works; the pitfalls of hasty emendations of the standard text based on dubious manuscripts; and the theological biases that often informed some of the highly tenuous readings and interpretations of these clerics. By the time Levi finished the third and final volume of the *Dissertations*, he had been stricken with palsy and had lost the use of his right hand; he died a year later. Despite his untiring efforts throughout his life, he had hardly made a dent in the grand enterprise of Kennicott, Lowth, and their successors to reconstruct the Hebrew Scriptures and to build upon it a new English translation, a true Christian rendering free of Jewish influence. The new "sacred criticism" had become firmly entrenched in the English literary and religious scene and was making great inroads on the continent as well, especially in Germany. It would eventually be superseded by the new "higher criticism" of the Welhausen school, which some Jews would later perceive to be the new "higher anti-Semitism." In this respect, Levi had anticipated some of their worst fears and forebodings.

Levi could hardly change the direction of English biblical studies and its impact on the larger religious community. But his *Dissertations* did not go unnoticed. As Richard Popkin has pointed out, they were widely read by Christian readers in England and in North America throughout the nineteenth century.[72] Through their republication in 1819 by the notorious John King,[73] they continued to play a role in responding to the well-publicized missionary campaigns of the early nineteenth century directed to the Jews. While Mendelssohn's translation and commentary of the Hebrew Bible into German generally addressed the challenge of Kennicott and the new Christian reading of the Hebrew Bible for the Jewish community in Germany, David Levi and his handful of colleagues in England tackled even more directly and openly the immediate threat that the En-

---

[71] Ibid., 2:297–98.

[72] Popkin. "David Levi, Anglo-Jewish Theologian," p. 98, mentions Henri Grégoire, Hannah Adams, Elias Boudinot, among others.

[73] On King, see T. Endelman, "The Checkered Career of 'Jew' King: A Study in Anglo-Jewish Social History," *Association for Jewish Studies Review* 7–8 (1982–83): 69–100. See also chapters 3 and 4.

glish divines had posed to the viability of Anglo-Jewry and its faith. With
little moral or financial support from an enlightened community of fellow
Jews who could embrace the project of defending the integrity of the Masoretic text and traditional Jewish interpretation of Scripture, as was the
case in Germany, Levi virtually singlehandledly assumed the role of critic
and advocate of the Jewish reading of the Hebrew Bible in English-speaking lands. When one considers the relative isolation in which he labored,
the economic hardships that he faced, and especially the powerful forces
of the Christian theological establishment with whom he contended, Levi
emerges as a remarkably heroic figure both in articulating a Jewish faith
for Jews in the English language and in upholding the right to define their
own voice and the integrity of their own sacred writings before the aggres-
sive claims of a new community of Christian biblical scholars and translators at the close of the eighteenth century.

Three

Deism and Its Reverberations in English Jewish Thought: Abraham Ben Naphtali Tang and Some of His Contemporaries

IN ONE of his many outbursts against the deists of his day in his study of the biblical prophecies, David Levi paused to consider the corrosive impact of deism on his own community and its faith:

> Before I quit this part of the prophecy, I must take the liberty to make one observation: which is, that those of the nation, that are deists, and who consequently, do not believe in revelation; as also those who are so indifferent about the truth of prophecy, and who never care for, nor desire a restoration; and in consequence laugh at the idea of a Messiah coming to redeem them: yet nevertheless, adhere to the body of the nation; and outwardly conform to the rites of the nation; they thus remain Jews; are denominated God's people; the same as the true believers of the nation; and in like manner, bear God's covenant in their flesh.[1]

Despite their apparent loss of faith, Levi could still view members of this group in a positive light for their peculiar adhesion to the Jewish people: "For notwithstanding all their impiety, they are still united to the body of the nation: they involuntarily remain within the pale of Judaism; for they have not the courage to secede from it. They are, as it were, withheld by some invisible power: they wish not to be shackled with the burden of the ceremonial law; because it lays them under such great restraints in the pursuit of pleasure: yet, have they not fortitude sufficient to renounce it entirely."[2] For Levi, their reluctance to leave the Jewish nation even when they had renounced its faith and ritual was surely a proof of the truth of prophecy. As God had predicted, although they had thrown off the yoke of the law, they continued to remain his people: "for even those of the nation that have not the least grain of religion in them, would yet be highly offended at being called Goy a Christian, or a Gentile: or Meshummad an Apostate."[3]

One of the great ironies regarding the subsequent dissemination of Levi's ideas is the fact that these very lines of Levi are found in his *Disser-*

[1] Levi, *Dissertations*, 2:232.
[2] Ibid., 2:233.
[3] Ibid., 2:234.

tations on the Prophecies of the Old Testament republished by John King in London in 1817, with a new introduction by the editor. King's "checkered career" in radical politics and in shady business transactions has been studied by Todd Endelman and others, and will also be considered briefly in the next chapter.[4] In many respects, King, "a lapsed Jew," fits the profile of Levi as a kind of Jewish deist. That he had reaffirmed his faith in Judaism some years earlier and had now taken on the formidable task of reissuing Levi's magnum opus in order to combat Christian missionaries and to pronounce the superiority of Judaism over Christianity was itself an incongruous and unusual development. That he had patently retained in his new reaffirmation of Judaism the unmistakable vestiges of his deist faith, despite his endorsement of Levi's unwavering Orthodoxy, was surely an even more bizarre twist of fate.

Levi would inevitably have shuddered at the temerity of his editor who dedicated his rambling preface to the chief sephardic rabbi of England, Raphael Meldola, while citing Bishop Newton on Jewish survival and the avowed deist Thomas Burnet's *Sacred Theory of the Earth*.[5] He would have even been more astonished by the closing remarks of King's introduction. King there revealed his motivation in republishing the Levi tomes to counter the propaganda of Anglican missionaries who spread their pernicious misreadings of the biblical prophecies. Then King offers the following remark: "Some counterpoise to a mistaken zeal is the rapid progress of Unitarianism, which is more successful as it employs no power but argument, and no influence but reason. With unparalleled perseverance, and unabated ardour, the Jews continue their adoration of ONE GOD." And finally he concludes with his endorsement of Levi coupled with one for the Unitarians: "The Unitarians have admitted the verity of the prophecies, their creed of the Unity seems to reproach the absurd notion of Christ being the Messiah; it is astonishing that infatuation and error

---

[4] Endelman, "The Checkered Career of 'Jew' King: A Study in Anglo-Jewish Social History," pp. 69–100; I. McCalman, *Radical Underword: Prophets, Revolutionaries, and Pornographers in London, 1795–1838* (Cambridge, 1988), pp. 35–39, 66–67, and "The Infidel as Prophet: William Reid and Blakean Radicalism," in *Historicizing Blake*, ed. S. Clark and D. Worrall (New York, 1994), p. 39.

[5] John King, "Dedication to the Reverend and Learned Raphael Meldola D.D. Chief Rabbi of the Great Synagogue of the Spanish and Portuguese Jews in England," in Levi, *Dissertations*, 1:ii–xv. He cites Newton on p. xi; Burnet on pp. vi–vii. On Burnet as a deist, see S. Mandelbrote, "Isaac Newton and Thomas Burnet: Biblical Criticism and the Crisis of Late Seventeenth-Century England," in *The Books of Nature and Scripture*, ed. J. Force and R. Popkin (Dordrecht, 1994), pp. 149–78; J. Force, "Biblical Interpretation, Newton, and English Deism," in *Scepticism and Irreligion in the Seventeenth and Eighteenth Centuries*, ed. R. Popkin and A. Vanderjagt (Leiden, 1993), pp. 294–95. In the same preface, King also exposes the rabbi to William Wollaston's writing (p. xii), another deist writer. On him, see Force, "Biblical Interpretation," p. 296.

should have sustained its influence for so many centuries; but the delusion has ceased, the incantation of Priestley sorcery is dissolved; sophistry no longer bewilders, and misrepresentation no longer deceives; the Unity of God will be asserted; and no preposterous doctrine longer blaspheme him."[6]

King's extolling Unitarians and other "infidels" for "serving as providential anti-Christian corrosives"[7] in Judaism's battle to protect the integrity of its faith in the unity of God would have undoubtedly rubbed Levi the wrong way in the light of his own polemic with Joseph Priestley.[8] Nevertheless, King's bewildering pronouncement of his Jewish faith consisting of a universal embrace of the divine unity in creation analogous to deism and Unitarianism, dramatically illustrated Levi's observation written some twenty years earlier that deists of Jewish descent did exist in England and that, despite their tenuous links to traditional Jewish faith and praxis, they "miraculously" retained their Jewish identity. King was no doubt an oddity among the Jews and Christians who knew him, but as this chapter attempts to demonstrate, his views and those summarized by Levi were not uncommon among Jewish intellectuals living in England in the eighteenth and early nineteenth centuries. Several Jewish thinkers, writing both in English and in Hebrew, were deeply impressed by the universalizing and rationalizing tendencies within English Christianity, the public debates between high and low churchmen, Orthodox and Latitudinarians, and so-called deists that had persisted for over a century. In the light of what they read and what they observed, they could no longer retain the naive and unwavering faith of Levi. The arguments in favor of a God universally present among all peoples, confirmed by nature and reason, and a faith liberated of meaningless ritual and the oppressive prescriptions of mindless clerics appealed to them immensely. Judaism, in their eyes, suffered from the same depravities and malaise that Christianity had experienced; it too required the liberating and liberalizing reformulations articulated so forcefully by deists and Latitudinarians. Jews could accordingly learn much from their inquiries and pronouncements. That several of these Jewish thinkers would adopt positions analogous to several of the more radical *maskilim* writing in Germany at the end of the eighteenth century does not suggest that these English Jews were influenced by their German coreligionists. On the contrary, these early English articulations of Judaism in a deistic key were autochthonous developments emerging from the rich encounter between English and Jewish thought. There were undoubtedly some intellectual links that later devel-

---

[6] King, introduction to Levi, *Dissertations*, 1: lxxiv, lxxvi.
[7] McCalman's phrase in "The Infidel as Prophet," p. 39.
[8] On the latter, see chapter 4.

oped between English and German Jews but the primary stimulus for deistic formulations of Jewish self-identity in England and even in Germany came from the larger religious discourse emerging on English soil that profoundly affected Jew and Christian alike. To these novel and virtually unnoticed constructions of Jewish faith by English Jews this chapter now turns.[9]

I

In 1778, Abraham Van Oven (d. 1778), physician of the Great Synagogue of London since 1767, published a seemingly odd book in English with his own Hebrew translation. The work in Hebrew was entitled *Derekh*

[9] Before proceeding, some clarification of the term "deism" used in this chapter and its relation to Latitudinarianism, or simply Anglican rationalism, and Unitarianism is in order. Clark's definition might serve as a starting point: "Deism is approximately identified as a reliance on natural religion, an attempt fundamentally to simplify traditional theology, distinguishing the major items of belief held in common between all religions and deriving a flexible and vague piety from the evidence of creation rather than from specific disclosures to mankind in revelation." See Clark, *English Society, 1688–1832*, pp. 279–81. Robert Sullivan has offered an extensive review of the term from Samuel Clarke's 1704 definition to Arthur Lovejoy's in the twentieth century. See R. Sullivan, *John Toland and the Deist Controversy: A Study in Adaptations* (Cambridge, Mass., 1982), pp. 205–76. He concludes that while the term generally defined an acknowledgment of the existence of God upon the testimony of reason and a rejection of revealed religion, it was usually meant as a term of reproach with little or precise meaning. Anglican rationalists inevitably adjusted to many of the positions generally labeled deistic as they embraced Lockianism, reinterpreted the Bible, and subordinated dogma to morality. Thus, for Sullivan, there is no intellectual coherence to deism. It is better to speak of a common discourse between Anglican rationalists, Unitarians, and deists rather than assume a clear-cut ideological divide between the three. James Force similarly speaks about the deist controversy in England as having a basic epistemological polarity between natural and revealed religions, but between the two poles there existed a variety of theological positions devoted to synthesizing these two epistemologies. See J. Force, "Newtonians and Deism," in *Essays on the Context, Nature, and Influence of Isaac Newton's Theology*, ed. J. Force and R. Popkin (Dordrecht, 1990), p. 46. Clark adds that while deism emerged as a self-conscious movement in the 1690s, spurred on by the indirect support of Locke's essays and by the strong articulations of Toland, Collins, and Tindal, it was already a spent force by the 1740s. Its later influence was due to its reimportation via Voltaire and other French thinkers. Unitarianism, and its close affiliation with the earlier Arianism and Socianism, focused primarily on anti-Trinitarianism and a denial of the divinity of Jesus Christ. Given the inherent difficulty of distinguishing between all of these groups and their similarly sounding arguments, I have refrained from labeling any of the Jewish thinkers treated here as "deists"; rather I speak of them as having deistic inclinations, by which I mean being part of a broad theological conversation common to all the groups mentioned here regarding the relationship between natural religion and revealed religious dogma. See also N. L. Torrey, *Voltaire and the English Deists* (New Haven, 1930); and especially the comprehensive essay of E. C. Mossner on deism in *Encyclopedia of Philosophy* 2 (New York and London, 1967): 226–36.

Ish Yashar Ha-Melamed le-Adam Da'at Aikh Yitnaheg Kol Yemei Ḥayyav le-ẓmo u-le-Aḥerim, while in English it read *The Oeconomy of Human Life Translated from an Indian Manuscript written by an Ancient Brahmin to which is Prefixed an Account of the Manner in Which the Said Manuscript was Discovered in A Letter from an English Gentleman now Residing in China, to the Earl of *****. The Hebrew title is not a direct translation but elaborates on the meaning of "The Oeconomy of Human Life" as a kind of guidebook for moral action, corresponding to the Hebrew genre of a *sefer musar*, even though Van Oven never utilized the term. The Hebrew title also embellishes the description by indicating that the manuscript was discovered in the state archives of Tibet at the extremity of eastern India and was published by the decree of the king of China. Van Oven adds that because of its great beauty he translated it into Hebrew.

From the perspective of the history of modern translations into Hebrew, Van Oven's early effort seems strangely out of place. With the exception of the equally odd translations of his contemporary Abraham Tang (to be discussed shortly), this translation seems so ill-conceived in an environment where most Jews could read English better than Hebrew, and where the appeal of a moral treatise allegedly written by an ancient Brahman teacher for a minuscule community of Hebraic readers had to be highly circumscribed, to say the least. Even if one assumes that Van Oven planned to circulate this work among his coreligionists on the continent, the text seems inappropriate, especially because of its accompanying English translation. What then prompted this physician to undertake the translation? The justification is found in the short introduction he penned in Hebrew.

Van Oven begins by underscoring the centrality of Hebraic wisdom in ancient times, then rehearses the sins of Israel, the destruction of Israel, and the theft of Israel's legacy by the gentile nations.[10] The wisdom of the Hebrew was then hidden in the archives of these peoples, copied into their languages and presented as originating with them rather than with Israel. In the case of this Indian work, Van Oven was apparently startled by the similarity of the Indian maxims to those of his own tradition and he thus concluded:

> As the reader will judge by this book which I translated from the far-off land of Eastern India, I declared I was not inferior to them [other people who enjoyed

---

[10] On this well-rehearsed theme, certainly by Van Oven's day, see, for example, I. Zinberg, *Toledot Sifrut Yisra'el* (Tel Aviv, 1960), 2: 395–398, appendix 2; J. Elbaum, "Editions of the Book *Ẓel Olam*," (Hebrew) *Kiryat Sefer* 47 (1971–72): 167, n. 44. Yehudah ha-Levi, *Sefer ha-Kuzari*, 2:66; Maimonides, *Mishneh Torah*; Hilkhot kiddush ha-ḥodesh, 17:24; *Moreh Nevukim*, 1:71.

its beauty by translating it] in embellishing a language. So I dressed it in the garments of holiness since all its utterances are based in pure gold foundations—the love of God and the love of man to his neighbor—and all its words are of molten silver, collecting the good flour in its strainer. And all who observe it shall recognize and know that it originated in blessed seed [see Isaiah 61:9] and was forgotten because it was composed long ago. Its descendants were the Emim, the Asshurim, the Letushim, and the Leummim, the descendants of Midian, Epha and Epher [see Genesis 25:3–4].[11]

Whether Van Oven actually believed he had rediscovered an ancient specimen of Hebraic wisdom long lost in the Far East and was simply returning it to its rightful owner, "the blessed seed" of the Jews, or was simply employing a well-tested convention to legitimate his audacious literary project is hard to determine. No doubt his sense that he had uncovered a Hebrew original was heightened by the English translation, which consciously strove to present the alleged wisdom of the Indian sage in the biblical style of Proverbs or Job. Be that as it may, Van Oven genuinely believed he had uncovered a work of profound moral worth meaningful to a potential audience of Jewish readers.

Although Van Oven faithfully translated the entire work, he conspicuously left untranslated the long English preface explaining the elaborate circumstances by which the manuscript reached the West from the priests of Tibet, through the mediation of a representative of the king of China. He also failed to translate the speculations of the English translator regarding the possible author of this treatise, either Confucius or Lao Kium, another Chinese philosopher and founder of the Tao sect, or the Brahmin Dandamis.[12] Perhaps he ignored this elaborate opening because it was secondary to his higher moral purpose in which the text itself was his only priority; or perhaps he failed to expend the effort at translation because he already knew how this work had come to light.

In reality, *The Oeconomy of Human Life* was the product of Robert Dodsley (1703–64), poet, playwright, bookseller, and literary midwife for many contemporary English writers. Dodsley was a central figure in the literary world of eighteenth-century London. By giving this work a Hindu or Taoist provenance, he clearly meant to suggest the universality of his ethical handbook. By translating it into the familiar style of the wisdom books, he wished to give this work a biblical patina that would be readily appreciated by his Protestant readership. He had already published a *Chronicle of the Kings of England* in the style of the Old Testament chronicler. Although wrapped in the aura of the exotic Tibetan

---

[11] Abraham Van Oven, *Derekh Ish Yashar* (London, 1778), pp. 18–19.
[12] Ibid., pp. 1–10.

Lamas, Dodsley's morality was highly conventional and nondenominational. More English than Indian in its value system, it placed reason and
sobriety at the center of moral action; the Aristotelian golden mean bal-
ancing extreme actions; a benevolent deity ordaining order, grace, and
beauty throughout the universe; the moral justification of wealth; and
the conventional social roles for women, who nevertheless are "man's
reasonable companion, not the slaves of his passion."[13] In short, while
mimicking a Christian morality, the book, in actuality, promoted a deistic
one, eschewing any ecclesiastical authority or textual tradition of the West
for a more universal foundation in the East. Being good in Dodsley's terms
was something innately human, normative in all societies that acknowledge the one God of creation and his reasonable and compassionate providence; it depended on no specific revelation nor was it mediated by any
clerical hierarchy.[14]

Despite the lack of Christian pedigree, Dodsley's work was a major
commercial success. No book published in the eighteenth century had
more separate printings. In a span of only fifty years (1750–1800), two
hundred editions were published and in the next century one hundred
more printings were issued. In the United States alone forty-eight editions
appeared by 1800. The work was also translated into every Western language and sold well on the continent. No English work sold more copies
in the eighteenth century other than the Bible.[15]

Van Oven was clearly charmed by the simplicity and beauty of Dodsley's creation. While obviously considering the work to be consistent with
Hebraic morality, even claiming that it probably originated in Israel, he
could not have been oblivious to its nondenominational and universal
character, its deistic underpinnings, its humanistic moral message tran-
scending any specific Jewish or Christian tradition. It taught "religion,"
not Judaism or Christianity; it addressed a God accessible through reason
and nature, not through the particular revelation of the church or synagogue. There is little known about Van Oven to explain his infatuation
with the deistic ethics of Dodsley other than the fact that he completed

[13] Ibid., p. 71.
[14] On Robert Dodsley and his *The Oeconomy of Human Life*, see J. Tierney, ed., *The
Correspondence of Robert Dodsley, 1733–1764* (Cambridge, 1988), especially pp. 10–11;
H. M. Solomon, *The Rise of Robert Dodsley: Creating the New Age of Print* (Carbondale
and Edwardsville, Ill., 1996), especially pp. 139–44; D. Eddy, "Dodsley's Oeconomy of
Human Life, 1750–1751," *Modern Philology* 85 (1988): 460–79, and "Dodsley's Oeconomy of Human Life: A Partial Check List, 1750–1800," *Cornell Library Journal* 7 (1969):
49–88. See also D. Pailin, *Attitudes to Other Religions: Comparative Religion in Seven-
teenth- and Eighteenth-Century Britain* (Manchester, 1984), pp. 114–16, who attributes
The Oeconomy not to Dodsley but to Philip Dormer Stanhope, the fourth earl of Chester-
field.
[15] See the works mentioned in the previous note, especially those of D. Eddy.

his medical degree in Leiden before settling in London and that he was an accomplished Hebraist and active member of the Jewish community both prior to and after his arrival in London.[16]

Perhaps a clearer idea of Abraham's own religious orientation can be gleaned from the writing of his more famous son, Joshua Van Oven (1766–1838). Joshua not only followed in his father's footsteps in entering the medical profession and in assuming the role of surgeon to the Great Synagogue, but lovingly collected and copied in 1789 a selection of his father's early personal letters and poems.[17] Joshua played a leading role as a communal leader in addressing the problems of the Jewish poor in London; he was also one of the founders of the Jews' Free School (fig. 4).[18] Surely as a result of his pedagogic concerns, he published in London in 1835 *A Manual of Judaism Detailed in a Conversation Between a Rabbi and His Pupil*. I shall return to this interesting catechism of the Jewish faith in a later chapter.[19] It is sufficient to point out here that Joshua's understanding of Judaism was surely consistent with that of his father and probably originated through his father's instruction and example. Like his father, he speaks generally about religious and moral instruction before ever mentioning Judaism. While his treatise culminates in several passages from Moses Mendelssohn's work and a traditional recitation of Maimonides' thirteen principles of faith, it is the preliminary sections of the work that clearly define its uniqueness as a teaching tool for the Jewish faith.

If David Levi had still been alive, he would have been highly uncomfortable with Joshua's citation of Joseph Priestley in his preface in support of quality instruction in the principles of religion.[20] He might have found equally awkward Van Oven's emphatic distinction between teaching about religion in general and "its peculiar Judaical arrangement" presently taught in a "stale, flat and unprofitable" manner.[21] But Abraham Van Oven would have had no scruples regarding his son's opening definition of the religious experience:

---

[16] Abraham's only other extant writing is found in a Hebrew manuscript found in the library of Hebrew Union College, ms. acc. 491, entitled *Sefer Keli Yakar be-khol Kodesh Ne'edar*, copied by Abraham's son in London and completed in 1789. The manuscript includes Abraham's medical diploma from Leiden both in the original and in Hebrew translation. The rest of the manuscript includes letters and poems written by Abraham between 1753 and 1769, dealing with communal affairs in Amsterdam and the Hague and letters of recommendation, many with only first names included.

[17] See the previous note.

[18] For more on Joshua Van Oven, see Endelman, *The Jews of Georgian England* (1979), pp. 231–37, 243–44. Also see chapter 6.

[19] See chapter 6.

[20] Joshua Van Oven, *A Manual of Judaism* (London, 1835), pp. viii–ix.

[21] Ibid., p. x.

Painted by S. Drummond A.R.A.   Engraved by T. Blood.

LONDON, Published by Jones & Aspere, N°. 12, Cornhill 1st April 1815.

Mr. Joshua Van Oven

הרופא כה׳ יהושע וואן אובן יחייהו השם
לעדתו יקר תפארה.
לאהביו עדיה ויעטרה.

4. Portrait of Joshua Van Oven, first published in 1815.

Religion is an inward feeling of awe and veneration, induced by the knowledge of the existence of an omnipotent and eternal God, the creator, preserver, and regulator of the universal, whom we strongly feel bound to worship and adore. . . . it may really become the rational result of deep reflection, or the consequence of great research exercised by contemplative minds. Thus it is, that we find some of the most distinguished among the ancient philosophers, had, by the efforts of their own reasoning, inferred the existence of a Cause of all causes, or that an exalted independent Supreme Power must necessarily have a being.[22]

Nor would he have objected to Joshua's statement regarding the evidence of a deity known to all men through the wonders of nature:

You must be impressed with the delightful appearance presented by the fields, the trees, and flowers, the fragrance and taste of the fruits; do you not observe how nimble the dog! how fleet the horse! how strong the ox! Noticing the sun appear every day cheering the earth with its warmth and light, until night comes on, when the moon, accompanied by myriads of bright stars, takes her station in the sky with admirable beauty! . . . Could all these things exist or move, unless there was some superior power who made them, and who still directs their course?[23]

Van Oven does not neglect the particularities of the Jewish religion in the remaining sections of his book: the special character of the Sinaitic revelation, the ritual laws, the year-round calendar of Jewish festivals and observances. The manual even closes with a listing of the 613 commandments incumbent on every traditional Jew. Nevertheless, they still appear to be in some tension with and even artificially grafted on to the author's general notion of religion, his evocation of a universal deity reflected in reason and nature, which all reasonable and morally sensitive people worship. As a textbook for a Jewish school, the presentation of Jewish ritual life was obligatory and expected. It was the deist opening that marks its special quality and links it directly to Abraham's earlier effort to inculcate Hebrew readers in a religious faith common to all humanity.

II

Abraham Van Oven was not alone among English Jews in his interest in the Far East and in the notion of universal religious faith. He was also not unique in his initiative to translate the writings of foreign authors into Hebrew. Abraham ben Naphtali Tang (d. 1792), probably the most

---

[22] Ibid., pp. 3–4.
[23] Ibid., p. 6.

original scholar and thinker among Anglo-Jewry of the late eighteenth century,[24] shared with Van Oven many of the same views regarding religion and Judaism and also shared his passion for translation. Among the many intellectual projects Tang completed but never published was even a translation of William Congreve's *Mourning Bride*. The tragedy, set in the context of the early conflicts between Granada and Valencia but most slightly related to any historical reality, was first performed in London in 1697. Unlike Van Oven's effort to translate Dodsley's moralistic compendium, there does not seem to be any compelling moral or pedagogic reason why Tang elected to translate this play. Its connection with the birthplace of sephardic Jews living in England was hardly significant; its moral or religious message is ambiguous at best. Although relatively popular in its day, it was hardly Congreve's most memorable creation. Nevertheless, Tang found it of cultural interest and faithfully, albeit awkwardly, transcribed it (fig. 5).[25]

More germane to his religious and moral agenda were Tang's Hebrew translations of sections of Voltaire's philosophical dictionary. Given the notoriety of this author, especially because of his biting critique of Judaism and the Jewish community, and because of his blatant deistic positions challenging the very foundations of Christian revelation, Voltaire was not an author that most Jews of good conscience could cite approvingly except to refute or condemn his damning accusations against their ancestral heritage.[26]

[24] On Tang, see C. Roth, "The Haskalah in England," in *Essays Presented to Chief Rabbi Israel Brodie on the Occasion of His Seventieth Birthday*, ed. J. Zimmels, J. Rabbinowitz, and I. Finestein (London, 1967), pp. 368–72. Sidney Leperer wrote his Ph.D. dissertation on Tang at University College London submitted in 1976 entitled "Abraham Tang as a Precursor of the Haskalah in England." From this work he published two essays: "Abraham ben Naphtali Tang: A Precursor of the Anglo-Jewish Haskalah," *Transactions of the Jewish Historical Society of England* 24 (1974): 82–88, and "The First Publication of *Pirkei Avot* in English," pp. 41–46. Leperer's work is an important foundation for this chapter. It is limited, however, in two ways. Leperer was unaware of Tang's major work *Behinat Adam*, considered in this chapter, as well as his *Discourse Addressed to the Minority* which I treat in the next. Leperer was also wedded to Roth's notion of an English *Haskalah* as a kind of transplant from Germany and used it as the primary explanation for Tang's intellectual development. As the rest of this chapter indicates, I do not agree with this explanation.

[25] See H. Davis, ed., *The Complete Plays of William Congreve* (Chicago and London, 1967), pp. 317–84; J. Schirmann, "The First Hebrew Translation from English Literature: Congreve's *Mourning Bride*," *Scripta Hierosolymitana* 19 (1967): 3–15.

[26] On Voltaire and the Jews, see W. Klemperer, *Voltaire und die Juden* (Berlin, 1894); L. Poliakov, *Historie de l'antisémitisme de Voltaire à Wagner* (Paris, 1968), pp. 103–17; A. Arkush, "Voltaire on Judaism and Christianity," *Association for Jewish Studies Review* 18 (1993): 222–43; A. Hertzberg, *The French Enlightenment and the Jews* (New York and London, 1968), pp. 268–313; J. Katz, *From Prejudice to Destruction: Anti-Semitism, 1700–1933* (Cambridge, Mass., 1980), pp. 34–47; and A. Sutcliffe, "Myth, Origins, Identity: Voltaire, the Jews and the Enlightenment Notion of Toleration," *Eighteenth Century* 39 (1998): 107–26.

5. Title page of Abraham Tang's Hebrew translation of William Congreve's *Mourning Bride*, Jew's College Hebrew MS 19, fol. 9a.

Tang's unusual Voltaire translations need to be viewed both in relation to Van Oven's project and in the larger context of Tang's extensive writings on Jewish theology and literature. The details of Tang's life are relatively scanty, however. He was the grandson of Abraham ben Moses Taussig Neungreschel (thus the acronym "Tang"), *dayan* of the lesser rabbinic court of Prague who died in 1699. His son Naphtali left Prague and settled in London, where he married the daughter of R. Nathan Apta of Opatow, rabbi of the Hambro Synagogue. Naphtali composed several rabbinic works that were never published, including an expansive commentary on the Ethics of the Fathers called *Eẓ Avot*.[27] That Abraham his son later chose to compose his own commentary on this rabbinical collection of ethical maxims, which he published in English, might be seen as an effort to please his father.[28] In another unfinished Hebrew work called *Kol Sinai*, a kind of commentary on "the root and foundation of those halakhot [as enumerated by Maimonides], their reasons and their inner meanings," Abraham mentioned explicitly his connection with his father. He explained that he had initiated this work at the same time he had been writing his most ambitious Hebrew composition *Beḥinat Adam*. His father had complained that "I had taught nothing there of the laws and that all my heart was devoted to non-Jewish learning. I was not pacified until I wrote this small work on the law according to Moses called *Kol Sinai*."[29] Apparently Naphtali knew his son well since even in this allegedly "traditional" project, Abraham also proved incapable of turning his attention away from non-Jewish sources, particularly from his beloved Voltaire, as we shall soon see.

The other important biographical detail about Tang is his relationship to Moses Minsk. The latter was appointed preacher and teacher of a small London congregation that first appeared in London in 1770 called Ḥevrat Sha'are Ẓioñn. The only information about its membership is gleaned from a collection of Minsk's sermons published in 1772 in London under the title *Sefer Even Shoham*. Minsk's successor, Phineas ben Samuel, published his own sermon collection in 1795 called *Midrash Pinḥas*. From the lists of subscribers to both volumes, it is possible to gain some sense of the community with which Tang probably affiliated. Among the sub-

---

[27] Naphtali's works are found in manuscripts in the Library of the London Beit Din, nos. 9, 31, 32. The entire collection has recently been sold and the whereabouts of these manuscripts as well as those written by his son are presently unknown. I have used microfilms of these mansucripts located in the National and University Library of the Hebrew University, Jerusalem.

[28] *The Sentences and Proverbs of the Ancient Fathers.*

[29] MS Cincinnati HUC 728/2 (Institute for Microfilmed Hebrew Manuscripts, National and University Library, Jerusalem no. 35913), fols. 11–12.

scribers was a certain Leib ben Naphtali Tang, probably Abraham's brother.[30]

Among the many texts Minsk discussed in his published sermons was the enigmatic story of the first-century Palestinian rabbi, Joshua ben Ḥananiyah, and his strange encounter with the sages of Athens in that city where he had been sent by invitation of the Roman emperor.[31] That Tang had actually heard that sermon or studied the text with Minsk is suggested by a remarkable composition Tang penned in honor of his teacher on the very same narrative. In Tang's hands, however, the text served no moral or homiletical purpose; rather, as we shall examine, it offered a lesson in political science. For Tang the learned rabbi had been employed for undercover work by the Roman emperor to undermine a political faction in Athens who posed a political threat to the stability of the Roman government. That Minsk would have accepted his clever student's explanation of the rabbi's behavior is doubtful.[32]

A good starting point for considering Abraham Tang's religious philosophy are his three aforementioned citations of Voltaire's philosophical dictionary, as well as two other isolated comments in which he mentions him by name. The two largest translations plus a significant comment on Voltaire are found in *Beḥinat Adam*, Tang's most original and extensive work, albeit unfinished, on the existence of God and the ways humans can know and acknowledge the divine presence. Tang first translated two complete entries from Voltaire's philosophical dictionary, his "Chinese Catechism" and his discourse on "God." He integrated both sections into his own discourse without comment. In the first case, he identified Voltaire by name; in the second, he failed to note the identity of the author.[33] And even more audacious was his citation from Voltaire's entry on circumcision regarding the pagan origin of the ritual, which Tang inserted, of all places, in his aforementioned *Kol Sinai*, a work meant to demonstrate his piety and to pacify his traditional father![34]

---

[30] See C. Roth, "The Lesser London Synagogues of the Eighteenth Century," *Miscellanies of the Jewish Historical Society of England* 3 (1937): 2–4; Leperer, "Abraham ben Naphtali Tang," p. 83.

[31] Moses Minsk, *Sefer Even Shoham* (London, 1772), pp. 15a–21a on B. T. Bechorot 9b.

[32] Abraham ben Naphtali Tang, *Sabei de-bei Atuna*, MS London Beit Din 35 (Institute for Microfilmed Hebrew Manuscripts, National and University, Jerusalem no. 4698), also completed in 1772, the same year Minsk's sermons were published.

[33] "The Chinese Catechism" is found in MS Frankfurt am Main (Stadt- und Universitaetsbibliothek) 8*59, fols. 128a-145b. MS St. Petersburg(Leningrad) RNL Heb. II A22, Saltykov Shehedrin Library, is incomplete and begins in the middle of the 3rd dialogue, fols. 86a–92b; the entry on "God" is found in the St. Petersburg MS, fols. 100a–102a.

[34] MS HUC Cincinnati 728/2, fols. 28–30, Hebrew Union College. Tang also cites Voltaire one more time in his *Discourse Addressed to the Minority* (London, 1770), pp. 34–35. On this work, see the next chapter.

Tang's translation of the "Chinese Catechism" immediately suggests an analogy to Van Oven's translation of *The Oeconomy of Life*. Voltaire, like Dodsley, articulates his views of the ideal religion by recourse to a fictional Eastern sage. In Chinese Neo-Confucianism, Voltaire, together with other *philosophes*, discovered an ideal prototype for an ethical deism, a nondenominational rational religion embracing a supreme deity whose natural laws govern the universe. Voltaire was particularly enamored of China's rational system of ethics independent of a belief in a personal God, in its enlightened and stable government, and in its gentle and tolerant citizenry, all of which provided a positive substitute for the "priest-ridden" societies of Christian Europe. Whether the empirical reality of Chinese religion and society actually fit the ideal Voltaire had constructed was immaterial to him. The critical role of his Sinophilism was to debunk his own religious heritage and to promote his own deistic positions.[35]

Voltaire's "Chinese Catechism" consists of six conversations between Ku-Su, a disciple of Confucius, and Prince Koo, son of the king of Loo, tributary of the Chinese emperor Gnen-Van.[36] Voltaire establishes the date of this encounter as 417 years before the common era and adds the following imaginative attributions: "Translated in Latin by father Fouquet former ex-Jesuit. The manuscript is in the Vatican library no. 42759," all of which is faithfully translated by Tang. The two fictional characters carry on a wide-ranging conversation about the meaning of God and his relation to nature and human society and plainly express sentiments central to Voltaire's philosophy. Thus, Ku-Su proclaims: "God has given you reason; neither you nor they should abuse it."[37] And later he gives his stamp of approval for the notion of immortality since it is an appealingly rational notion: "It is therefore necessary that good and evil be judged in

---

[35] On the image of China in the Enlightenment in general and for Voltaire in particular, see W. W. Davis, "China, the Confucian Ideal, and the European Age of Enlightenment," *Journal of the History of Ideas* 44 (1983): 523–48; V. Pinot, *La Chine et la formation de l'ésprit philosophique en France (1640–1740)* (Geneva, 1971); E. Leites, "Confucianism in Eighteenth-Century England: Natural Morality and Social Reform," *Philosophy East and West* 28 (1978): 143–59; A. Rowbotham, "Voltaire Sinophile," *Publications of the Modern Language Association of America* 47 (1932): 1056–65; Pailin, *Attitudes to Other Religions*, pp. 113–14; W. Appleton, *The Chinese Vogue in England during the Seventeenth and Eighteenth Centuries* (New York, 1951); S. Ching Song, *Voltaire et la Chine* (Aix en Provence, 1989). On the Chinese Catechism in particular, see A. Becq, "Le catéchisme chinois," *Aspects du discours matérialiste en France autour de 1770, Textes et documents* (Caen, 1981), pp. 267–75.

[36] I have consulted the edition of Voltaire's *Dictionnaire philosophique*, ed. B. Didier (Paris, 1994), and the English translation of T. Besterman, *Philosophical Dictionary* (London, 1972), from which I cite.

[37] Besterman, *Philosophical Dictionary*, p. 81.

another life. It is this idea, so simple, so natural, so general, that has installed in so many nations the belief in the immortality of our souls and in the divine justice that judges them when they have abandoned their mortal remains. Is there a system more rational, more agreeable to the divinity, and more useful to mankind?"[38] And Koo emphatically remarks "that god hasn't the slightest need for our sacrifices or our prayers, but we need to address them to him; his worship was not established for him but for us."[39]

Koo continues to ridicule "the madness of the sects," the fantasies preached by the bonzes "who beguile the people in order to govern them," and their ridiculous practice of celibacy.[40] Ku-Su underscores the true virtues, those which are useful to society "such as loyalty, magnanimity, beneficence, toleration , etc."[41] And Koo finally sums up with the following wishes: "I want to live in the practice of all these virtues and in the worship of a simple and universal god, far from the chimeras of sophists and the illusions of false prophets. Love of my neighbour will be my virtue on the throne, and the love of god my religion. . . . Woe betide the people so stupid and so barbarous as to think that there is a god for its province alone! . . . The divinity speaks to the hearts of all men, and the bonds of charity should unite them from one end of the universe to the other."[42]

In the second entry translated by Tang on the subject of God, Voltaire situates his two interlocutors, Logomachos, the sophisticated theologian from Constantinople, and Dondindac, a simple shepherd, in the remote region of Scythia. Predictably, Logomachos approaches the simple heathen prepared to ridicule his naive beliefs but is soon confronted with a penetrating wisdom he had not anticipated. Besieging Dondindac with a barrage of theological queries, the shepherd will say no more than "I've no wish to be a philosopher, I want to be a man."[43] And it is the Scythian shepherd who has the last word: "Before receiving your instruction, I must tell you what happened to me one day. I had just had a closet built at the end of my garden. I heard a mole arguing with a cockchafer: 'Here's a fine structure,' said the mole; 'it must have been a powerful mole who did this work.' 'You're joking,' said the cockchafer; 'its a cockchafter full of genius who is the architect of this building.' From that moment I resolved never to argue."[44] The theologian had met his match in the majestic simplicity of the righteous heathen.

[38] Ibid., p. 85.
[39] Ibid., p. 87.
[40] Ibid., pp. 87, 90.
[41] Ibid., p. 92.
[42] Ibid., p. 94.
[43] Ibid., p. 177.
[44] Ibid., p. 178.

Tang's decision to translate these two sections from *The Philosophical Dictionary* was certainly unusual for any Jew writing at the end of the eighteenth century, but it was hardly an impulsive or unthinking move on his part. In the first place, deism had declined considerably as an ideological force in England by the middle of the eighteenth century. The writings of Toland, Collins, or Tindal had lost most of their appeal. If deism had any new life in Tang's time, it was primarily due to the import of Voltaire's works and those of other French writers into England. Thus Tang's choice of texts to expose to his Hebrew readers was both timely and made perfect sense. The primary resuscitator of English deism in his day was indeed Voltaire. In the second place, "The Chinese Catechism" and the entry on God clearly captured to a great extent the message Tang himself wished to convey in his own writing on the divinity and religion, as we shall soon see. This choice to assign a central place to Voltaire's work in his *Behinat Adam* surely must have invoked some misgivings on his part. He failed to identify Voltaire by name in the section on God. And in his concluding remarks to his theological work, he further offers some tantalizing clues about his real attitude toward Voltaire.

In the midst of a rather enigmatic passage in which he lashes out against Jews who practice the minutiae of ritual law while lacking both moral character and intellectual substance, he speaks alarmingly of an impending spiritual disaster. The following lines then appear:

> The leprosy breaks out in everything and the priest of iniquity will purify us. He is as his name *Bal Tahor* [the purifier] Voltaire. They do corrupt and loathsome things in following after him, sacrificing and worshiping at his altar. But the sect who denies everything are the disciples of Spinoza with whom it is not appropriate to debate since their own folly proves this. However, the first [Voltaire] is the sweetener and deceiver, for sometimes he speaks truth to fortify a passageway broken by the second [Spinoza]. The fools who follow him fall into his net. But this thief will be seized by tunneling [Exodus 22:1] since the sun of truth doesn't shine on him. He testifies lies [Proverb 6:19] for his table lacks salt while reason is the redeemer. When the knowledgeable person fills the pot to boil, the dove of Israel will find refuge. They will burn the thistle and plaster his smitten house until the wound is healed.[45]

Whatever Tang's precise meaning is in this passage, it is clear that he related to Voltaire, in contrast to Spinoza, with marked ambivalence. "The sweetener and deceiver" could occasionally "fortify a passageway," and despite the misconceptions of his avid followers, his reflections were

---

[45] *Behinat Adam*, MS Frankfurt (Stadt- und Universitätsbibliothek),8*59, fol. 198a. See E. Roth and L. Priss, *Hebraeische Handschriften*, vol. 1 (Wiesbaden, 1982), no. 63 (Jerusalem no. 25906).

sometimes of value.[46] At the same time, his views were potentially dangerous, especially as articulated by his followers. That Tang still proceeded to
cite whole passages approvingly from Voltaire despite his own warnings
suggests at the very least a tacit endorsement of Voltaire's positions. A
more comprehensive look at Tang's attitudes toward God, Judaism, and
the Jewish community confirms that impression even more

III

Beḥinat Adam (An examination of man) is Tang's largest work, yet until
now it has been completely ignored by modern scholarship. It exists in
three manuscripts. The first two manuscripts, apparently copied by the
hand of the author, present the first part of the work in differing orders,
so that it remains difficult to reconstruct the text, and one is left with
the impression of an unfinished and unpolished composition. The third
manuscript presents the opening of the second part of *Beḥinat Adam*,
which was obviously unfinished and also includes another unfinished
composition, the aforementioned *Kol Sinai*. Given the significance of this
larger work for evaluating Tang as a religious thinker, it needs to be examined in its own right and in relation to his other writings, both in manuscript and in print (fig. 6).[47]

Tang offers his own assessment of *Beḥinat Adam* in the opening of *Kol
Sinai*:

> I lifted my hand in faithfulness to compose a large work comprising natural and
> divine matters and I named it *Beḥinat Adam*. It was written with the likeness of
> Ecclesiastes to which I added a commentary to interpret what was hidden in it,
> to present it in God's judgment. I called it [the commentary] *Beḥinat ha-beḥinah*

---

[46] Tang's attitude toward Voltaire might be favorably compared with that of Zalkind
Hourwitz who wrote: "It may well be that Voltaire had intended less the modern Jews than
the ancient ones, that is the trunk of Christianity against which he constantly takes aim.
Whatever it may be, the Jews pardon him all the bad he has said of them in favor of the
good he has done for them albeit without wishing it, perhaps even without knowing it. For
if they enjoyed a little rest during these last years, it is due to the progress of enlightenment
to which Voltaire in numerous works against fanaticism has surely contributed more than
any other writer." Cited in F. Malino, *A Jew in the French Revolution: The Life of Zalkind
Hourwitz* (Oxford, 1996), pp. 47–48. Elsewhere Hourwitz speaks of Voltaire's "seductive
eloquence" (Malino, p. 51) which sounds especially like Tang's remark.

[47] The three manuscripts of *Beḥinat Adam* are: St. Petersburg RNL Heb. II A22 (no.
63945 in the catalog of the Institute for Microfilmed Hebrew Manuscripts, University and
National Library, Jerusalem) and Frankfurt am Main 8*59, which contain only part 1 in
differing orders and with some parts in one missing in the other; Cincinnati HUC 728/1
(Jerusalem no. 35913), which contains the beginning of part 2 and the unfinished work
called *Kol Sinai*.

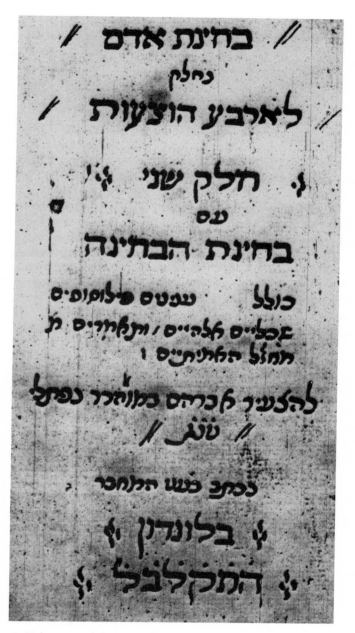

בחינת אדם //

נחלק

לארבע הוצעות //

חלק שני

עם

בחינת הבחינה

כולל   ענים פלוסופיס

שכליים אלהיים / ותלמודים מל

מחדל הלאתיותים ו

להעשיר אכרהם מווהרד נפתל

טנג //

נכתב משו המחבר

בלונדין

התקללבל

6. Title page of the second part of Abraham Tang's *Beḥinat Adam*, Hebrew MS Hebrew Union College 728, fol. 1.

[The examination of the examination] in which many of the statements of our true rabbis are elucidated, as well as stories and the rational homilies [*aggadot ve-ha-midrashim ha-sikhli'yim*] diffused throughout the four corners of [their] books. I drew them closer to the activity of the mind for which He chose us in love. When the enlightened reader reads it, he will look on us favorably because of it. Moreover, all the wise-hearted will know that the [Jewish] ancients were not inferior in all the disciplines and sciences and even in political science [*hanhagat ha-medinot*]."[48]

Tang goes on to praise his own composition on the political science of the rabbis, which we shall consider later, and the need to compose a work that focuses more on Jewish law to please his father. Of particular interest in this self-characterization of his project is the analogy he makes to the book of Ecclesiastes. In still another of his unfinished compositions, he devotes himself to an entire commentary on this biblical work, a favorite of several of his contemporaries.[49] This should also be seen together with his focus on examining "man," the entire human condition, not simply the Jews in the title. His stress on "rational" homilies, on the superiority of rabbinic knowledge of the sciences, and their fondness for the activity of the mind should also be noted.

In another remark, which was ostensibly meant to open the composition, he reveals the following: "This was written at a time when the author was on a sick-bed and stricken with scurvy [iskorvet?] without hope of recovery."[50] Although the title page of one of the two manuscripts gives the date of this composition as 1772,[51] it seems possible that Tang had worked on this important text for a considerably longer time, perhaps up until the time he died, probably in 1792.[52] Its unfinished and chaotic state might be explained by his untimely death although this is not certain.[53] Be that as it may, Tang's progressive illness and conceivable preoccupation with his own mortality might have contributed to the more probing nature and complexity of his reflections in this composition, as well as the imperfect manner of their presentation. All of Tang's other works were written in the late 1760s and early 1770s; if he began this work in

[48] MS HUC Cincinnati 728/2, fols. 10–11.

[49] Among the most relevant to Tang's are those of Moses Mendelssohn and Mordechai Schnaber Levison, which I consider in the appendix.

[50] *Beḥinat Adam* (St. Petersburg), fol. 3a; (Frankfurt), fol. 11a.

[51] *Beḥinat Adam* (Frankfurt), fol. 195b.

[52] Roth, in his "Haskalah in England," p. 372, identifies Tang with the Abraham, son of R. Naphtali, who was buried at the Lauriston Road cemetery of the Hambro Synagogue on the new moon of Ḥeshvan, in the autumn of 1792.

[53] The Frankfurt MS, fol. 11a, immediately following the line about the author's severe illness adds "And God cured me of my illness."

that period but continued to work on it up until the time of his death, it would reflect his most mature work.

Tang stresses one final point by way of justifying his composition. He writes:

> Regarding all this evil, I saw wise men in their own eyes, masters of assemblies [see Ecclesiastes 11:12], flying like foul capturing men without intelligence in their deception while distorting the truth. And particularly at this time they have had some success by the work of their hands although this did not come to them from wisdom. Regarding this I declared that everything is made known by examining it and its character, so for this reason I began to write the scroll [*megillah*] *Beḥinat Adam.*"[54]

It is uncertain to whom he was referring. Was it the followers of Voltaire alluded to earlier and their seductive but destructive aspersions against religious faith, or was it those religious leaders, unenlightened and oppressive, who became the brunt of his stinging barbs throughout this composition and in his others, as we shall soon examine? Perhaps, he meant the destroyers of Judaism both from within and from without. Whatever target he had in mind that stimulated him to write his most ambitious work, this opening sets the tone for what follows. Sometimes veiled and sometimes explicit, Tang's writing is overtly polemical; he constantly sees himself in tension with others, generally Jews, who view God and organized religion from different perspectives. Whether his biting satire and ringing denunciations of those with whom he disagrees qualify him as a "typical *maskil*," as one scholar has called him,[55] it is clear that Tang's ballistic and forensic style emerges directly from his intellectual and social encounters with both English culture and his own Jewish community in London.

In either manuscript version of the first part of *Beḥinat Adam*, one is hard-pressed to discern a coherent development of ideas. Rather than offer even a brief synopsis of the work, I consider in this chapter only several sections that appear relatively self-contained and relate directly to the subject of deism in general and to Voltaire's ideas in particular, as well as several of Tang's other compositions where these themes are also developed and highlighted.

Tang's translation of the two entries by Voltaire is located within a larger discussion of the notion of one God as found in the civilizations of both antiquity and the newly discovered inhabited world. Tang begins his discourse on proofs of God's existence in the following way:

---

[54] *Beḥinat Adam* (St. Peterburg), fols. 3a–3b (=9).
[55] I refer to Sidney Leperer's work cited in note 24.

As the existence of a creator is verified by his activities and by the reason of his existence, so too is he verified by the spread of this view [of his existence] in all the inhabited world, even among erring persons among the important ancient peoples. We are able to demonstrate from the writing of their activities and their histories that all humankind agreed on the existence of a creator. Thus we are obligated to believe this belief which is born out of a natural opinion implanted among as many human beings who are able to testify about it.[56]

Tang's claim that a belief in one god is "natural" and independently confirmed even outside the Jewish or Christian religions is supported by a formidable lineup of ancient luminaries from Seneca to Cicero to Maximus of Tyre to even Epicurus. Tang pauses to consider the derivation of the ancient Greek name of God *numen* from the Hebrew *na-amin* (we shall believe). He also claims that the multiplicity of God's names employed by the ancients did not indicate many Gods but only the many qualities that one god possessed. Citing a large array of sources from Seneca to Celsus and Julian, Tang has no hesitation that all of these "idolaters" ultimately acknowledged the one god.[57]

Tang's most recent source is the work of bishop Stillingfleet, from which he cites a long passage on the variety of pagan names of the deity. From the ancient world to the more recently discovered continents, the same argument is extended. Additional testimonies of one god are found in Madagascar, "Monomotapa," Muscovy, and Granganor. Still relying on Stillingfleet, Tang lists other African and American examples, refers to the reports of European travelers, especially Joseph Acosta, and singles out for special mention the case of Pero. He is even insistent that those reporters who claimed that the natives of the new world were unbelievers are mistaken. Such "witnesses" were ignorant of the language and customs of their subjects; coming as conquering enemies, they lacked the proper empathetic perspective to understand their subjects; and they confused the forms of external worship with personal belief.[58]

Tang also presents an elaborate response to those who emphasize the large number of nonbelievers in the ancient world like Theodorus, Epicurus, Democritus, Pythagorus, Leucippus, and others. He first claims that none of them lived in the time when the prophets were spreading their

---

[56] *Beḥinat Adam* (St. Petersburg), fol. 68a; (Frankfurt), fol. 120a.

[57] *Beḥinat Adam* (St. Petersburg), fols. 68a–70a; (Frankfurt), fols. 120a–123b. The rest of this section continues uninterrupted until, at 127b, it reaches the Chinese Catechism. The St. Petersburg MS breaks off suddenly when it reaches fol. 72b; see my subsequent discussion.

[58] *Beḥinat Adam* (St. Petersburg), fols. 70a–71b; (Frankfurt, fols. 124a–126a). He refers to Jose de Acosta (1540–1600), *The Natural and Moral History of the Indies*, which is probably cited from Stillingfleet. On the latter, see my subsequent discussion.

exalted teachings. Furthermore, as in the case of the disciples of Jesus, many were not actually nonbelievers but were only labeled as such by their enemies. In fact, Tang can only identify seven men who actually denied God's existence and these were truly bad and boorish people. At this point, Tang introduces his translation of the "Chinese Catechism."[59]

Later in his narrative, Tang returns to other ancient testimonies of God's existence citing Empedocles, Anaxagorus, and again Cicero. Relying on the testimonies of Ovid, Pliny, Herodotus, Varro, and Eusebius, among others, he offers a long discourse on the monotheistic features of the ancient Egyptian religion and its relation to the evidence of the biblical narrative. This leads him to translate his second selection from Voltaire on God.[60]

Tang's fascination with the ancient world, with pagan mythologies, and with comparative religion are hardly novel for any educated person living at the end of the eighteenth century. His gallery of pagans, both ancient and more recent, who consistently acknowledge the existence of one God and who confirm the "naturalness" of such a notion is also hardly new. Within Hebrew literature, however, such an initiative was rare. While Renaissance Jews had long appreciated the culture and religion of ancient paganism, while some had fully imbibed the notion of a universal core of religious truths commonly known as ancient theology, and while still others had searched for signs of the ten lost tribes and their monotheistic faith in the newly discovered civilizations of the New World,[61] Tang's enterprise was new in the impressive scope of his investigations, in his obsession with insisting that pagan mythologies were necessary reading for all educated Jews, and in the specific English background that informed his arguments and their sources.

At least since the first part of the previous century, Christian authors, especially in Holland and England, had built defenses of the Christian faith based on detailed explorations of pagan theology. Samuel Bochart, in his *Geographia sacra*, Sir John Marsham, in his *Chronicus canon aegyptiacus, ebraicus, & graecus*, and Gerard Vossius, in his *De theologia gentili*, had all built taxonomies of pagan traditions to reinforce Christian belief. Vossius especially produced a complete handbook of ancient and more recent mythology showing how a natural understanding of the one God remarkably coincided with that of Christian revelation.

---

[59] *Beḥinat Adam*: the text suddenly breaks off in St. Petersburg at fol. 72b. Its continuation is found in Frankfurt, fols. 127a–b.

[60] *Beḥinat Adam* (St. Petersburg), fols. 96a–100a; (Frankfurt), fols. 153b–156b.

[61] See, for example, D. Ruderman, *Kabbalah, Magic, and Science: The Cultural Universe of a Sixteenth-Century Jewish Physician* (Cambridge, Mass., 1988), especially chap. 9; or *The World of a Renaissance Jew: The Life and Thought of Abraham ben Mordecai Farissol* (Cincinnati, 1981), especially chap. 11.

In the second half of the seventeenth century, Ralph Cudworth, Edward Stillingfleet, and Isaac Newton drew from these earlier compositions to erect their own elaborate pagan testimonies that all peoples had been aware of the idea of God and that despite the different words and languages they used, they all pointed to the same monotheistic belief. Their monumental tomes represented a concerted effort to resolve a crisis of confidence in revealed religion. The flood of new information on other religions of the world and the new naturalistic explanations of religion offered by Hobbes and Spinoza raised serious questions about the viability and centrality of Christian revelation.

Of course, these elaborate collections were fraught with their own theological dangers in demonstrating that a natural religion of monotheism was common to all civilizations. Deists like Herbert of Cherbury or Charles Blount could utilize the material collected by Vossius and Cudworth not only to argue for an anti-Trinitarian Christianity but for a true ancient religion of the Gentiles, the authentic foundation of a deistic faith uncorrupted by Christianity and its priesthood. Herbert's five common notions of natural religion, gleaned from such taxonomies, served to substantiate the authentic roots of a natural reasonable faith independent of any unique Christian dispensation. To be sure, Bochart, Vossius, and the others insisted that their work served to emphasize by contrast the truth of Protestant Christianity. Bochart's attempt to demonstrate that most place-names in the ancient world derive from Hebrew, for example, was not meant to reflect on the inadequacy of Scripture or that the pagan sources had authority equal to that of the Bible. On the contrary, he contended, the pagan sources allow Christians to better understand the biblical references and thus fortify their faith in their truthfulness against the atheists and skeptics. Nevertheless, his work could be understood differently. According to Richard Westfall, this is precisely what happened to Newton when, like the deists, he placed pagan authorities on an equal footing with the Bible and thus was led to reject the idea that Scripture was uniquely divine. The weight of these pagan witnesses thus convinced Newton to view a reasonable natural religion as complete in itself without the explicit intervention of a special Christian revelation.[62]

---

[62] My observations are based especially on the following studies: R. Popkin, "The Crisis of Polytheism and the Answers of Vossius, Cudworth, and Newton," in Force and Popkin, *Essays on the Context, Nature, and Influence of Isaac Newton's Theology*, pp. 9–26; and, also in the same volume, R. Popkin, "Polytheism, Deism, and Newton," pp. 27–42; and J. Force, "Newtonianism and Deism," pp. 43–73. The last two essays attempt to refute R. Westfall in his "Isaac Newton's *Theologiae Gentilis Origines Philosphicae*," in *The Secular Mind: The Transformation of Faith in Modern Europe*, ed. W. Wagar (New York, 1982), pp. 15–34. See also C. Rademacher, *The Life and Work of Gerardus Joannes Vossius* (Assen, 1981); and F. Manuel, *The Eighteenth Century Confronts the Gods* (Cambridge, Mass., 1959), and *Isaac Newton, Historian* (Cambridge, Mass., 1963).

Tang probably had a general awareness of all of this material but singled out especially Bochart and Stillingfleet as his primary sources. He most likely relied heavily on Stillingfleet's *Origines Sacrae or a Rational Account of the Grounds of Natural and Revealed Religion . . . with an Answer to the Modern Objections of Atheists and Deists*, the revised and expanded edition published in Cambridge in 1701. Stillingfleet was a moderate Anglican who had once challenged Locke on his Christian faith and who firmly denounced Descartes and the deterministic implications of his system of mechanical laws of motion and matter. In the revised version of his *Origines*, he included not only the evidence of ancient philosophers but also that of recent accounts of the cultures of the New World. Obviously the source of Tang's remarks, Stillingfleet even offered a detailed criticism of some of these reports that claimed that the recently discovered natives were in fact atheists. On the contrary, Stillingfleet argued, such reports were not often reliable since the Spanish conquerors or mere seamen reporters were biased from the start and never really bothered to familiarize themselves with the natives or their languages and customs.[63]

Tang's explicit mention of Stillingfleet by name seems to suggest his caution in using the pagan taxonomies. It is not always clear where Tang's real sympathies lie: either in the deist or more moderate Christian Latitudinarian camps. And as the case of Newton suggests, the line between the two camps—between an advocacy of natural religion alone or between a unified appeal for both natural and revealed truth—is often hard to delineate. By disclosing his reliance on Stillingfleet, he seems to tip the scales in favor of a more middle-of-the-road position where the natural impulse of all peoples to acknowledge the one God may coexist with the unchallenged position of scriptural history and prophecy. Be that as it may, Tang's enlistment of pagan authorities to demonstrate "a natural opinion implanted" in all humanity[64] left him open to the notion that true religiosity was never the exclusive prerogative of Jews or Christians but rather a sentiment shared by all humanity.

Closely connected to his appeal to cultures outside Judaism to demonstrate the existence of God is Tang's particular understanding of the pa-

---

[63] On Stillingfleet, see S. Hutton, "Science, Philosophy, and Atheism: Edward Stillingfleet's Defense of Religion," in *Scepticism and Irreligion in the Seventeenth- and Eighteenth Centuries*, ed. R. Popkin and A. Vanderjagt (Leiden, 1993), pp. 102–20; R. Popkin, "The Philosophy of Bishop Stillingfleet," *Journal of the History of Ideas* 9 (1971): 303–19; R. T. Carroll, *The Common-Sense Philosophy of Religion of Bishop Edward Stillingfleet, 1635–1699* (The Hague, 1975). Tang especially consulted the *Origines Sacrae* (Cambridge, 1701), pp. 73–86.

[64] Of course, the notion of any doctrine implanted in human minds was unacceptable to Locke, a primary influence on Tang. See J. C. Biddle, "Locke's Critique of Innate Principles

rameters of faith and its relation to the senses and to reason. In the first place, Tang stresses over and over again the rational foundations of the Jewish faith, the public disclosure of the law, and the lack of inhibition to investigate rationally the principles of religion. The Torah would never require someone to believe in fantasies unsubstantiated by reason. Because God endowed all human beings with the natural faculty to distinguish between right and wrong, the Torah would never contradict our reasonable moral instincts. Furthermore, no prophet in Israel ever offered prophecies that contradicted reason; Abraham and Moses fully utilized their rational faculties in fulfilling their religious visions.[65]

Of course, there are limits to human knowledge, Tang confesses, and given these limits, a place for faith is to be located. Faith is defined as that which is received from God above and not through internal perception. It emerges to complete what is deficient by reason. But there are also limits to faith: "One can never find a true rational proof contradicting a true faith since both are from God."[66] Because faith cannot contradict reason, a belief in the Christian Trinity is simply untenable. Similarly, the fantasies of the kabbalists who imagine that their souls are connected to heavenly angels is equally repulsive. Tang adds: "I do not desire either them or their activities and all this ugly subject results from the deception of the imagination." Like the enthusiasts who are afflicted by melancholia, their false ideas and images are deleterious to Judaism where a "scholar is preferred to a prophet."[67]

Tang also emphasizes that all knowledge is based on our senses and our logical abilities to interpret their perceptions. He illustrates this truth with the story of an Indian man who claimed the world rested on a large white elephant. When asked to explain how the elephant was supported, he answered that it rested on a large fish. But when pressed to point out the fish's support, he could not answer. Although human beings cannot grasp the essence of things, our senses reveal something of the essence. But our senses cannot grasp the smallest particles of creation even with the aid of the microscope, thus underscoring the obvious limits to which human knowledge can reach.[68]

Tang's indebtedness to Locke's sensationalist epistemology is obvious in these discussions. His definition of faith as never contradicting reason is also reminiscent of Locke's formulation. His critique of mindless enthu-

---

and Toland's Deism," *Journal of the History of Ideas* 37 (1976): 411–22. On Locke, see my subsequent discussion.
   [65] *Beḥinat Adam* (St. Petersburg), fols. 38b–51b, 114a; (Frankfurt), fols. 64b–83b.
   [66] *Beḥinat Adam* (St. Petersburg), fol. 42b; (Frankfurt), fol. 64b.
   [67] *Beḥinat Adam* (St. Petersburg), fols. 45b–46a.
   [68] *Beḥinat Adam* (Cincinnati 728/1), fol. 16.

siasts and his support of reasonable prophets also shares with Locke the same ambiguity and uncertainty in determining the rational criteria of what distinguishes true from false prophecy. Tang's remarks are also quite similar to those of his contemporary, Mordechai Schnaber Levison, which we shall mention later.[69]

Having indicated his preference for a sober and rational religion sanitized of "the conceits of a warmed or over-weening brain," as Locke had labeled it, it only remained for Tang to stigmatize those aspects of Judaism and those leaders within the Jewish community who embodied those negative characteristics that were repugnant to him. His attitude towards the kabbalists was only one aspect of a larger critique. Throughout his long work, he speaks frequently of the ignorant rabbis (without specifying to whom he is referring) who fail to use their intelligence in opposition to those good Jews, "the learned philosophical Torah scholars." He criticizes their inability to distinguish between the minutiae of the law and the larger moral and cosmological questions religion should address, or as he puts it, "they cannot interpret [the Sabbath prayer] 'the sixth day [and the heaven and the earth] were finished' but only know a matter of no significance [*battel be-shishim*]" or "[They obsess] about the ritual obligation of the flame of the Hanukah candle but one *shemah* [the declaration of faith in one God] in its proper time, not one [of them] can recite [with understanding]."[70]

IV

These same preoccupations—pagan religions and their relation to Judaism; the nature of belief and its relation to rationality; and a critique of the enthusiasm, parochialness, and excessive legalism of rabbinic leadership—surface and resurface in Tang's many other writings. The last theme, his critique of rabbinic leadership, is most pronounced in one of his most unusual works, the *Sabei de-bei Atuna*, written in honor of his teacher Moses Minsk as a commentary on the enigmatic talmudic narrative [B.T. Bekhorot 8b] regarding Rabbi Joshua ben Ḥananiyah and the

---

[69] Tang explicitly referred to Locke's *Essay Concerning Human Understanding* in his introduction to his translation of William Congreve's *Mourning Bride*. See Schirmann, "The First Hebrew Translation," p. 6. On Locke's sensationalist epistemology and his view of religion and faith, see J. Yolton, *Locke: An Introduction* (Oxford and New York, 1985). On Levison's reliance on Locke, see Ruderman, *Jewish Thought and Scientific Discovery in Early Modern Europe* pp. 332–68.

[70] *Beḥinat Adam* (St. Petersburg), fols. 16a–b; (Frankfurt), fols. 197b–198a, from where the last quotation is cited.

scholars of the academy of Athens.[71] For Tang, as we have already mentioned, the real meaning of the rabbi's mission was political; he was sent
as an emissary of the Roman Empire to root out a seditionary element.
The contemporary message of the text soon becomes transparent in
Tang's preface to his beloved rabbi. There was once a time when rabbis
were thoroughly attuned to the ways of the world; they functioned effectively even in political and diplomatic roles; they were utterly different
from the present motley crew of uninspired and unenlightened religious
leaders.

> With my pen will I write of the height of wisdom evinced by Joshua ben Ḥanani-
> yah, a sage of Israel and an associate of royalty. One of expert knowledge of
> politics and its trickeries, called a philosopher in the eyes of the Greek and
> Roman peoples and influential at the court of the Emperor. Unlike the sages of
> our own generation whose wisdom is seasoned with emptiness, so that not with-
> out cause it is said that wisdom has perished from the "blind" [a pun on the
> Hebrew *ivri* and *iver*, "blind"]. They are babblers of the allegorical meaning of
> the Talmud like gushing waters while the modern compilations of the meaning
> of the homilies [*aggadot*] are forbidden to them as the stump of the lame. . . .
> How can he who is dubbed rabbi and who has spent the greater part of his life
> studying the laws of the *agunah* [the deserted wife] appreciate how a general
> should conduct his army in battle? Or how can another who has made a more
> profound study of the [section dealing with] 'leprous houses' . . . fully appreci-
> ate allegory and figurative speech that is splendidly and deliberately obscure?
> Then when you press them against the wall like the foot of the magician [cf.
> Numbers 22:25], they answer you arrogantly that the story is sealed [cf. Isaiah
> 29:11]. Truly they are like the ox which is muzzled as it threshes! Woe to you!
> Why don't you gird your loins and read the history and wisdom of the nations
> of the past? Do you think because they are written in a foreign language that
> God will be angry at you?[72]

Tang, however, considered Rabbi Moses of a different sort; he had engaged him in conversation about how one reads rabbinic texts; and he
found him open and intellectually honest. And he adds, again with bitter
sarcasm: "I have been drawn to you because of your intellect and not
because of your wearing a beard. For wisdom does not abide in the hair,

---

[71] The manuscript is listed as London Beit Din 35 (Institute of Microfilmed Hebrew
Manuscripts, University and National Library, Jerusalem no. 4698), written in Tang's own
hand in 1772. My English translations from this work are based mainly on S. Leperer's
translation (with some emendations) as found in his doctoral dissertation, listed in note 24.
I cite from this work.

[72] Leperer, "Abraham Tang," pp. 76–77 (MS London 35, fol. 2).

for since nature can also grant it to the ignoramus, it is possessed neither
of splendor nor physical beauty."[73]

True to his word, Tang treats Joshua ben Ḥananiyah's tale as a lesson
in the art of politics. His notes are studded with definitions of democracy,
aristocracy, monarchy, plebeians, and tribunes. He probes the political
mentality of the emperor in controlling the subjects of his large government and in stamping out potential insurrection. He is also quite aware
of the relation between religion and political control: "You must know
that religion has always been a force uniting the masses and through it
the sages ruled the masses. It is for this reason that the nobility has no
desire to quarrel with the priest. Thus when the conqueror wishes to destroy their religion or shatter their images, the priests quickly raise their
voices that . . . . they are fighting the battles of the Lord. It is for this
reason that the kings bribe the priests . . . since all the foolish masses have
faith in them."[74] Tang is also aware that the political role of the rabbis
will not be grasped unless one deconstructs their hidden allusions and
parables. By understanding that the whole purpose of politics is "guile,
trickery, and concealed lies" and that Joshua's goal of defeating the hated
Greeks coincided with the emperor's political strategy, the story can be
fully comprehended.[75]

It is unnecessary to enter into the details of Tang's fanciful and elaborate interpretation of the rabbinic parable. Even without its particulars,
it strikes me as remarkably unique in the history of rabbinic exegesis,
replete even with the trappings of footnotes and the scholarly apparatus
of comparing the various printed versions of the story. Tang fully expects
his rabbinic friend to treat his analysis with skepticism but he perseveres
nevertheless: "Do not repudiate its essential character, for I will not for-
give your so doing, but will declare that you are just like your associates.
I have prepared the way for you, therefore go to philosophy and history
and partake of them as one would partake of the pascal lamb on Passover
eve." He pleads that the story not be explicated esoterically: "Flee from
the kabbalah as you would from a searing brand, for a malignant fire
burns within it, and by my life, its devotees would compromise God's
very unity with their permutations." Finally, he reiterates his contempt
for the rabbis and their feigned piety: "God is in heaven and you are on
earth, so what difference is it to Him that you run to the house of prayer
until the sweat flows from the pores of your skin so that the cold air hits
you and dries up the core of your very being. Walk slowly, for that is how

[73] Ibid., p. 77 (MS London 35, fol. 3).
[74] Ibid., p. 102 (MS London 35, fol. 10).
[75] Ibid., p. 114 (MS London 35, fol. 15).

princes walk. For only soldiers rush and they get slaughtered when two or three barbed arrows are shot against them."[76]

Sidney Leperer, the only scholar to study this remarkable treatise, has viewed Tang's creation primarily as a clear illustration of the *Haskalah* approach to the *aggadah*.[77] But this does not seem to me to be the most fruitful way to approach this text. Given the early date of this composition (1772) and the relative isolation in which it was written, it is hard to imagine how Tang was connected with the early *maskilim* in Germany and central Europe. Of course his bitter satire against the rabbis is analogous to those of the *maskilim* both in the West and later in the East. But the genesis of Tang's thinking about religion, religious authority, and Judaism seems to be located elsewhere.

The primary concerns Tang raises in the quotes cited here might be summarized by the following. First, contemporary rabbis, unlike the ancients, are illiterate in the ways of the world, especially the art of politics. Second, they are poor readers of ancient texts: they either read literally and thus superficially or concoct mystical fantasies unrelated to the true meaning of the text, and they have no sensitivity to figures of speech, allegories, especially political ones. Third, they lack a knowledge of ancient history and culture and are afraid to read literature in foreign languages. Fourth, they fail to understand the place of religious ideology in political affairs.

Each of these concerns can be easily located in the literary sources at his disposal, in the deistic notions he had absorbed, and in English political culture, of which he saw himself an integral part. Whatever else singled Tang out, it was his passionate interest in ancient mythology, a passion that drove him to produce a mythological handbook for Jewish usage. He was also a student of mythography who recognized that the pagan myths were not mere stories but elaborations of ancient political truths. The narratives of the gods were essentially commemorations of the acts of real human beings on earth. In reading ancient myths euhemeristically[78]— and, by extension, rabbinic parables were also ancient myths—Tang

---

[76] Ibid., pp. 186–88 (MS London 35, fols. 47–48). See also p. 201, where Leperer offers a partial list of references to previous exegesis of the aggadah of Joshua ben Ḥananiyah and the sages of Athens.

[77] Ibid., pp. 225–40. Note that he does mention in passing the work's relationship to the anticlericalism of Voltaire and the political views of Machiavelli. He even speculates at one point (p. 229) that "Tang would have had the opportunity of perusing the *Dictionaire Philosophique*."

[78] On Euhemerist approaches to myth in the eighteenth century and before, see the classic study of Manuel, *The Eighteenth Century Confronts the Gods*, pp. 85–113; J. Seznec, *The Survival of the Pagan Gods: The Mythological Tradition and Its Place in Renaissance Humanism and Art* (New York, 1953), pp. 11–26.

could transform seemingly veiled parables into comprehensible events in the ancient political world. And ancient events often bore a striking resemblance to the politics of the eighteenth century as well.

As we have seen, Tang was a reader of deistic literature. He knew and appreciated Voltaire's views of religion, of the church, of the corruption of the priests, of the superstitions they inflicted on the masses. He also understood religion comparatively, which he had learned from the rich European literature on the subject from Bochart to Stillingfleet, to countless other authors he failed to mention. His criticisms of the rabbis, their narrowness and rigidity, their unenlightened postures, and their exclusive claims to interpret Judaism, patently mirrored the abusive rhetoric of Voltaire and his fellow colleagues.

Moreover, Tang could observe with his own eyes, without the aid of literary sources and historical antecedents, the close relation between governmental and church authority in England, the collusion of interests between the political leadership and the high Anglican clergy. He could also observe the close relationship between theological and political radicalism, that those who were church reformers were also involved in political dissent. Like the Latitudinarians and Unitarians, he could question the existing social and religious order on the grounds of reason and conscience, and on the basis of his own sophisticated reading of sacred texts unsullied by sacerdotal pretensions and clerical power. As we shall soon observe in the next chapter, Tang was also a political radical. The intimate connection between his political and religious radicalism seems obvious. Rather than explain the evolution of his views on the basis of some tenuous and vague tie to the radical *maskilim* in Germany, many of whom were clearly not so outspoken as early as the 1770s, it makes much more sense to contextualize him as a thinker within the literary and political culture of England. His peculiar views of Judaism emerged through his direct encounter with English Christianity, and within the forum of public debates between the establishment church and its boisterous critics.[79]

V

In addition to his treatise on Joshua ben Ḥananiyah, Tang began two commentaries on the opening verses of the book of Ecclesiastes. Given the poor condition of the manuscript, much of the text is illegible. Together with this project, he penned his *Ẓofnat Pa'aneaḥ*, a handbook of

---

[79] On the connection between religion and politics in eighteenth-century England and its impact on Jewish supporters of the establishment and Jewish dissenters, see the next chapter and the ample bibliography there.

classical mythology for the Jewish reader of rabbinic texts. Both compositions were written sometime between 1773 and 1776.[80] Despite the constant gaps in the text, Tang's impressive erudition in both Jewish and
classical sources is evident throughout. Especially worthy of mention are
his citations of the Spanish commentators of Ibn Ezra of the fourteenth
century who were particularly interested in astrology and the occult arts.
These same authors are also cited in his other works.[81]

Tang was hardly unique among eighteenth-century Jews for his special
interest in Ecclesiastes, a Jewish work of broad universal interest posing
the most challenging questions to traditional faith. He saw its author Solomon as holding views close to Aristotle and the ancient philosophers.
But Tang moves quickly from a consideration of this recondite narrative
to a broader strategy on how to understand rabbinic texts, specifically
midrash aggadah, the homiletical creations of the rabbis. Tang's original
contribution to this subject is his attempt to argue that a knowledge of
classical literature is a critical aid in the study of rabbinic civilization.
Furthermore, the methods of classical scholarship, its strategies in reading
texts, are useful in fathoming the deeper and more significant meanings
of the ancient rabbis. Both as a means of overcoming the shallow and
barren readings of contemporary rabbis, on the one hand, and the dismissive and mocking critiques of those who have fully abandoned Jewish
study, on the other, Tang offers a constructive alternative on how to make
sense of the ancient literature of his community.

In adopting a comparative method for reading the ancients, both Jews
and pagans, Tang has recourse to Jewish precedent. In the first place,
the ancient rabbis themselves, as we have seen in the case of Joshua ben
Hananiyah, knew Greek culture and its literature. It was out of their admiration for the latter, argued Tang, that they often dressed their homilies
in Greek allegorical style. In the second place, Tang has recourse to the
time-honored strategy of arguing that the wisdom of the Greeks ultimately derived from Judaism. "Do not reprimand me," he writes, "for
admiring the culture of the classical nations, for their wisdom is essentially
Jewish," which he proves by citing Maimonides. But neither the ancient
rabbis nor Maimonides could anticipate what Tang had in mind. As a
classicist, appreciative of the artistry of the great poets Homer, Hesiod,
Virgil, and Ovid, who presented their most lofty thoughts in obscure rid-

---

[80] These compositions are found in MS London Beit Din 7 (Jerusalem no. 4676).

[81] He cites such thinkers as Joseph Ibn Wakar, Samuel Sarza, and David Ibn Bilia. On
the importance of this group, see, for example, M. Idel, "The Magical and Neoplatonic
Interpretations of the Kabbalah in the Renaissance," *Jewish Thought in the Sixteenth Century*, ed. B. Cooperman (Cambridge, Mass., 1983), pp. 210–11.

dles impenetrable to the impatient masses, it was time to read *midrash* from a similar perspective.[82]

Tang is acutely aware of the challenge of finding a relevant message for Judaism in his own day, a challenge that contemporary Jewish preachers (*darshanim*) are incapable of meeting. "In our day" he writes, "alien philosophers arose who denied our God and Moses and spoke ill of the Torah and the words of the sages." They read ancient texts literally and assume simplistically that the ancient writers had no more to convey than what appears on the surface. Because they viewed all of their writings as vanities, they similarly dismissed their religious teachings. Within the Jewish community, a similar attitude prevails regarding *midrash*. And this problem is compounded by the absence of serious readers of these texts within the Jewish community. On the contrary, the so-called teachers of Judaism engender shame to Judaism by either interpreting these texts falsely or abdicating their responsibility by claiming that their secrets are incomprehensible.[83]

Tang's glossary of the ancient Gods is an attempt to provide enough information so that Solomon and the ancient rabbis can be understood in the context of their own times (fig.7):

> And truly an enlightened person must realize that in order to master these hidden things he must investigate the ancients thoroughly, mastering their method in riddles and proverbs according to the times and according to the place. And I have no doubt that Solomon learned non-Jewish wisdom from Hiram king of Tyre who was known as an astrologer and a great sage. It was certainly Solomon's strategy to effectuate a peace between himself and Hiram so that he could learn from him all he desired. . . . Thus he showed him all the ancient parables that were in his archives either regarding politics or other things.[84]

In the same manner one penetrates the meaning of Solomon's writings, one should approach rabbinic texts. Thus, for example, writes Tang: "I saw a wonderful thing when I examined many of the statements attributed to R. Yose the Galilean and his son and found in them remarkable higher insights. It is thus necessary to determine who is the speaker, to whom does he speak, at what time he is speaking, the events that took place in his time, and from whom he learned before one can interpret anything."[85] This literary approach is utterly different from the common practice of reading *midrash*. It requires a linguistic knowledge of Greek and Aramaic; and it demands a knowledge of folkways common to the ancient world

---

[82] MS London 7, fols. 72–80.
[83] Ibid., fols. 81–86.
[84] Ibid., fols. 87–88.
[85] Ibid., fol. 104.

צפנת פענח

...

Υἱὸν ἔχεις τὸν Ἔρωτα,
γυναῖκα δὲ τὴς Ἀφροδίτην· οὐκ ἄ
δίκαιως χαλκεῦ τὸν πόδα χωλὸς
ἔχεις.

...

Cupid is Vulcans Son, Venus his wife
no wonder then he goes lame all his life.

Æoly

Vulcania

Æolia

Momus

7. A page of Abraham Tang's handbook of classical mythology, *Zofnat Pa'aneaḥ*, originally MS London Beit Din 7, fol. 162, illustrating his citations in Greek, and his Hebrew and English translations.

in such matters as magic and amulets, even if one does not believe in them any longer. But despite this background critical in understanding talmudic civilization, there is no doubt that every rabbinic utterance has philosophical value, revealing the vast wisdom of their bearers. Tang concludes, "Thus the great masters of the *aggadah* wrote what they wrote in secrets and riddles as the custom of their times. Accordingly, one who is not familiar with the wisdom of these nations will be restricted in understanding their [the rabbis'] words in many places. And don't accuse me of calling it the wisdom of the nations since our words are in it in exile and actually the wisdom that the nations possessed was actually considered to be the wisdom of Israel."[86]

Tang thus concludes his introduction to his handbook of Greek and Roman deities, which immediately follows. Among the authorities he relies on are Hesiod, Plato, Plutarch, Varro, Cicero, Horace, Livy, Ovid, and Pliny, as well as Virgil, who is cited both in the Latin and in John Dryden's free English translation. Relying heavily on Samuel Bochart's *Geographia sacra*, which he cites explicitly, in finding common etymologies between the classical Gods and biblical personalities and events, there is little in his presentation of any original value. Nevertheless, in his attempt to "salvage" rabbinic literature by recourse to the substance and methods of classical scholarship, Tang had taken a daring and groundbreaking step. Viewed together with his political reading of an ancient rabbi, his taxonomies of pagan witnesses to monotheism, and his scathing critique of the religious and educational leadership of his community, the various components of his intellectual world meaningfully cohere. As a writer in Hebrew, ostensibly writing to a Jewish intellectual elite that he found wanting, his extensive though unfinished writing articulated fully his notion of a universal God, a rational faith, and a vision of a Jewish community socially and intellectually integrated within the larger cultural milieu of enlightened English society.

But Tang wrote not only within the narrow solitude of Hebraic scholarship and thought. On at least two occasions, he left the comfortable private space of his Hebrew manuscript writings in search of an audience of English readers, both assimilated Jews and Protestants alike. As a pioneering translator of foreign authors such as Voltaire and Congreve into Hebrew, he knew well the challenge of mediating between two relatively disparate and distant audiences. Were Tang's radical sentiments translatable into an English idiom and was there a greater need for self-censorship in publishing his thoughts for the first time? Would his public persona correspond to his private one? Finally, did his effort to publish in English constitute a conscious choice on his part to abandon the isolated world

---

[86] Ibid., fols. 104–9. The quotation is from fol. 106.

of the Hebrew intellectual for a participatory role in the larger society of authors and readers from which he had been excluded? Tang wrote two small works in English: the first, a translation and commentary of the rabbinic compendium of rabbinic moral maxims known as *Pirkei Avot*; and the second, a political treatise in support of the English radical John Wilkes. I consider the first immediately in this chapter, and the second at the beginning of the next.

VI

Tang published *The Sentences and Proverbs of the Ancient Fathers in Six Chapters called Abouth* in 1772, the first English translation (published together with the Hebrew original) of this classic rabbinic compendium of ethical statements. He signs the work "by a primitive ebrew" but identifies his real name in "A Soliloquey by the Translator" written in Hebrew. His English pen name perhaps signifies his ambivalence in promoting himself in English or suggests his own insecurity in adequately presenting the treasures of rabbinic literature to an English readership. On the other hand, he employs this name with a touch of irony. "Primitive" in the more romantic sense suggests exotic, mysterious, unspoiled. It implies the unsullied and pure state of humanity and religion at the beginnings of civilization. "A primitive ebrew" then wears both a badge of honor as well as a protective shield of self-deprecation (fig. 8).[87]

From Tang's initial words to the reader, it is apparent that the religious attitudes of his Hebrew works have been well rendered into English. Tang's highly apologetic tone is obvious throughout. Judaism, both in his introduction and in the subtle mistranslations and omissions of the English text,[88] is presented in the most rationalistic and moralistic way possible. Nevertheless, all of this is fully consistent with the positions Tang had espoused in his unpublished Hebrew writings. Here is how he opens the introduction:

> Courteous Reader the following proverbs and sentences, which I translated from the Ebrew . . . are neither enthusiastic, nor metaphysical, but simple morality, and sound philosophy, so as to be of utility to all and every rank of people: since the quintessence of the proceeding chapters are the scource [sic] and foundation of society, and the inlet of the true faith: a faith! divested from

---

[87] Note that Tang employs this name without reference to his Hebrew name in his political pamphlet discussed in the next chapter.

[88] These are well discussed by Leperer in "The First Publication of *Pirkei Avot* in English," especially pp. 43–44.

פרקי אבות

THE

SENTENCES AND PROVERBS,

OF THE

ANCIENT FATHERS.

In SIX CHAPTERS,

CALLED,

ABOUTH.

Written Original in EBREW,

And Compiled by Rabbi Surnamed R, JEHUDAH the Holy, *Anno Mundi* Three Thousand Nine Hundred and One.

And now Translated into the ENGLISH Language, with some of the Comments of the famous MAIMONIDES.

By a PRIMITIVE EBREW.

הולך את חכמים יחכם

He that walketh with Wisemen shall obtain Wisdom. Proverbs.

LONDON:

Printed in the Year M,DCC,LXXII.
And sold only at No. 17, and 67, Lemon-street, Goodman's Fields. *Anno Mundi.* 5533.

תקלב

8. Title page of Abraham Tang's translation and commentary of *Avot*, published anonymously "By a Primitive Ebrew" in London, 1772.

developments of indefatiguable ceremonies. . . . It will then serve to ominate that the learned amongst the Jews did preach up the superbest system of Ethics, that could be deduced from reason . . . for the omnipotent and omniscient God hath given one law and one faith to all his rational creatures. . . .The worship of God is chiefly the moral and inward duty, i.e., the duties of the mind: 'Tis not the outward application of certain maxims, which shall institute the good religious man; and of this hath Moses specified saying . . . and thou shalt love. . . . And since 'tis obvious that the moral duties do in rank preceed the ceremonious precepts, it doth follow that its knowledge ought to be in the like predicament: and that is what the sages named the duties of the mind.[89]

In these passages gleaned from the first pages of the introduction, Tang encapsulates several of his most cherished themes as he paints an ideal portrait of Judaism: the universality of its religious faith; its rationality and sound philosophy; the priority of its moral precepts over "indefatiguable ceremonies"; its lack of enthusiasm, and its stress on inward duties translated as "the duties of the mind" (*ḥovot ha-levavot*), recalling most likely the medieval philosopher Baḥya ibn Pakuda's famous work. Without a prior familiarity with Tang's religious ideas as expressed in his Hebrew writing, one might consider these lines as a mere exaggeration and distortion of Judaism and the rabbinical ethos, a presentation made to curry the favor of deists and other liberal Christians. But Tang is at least true to his own convictions, notwithstanding the fact that his rendering of *Avot* sometimes resembles Lord Henry, Charles Blount, and John Toland, as much as the original.

In a long note toward the end of the introduction Tang succinctly presents another of his favorite themes:

It is very needful for you to be informed. . . . mankind have divided themselves into three sects. The first, and such are the common run of learned people . . . they believe the passages of the wise Sages, to be understood literally, abstracted from any emblem, parable or figure, and with that sect all that is impossible, they hold to exist from necessity . . . though many of these passages that they so literally take, are so far from reason . . . and I do swear by the living God, that that sect are the destroyers of the beauty of the Law, and the obscurers of her pellucidness. . . . And I assure you, that most of the preachers of that sect pretend to acquaint the people, what they know not themselves . . . but by their arrogance they pretend to comprehend them. . . .

The second are numerous also, and such are those who have beheld the words of the wise men, and have taken them in the literal sense . . . and therefore that sect do pretend to ridicule them . . . and the most of these accusers pretend to be learned in Astrology and Medicine, and are wise in their own eyes, and

---

[89] Tang, *The Sentences and Proverbs of the Ancient Fathers*, pp. iii–vii.

pretend to much philosophical knowledge. But alas! how far indeed are they from intelligence . . . and indeed this sect are much baser than the first, and the major part of them are libertines that most accursed sect . . . and those vain fools, had they laboured to learn wisdom . . . as Divine philosophy ought to be written and placed, . . . they would then, indeed know whether the learned wise Rabbins were really wise. . . .

The third sect, and which I solemnly declare are but few indeed . . . and such are those people to whom the glory of the wise learned men hath been demonstrated, and have comprehended those latent meanings and figurative expressions, as meant by these wise men in their different scattered passages of the Talmud . . . and that sect are also satisfied that the several passages and orations of the wise men are not jeerings, but that they are both expressive as well as figurative, and that whenever the wise men were wont to treat respecting impossibilities, they spoke of them in a Parabolical and emlematical manner. . . . and thus is most of the book of Job parabolical. And . . . with respect to the dead that were raised by the prophet Ezekiel.[90]

Tang sees himself as belonging to and writes for the reader who identifies with the third sect. As he had done in both his treatises on Joshua ben Ḥananiyah and mythology, Tang had no patience for the literalists of either the traditionalist or "libertine" camps. For Tang, the only salvation for Judaism in an enlightened age was to learn how to read ancient texts with an eye to their larger context and with an ear for their oft-hidden message. Only as emblems or parables could the universal truths of Judaism be detected in the poetic language of the rabbis. Tang was not only announcing to his educated readers what he considered to be Judaism's essence; he was also prescribing for them a literary sensitivity to insure the continuing meaning and relevance of their heritage in a culture whose aesthetic and epistemological assumptions were radically different from those of their ancestors.

VII

Abraham Tang was certainly the most thoughtful and articulate English Jew at the end of the eighteenth century to embrace a version of Jewish theology closely associated with deism. His extended Hebrew writings in theology, ancient history and mythology, and comparative religion, as well as his limited English publications, entitle him to a serious place among Jewish thinkers of his era and inevitably suggest comparisons with some of the well-known Jewish radicals in Germany like David Fried-

---

[90] Ibid., pp. xxiv–xxix.

lander and Lazarus Ben David. But as David Levi clearly indicated, Tang was not the only English Jew of this period with deistic proclivities.

As early as 1746, Dr. Meyer Schomberg (1690–1761), the highly controversial but highly talented London physician, had written a short essay entitled *Emunat Omen*, either translated as "the True Faith" or "the Faith of a Physician."[91] Lacking the theological sophistication and erudition of Tang, Schomberg nevertheless offers a clear statement of his antitraditional and essentially deistic brand of Judaism. His view is important in its own right but also as a reflection of the attitudes of some of his sons, most of whom converted to Christianity. Obviously replying to accusations that he had publicly disrespected Jewish ritual observances and desecrated the Sabbath, Schomberg proceeded to justify his unorthodoxies by presenting his own understanding of the Jewish faith. This includes a recitation of the first seven principles of Maimonides' thirteen principles of faith, conspicuously omitting those dealing with the immutability of Jewish law, divine retribution, the messiah, and resurrection. These omissions, together with his insistence throughout that Judaism requires of its adherents only that they live virtuously and never demands their full allegiance to ritual law, suggest an unrefined adumbration of Tang's more weighty reflections some thirty years later. Schomberg closes his short essay with the following:

> Behold this we have investigated and it is so, the very essence of faith [*Emunat Omen*], that the wise and perfect man should know that his absolutely first duty is to believe that there is a God, an existent being that brought into existence everything that is before our eyes. . . . This straightforward faith will bring man fear and direct his heart to the service of God, the Maker of light and the Creator of everything. If he will investigate natural philosophy and look at His creations . . . then inevitably he will testify to the wondrous works of Him who is perfect in knowledge. . . . In our perfect Torah we find 613 commandments of which some concern religion and some behavior. . . . All of them were given from one source for man's salvation and his soul's advantage. But our lord, King David . . . came and reduced them to eleven principles . . . in one of his Psalms, the fifteenth. . . . After him came the prophet Isaiah and reduced them to six [Isaiah 33:15–16]. . . . Afterwards came Micah the prophet and reduced them to three principles, as he says Micah 6:8, "He has told thee, O Man, what is good; what does the Lord require of thee but to do justice and love kindness and walk modestly with your God."[92]

[91] I utilize the text and translation as presented in E. R. Samuel, "Dr. Meyer Schomberg's Attack on the Jews of London, 1746," *Transactions of the Jewish Historical Society of England* 20 (1959–61): 83–111.
[92] Ibid., pp. 109–10.

More substantial were the theological reflections of Mordechai Gumpel Schnaber Levison (1741–1797), who in many ways was Tang's intellectual equal and a potentially ideal intellectual and ideological colleague, even though there is no evidence that the two interacted with each other. I have treated him extensively as a thinker in another book,[93] and I will return to him below in several other relevant contexts. It will suffice here to offer only some brief remarks that underscore the linkages between his thinking and those of Tang and the other Jews with deistic leanings discussed in this chapter.

Born in Germany, Levison arrived in London from Berlin sometime in 1771 at the height of Tang's literary career. He was well versed in rabbinics, having studied with the distinguished Talmudist David Fraenkel. He was drawn to England by the wonderful opportunity for a young foreign-born Jew to study at the medical program of the famous surgeon and physiologist John Hunter and his equally famous brother William. Upon completion of his medical apprenticeship, he received an appointment as a physician at the General Medical Asylum of the duke of Portland in 1776. During this period he published his first major Hebrew work, *Ma'amar ha-Torah ve-ha-Ḥokhmah* (London, 1771), as well as two English medical texts. He eventually received a medical degree from the University of Aberdeen in Scotland.

Levison's professional career seems to have taken a bizarre direction through his contacts with August Nordeskjold, the Swedenborgian and Freemason, which eventually led him to Sweden, then again to England, briefly, and finally back to Germany, where he remained until his death. Leaving aside for the moment his allegedly clandestine Swedish connections and his exposition of Newton, to which we will refer later, let us recall his more theological musings in his more mature work published in Altona in 1792 under the title *Shelosh-Esre Yesodei ha-Torah*. Like Schomberg, Levison began with a putative discussion of Maimonides' thirteen principles of faith only to subvert them radically in the end. For Levison, like Schomberg and Tang, the primary issue was religious faith in general, not necessarily Judaism alone. Levison certainly did not obscure his Jewish commitments; after all, he published his work in Hebrew with a wide range of biblical, rabbinic, and kabbalistic citations. But like Tang, he was more interested in treating religion as a general cultural phenomenon where belief in one God, providence, or prophecy constituted general categories of religious experience accessible to all humankind. Levison's two major sources were the sensationalist epistemol-

---

[93] Ruderman, *Jewish Thought and Scientific Discovery in Early Modern Europe*, pp. 332–68. My summary here is essentially based on this work, but see also chapter 5 and the appendix.

ogy of John Locke, on the one hand, and the physicotheology of Carl Linnaeus, on the other, reflecting respectively the formative intellectual environments—London and Stockholm—of his professional career.

For Levison, Jewish faith rested on a single foundational principle of knowing God, a knowledge based solely on human sensation and cogitation as practiced in the scientific laboratory. The primary evidence of God's existence is an intimate knowledge of how the world functions, specifically the remarkable system of balance and compensation operating throughout the universe. Drawing freely from the writings of Carl Linnaeus and the formidable English tradition of physicotheology, Levison elaborated for his readers "the great chain of being," a naturalistic understanding of divine providence based on the maintenance of equilibrium in nature, while ignoring traditional views of heaven and hell or divine revelation specifically bestowed on the Jewish people. Levison displayed a marked indifference to justifications of ceremonial law or the particularity of Jewish existence. Despite his sharp denunciation of Spinoza, his defense of Mosaic chronology based on the well-known works of Martini and Bochart, and his promotion of Hebrew as the original language, Levison's allegiance to traditional faith and praxis was tenuous at best. He had virtually transformed a Maimonidean theology of the twelfth century into a conventional deism of the eighteenth. He was truly a kindred spirit of Abraham Tang. Despite their obvious differences and eventual physical separation, both men were products of the scintillating intellectual climate of London in the 1770s.

Before concluding this chapter, we need to consider one of London's most famous Jews, Isaac D'Israeli (1766–1848), literary historian and critic, author of the well-known *Curiosities of Literature,* full-fledged member of the so-called Murray circle of writers, and father of Benjamin Disraeli (fig. 9) D'Israeli's relationship to Judaism has been discussed by others and does not require a full review here. I should only point out that Isaac, unlike his son, was never baptized, maintained his synagogue membership through most of his life, and despite his bitter denunciations of rabbinic Judaism, still retained a positive sense of his Jewish identity.[94] Was D'Israeli a deist and would he have felt a common ideological bond with the others discussed here?

In Todd Endelman's most recent assessment, D'Israeli could be labeled a deist because of his "Voltaire-like, deistic critique of Judaism."[95] This

[94] See the standard work of J. Ogden, *Isaac D'Israeli* (Oxford, 1969). On the *Curiosities,* see pp. 95–113; on the "Murray Circle," see pp. 114–37; and on D'Israeli and Judaism, see pp. 192–206.

[95] T. Endelman, " 'A Hebrew to the End': The Emergence of Disraeli's Jewishness," in *The Self-Fashioning of Disraeli, 1818–1851* ed. C. Richmond and P. Smith (Cambridge, 1998), p. 107.

Alfred Croquis delt.

I D'Israeli

AUTHOR OF "LIFE & CHARACTER OF CHARLES I"

9. One of the many portraits of Isaac D'Israeli.

same impression is also confirmed by his primary biographer James Ogden, who particularly underscores D'Israeli's passionate attachment not only to Voltaire, but to Rousseau, Montisquieu, and Bayle.[96] Endelman has mentioned the various places in his writing where his Jewishness becomes an issue and has even identified a significant part of Isaac's library that dealt with Jewish themes.[97] I would like to focus briefly on his most sustained exposition of Judaism, his book *The Genius of Judaism*, published anonymously in 1833.[98]

The most difficult challenge in reading this fascinating work, as Ogden points out,[99] is to determine what D'Israeli actually likes about Judaism, what in fact is its "genius," and what does he actually believe in. He is quite explicit about his dislikes, about "the infinite multiplicity of customs, of gross superstitions, as ridiculous as once were those of witchcraft, the mere inventions of their Talmudical doctors [that] are incorporated in their faith, in their ceremonies, and their daily customs."[100] He questions the "dubious authority" of the oral law,[101] denounces the parochialism and "barbarous disdain of all foreign learning . . . long the haughty distinction of the Synagogue",[102] and praises the Karaites, those "Jewish Protestants" and their revolt against the tyranny of the rabbis.[103] His exposure to rabbinical Judaism is secondhand, acquired through his reading of the summaries of Leon Modena, Isaac Cardoso, and even David Levi. He treats the last disdainfully, pointing to his unwavering allegiance to traditional Judaism's twofold law: "Yet the immutable orthodoxy of the true Rabbinist, in our own times, returns us back to the twelfth century, asserting that the written and the oral law were 'delivered by the great Legislator in the same order he received both from God in the Mount.' "[104] He is especially caustic about the dietary laws and the social barriers the rabbis have erected that generate unrestrained hostility to Jews through the ages.[105]

What he says positively about Judaism and what ultimately represents Judaism's genius for him lies beneath the surface of his bitter excoriations. If Judaism has been totally corrupted by the "dictators of the human intel-

---

[96] Ogden, *Isaac D'Israeli*, p. 10.

[97] Endelman, " 'A Hebrew to the End,' " pp. 107–9, 128–30.

[98] I have used the second edition of *The Genius of Judaism* (London, 1833), where the author's name appears.

[99] Ogden, *Isaac D'Israeli*, p. 202.

[100] D'Israeli, *The Genius of Judaism*, p. 263.

[101] Ibid., p. 83.

[102] Ibid., p. 94.

[103] Ibid., p. 104.

[104] Ibid., p. 83. He cites Levi's *Ceremonies*, p. 224.

[105] See especially D'Israeli, *The Genius of Judaism*, pp. 146–77.

lect, the Rabbins,"[106] it stands to reason that, at its original core, it was once uncorrupted, resting solely on a belief in God and a genuine moral concern for other human beings. Moreover, it must have valued freedom of thought, the acquisition of all learning, and the common good of all society. Nowhere is this said explicitly in his verbal assault on the rabbis who "from age to age . . . went on corrupting the simplicity of the ancient creed."[107] Yet the assumption, of course, is that there was "an ancient creed" worth preserving, and that "the first principle of Judaism was the worship of the Divine Being," although it eventually "sunk fast into a new sort of idolatry of customs and ceremonies."[108]

Besides this vague articulation of what the genius of Judaism represents, D'Israeli affirms his conviction that Jews should "begin to educate their youth as the youth of Europe"[109] and that "the enlightened Christian should not indeed persecute his ancient brother, since Christianity and Judaism rest on the same foundation; nor is the faith of either in danger from the other."[110] Jews, he proclaims, are the most zealous patriots of any state and their enjoyment of civil rights "will neither endanger the genius of Judaism nor the genius of Christianity."[111] Most remarkably, D'Israeli's commitment to enlightenment ideals and his repudiation of rabbinic obscurantism and ritualism still left room for a positive affiliation with his ancestral heritage. Hardly articulate and self-discerning about his own Jewish identity, and highly reminiscent of John King in his confused utterances on the Jewish faith, D'Israeli also fit precisely the perspicuous characterization of the deists offered by Levi. Indeed, D'Israeli was definitely the type of Jew Levi had in mind, who, notwithstanding all of his impiety, still remained tied to "the body of the nation," as if he was "withheld by some invisible power" to remain within the Jewish fold.[112]

Accordingly, David Levi indeed had spoken neither imaginatively nor speculatively when he pointed to the actual existence of deists of Jewish ancestry in London at the end of the eighteenth century as the thinking of Tang, Levison, Schomberg, the Van Ovens, King, and D'Israeli clearly demonstrates. This evidence also reveals the longevity of this phenomenon at least beginning with Schomberg in midcentury and reappearing with John King, Joshua Van Oven, and Isaac D'Israeli well into the second decade of the next, and probably beyond. The thinkers treated in this

---

[106] Ibid., p. 78.
[107] Ibid., p. 264.
[108] Ibid., p. 176.
[109] Ibid., p. 265.
[110] Ibid., p. 211.
[111] Ibid., pp. 250, 266.
[112] See David Levi's full statement at the beginning of this chapter.

chapter constitute the rare examples of individuals capable and interested in articulating their thoughts on paper. They represent a significant range in their sophistication and erudition. Schomberg, King, and D'Israeli offer the least-refined self-presentations of their Jewish faith. Abraham Van Oven does little more than translate the conventional ethics of Dodsley into Hebrew. His son Joshua presents his remarks in a simplified way appropriate to young students. Only Tang and Levison provide well-informed and elaborate discussions of their religious philosophies. Surely Levi had in mind more than these seven; he certainly referred to countless other Jewish intellectuals, like Ralph Schomberg or Emanuel Mendes da Costa (see chapter 5), who shared their views without the capacity or inclination to present them in written form.

Levi's orthodoxy and avid defense of traditional Jewish faith and practice thus stood in sharp contrast to many of the most creative spirits of Anglo-Jewry. And his conservative temperament also stood at loggerheads with some of them in the political arena as well. The intimate connection between religious radicalism and political radicalism and the opposition to both from a religious-political establishment, as especially manifest in England, has already been noted in passing. For Levi, Judaism's good name was blackened both by Jews espousing deist beliefs and by Jews associated with radical causes, and sometimes both expressions of dissent could emanate from the same source. We examine this other source of Levi's consternation as well as his own complicated stake in the political world of his day in the next chapter.

Four

Between Rational and Irrational Dissent: Political Radicalism in Anglo-Jewish Thought

WHEN THE irrepressible David Levi was given a pamphlet in 1795 by one of his Christian students regarding the authenticity of the self-styled prophet Richard Brothers, the so-called Prince of the Hebrews and Nephew of the Almighty, written by the hand of the distinguished Orientalist Nathaniel Brassey Halhed, he could not restrain himself from replying immediately. But he was scrupulously careful in commenting only on the religious and scriptural foundation of this alleged visionary and not on his radical politics. As he put it:

> As to what you observe concerning the question of "Peace or War," and which serves you as an introduction to your Testimony, I have nothing to say; because we [the Jewish nation] never enter into the Political disputes of the different nations among whom we dwell; but indeavour strictly to abide by the admonition of the Prophet Jeremiah [29:7], "And seek the peace of the city, whither I have caused you to be carried away captive, and pray unto the Lord for it, for in the Peace thereof shall ye have peace." This Sir, is the reason that you will not find in History, any account of the Jews ever being concerned in any rebellion, sedition, or treasonable practices, towards the different governments w[h]ere they have resided, notwithstanding the most unexampled oppressions and cruelties which they have suffered . . . and which is a manifest proof, of their strict adherence to the command of God by the hand of the Prophet."[1]

Todd Endelman, in his comprehensive study of the Jews of Georgian England, cites this same passage in arguing that Levi's view was emblem-

---

[1] David Levi, *Letters to Nathaniel Brassey Halhed M.P. in Answer to his Testimony of the Authenticity of the Prophecies of Richard Brothers and his Pretended Mission to Recall the Jews* (London, 1795), pp. 4–5. On Brothers's mission and Halhed's involvement with him, see J.F.C. Harrison, *The Second Coming: Popular Millenarianism, 1780–1850* (London and Henley, 1979), chap. 4; C. Garrett, *Respectable Folly: Millenarians and the French Revolution in France and England* (London, 1975); C. Roth, *The Nephew of the Almighty* (London, 1933). Halhed published *The Whole of the Testimonies to the Authenticity of the Prophecies and Mission of Richard Brothers* (London, 1795). A positive reaction to Brothers's mission by a former Jew was written by Moses Gomez Pereira, *The Jew's Appeal on the Divine Mission of Richard Brothers and N. B. Halhed, Esq. to Restore Israel, and Rebuild Jerusalem with a Dissertation on the Fitness, Utility, and Beauty of Applying Ancient Predictions and Allegories to Modern Events and a Singular Prophecy Relative to the Present and*

atic of Anglo-Jewry's position in general: "At a time when ideological concerns were reanimating British political life, and hitherto politically disenfranchised groups were demanding radical reforms of the established order, Anglo-Jewish writers were reemphasizing the loyalty and the political quiescence of their coreligionists." In another passage he is even more emphatic: "The number of English Jews who took an active part in political life during these decades of heightened political consciousness (1770–1815) was minuscule." And after noting a few exceptions, principally the aforementioned John King and the rabbi Emanuel Nunes Carvalho, who left London in 1799 for Barbados, Endelman concludes: "Further research might reveal another nine or ten similar examples, but even then such isolated instances hardly would permit one to speak of Jewish political activity."[2]

One wonders, however, whether Englishmen living at the end of the eighteenth century would have drawn the same unambiguous conclusion as that of Endelman. Take, for example, the three fascinating pieces of evidence linking enthusiastic prophecy and radical politics with Jews and Judaism dramatically presented by Iain McCalman.[3] The first example is a caricature entitled "The Repeal of the Test Act. A Vision," created by the London engraver James Sayers in 1790. Sayers satirizes the efforts of radicals to repeal the Test and Corporation Acts of that year by expressing his hostility toward those dissenters like Joseph Priestley, Theophilus Lindsey, and Richard Price for attacking the church and the English constitution and for supporting the French Revolution. Here is McCalman's evocative description of the print:

> While Price prays for the patriot members of the French National Assembly, Priestley appears to vomit airy flames of Atheism, deism, Socinianism and Arianism, blasting a passing angel in the process. Below cavort a hideous cast of ratbags and revolutionaries—demons carrying American and Cromwellian favours, the English Jacobins Fox and Paine, the failed regicide enthusiast Margaret Nicholson and, significantly, a Cromwellian soldier watching a bearded Jew destroy the sacred symbols of the Established Church.[4]

Ensuing Century (London, 1795). Pereira claimed that Brothers interpreted Scripture "in a rabbinic manner" (p. 16).

[2] Endelman, *The Jews of Georgian England*, pp. 274, 276. Referring to the first part of the eighteenth century, David S. Katz writes: "The Jews in early eighteenth-century English politics would provide material for a very short chapter indeed." See Katz, *The Jews in the History of England, 1485–1850* (Oxford, 1994), p. 215.

[3] McCalman, "New Jerusalems," pp. 312–35, especially 312–15.

[4] Ibid., p. 312. See also M. Fitzpatrick, "Priestley Caricatured," in *Motion towards Perfection: The Achievements of Joseph Priestley*, ed. A. T. Schwartz and J. G. McEvoy (Boston, 1990), pp. 161–218.

McCalman's second example from the same year is Edmond Burke's well-known vituperative outburst directed at the recent notorious convert to Judaism, Lord George Gordon:

> We have Lord George Gordon fast in Newgate; and neither his being a public proselyte to Judaism, nor his having in his zeal against Catholic priests and all sorts of ecclesiastics, raised a mob . . . which pulled down all the prisons, has preserved to him a liberty of which he did not render himself worthy. . . . We have rebuilt Newgate, and tenanted the mansion. We have prisons almost as strong as the Bastile, for those who dare libel the Queen of France. In this spiritual retreat, let the noble libeller remain. Let him there meditate on his Thalmud, until he learns a conduct more becoming of his birth and parts and not so disgraceful to the ancient religion to which he has become a proselyte.[5]

Finally, McCalman offers a series of three prints produced by Sayers's chief professional rival James Gillray inspired by Richard Brothers's well-publicized prophecies of 1795, which had irked David Levi. In these prints Gillray similarly links Jacobin prophecies, irreligion, religious dissenters, and pro-French revolutionaries with Judaism in a most disparaging way.[6]

How might we explain the apparent discrepancy between the violent images of Sayers and Gillray and the angry rhetoric of Burke with Levi's categorical assertion that Jews never involve themselves "in any rebellion, sedition, or treasonable practices towards the different governments where they have resided." Endelman offers one resolution of this quandary by suggesting that Levi was merely countering the widespread impression generated by conservative writers on the continent that the despised French revolutionaries were responsible for emancipating the Jews. While this association was not yet common in England, he claims, it was made frequently enough to unsettle English Jews, to put them on the defensive, and to encourage them to demonstrate beyond any shadow of doubt their unwavering loyalty to the English crown.[7] Is this incongruity then the mere result of a divergence between the images promoted by xenophobic loyalist propaganda on the one hand, as distinct from the actual reality of quiescent or obsequious political behavior of Anglo-Jews on the other?

On the basis of some new evidence as well as some further reflection on material long studied, I wish to reexamine the question of Anglo-Jew-

---

[5] Edmund Burke, *Reflections on the Revolution in France* . . . (London, 1790), pp. 124–25, and cited by McCalman, "New Jerusalems," p. 312. On Gordon as a Jewish dissenter, see my subsequent discussion.

[6] McCalman, "New Jerusalems," p. 314. See also Felsenstein, *Anti-Semitic Stereotypes*, pp. 96–98.

[7] Endelman, *The Jews of Georgian England*, p. 275.

ish dissent in the last decades of the eighteenth century, primarily from the perspective of Jewish self-perception: how conscious were English Jews of the political environment in which they lived, how did it affect their own sense of self identity, and under what circumstances, if any, were they actually drawn into political life, especially into the radical or dissenting camps? Of particular significance in this regard is the considerable attention paid to the problem by David Levi in many of his writings but especially in his exchanges with Joseph Priestley, Thomas Paine, and the aforementioned Nathaniel Brassey Halhed, along with an even larger group of other Christians, primarily clerics, with obvious political and religious agendas. At the very least, rethinking the question of Jewish dissent through Levi's eyes might allow us to see the issue slightly differently. But Levi's own writing is not all we can utilize to reopen the question, as we shall soon see.[8]

It is clear that the popular image of the despised Jewish radical tinged with anti-Semitic stereotypes loomed considerably larger than the reality behind it. Yet it would be wrong to hastily conclude that those who believed there were Jewish elements among the dissenters were merely hallucinating. Was the figure of Lord Gordon an aberration or symptomatic of a larger phenomenon connected to the actual presence of Jews in England? How are we to understand Richard Brothers from the viewpoint of the Jewish community itself? And what are we to make of the most mysterious Jewish figure in late-eighteenth-century England, Rabbi Samuel Falk, the so-called *Ba'al Shem* of London, and his alleged involvement

---

[8] On the place of dissent and radical politics in English culture at the end of the eighteenth century, I have gained especially from the following in writing this chapter: Haakonssen, *Enlightenment and Religion*, especially the introduction by the editor and the essays by John Seed, John Gascoigne, Alan Tapper, and Ian McCalman; M. Fitzpatrick, "Heretical Religion and Rational Political Ideas in Late Eighteenth-Century England," in *The Transformation of Political Culture: England and Germany in the Late Eighteenth Century*, ed. E. Hellmuth (Oxford, 1990), pp. 339–74; M. Philip, "Rational Religion and Political Radicalism," *Enlightenment and Dissent* 4 (1985): 35–46; Hole, *Pulpits, Politics, and Public Order in England, 1760–1832*; D. W. Lovegrove, *Established Church, Sectarian People: Itinerancy and the Transformation of English Dissent (1780–1830)* (Cambridge, 1988): McCalman, *Radical Underworld: Prophets, Revolutionaries, and Pornographers in London*; J. Mee, *Dangerous Enthusiasm: William Blake and the Culture of Radicalism in the 1790s* (Oxford, 1992); W. H. Oliver, *Prophets and Millennialists: The Use of Biblical Prophecy in England from the 1790s to the 1840s* (Auckland, 1978); Garrett, *Respectable Folly*; Clark, *English Society, 1688–1832*, and his review of Haakonssen, *Enlightenment and Religion*, in *American Historical Review* 103 (1998): 176–77; Bradley, *Religion, Revolution, and English Radicalism*, R. Porter, *English Society in the Eighteenth Century* (London, 1982); J. Fruchtman Jr., *The Apocalyptic Politics of Richard Price and Joseph Priestley: A Study in Late Eighteenth-Century English Republican Millennialism*, Transactions of the American Philosophical Society, 73 (Philadelphia, 1983), part 4. Other works are listed subsequently.

with radical political elements? On the assumption that David Levi knew more than what he cared to reveal to Mr. Halhed, I offer here a fresh look at these fascinating questions.

I

I begin this inquiry by returning to the central figure of the preceding chapter, Abraham ben Naphtali Tang. Among the few compositions he published in his lifetime is a previously unnoticed pamphlet written in English, recently discovered by Shmuel Feiner in the massive collection of Anglo-Judaica at the Jewish Theological Seminary in New York. The work bears the ambiguous title *A Discourse Addressed to the Minority* and appeared in London in 1770. Tang omits his name but signs the work simply "by a primitive Ebrew," the identical way in which he signed his commentary on *Avot*, and probably in other English works yet to be discovered.[9]

The reader of Tang's pamphlet familiar with the English political scene of 1770 cannot miss the context of this writing. It addresses the affair involving the infamous John Wilkes, the ambitious politician who had recklessly challenged the government of the earl of Bute from the early 1760s, who had carried on a vicious press campaign against the government, had been arrested and forced to exile himself to France, had then returned to England only to win reelection to Parliament despite the strong opposition he had engendered. Wilkes was again arrested on charges of blasphemy despite his apparent protection from such action as a newly elected member of the House of Commons. To clear the way for his prosecution, the governmental ministers manipulated the House to expel him. The action soon precipitated a major assault from the press arguing the unconstitutionality of this expulsion, its affront to liberty and to the independence of the House of Commons. In a period of growing conflict with the American colonies, a common thread between the Wilkes

---

[9] In *The Sentences and Proverbs of the Ancient Fathers*, Tang again hides his real name from the cover page but later fully identifies himself in a Hebrew page inserted at the end of his English introduction. There is no doubt the unsigned *Discourse* and this work are by the same author. On Tang and this commentary on *The Ethics of the Fathers*, see the previous chapter. I have also come across another document with the signature "A Primitive Hebrew" (note the different spelling) in a special edition of J. Picciotto's *Sketches of Anglo-Jewish History* (London, 1875), with insertions of photographs and documents in two leather bound volumes, 2:368, housed in the Mocatta Collection, University College London. The document entitled *Yisr'ael Nosha* but written in English calls for a general reform of the synagogue, apparently at a considerably later time. It is doubtful that this could have been written by Tang, although there is nothing in it with which Tang would have disagreed.

affair and the constitutional rights of the Americans was discernible to many.[10]

Wilkes seemed to be emboldened by this incident rather than subdued. For him the issue at stake was no less than the future of democracy in England: "If ministers can once usurp the power of declaring who shall not be your representative, the next step is very easy, and will follow speedily. It is that of telling you whom you shall send to Parliament, and then the boasted Constitution of England will be entirely torn up by the roots."[11] Wilkes's supporters were chiefly small merchants and craftsmen and less the gentry and the moneyed classes. Although the Rockingham Whigs, the leading group within the parliamentary opposition, initially supported Wilkes's cause, they eventually distanced themselves from the more radical opposition connected with the Society of Supporters of the Bill of Rights. In the same year that Tang published his own statement about the affair, Edmund Burke penned his own partisan "Thoughts on the Cause of the Present Discontents," a Rockingham's eye view of the politics of the 1760s condemning the political corruption of an alleged secret cabal of government ministers who had undermined the system. Burke was, in turn, criticized for his limited view by the more radical group among the opposition, led by the historian Catherine Macaulay and the London book seller John Almon.[12]

Almon had written his own version of the events leading up to the Wilkes explosion as early as 1765 in a book entitled *History of the Late Minority*.[13] In it he excoriated the earl of Bute as the chief villain in the undermining of England's democratic traditions. In lamenting the process by which the government fell into the hands of a leadership of privilege

[10] There is an enormous bibliography on the Wilkes affair. I have found most useful the following: I. R. Christie, *Wilkes, Wyvill, and Reform: The Parliamentary Reform Movement in British Politics, 1760–1785* (London and New York, 1962); G. Rude, *Wilkes and Liberty: A Social History of 1763–1774* (Oxford, 1962); P.D.G. Thomas, *John Wilkes: A Friend of Liberty* (Oxford, 1996); R. Pares, *King George III and the Politicians* (Oxford, 1953); J. S. Watson, *The Reign of George III, 1760–1815*, in *The Oxford History of England*, vol. 12, ed. G. Clarke (Oxford, 1960); J. E. Bradley, *Popular Politics and the American Revolution in England: Petitions, the Crown, and Public Opinion* (Macon, Ga., 1986); and L. Sutherland, *The City of London and the Opposition to Government, 1768–1774* (London, 1959).

[11] *Public Advertiser*, 4, February 8, 1769, quoted in Christie, *Wilkes, Wyvill and Reform*, p. 32.

[12] For Burke's work, see P. Langford, ed., *The Writings and Speeches of Edmund Burke*, vol. 2, *Party, Parliament and the American Crisis, 1766–1774* (Oxford, 1981), pp. 241–323; see also S. Ayling, *Edmund Burke, His Life and Opinions* (New York, 1988), especially pp. 39–53.

[13] J. Almon, *The History of the Late Minority Exhibiting the Conduct, Principles and Views of That Party During the Years 1762, 1763, 1764 and 1765* (London, 1765; reprint, 1766). I have used a copy of the original edition in the Rare Book Collection of the University of Pennsylvania Library.

and corruption, he singled out the honest independence of the opposition, "the true friends of liberty,"[14] who had protested the illegality of arbitrary warrants and who had supported the just cause of John Wilkes. This "late minority" who had resisted the power of Bute by opposing and censuring all the arbitrary violations of his ministers had been crushed and "broken-hearted."[15] They would eventually receive a new lease on life only five years later when the Wilkites would again challenge the unbridled power of the majority government.

Tang apparently meant the same minority that Almon had eulogized in his well-known book and which now, some five years later, had returned to center stage of the volatile political scene as a result of the removal of Wilkes from his elected seat in Parliament. For an obscure Jew, "a primitive ebrew," to jump into the commotion of this national debate not only was an act of daring on his part but suggested a sense of participation, of identification with England and its political traditions unparalleled in the Jewish European world of 1770.

Tang opens his pamphlet in a cautionary tone that soon allows him to express his own political and religious credo:

> I pray that when you come to peruse this small pamphlet, that ye divest yourselves from all prejudices, a grand and necessary object in religion, as well as politics. I do openly avow that I have done the same; be not quick in judging that my intention was to raise a tumult or to censure particular people for the sake of calumniating them; let me therefore tell you my creed. I believe in the Omnipotent supreme being, that knoweth the secrets of the heart, and to him all mysteries is ever open. I pay a due respect to my country wherein I drew my breath, as far as consistent with nature, and justifiable by law; I revere the legislature of my country, I love the king, I pray earnestly that God may ever emit that pellucid ray of truth and justice on him."[16]

While underscoring his supreme religious faith, he chooses to emphasize how religion should bind humankind, not divide it: "I earnestly wish that the word RELIGION may not be impiously and craftily converted to destroy the tranquillity of men. O Lord, with thy goodness, send forth to men that happy dawn of reason, that they may love and esteem each other without any distinction to mere terms of their several Faiths. O Lord, send forth thy calming SPIRIT into this land, now so fomented, and let every man dwell again in peace upon his woolpack."[17]

---

[14] Ibid., p. 223.

[15] Ibid., p. 310.

[16] Tang, *A Discourse Addressed to the Minority*, "To the Reader, the Man, and the Critick,", pp. v–vi.

[17] Ibid., p. vii.

His calming ecumenical opening, however, is soon punctured by his piercing battle call against the enemies of liberty:

When the heavens tremble . . . when laws are no farther observed than what will answer certain ends; when a good [kin]g is surrounded by deluded ghosts of M[inister]s who sheer off and strike at LIBERTY, as at the Cry of the Cok: In a time when it is even dangerous to call the culprits to an account: when flattery seemeth to be the spreading genius of the great, and reason becomes a victim to the lewdness of the impious; when the laws of our ancestors are forgotten, and new ones take their place; when M[i]n[iste]rs say to Magna Charta, "begone from us, and your ways we see not!" When a nation is come to such a crisis, as to behold part of her friends betraying her . . . when the common people are sacrificed to the caprice of a few tyrannical men, gratifying their own lusts at the expense of the juices of consumpted Britons . . . O! I lament for my people, I will mourn for her innocent youths that were slain. O! unhappy family of this island, it is high time that thy father, the [kin]g, whom God hath blessed with intellect and perspicuity, looketh forth from his window, and be roused from that opiate draught which the M[inister]s have given him to drink. The time is critical: they are, indeed Shakespeare saith, "out of joint."[18]

Conspicuously displaying his Jewish affiliation, Tang proceeds to offer an inventory of biblical citations in both Hebrew and English translation that highlight the crisis of moral authority and the compelling religious reasons for regal intervention.[19] "It is even wrong in the eyes of Providence," he writes, to remove "a certain great L[egislato]r."[20] Evoking Isaiah's testimony, even the government of Jerusalem was similarly guilty of removing honest judges and ministers. But at least there was a proper pretext for such a removal. In the case of Wilkes, there was no proper cause for his dismissal other than "the chimerical pleasure of M[inisters] to change."[21] The ultimate issue is whether the government of England is "a Democracy, or visa versa,"[22] whether its representatives in the House of Commons truly represent the will of the people who elected them.

Tang again returns to the theme of religion, one that unites all creeds and is devoid of ceremony or dogma: "Friends and countrymen, be not baffled or dwindled into fright. . . . Remember that men, be they as great in power as they can, are but men. I would now remind you, when you come to inquire into the character and conduct of your leaders, never to intermix religion therewith; look only whether the talk he hath under-

[18] Ibid., pp. 1–4.
[19] See especially ibid., pp. 4–6.
[20] Ibid., p. 11.
[21] Ibid., pp. 12–13.
[22] Ibid., p. 15.

taken be just. . . . No, be not deceived with the naked word of religion; look out for the plain meaning man for your country; and know that God judges men simply, without ceremonial or dogmatical laws."[23] Transparently vindicating his own intervention into politics, he clearly asks his reader to judge him not as a Jew but one who speaks for the simple religion of all humankind. And as a way of bolstering his credibility, he casts aspersions both on atheists and Jesuits.[24]

But all the preceding is just a prelude to his gushing peroration on the glories of his English homeland:

> As directed chance hath given me my prima mobile in this blessed country; whose laws are founded on the basis of reason; That grand reason which sucked the milk of nature, formed by that stupendous hand; that glorious spot where her people will not suffer imposition; where the laws are equal to the native and the sojourner [i.e., the Christian and the Jew]; knowing that my country is armed with such noble weapons, makes me truly happy, and I say with the wise: Blessed are thou, O land, where they king is free, and thy princes eat in due season.[25]

Tang winds up in true homiletic form drawing the direct parallel between Jeremiah's cry for righteousness and his own: "The City of Jerusalem we are told was destroyed, because of no justice being rendered there: I hope we don't labor under such circumstances. Jeremiah, who was present at the destruction of the Jews, did exhort them to be righteous, to keep to their Magna Charta."[26] The last words he ironically reserves for one of his favorites, "M. de Voltaire," on the meaning of "Country."[27] In a final outpouring of rallying cries, Tang finally evokes by name the victim he is championing: "Accept Wilkes' Ctechism," as he closes with the words: "For every blessing must come authorized and manifested."[28]

Seen in the light of his other writings considered in the previous chapter, the close connection between Tang's religious and political radicalism seems obvious. Tang openly affirmed the democratic ideal simultaneously as a Jew and as a member of the English nation. He had shown himself to be a student of political science; but he was also a practitioner of the art of political rhetoric. He sincerely believed, even as a Jew, that he had the right, indeed the responsibility to voice his concerns regarding the Wilkes affair, and to publish them in the public forum of pamphlets flood-

---

[23] Ibid., pp. 27–29.

[24] Ibid., pp. 28, 30.

[25] Ibid., pp. 30–31.

[26] Ibid., pp. 33–34.

[27] Ibid., pp. 34–35. For a discussion of Tang's other citations from Voltaire, see the previous chapter.

[28] Ibid., pp. 35–36.

ing the political world of London politics. Who read this pamphlet and did it have any impact on public opinion are questions to which we have no answer. Nevertheless, the intention of the author and his success of printing his views speaks for itself.

It is hard to conceive of a similar work written by any Jew at the end of the eighteenth century. But how then should we view it in the context of the alleged absence of Jewish political activity in England? Is it merely another isolated example of Jewish political consciousness, another exception to the general trend? I am prepared, in the absence of other compelling evidence, to assume that Tang's remarkable publication, his identification with the radical Wilkites, his forceful rhetoric on behalf of democratic principles, his articulation of a deistic faith that safeguards the rights and opinions of even "primitive ebrews," and his emotional attachment to his British homeland cannot be used to generalize about the mood of Anglo-Jewry as a whole. Nevertheless, it demonstrates, at the very least, the radical potential of English Jewish self-consciousness. And if it is unusual even for Anglo-Jewry, how much more singular does it appear from a continental perspective? Mendelssohn's public meekness and Tang's (as well as Levi's) brazenness remain in the end dramatic studies in contrast in assessing the degree of confidence each Jew had in the goodwill of his government and political culture.

II

The only other English Jew whose political behavior offers a close comparison with that of Tang is John King. Writing some fifteen years after Tang, he bitterly complained of the corruption of certain governmental ministers, the high taxes and tariffs, and the monopoly of the East Asia Company. His close contact with social reformers like Alexander Galloway, Richard Hodgson, Thomas Hardy, and William Godwin placed him at the center of radical politics of his day. As editor of *Argus*, King even supported Thomas Paine and the London Corresponding Society against the policies of William Pitt's government in the early 1790s. But the erratic King soon retreated from his most radical positions in reversing himself in support of Pitt, in defending the English constitution, and in distancing himself from the violence of the French Revolution.[29] Writing in 1792, he declared: "Some reform is certainly wanted but let it be fought for

[29] On King and his politics, see Endelman, "The Checkered Career of 'Jew' King: A Study in Anglo-Jewish Social History," pp. 69–100. See also McCalman, *Radical Underworld: Prophets, Revolutionaries and Pornographers*, pp. 35–39, 66–67, and "The Infidel as Prophet," pp. 34–39.

N.º XIX. *N.º XX.*

The Degenerate Countess. *The Fugitive Israelite.*

London. Published as the Act directs by A. Hamilton Jun.º Fleet St.ª Aug.1.1787.

Lady Lanesboró *John King*

10. Portrait of John King with that of his second wife, the widowed countess of Lanesborough, underscoring the unseemliness of the union between this notorious Jew and a Christian countess.

constitutionally, let it go to the king through the representatives of the people; when was he ever yet known to refuse redress of grievances? But shall we be passive when we see men begin what they call a reform, by deluging their country in blood?"[30] And to Paine he wrote in the following year: "Let us, in England, Paine, enjoy our liberty. . . . Let us continue our trials by jury while your's are conducted by the mob; and let us continue to defend our country, while you are desolating France (fig. 10)."[31]

As we have seen, King also approached Tang's religious views in praising Unitarianism in his preface to David Levi's work, and even more explicitly in his *Apology* published in 1798 where he wrote: "Why do we hold Judaism in detestation, since divested of its ceremonies, it is but a religion of deism . . . pretending to no preternatural illumination, to no illapses of the spirit, I am obliged to follow the dictates of reason, and

---

[30] J. King, *Mr. King's Speech at Egham with Thomas Paine's Letter to Him on It and Mr. King's Reply*, 3rd ed (Egham, 1792–93), p. 6.
[31] Ibid., p. 16.

square my life by natural instruction; the aphorisms of common ethics are simple and intelligible, they are assented to without effort."[32]

If King's work "marks one of the earliest occasions that a Jew anywhere in Europe sought to participate in national political life in pursuit of goals unrelated to Jewish communal needs,"[33] Tang's work is even earlier, as early as that of Isaac de Pinto whose French writings appeared in the 1760s and 1770s on the continent. But the difference between these English Jews is not only a matter of the time they wrote or the specific political cause they espoused. Tang, unlike King, was an accomplished Hebraist, a scholar of rabbinic literature, whose cultural world was still intimately linked to that of his traditionalist father and traditionalist teacher Moses Minsk. His English publications and his embrace of the Wilkites constituted dramatic departures from the cultural milieu in which he was rooted. King, on the other hand, the son of a humble street trader, had only a rudimentary Jewish education, wrote only in English, and was far removed physically and psychologically from the Hebrew literary world in which Tang claimed membership. That both of them could end up in the same theological and political camps, given their contrasting backgrounds, is quite remarkable. That Tang's radicalism evolved from his "insider" position, involving as well a thorough and searching critique of Jewish culture, past and present, was, of course, even more extraordinary.

Although Tang and King were exceptional in their politics of dissent, they were not alone among Anglo-Jews in publicly demonstrating their political views. Throughout the eighteenth century, both the organized Jewish community and individual Jews went out of their way to praise the political establishment and to celebrate liturgically and homiletically their good fortune of living under the British crown. These forms of public flattery, of prayers on behalf of the host governments, have long histories in Jewish political life and are hardly unique in themselves. Nevertheless, the rhetoric of these Jewish approbations to the king and his ministers reflects a special English ambience where an absolute identification with the royal government and a sycophantic demonstration of utter loyalty to it are effortlessly expressed. I offer only a few interesting examples of this phenomenon.[34]

---

[32] J. King, *Mr. King's Apology or a Reply to his Calumniators* (London, 1798), p. 41. On his other comments on Unitarianism, see the previous chapter.

[33] Endelman, "The Checkered Career of 'Jew' King: A Study in Anglo-Jewish Social History," p. 89.

[34] For a longer list of such special prayers to the king and his government, see Roth, *Magna Biblioteca*, pp. 311–21.

On Friday February 16, 1759, on the eve of a major naval campaign against the French troops in Canada,[35] and in support of a general fast in support of Britain's war efforts, the sephardic rabbi Reverend Moses Cohen de Azevado offered the following words to King George II from his pulpit in the Bevis Marks Synagogue:

> To thee, O gracious Lord, are all praises due, for the great progress the arms of our Sovereign made in the course of this year; and as it is notorious that our pious monarch does not make war but for the just defence of his dominions, may that be, O righteous Judge, a motive that you may be pleased to continue your auspicious protection to his royal person: May his arms again obtain glorious victories by sea and land; assist his honourable ministers and counsellors with thy grace . . . preserve and prolong, O Eternal Father, the precious life of our sovereign lord, king George the Second, for many and happy years.[36]

In the wake of a failed attempt to assassinate King George III "as he passed to the Parliament House on Thursday, the 29th of October [1795]," the Reverend Moses Myers composed a Hebrew prayer to be recited in "the German Jew's Synagogue of London." The prayer was translated by David Levi into English and reads in part:

> And how excellent is thy loving kindness which thou hast exercised towards us, and all the inhabitants of Great Britain, among whom we dwell, and take heed of our gracious and pious king, George the Third, whose glory may be exalted; for he seeketh the peace of his people; and earnestly desireth the peace of all his neighbors . . . for his affection towards us is that of a father; and in his enjoyment of peace, we have peace. . . . Wicked sons of Belial rose up, and put forth their hands against our lord and king, the Lord's Annointed . . . but God protected him.[37]

Having categorically insisted to Mr. Halhed that Jews never involve themselves in political disputes and rebellions, Levi apparently had no qualms about going to the other extreme in declaring hyperbolically that

---

[35] On this, see I. S. Leadam, *The History of England From the Accession of Anne to the Death of George II (1702–1760)* (London, 1909; reprint, New York, 1969), p. 459.

[36] Moses Cohen de Azevedo, *Sermon Preached in the Portuguese Jews Synagogue on Friday, the 16th of February, 1759, etc. Translated from . . . Spanish* (London, 1759), pp. 21–22. I have used a copy found in the library of the Jewish Theological Seminary in New York.

[37] *A Form of Prayer and Thanksgiving to the Almighty for his Providential Care in the Preservation of the King's Majesty from the Late Outragious and Desparate Attempts Against His Person as He Passed to the Parliament House on Thursday, the 29th of October, i.e., the 17th Day of the Jewish Month Cheshvan to be used at Morning and Evening Service in the German Jew's Synagogue in London* (London, 1796). Levi was also the publisher of the pamphlet that appeared in 1795 and 1797.

George III was "the Lord's Annointed." But apparently such a style of unctuous tribute had the official sanction of the sacerdotal leadership of English Jewry, and Levi was merely acting as a willing servant of his community. But such political tributes were also not the exclusive preserve of community officials.

The books of Dr. Ralph Schomberg, the assimilated son of Meyer, physician in his own right and aspiring author of prose and poetry, provide a graphic example of the use of political flattery by an individual writer. We shall have occasion to return to Ralph again and his close friendship with the scientist Emanuel Mendes da Costa.[38] Ralph never quite "made it" as a writer despite the relatively large number of books he published. In one instance he suffered the humiliation of being accused of plagiarism but even this did not dampen his spirit to win acclaim in the literary community. He dedicates several of his works to political figures in an apparent attempt to curry favor with the political-cultural establishment. He opens his *The Life of Maecenas*, published in 1767 with a dedication "to the Right Honorable William Pitt":

> You resemble him [that is, Maecenas] most. The glory of his king, the honor of his country, and the good of the Roman people, were the constant objects of his attention: So have they ever been, and are still yours. In his ministry he was uncorrupt, diligent, and resolute; in his counsels to Augustus, open, disinterested and sincere; in his expeditions against the enemies of Rome, cool, determined, and successful. All the world must see and acknowledge the striking likeness; his superior talents and surprising abilities, secured to him, the favour of his Prince, the esteem of his country, and the love of the people; yours, sir have had the same happy influence.[39]

And not a bit disingenuiously, he adds: "I scorn a menial compliment and am above a servile expectation. I have neither the happiness nor honor to know, or to be known to you. My address is your virtue, not to the minister, the great champion and assertor of British liberty."[40] Similarly, in his *Critical Dissertation on the Character and Writings of Pindar and Horace*, published in 1769, Schomberg addresses the "the Right Honourable the Earl of B[ute]," one of the chief targets of the political opposition: "I could not avoid giving your Lordship this public testimony of my respect; adulation is not my province: If the strictures I have thrown

---

[38] On Ralph Schomberg, see the previous chapter on his father Meyer and his deist beliefs. See also the next chapter where his letters with da Costa are discussed with additional bibliography.

[39] Ralph Schomberg, *A Life of Maecenas with Critical, Historical, and Geographical Notes, Corrected and Enlarged by Ralph Schomberg, M.D., Fellow of the Society of Antiquaries*, 2nd ed. (London, 1767), pp. iii–iv.

[40] Ibid., pp. iv–v.

together, in pursuance to your Lordship's request meet with your approbation, I shall esteem the time I bestowed upon them, not to have been
disagreeably employed."[41]

Even more self-serving was Schomberg's *An Ode on the Present Rebellion Dedicated to Her Royal Highness the Princess of Orange* published
in 1746 when Schomberg was residing outside England. This poem was
composed immediately after the Jacobite invasion of Scotland in 1745
led by "the young pretender," Charles Edward Stuart, whose forces first
penetrated to within eighty miles of London until they were driven back
and defeated. He introduces his elegy to the legitimate Hanoverian king
and his noble family with the following:

> The present unnatural rebellion with which your Royal father is audaciously
> attack'd, is an incident which has rais'd the amazement, as well, as engross'd
> the conversation of all neighbouring nations: Who can see without astonish-
> ment the imperial crown of England claim'd by a popish pretender, when the
> universal voice of the people, & a parliamentary right, agreable to the ancient
> constitution of our country, maintain'd thro' ages at the price of so much blood
> had plac'd it in your royal house, with the great view of preserving to us our
> Liberty & Religion?
>
> Future ages will scarce believe that we had men against us, base enough to
> dethrone their monarch at the very time, when his greatest care was generously
> emply'd in defending the Liberties of Europe against the ambitious views of
> tyranny & oppression; & who was ever wakeful for the happiness & welfare
> of his people. . . . As my residence abroad put it out of my power to give per-
> sonal proofs of my loyalty to his Majesty, I thought it at least my duty to express
> my zeal in writing; conscious, that nothing cou'd recommend me so much to
> the esteem of all true patriots, as my honest intentions in choice of a subject, in
> which our civil & religious liberties are so nearly concern'd, & the approbation
> of your royal Highness, with which you have been most graciously pleas'd to
> honour me. Your royal Highness's most obedient & most devoted humble ser-
> vant R. Schomberg.[42]

Schomberg's fawning encomiums to William Pitt, the earl of Bute, and
George II and his denunciation of the Jacobite invasion of 1745 hardly
bespeak a lack of interest in English political life on his part. Together
with the incessant flow of Jewish blessings in praise of the monarchy emanating from the Jewish clergy throughout the century, it suggests an acute
awareness of the powerful forces dominating English society to which the

[41] Ralph Schomberg, *A Critical Dissertation on the Character and Writings of Pindar
and Horace in a Letter to the Right Honourable the Earl of B[ute]* (London, 1769), p. 7.

[42] Ralph Schomberg, *An Ode on the Present Rebellion Dedicated to Her Royal Highness
the Princess of Orange* (Rotterdam, 1746), dedication pages.

Jewish collective and its individual members were beholden. Schomberg's politics were diametrically opposed to those of Tang and King but all three shared the same obvious passion for their political heroes and the causes of liberty and the constitution, however they were interpreted. Although it would appear that most Jews faithfully followed the "party line" of the Jewish community in zealously supporting the crown while distancing themselves from the dissenters, their loyalty should not necessarily be interpreted as an aloofness or indifference to politics in general. Perhaps Tang's behavior then is not as unusual as it might first seem.

III

In a provisional list of Jewish Freemasons in England of the eighteenth and early nineteenth centuries prepared by Morris Rosenbaum and eventually published in 1977 by John M. Shaftesley, the name "Abraham Abrahams" appears no less that five times.[43] "Abraham Abrahams" was the name by which Abraham Tang was known in English society. Two of the entries—one that lists Abrahams a member of the Atholl Register Lodge no. 145 in 1766 and the other with a listing of an Abrahams for 1771 for the Fortitude Lodge—conform precisely to the years in which Tang's literary career was in full bloom, the late 1760s and early 1770s.[44] It therefore seems plausible to suggest that Tang was a Freemason and that his notions of natural religion, of civic life and secular fraternizing, and especially his commitment to democratic principles as exemplified by his support of John Wilkes, may have been shaped, at least in part, by his involvement in these new enclaves of sociability that emerged in England by the early eighteenth century.

[43] J. M. Shaftsley, "Jews in English Regular Freemasonry, 1717–1860," *Transactions of the Jewish Historical Society of England* 25 (1977): 150–209. Rosenbaum's list is found on pp. 169–209. The entries on Abrahams are on p. 170. Shaftsley, who was a regular Freemason, also published a companion piece, "Jews in English Freemasonry in the Eighteenth and Nineteenth Centuries," *Ars Quatuor Coronatorum* 92 (1979): 25–63.

[44] On my own visit to the United Grand Lodge of England on Great Queen St. in London, in January 1998, I also examined the handwritten Athol Register F, vol. 6, 1768–95, of the Grand Lodge of the Antients. Lodge no. 145 is listed in the index as "Jews Lodge" and among its fourteen initial members, the names of Abraham Abrahams and David Levi appear. If this Abrahams is the same Abraham Tang, then David Levi was acquainted with him, which seems likely in any case. I also inspected the Register of the Grand Lodge of the Moderns 1768–1813, specifically the listings for Hiram's Lodge, Swan St., fols. 405–6, 476–77, where the following names are also listed: Phinoas Netto (son of Isaac Nieto), residing in Bevis Mark; Simon Baruch, age thirty-five; Daniel Baruch, listed in 1798 (on Raphael Baruh, their relative, see my previous discussion); Jacob Hart, silversmith, listed in 1801 as age forty-five (on him, see the next chapter). I want to thank John Ashby, deputy librarian and curator of the United Grand Lodge for his valuable assistance.

Of course, Freemasonry and its role in absorbing Jews into European society is hardly a new story, at least since the pioneering work of Jacob Katz, first published in 1968.[45] But Katz's book is primarily a history of the attitudes of German Freemasons to the Jews, the promise Freemasonry initially held for Jews seeking social acceptance, the obstacles constantly encountered in their struggles for civil emancipation in Germany, and ultimately the utter failure of these new social networks to integrate successfully their Jewish members. The primary message of Katz's research was that despite its idealistic beginnings, in the end the principle of Christian exclusivity remained firmly entrenched in German Freemasonry.[46]

Despite a brief description of English Masonry, Katz did not concentrate on the English scene except in considering the impact of English policies on German lodges. Indeed, as Katz openly pointed out, he could not even gain access to London's Grand Lodge and thus his sources were almost exclusively continental, reflecting a considerably different story than the one still to be fully told for England.[47] The subject of English Freemasonry and its attitude to Jews during the period of the Enlightenment and beyond provides still another dimension for considering the uniqueness of the English ambience and its notable contrast with that of Germany. Furthermore, there is an acute difference in the relationship between Freemasonry and Jewish self-reflection in both societies. As Katz clearly pointed out, there never existed any relationship between the Masonic lodges and Mendelssohn's circle. Mendelssohn was not only suspicious of Lessing's involvement with Masonry; he even taunted him about the alleged secrets the Masons preserved. Mendelssohn's primary objection to Lessing's allegiance to Freemasonry was the presumption that he possessed a secret knowledge, which he would not even share with his faithful ally in the search for truth.[48] In striking contrast, Freemasonry in England appears to be an important factor in the shaping of Jewish self-consciousness. Among the Jewish thinkers I have identified in England at the end of the eighteenth century and beyond, almost all of them were active Freemasons or, at the very least, were connected to Freemasonry through close associates or relatives. I would thus argue, at least tentatively on the basis of the limited evidence I now possess, that the new sociability afforded through English Freemasonry was not only important as a factor in Jewish social acceptance; it may also have had an impact

---

[45] J. Katz, *Jews and Freemasons in Europe, 1723–1929* (Cambridge, Mass., 1970). The book was first published in Hebrew in Jerusalem in 1968 as *Bonim Ḥofshi'im ve-Yehudim: Kishrehem ha-Amiti'im ve-ha-Medumim*.

[46] See especially Katz, *Jews and Freemasons*, p. 72.

[47] Ibid., p. 6.

[48] Ibid., p. 24.

on the history of English Jewish thinking as well. Let me elaborate a bit more on both points.

Margaret Jacob and others have eloquently argued for the critical role of English and Dutch Freemasonry in the formation of modern civil society.[49] The lodges, together with the philosophical and scientific academies (on these, see the next chapter), became the underpinning for republican and democratic forms of government. The culture of Freemasonry, Jacob maintains, was unrelentingly nonsectarian, offering membership to often the least socially acceptable, and identified with the English republican tradition that merit and not birth constitutes the foundation of the social and political order. Especially in Britain, Masonic civic life and its governmental structure actually mirrored the larger political and constitutional order. The democratic rhetoric as articulated in the lodges came to bind men of diverse social rank and power, even in times of ideological tension such as that of the Wilkes affair. Along with notions of English constitutionalism, the bill of rights, majority rule, and representative government, Freemasonry also displayed a peculiarly English religiosity with its emphasis on natural religion, Lockean psychology, and Newtonian cosmology. This British coloring was often left behind as Freemasonry migrated from England to the continent.[50]

Whereas Jacob has primarily emphasized the enlightened side of Masonry, others have focused more on its more mysterious character, its syncretistic symbols, its hermeticism and kabbalism, its preoccupation with ancient architecture, especially the Solomonic Temple. Perhaps Masonry's power lay in its remarkable blending of old and new meanings, its simultaneous embrace of ancient mysteries and modern science, and its uncanny ability to mediate between the traditional and the revolutionary, which,

---

[49] See especially M. Jacob, *The Radical Enlightenment: Pantheists, Freemasons, and Republicans* (London, 1981), and *Living the Enlightenment: Freemasonry and Politics in Eighteenth Century Europe* (Oxford, 1991). See also on the early history of Freemasonry, D. Stevenson, *The Origins of Freemasonry, Scotland's Century* (Cambridge, 1989); J. Hamill, *The Craft* (London, 1987); R. W. Weisberger, *Speculative Freemasonry and the Enlightenment: A Study of the Craft in London, Paris, Prague, and Vienna*, Eastern European Monographs (New York, 1992). S. C. Bullock's recent *Revolutionary Brotherhood: Freemasonry and the Transformation of the American Social Order, 1730–1840* (Chapel Hill and London, 1996), has a good opening chapter on English Freemasonry.

[50] Jacob, *Living the Enlightenment*, pp. 4–72. On the connection between the Freemasons and Wilkites and the tensions the Wilkes affair engendered within the London lodges, see ibid., p. 57; Jacob, *The Radical Enlightenment*, pp. 175, 263; and J. Money, "The Masonic Moment; Or, Ritual, Replica, and Credit: John Wilkes, the Macaroni Parson, and the Making of the Middle-Class Mind," *Journal of British Studies* 32 (1993): 358–95. In the library of the United Grand Lodge in London, I examined a pamphlet written by A. M. Broadly entitled *Brother John Wilkes, M.P. (1727–1797), Alderman, Chamberlain, and Lord Mayor of London, as Free Mason, "Buck", "Leech" and "Beefsteak"* (Weymouth, 1914).

on the surface, seemed to be rapidly diverging, but could be creatively linked in the Masonic universe of discourse.[51]

For English Jews, the lure of Freemasonry, as pointed out by Jacob Katz and others, was obvious.[52] It offered the potential for meaningful relationships with non-Jews and for instant social prestige. It also offered intellectual stimulation as well as "an escape from the drudgery of everyday life into a glamorous world of exotic ritual," as Todd Endelman put it.[53] Moreover, Jews could not help but be impressed by the smatterings of Jewish cultural artifacts located within the discourse and symbols of Freemasonry: Hebrew sounding words, biblical references, obscure kabbalistic connections, and especially the lionization of Solomon and his Temple of perfection. When the sephardic Jew Jacob Judah Leon of Amsterdam (1602–75) produced a model of the Temple and a treatise on its specifications, it was eventually appropriated by Masonic circles, brought to London where it was displayed as late as 1760, and became an essential part of Masonic lore. Rabbi Leon, in the mind of Lawrence Dermott, the grand secretary of the Grand Lodge of the Antients in London, writing in 1764, was a true brother of the fraternity who had accurately described the origins of the coat of arms of the Grand Lodge. No doubt even the most assimilated Jewish member of a London lodge could not help but warm to the notion that the most prestigious symbol of Masonry was of Jewish pedigree.[54]

Of course, with the appearance of distinctly Jewish lodges by the middle of the eighteenth century, the social and cultural utopian promise of Freemasonry had somewhat evaporated. Lodges catering to an exclusive clientele of Jewish shopkeepers and artisans, serving kosher meals, and following the Jewish calendar could never meet the expectations of those Jews who had dreamed of enhanced contacts with prominent members of London's Christian social aristocracy. The adoption of Christian ritual and prayer by some lodges, or even occasional anti-Jewish resolutions, could also alienate potential Jewish members. Nevertheless, as John Shaftesley has already pointed out in his reaction to Jacob Katz's book, the latter "had the effect of directing my attention to the differences between English and German freemasonry."[55] Despite the occasional setbacks in en-

---

[51] On the more mysterious side of Freemasonry, see Stevenson, *The Origins of Freemasonry* and the extensive bibliography he cites. See also the review of Jacob's *Living the Enlightenment* in the *Times Literary Supplement* by N. Hampson, for June 12, 1992; and see the useful discussion of Bullock, *Revolutionary Brotherhood*, pp. 20–40.

[52] See notes 43 and 45.

[53] Endelman, *Jews of Georgian England*, p. 270.

[54] In addition to the two articles of Shaftesley cited in note 43, see also A. L. Shane, "Jacob Judah Leon of Amsterdam (1602–1675) and his Models of the Temple of Solomon and the Tabernacle," *Ars Quatuor Coronatorum* 96 (1983): 145–69.

[55] Shaftesley, "Jews in English Freemasonry," p. 56.

gendering a true social mix between Christians and Jews in English Freemasonry, the experiment in England often worked. Jews and Christians
could inhabit the same neutral social space and could realize to a great
extent a new sociability unimagined in previous centuries. And the record
of the German failure at equal coexistence highlights the incredible success of the English model even more. To the extent that English Freemasonry succeeded in establishing a place for Jews, it was acting out the
political and social ideals embedded in the democratic vision of English
society as a whole.

That so large a proportion of Jewish intellectuals—both the assimilated
and the more traditional, both the sephardic and the ashkenazic—embraced Freemasonry provides ample testimony to the relative success of
this social structure in enhancing social mobility and in providing intellectual stimulation. Notions of belonging to an elite who shared a concern
for society as a whole appealed particularly to Jewish intellectuals with a
cosmopolitan outlook and a social conscience. In many respects the new
fraternities were mere extensions of the traditions of social volunteerism
embedded in the Jewish confraternities of the past. They represented
merely the expansion of the notion of "brotherhood," an overcoming of
a suffocating parochialism for the benefits of a restructured community
increasingly universal in spirit if not always in practice. For, in fact, even
the more segregationist Jewish lodges were in some form linked to a larger
universal fraternity where "all Masons are as Brethren upon the same
Level."[56]

By merely consulting Rosenbaum's extensive list, one encounters the
name of not only Abraham Abrahams (Abraham Tang), but also David
Levi and Jacob Hart (Eliakim ben Abraham).[57] Levi and Hart, in contrast
to Tang, were both conservative and strong defenders of Jewish traditional values.[58] Samuel Falk and Mordechai Gumpel Schnaber Levison
are not on the list but most likely had connections with Freemason and
Swedenborgian circles in London, as we shall discuss later.[59] David
Nieto's grandson and son of Isaac, Phineas, was a Freemason; so was
Joshua Van Oven, Joseph Salvador, Meyer, Isaac, and Ralph Schomberg.[60]
Although Emanuel Mendes da Costa (see chapter 5) is not listed, a large
number of his relatives besides Salvador are.[61] Raphael Baruh, the sephar-

---

[56] A line from the constitutions of 1723 quoted by Bullock, *Revolutionary Brotherhood*,
p. 39.

[57] Shaftesley, "Jews in English Regular Freemasonry," pp. 180, 182.

[58] On Hart, see the next chapter. See also note 44 on him and the other names mentioned.

[59] On Levison, see my previous discussion as well as the next chapter and appendix. Falk
is discussed later in this chapter.

[60] See Shaftesley, "Jews in English Regular Freemasonry," pp. 185, 186, 187, 188.

[61] Ibid., p. 176.

dic biblical scholar, is not mentioned but several of his family are included.[62] Many of the Jewish names are those of physicians, hardly unexpected for a fraternity that always boasted a high percentage of doctors
in its ranks.[63] In short, Freemasonry provided a stimulating cultural environment and hospitable social setting for a wide range of Jewish intellectual figures. Freemasonry could offer them either an outlet to escape from
the burdens of their ancestral tradition or simply a nonthreatening ambience where their Jewish identity was respected and could even be preserved intact.

Of course, several related questions remain regarding the Jewish engagement with Freemasonry, questions especially pertinent to the subject
of this chapter. What was the precise connection between Freemasonry
and radical politics? Did Freemasonry provide a conducive social environment and support system for those critical of the political-religious establishment? And were radical Jews like Abraham Tang, as well as several
others to be considered here, primarily stimulated by their associations
with Freemasonry in pursuing their political and religious agendas? An
unequivocal answer to any of these questions is not easily forthcoming
given the sheer diversity of the lodges in England and the wide range of
political attitudes held by their memberships.

John Money offers a particularly cautionary perspective against facilely
identifying English Freemasonry with political radicalism. Money examines the peak period of Freemasonry's growth in the 1760s in London,
followed by its decline and subsequent development in the provinces.
While modern Freemasonry was generally "latitudinarian in theology,
deist in metaphysics, and whig in politics," a great variety of views persisted among lodge members including radical and Jacobite loyalties. But
Freemasonry's prohibition of overt political discussion, as Money explains, and its message of natural religion and rational tolerance "made
it ideal for diffusing the non-partisan patriotism of Country ideology
among the emerging professional and entrepreneurial elements of provin-
cial society." Accordingly, it is easy to exaggerate the extent of deism and
to ignore the retention of historic Christian orthodoxy in actual Masonic
practice. Freemasons were just as likely to be conservative religiously or
politically as they were to be secular or radical. Money concludes that
although Freemasonry did contribute at times to radicalism, this was
often balanced by a leadership espousing conservative values. From the
mid-1770s, it is more accurate to characterize the prevailing tendencies
within the lodges as those of "pride in civic aspiration and achievement,

---

[62] See ibid., p. 173. On Raphael Baruh, see my previous discussion.
[63] See J. R. Clarke, "The Medical Profession and Early Freemasonry," *Ars Quatuor Coronatorum* 85 (1972): 298–311.

a growing veneration of tradition, and a reverence for national associations, church and state and king."[64]

Money's position stands in sharp contrast to that of Marsha Keith Schuchard who focuses especially on the clandestine network of Franco-Scottish Ecossais Masonic lodges established by exiled supporters of the deposed Stuart regime who sought to overthrow their firmly entrenched Hanoverian rivals. The followers of "antient" Stuart Freemasonry in London were forced to retreat into a kind of underground status in the eighteenth century with the rise of the "modern" Grand Lodge vowing loyalty to the Georgian governments and expressing Whig patriotism. Thus, according to Keith Schuchard, "Jacobites and Hanoverians maintained rival Masonic systems that struggled for dominance in Britain and abroad. Though Masonic histories in English have tended to glorify the Modern Grand Lodge system in Britain, Continental historians argue that the 'Ancient' Jacobite system attracted more recruits in the rapidly expanding Ecossias lodges in Europe and the New World."[65]

Because Rosicrucian and "Cabalistic" traditions were primarily cultivated in the Jacobite system of Freemasonry, Keith Schuchard claims that these concealed conventicles of ritualistic and political activity were the source of Jewish involvement in radicalism. Focusing especially on the Jewish convert Lord George Gordon and the mysterious Jewish magician Samuel Falk, Keith Schuchard has vigorously argued for the critical role of Jews and Judaism in the radical politics of the eighteenth century both in England and in western and eastern Europe, and throughout the eighteenth century and well into the nineteenth. A review of both remarkable figures and her enthusiastic claims about each, as well as the links between the two, is in order.

IV

The highly publicized conversion of Lord George Gordon (1751–93) to Judaism sometime in the 1780s has been discussed on more than one

[64] J. Money, "Freemasonry and the Fabric of Loyalism in Hanoverian England," in Hellmuth, *The Transformation of Political Culture*, pp. 235–72. The citations are from pp. 256, 257, and 266.

[65] I cite from a still unpublished paper, "Dr. Samuel Jacob Falk: A Sabbatian Adventurer in the Masonic Underground," p. 8, delivered by Marsha Keith Schuchard at a symposium on Millenarianism and Messianism in Early Modern Europe and America at the Clark Library, University of California at Los Angeles, November 16–17, 1997. The paper is to be published in *Jewish Messianism in the Early Modern Period*, ed. M. Goldish and R. Popkin (Dordrecht, 2000). My thanks to Professor Keith Schuchard for sending me the final version of this essay.

11. Depiction of Lord George Gordon in Newgate Jail by the Hanoverian artist Johann Heinrich Ramberg, surround by caricatured Jews serving him kosher food.

occasion, beginning as early as 1795 in the biography of Gordon penned by his close associate Dr. Robert Watson.[66] Prior to his seemingly inexplicable decision to be ritually circumcised and to assume faithfully the religious regimen of an observant Jew, Gordon had sensationally entered the public arena of radical politics through his early election to Parliament, through his rise to the presidency of the United Protestant League, and especially through his instigation of the riots of 1780 that soon were to bear his name, unleashed against Roman Catholics, the wealthy aristocracy, and the Bank of England (fig. 11).[67] Watson was probably in as good a position as anyone to understand Gordon's mind-set in converting to Judaism. Here is how he tries to isolate the factors that led to his friend's bizarre decision:

[66] Robert Watson, *The Life of Lord George Gordon: With a Philosophical Review of His Political Conduct* (London, 1795). See also P. Colson, *The Strange History of Lord George Gordon* (London, 1937); I. Solomons, "Lord George Gordon's Conversion to Judaism," *Transactions of the Jewish Historical Society of England* 7 (1915): 222–71; Katz, *The Jews in the History of England*, pp. 303–11; Felsenstein, *Anti-Semitic Stereotypes*, pp. 114–18.

[67] See J. de Castro, *The Gordon Riots* (London, 1926).

Lord George, who was constitutionally religious, had acquired a serious, contemplative turn of thinking. . . . He had long entertained serious doubts about the truths of Christianity, and observed "that its professors were both at variance with revelation and reason; whilst the Jews literally adhered to the laws of Moses." . . . [H]is conversion may have been due to his disappointments in life, which had soured his temper, and men in this state of mind from sympathy generally love to associate with victims of persecution. Perhaps he hoped to give celebrity to his favourite scheme of finance by embracing Judaism; perhaps he expected to have led back the Israelites to their fathers' land. . . . Perhaps his conviction arose from internal evidence; or perhaps he chose rather to be considered as the leader of the Jews than the humble disciple of Christ. But whether one or all these motives had any influence upon his conduct, I must confess, though I have talked a thousand times with him on the subject, I was never able to discover.[68]

Watson's bundle of possible motives—psychological, religious, and political—still betray an inability to penetrate Gordon's ultimate conviction. No doubt Gordon's Judaizing sympathies were clearly discernible long before his full embrace of the Jewish faith. He had previously berated Emperor Joseph II regarding his poor treatment of his Jewish subjects. In a letter of 1785, he complained about the "approaches, insults, and injuries" leveled at him by the emperor's associates in London "because I loved the Jews."[69] Gordon's correspondence with Elias Lindo, a *parnas* of London's sephardic Jewish community, and with Nathan Solomon of the ashkenazim and business partner of the wealthy Jewish businessman Abraham Goldsmid reveals a solidarity with Jews and Judaism well beyond the ordinary. Interspersed among his ravings about Jesuits and Catholics and his demand for Jewish support for the Protestant cause in Europe and in America is a string of biblical phrases in English and Hebrew: Shemah Israel; Shemah Koli; the God of the Philistines; the long blast with the ram's horns; there is no rest for the wicked; the sceptre of their government is not the *shebet* of righteousness; Jehovah-Jireh; and so on.[70] Gordon's interactions with individual Jews both before and after his conversion are well documented: his encounter with Isaac Titterman in Ipswich;[71] his letter to Rabbi Tevele Schiff, who refused to convert him;[72] his frequenting of Jewish homes in Birmingham, including his residence "in

---

[68] Cited in Solomons, "Lord George Gordon's Conversion," pp. 240–41, from Watson, *The Life*, pp. 79–80.

[69] Ibid., p. 229.

[70] Ibid., pp. 235–37.

[71] Ibid., pp. 239–40.

[72] Ibid., pp. 241–42.

one of the dirtiest homes in Dudley Street";[73] his study of Jewish texts and meticulous observance of Judaism as reported by his Jewish teacher Myer Joseph;[74] and his proud affirmation of wearing a Jewish beard in his letter to Angel Lyon.[75] In the latter case, Gordon even directs his stinging barbs at the affluent London Jews who appear to be ashamed of their outward Jewish appearance:

> The richer sort are ashamed of appearing with beards before the Christian merchants at the Exchange, and the nobility at the Playhouses. The souls of these men are lifted up unto vanities, their pride is testified by their faces, they set them towards the Ammonites and not against them. They are ashamed of the outward and visible sign, given unto them by God himself, and commanded to be preserved by Moses, because it distinguishes them as Jews, in public, from the nobility and gentry of these lands.[76]

For Marsha Keith Schuchard, Gordon was more than a radical politician; more than a pacifist; more than a critic of the penal system, slavery, and of the deceptive use of Catholic relief by the English government to recruit more troops to fight the American rebellion; and certainly more than a simple convert to Judaism. He "was almost certainly a freemason" and many Masons were implicated in the Gordon riots of 1780. Following the suggestion of Perry Colson and Cecil Roth, Keith Schuchard also claims that Gordon became involved with Samuel Falk, "a Sabbatean kabbalist" and "radical freemason," who was working "on a secretive effort to develop a Jewish-Christian masonic order, which became known as the Asiatic Brethren." Falk gained the financial support of rich Jewish families like the Boas in Holland and the Goldsmids in England who were also Freemasons. Gordon's two Jewish correspondents, Elias Lindo and Nathan Solomon, were also probably Freemasons, according to Keith Schuchard.[77]

The evidence that Falk actually met Gordon is highly circumstantial but there exists a clear connecting link between the two in the person of Joseph Balsamo (1745–94), known as Count Cagliostro, Sicilian adventurer, Freemason, and radical politician. Cagliostro had been imprisoned by Marie Antoinette and then banished from France. Arriving in

---

[73] Ibid., pp. 242–47; the citation is from p. 246.

[74] Myer Joseph's letter is found in M. Margoliouth, *The History of the Jews in Great Britain* (London, 1851), 2: 122–24.

[75] Solomons, "Lord George Gordon's Conversion," pp. 251–55.

[76] Ibid., p. 252.

[77] M. Keith Schuchard, "Lord George Gordon and Cabalistic Freemasonry: Beating Jacobite Swords into Jacobin Ploughshares," typescript, to be published in *Secret Conversions to Judaism in Early Modern Europe*, ed. M. Mulsow and R. Popkin. The citations are on pp. 7, 17, 20. My thanks to Professor Keith Schuchard for sharing her paper with me.

London he met Gordon who took an instant liking to him. During the same period Cagliostro had also visited Falk in his home in London in Wellclose Square where they developed a close relationship. Thus, through this hero of the Freemasons, Keith Schuchard speculates that Gordon too was initiated in the secrets of kabbalistic Freemasonry and developed a tie to the shadowy radical underground in which Falk was a central figure. She also mentions James Gillray's satiric print entitled "A Masonic Anecdote, designed by a Brother Mason," conjoining Cagliostro, Gordon, and radical Freemasonry.[78]

We shall consider more directly Keith Schuchard's elaborate reconstruction of Falk and his associates. But before turning to this more obscure personality, her ideas about Gordon and his alleged relationship to Falk's circle require further comment. Cagliostro indeed is an important bridge between the Jewish magician and the Jewish convert. Cagliostro's clear association with radical Masonry at leasts suggests a possibly similar affiliation for Gordon. What is more problematic, however, is the nature of Gordon's Jewish identity as displayed in the aforementioned sources of his life in contrast to Keith Schuchard's assumptions about him.

Gordon's religiosity, in comparison with that of Falk, was that of a person deeply serious about ritual practice and about external appearance as manifest in a long beard, and who identified with the Jewish poor and disadvantaged. His Jewish literacy was heavily biblical with a tinge of apocalyptic rhetoric regarding the return of the Jews and the approaching millennium. There is no hint of kabbalistic interest, no suggestion of a Sabbatean loyalty, no relationship whatsoever to magical activity. Rather Gordon's Jewish identity is what one would expect from a convert coming from a Protestant upbringing, one that is primarily biblically based and ritually focused. For Gordon, it seems, the best anti-Catholic Protestant is a Jew and loyalty to Judaism is the purest expression of protest about the injustices and iniquities of "popish" Christianity. Perhaps Edmond Burke in his remarks on Gordon came closest to defining his Jewishness by referring to him as "the Protestant rabbi."[79] But that appellation should not imply a merger or collaboration between Judaism and Christianity. On the contrary, Gordon's acceptance of the Jewish faith was a clear repudiation of Catholicism and Anglicanism. Judaism was for him the most natural culmination of his dissent from the repressive political and religious order of Christian England. Whether Gordon was ac-

---

[78] This is all discussed in her article in the previous note. On Cagliostro, see also Keith Schuchard, "Yeats and the 'Unknown Superiors': Swedenborg, Falk, and Cagliostro," in *Secret Texts*, ed. M. Roberts and H. Ormsby-Lennon (New York, 1995), pp. 114–67, and "William Blake and the Promiscuous Baboons: A Cagliostroan Séance Gone Awry," *British Journal for Eighteenth-Century Studies* 18 (1995): 185–200.

[79] See note 5. My thanks to Professor Stuart Semmel for helping me to clarify this point.

quainted with Falk is uncertain; whether he identified with the kind of Judaism he espoused is surely doubtful.

Samuel Jacob Ḥayyim Falk (c. 1710–82), known as the *Ba'al Shem* of London, represents the other prominent Jew in London to be identified by Keith Schuchard with the cause of political and religious dissent (fig. 12). Whereas Gordon's political activity was highly publicized, Falk's alleged involvements were practiced in the secrecy of dissenting Masonic brotherhoods. Whereas Gordon's Jewish behavior, as I have suggested, was fairly straightforward and conventional as a new convert, Falk's mystical-magical beliefs and praxis were shrouded in mystery. Yet the common denominator for both, as Keith Schuchard has claimed, was a strong posture of dissent against the political and religious establishment of their day, not only in England and France, but throughout the rest of Europe.

In recent times, Falk's life and activity has been studied intensely not only by Marsha Keith Schuchard but also by Michal Oron.[80] Coming from remarkably different perspectives—Keith Schuchard from the standpoint of the history of Freemasonry, Swedenborgianism, and radical politics; Oron from that of the history of the kabbalah and Sabbateanism—each has focused on different sources and arrived at somewhat different conclusions. Keith Schuchard's understanding of Falk's seminal role in Ecossais "illuminist" Freemasonry, in Swedenborgianism, and in the shadowy underground of Jacobites, Jewish-Christian Rosecrucian syncretists, and kabbalistic and Sabbatean Jews, is based on a wide reading in non-Hebraic sources, in Masonic documents in England and throughout Europe. She claims understandably that in studying such a subject as Falk and his cohorts, the sources at her disposal can never give us a clear and overt picture of their ideology and activities. Nevertheless, "the thicket of

---

[80] Keith Schuchard's principal essays on Falk have been mentioned in notes 65, 77, and 78. In addition, see her "Swedenborg, Jacobitism and Freemasonry," in *Swedenborg and His Influence*, ed. E. J. Brock and J. Williams-Hogan (Bryn Athyn, Pa., and London, 1988), pp. 359–79; and her 1975 doctoral dissertation from the University of Texas entitled "Freemasonry, Secret Societies, and the Continuity of the Occult Tradition in English Literature." Michel Oron has two overlapping essays: "Mysticism and Magic in London in the Eighteenth Century: Samuel Falk the Ba'al Shem of London" (Hebrew), in *Sefer Yisra'el Levin: Kovez Meḥkarim be-Sifrut ha-Ivrit Le-Doroteha*, ed. R. Zur and T. Rosen (Tel Aviv, 1995), pp. 7–20, and "Dr. Samuel Falk and the Eibeschuetz-Emden Controversy," in *Mysticism, Magic, and Kabbalah in Ashkenazi Judaism*, ed. K. E. Grozinger and J. Dan (Berlin, 1995), pp. 243–56. Oron is also completing a critical edition of the diaries of Falk and his servant Hirsch Kalisch. Keith Schuchard, in her recent paper on Falk, also mentions her forthcoming book entitled *Restoring the Temple of Vision: Cabalistic Freemasonry and Stuart Culture*. See also H. Adler, "The Ba'al-Shem of London," *Transactions of the Jewish Historical Society of England* 26 (1902–5): 148–73; C. Roth, "The King and the Cabalists," in his *Essays and Portraits in Anglo-Jewish History* (Philadelphia, 1962), pp. 139–64; and Katz, *The Jews in the History of England*, pp. 300–303.

צורת מרן הבעל שם טוב זי"ע וחתימה יד קדשו
(חג השבועות תק"כ)

12. The famous portrait of Samuel Falk incorrectly attributed to John Sin-
gleton Copley. This picture of the *Ba'al Shem* of London was commonly
confused with that of the founder of Hasidism, the *Ba'al Shem Tov*, as the
Hebrew caption indicates.

multi-layered political and Masonic intrigues [surrounding Falk], which are almost impenetrable to scholars because of the deliberate secrecy and the destruction of the documents demanded of participants," cannot be dismissed as "mere figments of the Rosicrucian imagination."[81] By an exhaustive search for hints in the sources she has identified, many of them unearthed in the remotest of archives, and by a rich dosage of imaginative speculation regarding often unspecific and circumstantial evidence, Keith Schuchard has energetically attempted to reconstruct the clandestine Falk and his radical religiosity and politics.

Oron, on the other hand, has primarily considered the place of Falk in the history of Sabbateanism in Europe, focusing primarily on three Hebrew documents: the evidence and stinging commentary on Falk by the archenemy of the Sabbateans, Rabbi Jacob Emden;[82] the diary of Falk's personal valet Hirsch Kalish, preserved in a Hebrew manuscript in the Jewish Theological Seminary of New York; and one of Falk's own kabbalistic notebooks preserved in the Rabbinical Seminary of London.[83] Despite the stigma associated with Falk's magical activity on the continent and then in London, and the abuse hurled at him by Emden, Oron cannot identify any specific clue directly linking Falk with Sabbateanism in any of his writings.

Oron traces Falk's activity from his birth in Galicia to his arrival in Podhayce and then in Fürth, towns associated with two well-known Sabbateans Judah the Pious and Moses David of Podhayce. Falk moved on to Westphalia, functioning as a Ba'al Shem, a kabbalistic magician, where he was accused of witchcraft and sentenced to death. He escaped and ended up in London in 1742. Establishing his home and private synagogue in Wellclose Square and a kind of magical-alchemical laboratory on London Bridge, he attracted considerable attention from Jews and non-Jews alike. In the diary of Hirsch Kalish recorded between 1747–51, one finds explicit descriptions of his magical activities, his strained relation with his wife, and even his extramarital affair with his maid-servant Sophie. Kalisch also reports about the initial discomfort of the London Jewish community regarding his activities and its attempt to ostracize him. By the end of his life, however, he appeared to be on better terms with the community and even gained the support of the powerful Goldsmid family.

[81] Keith Schuchard, "Yeats and the 'Unknown Superiors,' " p. 116.

[82] The text is essentially translated from Emden's *Gat Derukha*, in Adler, "The Ba'al Shem of London," pp. 168–71.

[83] Kalisch's diary is found in MS JTSA, Jewish Theological Seminary of America, New York, Mic. 3599; Falk's is listed in A. Neubauer's catalog of the Jewish Museum in London, no. 127.

In contrast to the relative silence of Jewish contemporaries in London regarding Falk, he was considered a legend among Christian Freemasons interested in the occult. He was visited by a steady stream of adventurers, dissenters, and occultists. He was in touch with Baron von Neuhoff, the king of Corsica, the Polish prince Adam Czartoryski, the duke of Orleans, the marquis de la Croix, the Danish count George Rantzow, and several others. In addition to his close association with the aforementioned Cagliostro, Keith Schuchard proposes, on the basis of a single obscure reference in Falk's writing, that he even taught Swedenborg directly.[84]

In Emden's discussion of Falk, he includes a letter of Susman Shesnowzi who describes a typical magical ceremony performed by Falk, including the lighting of candles, the pronunciation and writing down of holy names, and the holding of the event in a forest or near water. His activities often seem to have an alchemical dimension as well; in the case of several visitors, large sums of money seem to have been exchanged. Shesnowzi also points out that he was a close friend of Moses David of Podhayce, who in turn was associated with Rabbi Jonathan Eybeschuetz and his son Wolf. Emden, the primary accuser of Eybeschuetz for his Sabbatean proclivities, could not help but comment on this connection: "The fact that he is allied with Moses David, the friend of the Eybschuetzer, testifies against him." Indeed, in 1759, Moses David even visited Falk in London.[85]

Unlike Oron and the other scholars who have written on Falk, Keith Schuchard views Falk not only as an occultist and kabbalist but also as a dissenter with a clear-cut ideology. Especially in the last five years of his life, she claims, Falk played a significant role in an ambitious effort to develop a new form of Judeo-Christian Freemasonry in which there would be no conversionary pressures. She insists that this new religious syncretism went far beyond the basic tolerance of the English Grand Lodge system "for it involved the development of a new mystical religion which would utilize Cabbala to transcend all sectarian divisions."[86] She accepts Emden's characterization of Falk as Sabbatean and then refers repeatedly to a Sabbatean theosophy that infused certain systems "of irregular high-degree Masonry."[87] The latter was then linked to the Jacobite opposition to England's Hanoverian government, the philo-Semitic activity of the Moravian brotherhood, and the celestial arcana of the Swe-

---

[84] On the Swedenborg-Falk connection, see Keith Schuchard, "Yates and the 'Unknown Superiors,' " pp. 140–41.

[85] See Adler, "The Ba'al Shem of London," pp. 158–61. The citation from Emden is on p. 161. R. Patai in his *The Jewish Alchemists* (Princeton, 1994), pp. 455–62, stresses the alchemical context.

[86] Keith Schuchard, "Yeats and the 'Unknown Superiors,' " p. 117.

[87] Ibid., p. 118.

denborgians. At one point she refers to "the ecumenical Kabbalism of Shabbetai Zevi";[88] at other times she refers to Frankism, the movement initiated by the radical Sabbatean Jacob Frank who encouraged his following to convert to Christianity.[89] In sum, in Keith Schuchard's amazing reconstruction, Samuel Falk was the main Sabbatean representative in England. He worked with Caligliostro and William Bousie, a wealthy Anglo-French merchant, to develop a new system of "Egyptian" Masonry that would merge Sabbatean kabbalism and Swedenborgian theosophy.[90]

Keith Schuchard's intriguing portrait of Falk and his Judeo-Christian political circle is both impressive in the scope of her researches and in her uncanny ability to notice subversive connections not apparent to the casual reader of the texts she treats. Nevertheless, there remain serious questions about her understanding of Falk and his actual involvement in secret political and religious activity. In the first place, as Oron has argued, the evidence for his Sabbatean loyalties is hardly conclusive. Nowhere in his own writing does he make reference to Shabbetai Zevi nor does he offer any allusions to Sabbatean beliefs and practices. Emden, of course, had named him a Sabbatean primarily on the basis of his direct relationship with Moses David of Podhayce and his indirect relationship with Jonathan Eybeschuetz, his archenemy.

The connection with Moses David is indeed a fascinating one in the light of the study of him by the late Chaim Wirshubski written some fifty years ago.[91] Moses David's creation of an amulet made of a cross, his enigmatic juxtapositions of the names of Shabbetai Zevi and Jesus, and his general syncretistic orientation which Wirshubski attributed to the influence of the Sabbatean ideologue Brukhiah, head of the Doenmeh who converted to Islam, all testify to an orientation linking Jewish messianism with some fundamental Christian beliefs. This unique ideology was quite different from that of the Frankists, as Wirshubski also points out. The latter converted to Christianity as an instrument to reach their own secret faith. Christianity, in its externality, had little attraction to them; they converted in order to subvert its basic convictions. Keith Schuchard's loose linkages between the Frankist faith and that of Moses David are accordingly misleading and confusing. The Frankists were hardly ecumenical, as the Inquisition in Warsaw in 1760 quickly noticed and accordingly arrested them. Of course, the Frankists were not totally homogenous in their views and practices, and one should not expect them to be fully

---

[88] Ibid., p. 123.

[89] See, for example, ibid., p. 139.

[90] Ibid., p. 146.

[91] C. Wirshubski, "The Sabbatean Kabbalist R. Moses David of Podhayce" (Hebrew), *Zion* 7 (1942): 73–93.

consistent in their ideas about Christianity and their political connections. Nevertheless, they would have distanced themselves, at least initially, from Moses David or from his colleague Jonathan Eybeschuetz.[92]

More recently, Yehudah Liebes has added a new twist to the notion of Sabbatean ecumenicism. He argues that there existed a secret Jewish-Christian sect emerging from Sabbatean circles in Prague in the 1720s. Whereas in its early stages Sabbateanism was antagonistic to all existing religions, in its later phases it moderated its nihilistic tendencies for a more syncretistic posture. Liebes refers not only to the Christian dimensions in Moses David's thinking but also to similar tendencies in the writing of Nehemiah Ḥiyyah Ḥayyon and Eybeschuetz himself, among others. Sid Leiman has recently refuted Liebes in an unpublished paper I have not been able to see.[93] Nevertheless, whatever the accuracy of Liebes's assertion that there was an actually defined group with a distinct ideology of Judeo-Christianity among the Sabbateans, the general thrust of his argument lends credence to Keith Schuchard's argument that Falk, through his association with Moses David, had similar inclinations. Perhaps Emden knew exactly what he was talking about.[94]

It is at this point, however, that the representation of Falk offered by Oron and that of Keith Schuchard appear to clash. There is little sense in Falk's own writings that he was a great intellectual, that he had a clear ideology of Judaism, let alone Christianity, that he was capable of articulating a syncretistic religious philosophy weaving together Swedenborgian and Masonic themes with those of the kabbalah. He was clearly a practical magician, a *Ba'al Shem*, a great performer who was sometimes successful in extorting huge sums of money from his Christian and Jewish supporters. But this hardly suggests a deep student of the kabbalah, or of

[92] Yehudah Liebes does suggest, however, that the boundaries between the Frankists and the circle of Eybeschuetz were not always clear-cut and their relations require more investigation. See Y. Liebes, "On a Secret Jewish-Christian Sect Whose Source Is in Sabbateanism" (Hebrew), in his *Sod ha-Emunah ha-Shabbeta'it* (Jerusalem, 1995), p. 222.

[93] Professor Leiman, in personal correspondence (May 20, 1998), expresses his skepticism about the logic of a Jewish-Christian position in general. Either Jews converted to Christianity or some Christians converted to Judaism. Regarding the specific evidence of Liebes, he writes: "My critique of Liebes dealt specifically with an alleged Jewish-Christian sect in Amsterdam in the eighteenth century. Liebes did not see copies of the original documents relating to this 'sect'; he saw only a late-nineteenth-century summary of the evidence. I gained access to the original documents, which prove that Liebes's reconstruction of the history of the 'sect' is imaginary. So any theories you or others may have may be perfectly true, so long as they are not based on Liebes' essay."

[94] See the Liebes article in note 92, pp. 212–37, and generally in his *Sod ha-Emunah ha-Shabbeta'it*, pp. 103–211. Oron, in "Dr. Samuel Falk," pp. 253–54, also mentions the interesting notice of a "Christ Jew" in *Gentleman's Magazine* as perhaps referring to Falk and possibly indicating Falk's syncretistic orientation and connection with Moses David and Eybeschuetz.

comparative religion, or of radical politics. Although his magical aura may have elevated his stature among Christian "illuminated" radicals, there is little basis to suggest that he was capable of constructing and articulating a complex ideology of Jewish-Christian merger fused with radical political activity.

There is also no evidence to suggest that he even looked favorably at Christianity. In his own commonplace book, he mentions that he owned two polemical works against Christianity: the *Sefer Nizzaḥon* and *Ḥizzuk Emunah* of the Karaite author Isaac of Troki.[95] And more revealingly, in the only account of his ideas on Judaism and Christianity, written by Count Rantzow as early as 1736, several years before Falk's arrival in London, Falk is reported to have said the following:

> I am so little in error and love it so little, that I work at freeing all my brothers from [the New Testament]. They are waiting for somebody to liberate them from the oppression and the slavery in which they are. The time is approaching, but I cannot say more about it. Your law assumes they we are rejected by the people elected by God. But one would have to prove to me that God, who is immutable, could change His decrees. It is quite apparent that He has not changed them with regard to our people, that we are actually under His hand which beats us on our heads like the hands of a father who punishes his children. The Christians bask in the glory of the world. The Jews are in ignominy, so that in a true sense they are the only Christians. The death of Jesus Christ has come about in order to announce to us a humiliating state, after which we must fill the earth, to the very ends of the universe, with the cry of the magnificence of God and the glory of the Jewish nation. This nation has withstood the injuries of all times, it preserved its name, its unity, despite all the efforts of the powers of the earth. Unsuited to perform impostures, and very indifferent to the politics of the century, we do not count except in the thunder of heaven that will be detonated by the ministers of His vengeance. One should not say that we are blind. We always see the finger of God over our heads. Would you, Monsieur, cease to recognize your father as your father because he punishes you? Is it not that chastisement is the most beautiful sign which the true tenderness of a father can give? When all the Jews will be humble of heart, in sackcloth and ashes, He shall respond with their deliverance.[96]

This unusual citation in referring to Jews as the true Christians and as Jesus' death as a sign of Jewish humiliation followed by deliverance might suggest a kind of ecumenical perspective. On the other hand, there is also a clear sense of Jewish pride, of utter defiance, of unwavering trust in the

---

[95] See Adler, "The Ba'al Shem of London," p. 166.
[96] Cited from Patai's translation in *The Jewish Alchemists*, p. 457.

imminent redemption of Israel. The Jewish nation is perceived as glorious because it preserved its integrity against "the injuries of all times." Unlike Christianity, Falk adds, it is "unsuited to perform impostures"; and the politics of the century are not of interest to Jews. Are these the words of an architect of Jewish-Christian syncretism, of a radical interested in overthrowing the existing political order? Rather, they are the declarations of a firm believer in the authenticity of Judaism and the Jewish people who have stood the test of time and await patiently the messianic future. David Levi could not have said it better.

Many of Marsha Keith Schuchard's other assumptions also remain unproven. What elements of Sabbatean theosophy were actually appropriated into Masonry? What texts were studied, what doctrines were espoused, and how were Sabbatean ideas conjoined with both ecumenicism and political radicalism? Not only does Falk's relationship with Swedenborg remain uncertain; the larger question of the relation between kabbalah, Sabbateanism, and Swedenborgianism still requires further study and clarification. While some have already suggested connections between Swedenborg and the kabbalah in general,[97] this is not the same as claiming an affinity with Sabbatean theosophy, particularly its antinominan impulses. How a mood of cosmic harmony and ecumenical spirituality can coexist with radical dissent and nihilism under the umbrella of Sabbatean-Swedenborgian-Jacobite associations is not yet fully comprehensible. Nor should it necessarily be assumed merely on the basis of the supposed proximity and mutual interests of each of these constituencies.

On the other hand, Keith Schuchard's grandiose reconstruction cannot be dismissed out of hand. She has imaginatively pointed to connections that might indeed exist. She has marshaled strong evidence for an image of Falk far more important to an international circle of Christian radicals and illuminati than to his own coreligionists. She has raised the intriguing question of how Jewish magicians and charlatans like Falk could leave a greater impact on the politics and culture of their times than the more sober and conventional of his Jewish contemporaries. And she has correctly underscored "the perennial vitality of the Jewish visionary tradition that nourishes and regenerates both Rabbinic and Christian orthodox-

---

[97] See the interesting parallels between Swedenborg and the kabbalah mentioned by M. Idel in "The World of Angels in the Image of Man" (Hebrew), *Meḥkharei Yerushalayim be-Maḥshevet Yisra'el (Sefer Tishbi I)* 3 (1984): 64–66. See also E. Wolfson, "Constructions of the Shekhinah in the Messianic Theosophy of Abraham Cardoso with an Annotated Edition of *Derush ha-Shekhinah*," *Kabbalah* 3 (1998): 56, n. 141, on the kabbalistic ideas of Johann Kemper, formerly Moses ben Aaron of Cracow, the teacher of Swedenborg. Wolfson announces a forthcoming study on Kemper, Swedenborg, and the kabbalah. See also on Kemper, H. J. Schoeps, *Barocke Juden* (Bern, 1965), pp. 60–82.

ies,"[98] and, I might add, puts an entirely different cast on the meaning of the crisis of modernity for Christians and Jews alike.

In the end, even Keith Schuchard cannot decide whether Falk "was genuine or a knave,"[99] whether he was a true believer who championed the ideals of political and religious reform or a mere impostor deceptively acting out a theatrical performance for gullible Christians while laughing all the way to the bank. Even some of his more informed Jewish contemporaries could be taken in by his mysterious demeanor, as the case of the Goldsmids indicates. Levi remained curiously silent about Falk, but it would be safe to assume he was obviously uneasy with so unpredictable and dangerous a character. Tang probably dismissed him outright as a fraud, although it is unclear how Levison might have reacted to him, given his own apparent flirtation with the Swedenborgians and alchemical laboratories.[100] But whatever their reactions to him and to Gordon, they could do little to suppress the common notion among some contemporary observers of an intimate connection between Judaism and radicalism, a perception primarily fueled by the image both men had cut within English society at the close of the eighteenth century.

V

Having come full circle in finally returning to consider David Levi, one might be tempted to ask, What did David Levi have to do with dissent? Of all the Jews of his generation, he fully identified politically and socially with the Anglican establishment and with the English crown, even translating elegiac prayers on behalf of George III. In fact, Levi became the quintessential Jewish opponent of the dissenters, taking on in the last decade of his life Joseph Priestley, Thomas Paine, and Richard Brothers, three of the most prominent dissenters, and crossing swords with three primary streams of dissent, Unitarianism, deism, and millenarianism. At

---

[98] See Keith Schuchard, "Yeats and the 'Unknown Superiors,' " p. 156.

[99] Keith Schuchard, "Dr. Samuel Jacob Falk," p. 21.

[100] On Levison's possible connections with Falk through August Nordenskjold, see Keith Schuchard, "Yeats and the 'Unknown Superiors,' " p. 133; her "The Secret Masonic History of Blake's Swedenborg Society," *Blake: An Illustrated Quarterly* 26 (1992): 40–51; and her "Dr. Samuel Falk," p. 16, as well as the references she cites. Although the personal connections she underscores between Levison and Swedenborgian and Masonic figures are intriguing, her imaginative conclusions ultimately reach beyond the evidence. Her claim that Levison's Hebrew work on law and science (or any of his works, for that matter) shows the influence of Swedenborg as well as Linaeus's "Cabalistic [sic] theory of correspondences" is totally unfounded. For an analysis of this work, see Ruderman, *Jewish Thought and Scientific Discovery in Early Modern Europe*, pp. 345–68.

the very least, Levi's writing against the dissenters represents a rich reposi-
tory of arguments by their opponents. It reveals a degree of familiarity
with political and religious dissent unparalleled among other Jewish contemporaries. Furthermore, there is more to Levi's arguments against the
dissenters than rigid opposition. At times, he adopts their forms of argu-
mentation, partially agrees with them, even evokes a certain sympathy
with their stands. Finally, there is a deeper sense in which one might even
understand Levi's political and religious stances as being aligned with
those in the dissenting camp, as we shall soon observe.

This is not the place to review the circumstances, the detailed arguments
and counterarguments between Joseph Priestley and David Levi, as well
as the flurry of pamphlets that appeared both for and against Priestley in
the wake of their highly public confrontation.[101] I would simply like to
comment on several aspects of Levi's two responses to Priestley, on those
to some of his later critics and those of Priestley, and on the final outcome
of their disputation immediately prior to Levi's death in 1801. As has been
pointed out by others, Priestley was genuinely interested in embracing the
Jewish community because he admired Judaism as a historical faith and
because he truly believed that the differences separating Judaism and Unitarian Christianity were so minimal that a rapprochement between the
two was actually possible. Already in his first address to the Jews he
wrote:

> If you examine impartially what Christianity really is [that is, Unitarianism],
> and not what is has been represented to be, you will find in it nothing at which
> your minds ought to revolt. . . . Christianity inculcates as fully as Moses him-
> self, the doctrines of the divine unity, and that of his placability to returning
> penitents, and it asserts with peculiar clearness and energy that fundamental
> article of all practical religion, the revelation of a future life. . . . Your whole
> nation is to be the head of all the nations of the earth, in order to its being
> the medium of communicating happiness to all mankind, who are equally the
> offspring of God and the care of his providence with yourselves. Let then this

[101] See especially, Popkin, "David Levi, Anglo-Jewish Theologian"; J. Van den Berg,
"Priestley, the Jews, and the Millennium," in *Sceptics, Millenarians, and Jews*, ed. D. Katz
and J. Israel (Leiden, 1990), pp. 256–74; Garrett, *Respectable Folly*; Fruchtman, *The Apocalyptic Politics of Richard Price and Joseph Priestley*; Katz, *The Jews in the History of
England*, pp. 296–300. On Priestley in general, see R. E. Schofield, *The Enlightenment of
Joseph Priestley: A Study of His Life and Work from 1733 to 1773* (University Park, Pa.,
1997). I have focused primarily on the Levi-Priestley interchange and its aftermath. On
Levi's encounter with Paine, see R. Popkin, "*The Age of Reason* versus *The Age of Revelation*: Two Critics of Tom Paine," in *Deism, Masonry, and the Enlightenment*, ed. J. A. Leo
Lemay (Newark, Del., 1987), pp. 158–70; and E. Davidson and W. Scheick, *Paine, Scripture, and Authority: The Age of Reason as Religious and Political Idea* (Bethlehem, Pa.,
1994). On Levi's response to Brothers, see the references in note 1.

13. One of the many portraits of Joseph Priestley, published in 1792.

great, this rational, and desirable pre-eminence content you, and let all idea of
opposition, and difference of interest, cease. We will receive and honour you as
our elder brethren, in the great family of God. Acknowledge us as your younger
brethren (fig. 13).[102]

Levi, of course, would have nothing to do with such a solicitation. He
proceeds to attack Priestley for the inauthenticity of his Christian faith.
The argument is made for tactical reasons in embarrassing Priestley and
putting him on the defensive. It also represents, I would contend, an honest reflection on Levi's part about the truth of revelation, whether it be

[102] Joseph Priestley, *Letters to the Jews Inviting Them to an Amicable Discussion of the
Evidences of Christianity* (Birmingham, N.Y., 1794), pp. 45–47.

Christian or Jewish. Whatever else Levi was, he was a traditionalist who believed in the notion of a divine revelation and the sacredness of Scriptures. To recast Christian orthodoxy into a liberal rational faith consistent with deism and devoid of Trinitarian doctrine was for Levi a repudiation of Christianity's essential character. Judaism could only be true to itself, and by extension so too Christianity, if it took the words of its revealed writings at face value instead of misrepresenting them to fit some rational preconceptions. Levi was a literalist and the essence of his explanation of Judaism was a defense of what the actual biblical text was saying. This meant that he would subject the New Testament to the same kind of reading to which he was accustomed in reading the Old, and by so doing, Priestley's interpretations would prove wanting. Accordingly, he proclaims to Priestley:

> For your doctrine is so opposite to what I always understood to be the principles of Christianity, that I must ingeniously confess, I am greatly puzzled to reconcile your principles with the attempt. . . . For if you, and the other writers of your sect, have not been able to convince those that account themselves Orthodox Christians, of the true unity of God; nor they you, of the divinity of Christ, how shall a simple Jew, (who is perhaps despised by both) be able to convince either?[103]

Having familiarized himself with the extensive polemical literature between the Orthodox and Dissenters, Levi enlists its support in undermining Priestley's claim to represent himself as a true Christian. Citing Theophilus Lindsey, Priestley's close colleague and founder of the Unitarian Church of London, in his debate with the fundamentalist William Romaine, Levi cleverly points out that the Reverend Romaine had condemned the Jews for being atheists in rejecting the Trinity, while Lindsey had excoriated Romaine for believing in the Trinity.[104] To the Jewish outsider in this debate, the choices seemed stark indeed. Levi also seemed to relish the opportunity of citing the testimony of one of Priestley's staunchest opponents, Josiah Tucker, in delegitimizing the faith of Unitarianism:

---

[103] David Levi, *Letters to Dr. Priestley* (London, 1793), p. 10.

[104] Ibid., pp. 74–76. On Theophilus Lindsey (1723–1808), his fight with the Anglican establishment, and eventual departure from the Church of England, see Clark, *English Society*, pp. 313–15; H. Mclachlan, ed., *The Letters of Theophilus Lindsey* (Manchester, 1920); Fitzpatrick, "Heretical Religion and Radical Political Ideas," pp. 351–52; J. Seed, in Haakonssen, *Enlightenment and Religion*, pp. 165–67; and in the same volume, J. Gascoigne, pp. 230–34; and the Sayer's engraving linking him to Priestley and Price in the McCalman essay in the same volume, pp. 312–13. On William Romaine (1714–95) and his role in the debate over Jewish naturalization in 1753, see Katz, *Jews in the History of England*, pp. 250–51; Perry, *Public Opinion, Propaganda, and Politics*, pp. 91–92; and Roth, *Magna Biblioteca*, p. 222.

"That if this system [the Unitarian] be really true, the Scriptures of course must be false, and Christ and his apostles be ranked among the greatest hypocrites and impostors that ever appeared on earth."[105]

In his second batch of letters to Priestley, Levi is just as unrelenting in exposing the un-Orthodox nature of Unitarianism. In reference to Mosaic law he writes: "As soon as a Jew begins to trifle with it, by calling into question the authenticity of any part thereof, he is no longer considered a Jew in the strict sense of the word; and in like manner, I am clear, that whoever calls into question the authenticity of any part of the New Testament, cannot with propriety be called a Christian in the strict sense of the word . . . and therefore, if once the partition wall is thrown down, who shall be able to draw the line, and say, so far thou shalt go and no farther?"[106] In the light of his notion of the distinct impermeable characters of the two faiths and their unambiguous delineation from each other, Levi is incapable of comprehending Priestley's proposal for a Jewish church, a kind of syncretistic faith drawing from the most liberal and rational elements of both Judaism and Christianity. So he proclaims: "But such a church as you have described, I think never was heard of, as I verily believe it is neither Jew, nor Christian, and for which I am really at a loss to find a proper name; however, that is what you call Christianity."[107]

Citing Priestley's friend (John Buncle)[108] and foe (Samuel Horsley)[109] alike to confirm his observation about the alarming schisms within Christianity, Levi reserves his most damaging testimony for the last of his letters on the alleged divine mission of Christ compared with that of Moses. Here he brings the opinion of Dr. Conyers Middleton, the Anglican cleric who attempted to adduce historical arguments to demonstrate the pagan origins of the putative miracles of the early church. If indeed a Christian

---

[105] Levi, *Letters to Dr. Priestley*, p. 89. On Tucker and his view of Jewish naturalization, see Endelman, *Jews of Georgian England*, pp. 37–38; and on his critique of Priestley and Price, see G. Shelton, *Dean Tucker: Eighteenth-Century Economic and Political Thought* (London, 1981).

[106] Levi, *Letters to Dr. Priestley in Answer to His Letters to the Jews*, part II, p. 15.

[107] Ibid., p. 21.

[108] Ibid., p. 19. James Lackington, the bookseller, who often invited Levi to dine with him and their mutual friend Henry Lemoine, mentions that he had read the Memoirs of Buncle, which he called a pernicious work, and adds: "Having, like John Buncle, given up the doctrines of the Trinity, original sin, atonement made by Christ, the obligation of the Sabbath, &c." See James Lackington, *Memoirs of the Forty-Five First Years of My Life of James Lackington* (London, 1794), p. 4.

[109] Levi, *Letters*, part II, p. 20. On Samuel Horsley (1733–1806), chaplain of Bishop Lowth and friend of Samuel Johnson, well known for his exchanges over Priestley's *History of the Corruptions of Christianity*, see Clark, *English Society*, pp. 230–34, and F. C. Mather, *High Church Prophet: Bishop Samuel Horsley (1733–1806) and the Caroline Tradition in the later Georgian Church* (Oxford, 1992).

clergyman could demonstrate the fraudulent character of Christian miracles, it was incumbent on a Jew to cherish the true miracles publicly bestowed on his forefathers at Sinai.[110]

Although most of the reactions to the Levi-Priestley debate were negatively disposed toward Levi's position, there were at least two respondents who fully appreciated Levi's position and tacitly agreed with him. The first was probably George Horne, whom we have already encountered as a supporter of the Hutchinsonians against the followers of Kennicott. Writing under the fictional name of Solomon de A.R. and unconvincingly presenting himself as a Jew, Horne dashed off a quick and nasty response to Priestley entitled *The Reply of the Jews to the Letters Addressed to Them by Doctor Joseph Priestley*. Horne easily concurs with Levi that the Gospels plainly teach the Trinity. His defense of orthodox doctrine seems to echo Levi precisely: "Do they cease to be doctrines of the Christian Gospel because they do not believe them? . . . If we forsake the religion of our fathers, and do not embrace [the Doctrines of the Gospel], what else we may become, we certainly do not become Christians." And later he continues, still speaking as a Jew: "Assuredly you have acted a very unwise part in inviting us to be of a religion which it does not appear you have adopted yourself; and in recommending us to be governed by a book, to which, in the most material articles of it, you professedly give no kind of credit."[111]

Horne recognizes that if Priestley's faith is so close to Judaism, as he himself indicates, then the logic of his conversion to Judaism makes more sense than the Jew's conversion to an inauthentic version of Christianity: "Be bold, and openly profess the religion of which you think such great things, and no longer let your name be numbered among the uncircumcised. . . . Submit to the operation. . . . How then can there be any danger in it? You fancy the operator's hand may slip, and so you might receive irreparable damage. . . . if you preserve yourself calm, without turbulence or refractoriness, I no not see how any possible evil can happen from your being circumcised, let your age be what it will." And as if to add insult to injury, Horne confesses that the Jew would not accept Priestley either

[110] Levi, *Letters*, part II, pp. 42–47. On Dr. Conyers Middleton (1683–1750) and his influential *Free Inquiry into the Miraculous Powers which are supposed to have subsisted in the Christian Church from the Earliest Ages through Successive Centuries* (London, 1749), which Levi cites, see Mossner in *Encyclopedia of Philosophy*, p. 33, s.v. "Deism"; Harrison, *"Religion" and the Religions in the English Enlightenment*, p. 144; and G. Rupp, *Religion in England, 1688–1791* (Oxford, 1986), index.

[111] On George Horne and his role in the Kennicott debate, see chapter 1. The identification of the author of this pamphlet with Horne seems to have been first made by Cecil Roth. See his *Magna Biblioteca*, p. 260. See Solomon de A.R., *The Reply of the Jews to the Letters Addressed to Them by Doctor Joseph Priestley* (Oxford, 1787), pp. 10–11, 19.

because "it is a maxim among the Turks that a bad Christian will never make a good Mussulman." So he concludes rather abusively: "Try to become a Turk or if desperate, circumcise yourself!"[112]

Jacob Barnet, a recent convert to Christianity, in his *Remarks upon Dr. Priestley's Letters to the Jews*, similarly cautions the Jews, to refrain from converting to a faith that misrepresents the true Christian doctrine: "You may fall into a species of idolatry by looking up to Dr. Priestley, exalted into a saint of superior order, power, and beatitudes, for converting you according to his own description . . . so that . . . it is best, perhaps, for you to invite Dr. Priestley to come over to you, and be circumcised, or remain as you are, in humble expectation, till it shall please God to call you in his own appointed time, and convince you of the truth, as it is in Jesus."[113]

Priestley was apparently hurt by Levi's stern reply to him. In the second installment of his letters, he failed to mention Levi by name, a slight that Levi would not allow to go unnoticed in his later rejoinder to him. But Priestley remained restrained throughout and earnestly tried to address the Jews deferentially: "I do not address you as a disputant, desirous of triumphing in any advantage I may have in the argument, but from the truest respect to your nation . . . and from the most earnest wish to promote your welfare, here and hereafter."[114] Despite their initial agitation, the two ultimately developed a mutual respect for each other. After Priestley had left England for Northumberland, Pennsylvania, he published there *A Comparison of the Institutions of Moses with Those of the Hindoos and Other Ancient Nations* in 1799, and appended *An Address to the Jews on the Present State of the World and the Prophecies Relating to It*. In this work he defends himself against charges of being a Freemason and atheist, although he persists in believing that the French Revolution was ultimately a positive development for humankind: "Despite all the evil that has taken place, I shall trust that the consequence of that revolution will be great and happy and that the final issue of the present disturbed state of the world will be that glorious and most desirable state of things which is subject of so many prophecies."[115]

Turning to the Jews, their faith and ritual customs, Priestley has nothing but genuine admiration for them. He singles out their moving liturgy, their reverence for Scriptures, their charity, even their tenderness to animals.

---

[112] Solomon de A.R., *The Reply of the Jews*, pp. 26–33.

[113] Barnet, *Remarks upon Dr. Priestley's Letters to the Jews*, pp. 7–8.

[114] Joseph Priestley, *Letters to the Jews Part II Occasioned by Mr. David Levi's Reply to the Former Letters* (Birmingham, 1787), p. 53.

[115] Joseph Priestley, *A Comparison of the Institutions of Moses with Those of the Hindoos and Other Ancient Nations . . . and An Address to the Jews on the Present State of the World and the Prophecies Related to It* (Northumberland, 1799), pp. xv–xvi.

Drawing his account from Buxtorf and Leon Modena, he acknowledges "the great superiority of their religion, and customs, to those of any heathen nation."[116] He then addresses the Jews directly: "Be not offended at a Christian, who from his early years has entertained the greatest respect and veneration for your nation, and who in this work has endeavored to vindicate the honor of your religion, and to evince its superiority to all other ancient religions, to address you on the present extraordinary situation of the world at large has, in the great plan of providence always borne a particular relation to you, as the peculiar people of God."[117]

He has in mind "there being evident symptoms of the time of your deliverance being at hand." In the aftermath of the fall of France and other European monarchies, and with the decline of papal power, "Palestine, the glory of all lands, which is now part of the Turkish empire, is almost without inhabitants. It is wholly uncultivated, keeping its Sabbaths, empty, and ready to receive you." This is not the time for arrogance or animosity toward contemporary Christians on the part of the Jews, he insists, since "your persecutors have been long dead, and all sincere and intelligent Christians, notwithstanding all that their ancestors . . . have suffered upon you, bear you the greatest good will, and feel the most sincere compassion for you."[118]

He finally acknowledges his previous encounter with the Jews and with Levi specifically: "I formerly took the liberty to address you on this subject [on their conversion], and had the happiness to find you were satisfied that I wrote from the purest motives and a sincere respect and good will to your nation. . . . But I cannot help observing that, tho' one of your nation, a person whom I well know and respect, replied to me, he did not undertake to refute my principal argument. . . . He did not pretend to point out any defect in the arguments that I advanced for Jesus having wrought real miracles of his having died, and having risen from the dead." Unwilling to acknowledge the force of Levi's rebuttal, he presses forward: "Your restoration cannot fail to convince the world of the truth of your religion; and in those circumstances your conversion to Christianity cannot fail to draw after it that of the whole world. . . with the greatest respect and affection I subscribe myself your brother in the sole worship of the God of your fathers, J. Priestley."[119]

This would appear to have been the final word between the two formidable adversaries since Levi never again directly responded to him. Yet there is one more extraordinary piece of evidence to suggest that the two

---

[116] Ibid., p. 260.
[117] Ibid., p. 393.
[118] Ibid., pp. 397, 411, 413–14, 416.
[119] Ibid., pp. 426–28.

had made their peace despite Priestley's unrelenting missionary exhortations. In 1801, months before Levi's death, Priestley's *An Inquiry into the Knowledge of the Antient Hebrews Concerning a Future State* appeared in London. Remarkably, it was "printed for J. Johnson, St. Paul's Church Yard by D. Levi, Green Street Mill End, New Town." That a Jew of Levi's stature would dare to publish an exegetical work on Hebrew Scripture by a Christian is curious in itself; that it was Levi publishing Priestley, without any apology or explanation on his part, is quite phenomenal. It suggests a noticeable appreciation of Priestley and his respect for Judaism, despite their strong disagreements of the past and Levi's firm repudiation of Priestley's proselytizing efforts.

One may also surmise that Levi had other reasons for publishing Priestley's excursus on Isaiah 18. In this work, Priestley offers strong textual support for the fact that the Jews always believed in the doctrine of resurrection and in spiritual retribution. We should recall how Levi began his literary career with an ambitious critique of Humphrey Pridaeux's claim that the Jews were inferior to the Christians because they lacked such beliefs.[120] Levi had been finally vindicated by a formidable Christian supporter of his position. Levi surely was most favorably disposed to another of Priestley's positions, his tepid support for and clear reservations regarding the biblical emendations of Benjamin Kennicott. As Priestley explained: "Even conjectural emendations, without the authority of any antient version, or ms., may sometimes be allowed, though this should be done very sparingly; since many of the most plausible of those emendations have appeared, on further consideration, to be unnecessary; the present text being capable, on a more critical examination, of a clear and unexceptional interpretation."[121] In the end, Levi, the proud and unrepentant Jew, had discovered a common ground with his former antagonist. Years after their first skirmish, Levi could selectively affirm some of Priestley's ideas while still resisting the blandishments of his missionizing disposition.

Surprisingly, Levi was also moving closer to Priestley on another issue to which neither could be oblivious. Priestley, as we have seen, had repeatedly found spiritual significance in the radically changing political climate of Europe, the French and American revolutions, and the real possibilities of Israel's restoration to the Holy Land in the wake of Napoleon's entrance into the Middle East. Levi was more reticent to express himself forcefully on this issue given the dangerous consequences of unbridled

---

[120] See David Levi, *A Succinct Account of the Duties, Rites, and Ceremonies of the Jews*, pp. 252–76. Also see chapter 2.

[121] Joseph Priestley, *An Inquiry into the Knowledge of the Antient Hebrews Concerning a Future State* (London, 1801), p. 56.

millenary passions as exemplified in the lunatic frenzy of Richard Brothers and other self-styled prophets. But he too had noticed the instability of the political world in which he was living and could not help but react to it. In his *Dissertations*, he writes: "And at the present time, the year 1793, almost all Europe is engaged in a more horrid and dreadful war; in which, such enormous excesses are committed, as is scarce credible of human beings; especially of civilized mortals enlightened by revelation. Whence it is evident, that it remains to be fulfilled all the restoration of the Jews by the true Messiah, when it shall please God in his mercy, to redeem them." And he is more forceful when again noting the dreadful condition of Europe, Napoleon's attempt to conquer Egypt, "the clang of guns and trumpets, of arms and armies rushing to dreadful combat . . . which seem so much in accord with the events, that the different prophets have predicted are to take place at. . . . I cannot but consider all these occurrences, as indications of the near approach of the redemption of our nation."[122]

Levi then, although a staunch opponent of deists, Unitarians, and millennial enthusiasts, could identify some points of agreement with them that ironically softened somewhat his opposition to their dissenting voices. While outraged at Paine's irresponsible assault on the Bible, he could at least appreciate that deists within his own community had not fully deserted the fold and still identified themselves as Jews; that Unitarians like Priestley shared some common notions that endeared them to the Jews; and that fanatic restorationists could not be dismissed out of hand in the topsy-turvy world of the end of the eighteenth century.[123] Yet there still remains one fundamental way in which Levi identified with all of these dissenting parties, despite his seeming antagonism to them and to their principles.

Jack Fruchtman Jr., in a recent paper on Levi's confrontation with Priestley, makes an important point in arguing that by merely entering into a public, rancorous debate with the famous theologian and scientist,

---

[122] Levi, *Dissertations*, 1:299–98; 3:140, 240.

[123] Regarding this last point, Ian McCalman, in his "New Jerusalems," pp. 317–18, has pointed out the rather bizarre nature of Levi's close Christian friends beginning with his loyal Henry Lemoine. Lemoine was a restorationist interested in mystical and magical writings, and especially ghost experiences. McCalman even cites Thomas Hastings to the effect that Levi was "a kind of conjurer, an adept in the abstruse science of physiognomy . . . a profound critic, and a rigid reviewer of whims, dreams, riddles, romances, enigmas, tales of ghosts, hobgoblins, and so forth." (See Thomas Hastings, *The Regal Rambler; or Eccentrical Adventures of the Devil in London* [London, 1793], pp. 3–6, cited from McCalman, p. 318.) As McCalman points out, this description of Levi seems to fit Lemoine more closely. It is hard to imagine Levi having any interest whatsoever in such matters but given his close relation with Lemoine, Lackington, and their "circle of plebeian freethinkers and mystics," as McCalman calls them, some positive attitudes toward enthusiasts and restorationists on Levi's part should not be ruled out of hand.

Levi had helped legitimize Judaism's place in late-eighteenth-century English society and culture. While Jews in Levi's lifetime had practiced their religion to the extent that their English Gentile compatriots tolerated them, Levi's bold entrance into the public arena in defense of Jewish interests "singlehandedly inspired the transformation of religious toleration to English religious liberty."[124]

Before concluding this chapter, I would like to explore Fruchtman's insight from a slightly different vantage point. Levi, as we have seen from the very beginning of our discussion, carefully separated his religious from any political dissent. In his opening remark to Halhed, he clearly stressed the supreme loyalty of the Jewish subjects of the English crown and their inhibitions to even enter into political discussion in the first place. But given Levi's remarkable public persona and his obvious lack of restraint in challenging the Goliaths of his world from Priestley to Paine to Halhed, it seems rather disingenuous on his part to insist on so neat a demarcation between the religious and political spheres. As J.C.D. Clark and others have long indicated, all forms of radicalism in early modern England had a religious origin. Any discussion of religious doctrine could not be separated from the question of political authority and power.[125] In openly attacking Christianity in public, in mocking the inability of Catholic or Protestant Christians to reach any consensus on the nature of their faith, in ridiculing Christian leaders for their lack of knowledge in understanding and translating biblical prophecies, and even in presuming to defend religion in general before such adversaries as Thomas Paine, Levi was consciously pressing the culture and power structure of his Christian majority to allow Jews like himself to speak their mind, to overcome their self-defensive postures of passivity and meekness, and to take full advantage of the free speech a democracy was supposed to guarantee all its citizens, even Jews. And by insisting that Jews had the right to express themselves even at the expense of Christian sensibilities, he was singlehandedly assuming the right to change the rules of the game, that is, the way Jews were to conduct themselves in an enlightened Christian society.

Already in the opening to his first response to Priestley, Levi was fully self-aware of what he was doing. In pointing out that the other leaders of his community had declined to answer Priestley, he explains their behavior on account of the aversion they have "towards any of their body entering into religious disputes, for fear, that anything advanced by them,

[124] See J. Fruchtman Jr., "Philosemitism and Millenarian Thought in the Late Eighteenth Century: David Levi Confronts Joseph Priestley," paper presented to the conference on Millenarianism among English Protestant Thinkers, 1600–1800: Science, Liberal Politics, Philosemitism and Millenarian Thought, University of California at Los Angeles and William Andrews Clark Library, February 20–21, 1998. The citation is from p. 4.

[125] See especially Clark, *English Society*, pp. 277–78.

might be construed as reflecting on, or, tending towards disturbing the national religion, as by law established." He dismisses this argument as groundless

> for although they may justly have been apprehensive of the consequences of such disputes in the dark ages of Popery, when, on the least surmise, or most groundless accusation (as the crucifying of children &c.) thousands were massacred in England. . . . Yet, ought they not at present, to entertain any such apprehensions, thanks be to God, the Reformation, and glorious Revolution. Besides, we live in an enlightened age, in which the investigation of theological points is accounted laudable; and so they really are, if not carried to a licentious height.[126]

Levi's detractors also noticed and commented harshly on not merely the substance of his arguments but that he dared to make them in the first place. John Hadley Swain could not fail to note the irony of Levi's fearless attacks: "And let the Jew know, that it is owing to the benevolent spirit of that religion [Christianity] whose author he treats with contempt, that he not only enjoys his liberty, and has his property well secured, but can sit down, write, and publish with impunity whatever his pen has produced against that very religion." And Swain continues: "Upon one thing I congratulate him, that he lives in a country, and at a time, that he may write against the religion that protects him, and grossly abuse the author of it, without endangering his liberty, his ears, or his pocket. But I cannot promise him, that his character will be equally secure. For if a man will do silly things, perhaps it cannot be avoided, but that contempt will be his portion."[127]

It was left to Anselm Bayly, however, to articulate the full consequences of Levi's actions. Bayly, as we have seen in previous chapters, was a Christian cleric who displayed a full appreciation for rabbinic scholarship and even prided himself on his close acquaintance with contemporary English Jews. He was a good Anglican with even some sympathies for the Hutchinsonians, as we have seen, and could therefore not countenance the dissenting religious creed of Joseph Priestley. Therefore, it is quite ironic to discover that he, more than any other cleric, was incensed by Levi's temerity in criticizing Priestley's overture to the Jews.

Bayly begins by laying out his proper credentials in indicating that no common anti-Semite was addressing Levi; indeed, as he patently indicated, some of his best friends were Jews: "I know myself three Gentle-

---

[126] D. Levi, *Letters to Dr. Priestley in Answer to those he Addressed to the Jews* (London, 1787), pp. 4–6.

[127] John Hadley Swain, *The Objections of Mr. David Levi to the Mission, Conduct, and Doctrine of the Lord Jesus Christ Examined* (London, 1787), pp. 36, 76.

men, named Messrs. Belisario, Baruh, and De Paz[128] who are more learned, respectable, and more accurate than himself in the idiom and phraseology of the English language." He then proceeds to offer his own observations about English Jews whom he has known and about the ideal relations that should ensue between them and their Christian neighbors: "both are neighbors and brethren in expectation of blessings, and therefore ought to be friends, as much as possible, and love one another. . . . For my own part I am glad to embrace this opportunity of declaring, that I ever loved your nation as the receivers of God's gracious promises, and the careful preservers of his precious oracles, and also for the many civilities I have for many years received from several individuals, persons of politeness, honour, and virtue."[129]

While belittling a large inventory of Jewish customs and ceremonies, he singles out "one neat, decent, and brotherly ceremony, the Sabbath *kiddush* and breaking of the bread." He compares it to the "sacrament administered in the Church of England" and relates that "I have more than once took the *kiddush* with my late worthy friend Furtado, and with another worthy Jew now living." He laments the fact that so many Jews in his day ignore this lovely ceremony and "are disposed to embrace deism."[130]

If it is not his antagonism to Jews and Judaism that motivates Bayly to attack Levi, it is likewise not his appreciation for Priestley and his ideology. For Bayly, Priestley is a blasphemer "who threatens the king, the minister (Pitt), and both houses of Parliament" and who ridicules all the bishops and considers them "a pack of ignorant, dastardly, dumb dogs, fast asleep." In Bayly's opinion, Priestley "ought immediately to be hanged, for putting the three Estates of the realm in bodily fear."[131]

---

[128] On Baruh, see chapter 1. Bayly had referred to Isaac Mendes Belisario as well as Baruh in the introduction to his Hebrew grammar mentioned earlier. On the de Paz family, see S. Oppenheim, "Memorial of the Solomon and Elias De Paz on the Capture of their Ship in 1728–29 off Jamaica by the Spaniards," *Publications of the American Jewish Historical Society* 26 (1918): 248–49. An A. de Paz had revised and corrected Jacob Castro's *Grammatica Anglo-Lusitanica & Lusitano-Anglica; or a new grammar, English and Portuguese, and Portuguese and English*, 5th ed. (London, 1770). This is likely the man Bayly had in mind. See Roth, *Magna Biblioteca*, p. 409.

[129] Antisocinus [Anselm Bayly], *Remarks on David Levi's Letters to Dr. Priestley in Answer to Those He Addressed to the Jews* (London, 1787), pp. 19, 34–35.

[130] Ibid., pp. 36–37. Bayly might have meant Isaac Mendes Furtado, who attacked the elders of the sephardic synagogue in justifying his unruly behavior on Purim, 1783, and subsequently baptized his children. If this was indeed Isaac, Bayly's testimony that this assimilated Jew still observed the *kiddush* would be most interesting. See J. Picciotto, *Sketches of Anglo-Jewish History* (London, 1956), pp. 195–96.

[131] Antisocinus, *Remarks*, pp. 38–40.

If Bayly loved Jews and despised Priestley, what provoked him to label Levi "a dogmatical, dictatorial, categorical, audacious Egotist?"[132] It was Levi's manner rather than the substance of his charges that triggered Bayly's ugly reaction:

> Dr. Priestley, pitying your sufferings was in some sort for healing your grievances; in his way he presented you balm, wine, and oil, which he would pour into your wounds, and bind them up; you with rudeness tear off the bandages and cast them in his face; and is it to be expected, that while you throw darts and fire brands, we should stand quietly by and laugh at the sport? You might have refused Dr. Priestley's offers with civility, and perhaps would have been thought wise in so doing or at least to have shewed some good breeding.

But there is more here than the matter of bad manners: "You, Dr. Priestley, and others, give me leave to say it, make not a generous and proper use of toleration, but audaciously abuse it, flying in the face of the reformation and revolution; while you are pleased to compliment it with the title of glorious, for giving you the liberty forsooth of writing whatever, and in what manner, you like: commendations from such mouths comes with an ill grace."[133]

But Levi's unacceptable behavior derives ultimately from overstepping the proper limits of how Jews should conduct themselves in a Christian society: "Behave as good Jews till it please God to call you to be Christians, and in the meantime I will protect you in the utmost of my power; and if I had the authority I once had, I would protect your unhappy nation in the peaceful and quiet practice of your religion."[134] When Jews don't practice their religion "peacefully and quietly," they not only will relinquish their right to protection from the good pastor, they will subject themselves to the worst of Bayly's stinging barbs emanating from the basest of Christian stereotypes: "Here David Levi, Shiloc like, demanding the execution of his bond, earnestly and rigorously contends for the letter of the law, which killeth without the least regard to equity and the spirit of it, which giveth life. This is Rabbinism and superstitious bigotry in the extreme, not humanity and charity, which he so much boasts of, as the characteristic of himself and his people."[135]

Anselm Bayly thus understood the ultimate gravity of Levi's presumption. Jews could be tolerated as long as they practiced their religion "peacefully and quietly" and observed their quaint sacraments like the *kiddush* to the delight of curious Christian spectators. But when they

---

[132] Ibid., p. 19.
[133] Ibid., pp. 15–16, 21.
[134] Ibid., pp. 42–43.
[135] Ibid., p. 53.

overstepped their limits, when they dared to pronounce publicly their deeply cherished beliefs, when they endeavored to reject the overtures of Christian proselytizing, when they presumed to correct Christian misreadings of sacred scriptures, and when they had the audacity to even ridicule Christian articles of faith and recall those embarrassing disagreements among Christians themselves, they had crossed the line of civility and proper Jewish behavior. Toleration meant servility and meekness, not brashness and unfettered speech. "Being good Jews" was the rule of the day and, in Bayly's view, Levi had broken it. His genuine loyalty to the English system notwithstanding, David Levi should be considered ultimately the primary Jewish dissenter of his day.

Five

Science and Newtonianism in the Culture of Anglo-Jewry

ONE OF THE unique features of Jewish thought in eighteenth-century England was its attentiveness to Sir Isaac Newton and the impact of his ideas on religious culture. Just as Newtonianism had pervaded the social, theological, and political fabric of English society prior to its later repercussions throughout the rest of Europe, Anglo-Jewish writers were similarly the first among European Jews to take notice of its cultural importance and the primary protagonists to wrestle with its implications for Jewish faith.[1] I have already discussed elsewhere the impact of Newtonianism on two Jewish thinkers writing and publishing in England: David Nieto, the rabbi of the Bevis Marks Synagogue at the beginning of the eighteenth century,[2] and Mordechai Gumpel Schnaber Levison, the illustrious physician and prolific medical writer at the end of the eighteenth century.[3] Matt Goldish has recently studied the significant weight of Newton's ideas on the writing of Dr. Jacob de Castro Sarmento, Nieto's chief disciple who eventually abandoned Judaism as a result of a sense of spiritual and intellectual alienation that he never fully articulated.[4]

After reviewing the dialogues of these three and their relation to Newtonianism, I consider a fourth thinker clearly affiliated with the small circle of Jewish intellectuals in London at this time: Eliakim ben Abraham,

---

[1] For a useful recent overview of Newton and Newtonianism, see B.J.T. Dobbs and M. Jacob, *Newton and the Culture of Newtonianism* (Atlantic Highlands, N.J., 1995), especially its extensive bibliography. See also Force and Popkin, *Essays on the Context, Nature, and Influence of Isaac Newton's Theology*; M. Jacob, *The Newtonians and the English Revolution* (Ithaca, N.Y., 1976); J. Gascoigne, "From Bentley to the Victorians: The Rise and Fall of British Newtonian Natural Theology," *Science in Context* 2 (1988): 219–56.

[2] D. Ruderman, "Jewish Thought in Newtonian England: The Career and Writings of David Nieto," *Proceedings of the American Academy for Jewish Research* 58 (1992): 193–219, and reprinted with minor changes in Ruderman, *Jewish Thought and Scientific Discovery in Early Modern Europe* , pp. 310–31.

[3] Ruderman, *Jewish Thought and Scientific Discovery in Early Modern Europe*, pp. 332–68.

[4] M. Goldish, "Newtonian, Converso and Deist: The Lives of Jacob (Henrique) de Castro Sarmento," pp. 651–75. See also R. Barnett, "Dr. Jacob de Castro Sarmento and Sephardim in Medical Practice in Eighteenth-Century London," *Transactions of the Jewish Historical Society of England* 27 (1978–80): 84–114.

known in England as Jacob Hart. Hart wrote exclusively in Hebrew and published several of his books both in England and in Germany. Like the other three, he displayed a broad familiarity with Newton's scientific ideas as well as with the theological hurdles they posed to traditional revelation. His particular reaction to Newtonianism, both his enthusiasm for Newton's contribution to the sciences and his sense of alarm about the uses of Newtonianism by deists, atheists, and even some Latitudinarians, is unique among his Jewish contemporaries both in his awareness of English ideas and authors generally unknown to a Jewish readership, and because of the conservative positions he adopts in his "wars" on behalf of the Jewish faith. Hart was surely a less significant thinker than either Abraham Tang or David Levi, both with respect to the quantity as well as the profundity of his reflections. Nevertheless, Hart represents a highly interesting intellectual figure in modern Jewish thought because of his engagement in a discourse, although far removed from the consciousness of most of his coreligionists, still very much at the heart of a larger conversation taking place among ever widening circles in western Europe of his day.

I

David Nieto (1654–1728), the *ḥakham* of the Spanish and Portuguese congregation of London at the beginning of the eighteenth century was apparently the first Jewish thinker in Europe to grapple with the impact of Newtonianism on his community and its faith.[5] Arriving in England in 1701 to assume his new rabbinic post, and although armed with a prestigious medical degree from the University of Padua, he was patently unprepared to understand fully the intellectual and cultural world of English society and was even limited by his inability to communicate freely in the English language. But Nieto was a quick study, and probably because of his solid grounding in medicine and the sciences, he was fully capable of appreciating the fertile discussions about science and religion that Newton's work had stimulated in England by the turn of the eighteenth century.

Nieto never mentioned Isaac Newton by name, but he seems to have been fully cognizant of the ideas of the Christian Anglican proponents of Newtonian science. He appears to have fully identified with their vision of religious faith as a natural religion that glorified the new scientific discoveries but repudiated the outmoded Aristotelianism of the past or the

---

[5] The information found in the following paragraphs on Nieto is essentially gleaned from my work mentioned in note 2. I list there earlier scholarship on him as well.

materialistic and potentially atheistic philosophies of Hobbes and Descartes. He was equally sympathetic to their notion of a mechanical philosophy requiring God's active engagement in the workings of nature. What Nieto found the most useful in creating a theology of Judaism to fit the needs of his new fledgling community emerging on English soil was the arsenal of informed arguments aimed at the enemies of religious faith: the atheists, the deists, the freethinkers, and the enthusiasts of his day. Judaism too, Nieto discovered, had its own versions of these antagonists of true religiosity in the form of Spinozaists, Jewish deists, and Sabbatean prophets. Seemingly taking as his primary script the formidable Boyle lectures of Samuel Clarke of 1704–5 on the being and attributes of God and on the relationship of natural religion and Christian revelation, Nieto constructed his own vision of traditional Judaism that clearly paralleled that of Clarke and his Newtonian circle. In so doing, he effectively argued for the active engagement of God in the natural world in his *De la Divina Providencia*, demonstrated the affinity between Judaism and science in his *Mateh Dan*, and forcefully challenged the Sabbatean enthusiast Nehemiah Ḥiyyah Ḥayon and his effort to undermine rabbinic authority in his *Esh ha-Dat*.

Jacob (Henrique) de Castro Sarmento (1691–1762), a Portuguese converso trained in philosophy and medicine, arrived in London about 1720 and immediately associated himself with the sephardic Jewish congregation and with Nieto directly.[6] Despite some initial difficulties, Sarmento was admitted to the Royal College of Physicians and elected to the Royal Society some years later. In 1737 Sarmento published in London his *Theorica Verdadeira das Mares, conforme a Philosophia do incomparavel cavlhero Isaac Newton*, demonstrating his enormous indebtedness to Newton on the causes of the tides. Clearly promoting himself as a major exponent of Newtonian science in his former homeland of Portugal, Sarmento not only treated a specific scientific problem using Newtonian assumptions but included as well a flattering biography of his master and a succinct account of his general scientific conclusions, especially the theory of universal gravitation. He also displayed his awareness of the work of Jean Theophile Desaguliers, one of the most important of the experimental Newtonians of his day.

Sarmento's effort to integrate his enthusiasm for Newtonian science with a return to Jewish faith and practice ultimately ended in failure, however. Despite his close contact with David Nieto and his delivery of several sermons in the synagogue, including a eulogy he preached on the death of his beloved Jewish teacher, Sarmento gradually drifted away from the organized Jewish community, severing his ties altogether by

---

[6] I summarize in the following the work of Goldish and Barnett mentioned in note 4.

1758. As Goldish puts it, Newton eventually replaced Nieto as his true hero. His skeptical and religious crisis as a converso attempting to return to the Jewish fold was ultimately resolved through Nieto's death, his complete repudiation of confessional religion in general, and his full embrace of radical deism. Sarmento had surpassed Nieto in displaying a significant knowledge of the Newtonian corpus and in applying it in his own original research. But in so doing, he had fully rejected the theology and communal loyalties of his former mentor for what he called "the general society of men of honor and probity."[7] Sarmento was the first Jewish casualty of the Newtonian Enlightenment.

We have already encountered Mordechai Gumpel Schnaber Levison (1741–97) in previous chapters regarding the deistic elements of his Jewish philosophy and his possible connections with Swedenborgian ideas.[8] We shall also return to him briefly in reference to his notions of physico-theology and ecological balance in nature. In this context, it is sufficient to focus on his contribution to the study of Newtonian physics.

Levison published his *Ma'amar ha-Torah ve-ha-Ḥokhmah*, which he referred to in English as "A Dissertation on the Law and Science," in London in 1771. Writing many decades after Nieto and Sarmento, arriving in England from Germany at the invitation of the renowned Hunter brothers to study and practice medicine, and deriving from pure ashkenazic ancestry, he apparently discovered Newton on his own rather than through the mediation of either of his sephardic predecessors. While his general theological orientation seems to have been shaped more by Locke and Linnaeus than by Newton, Levison was still deeply impressed by the latter and devoted a special place for him in his writing.

The *Ma'amar ha-Torah ve-ha-Ḥokhmah* opens with an essay extolling the majesty of nature and with the claim that the study of the sciences is not deleterious to religious belief. It then proceeds to present an introduction to all the physical and life sciences, Originally planned as a double volume, Levison never succeeded in treating the mineral, plant, and animal worlds and the study of the human body. He does include a description of the Copernican universe, including separate chapters on the Sun, Moon, and the planets. He narrates throughout the mechanical experiments of a variety of seventeenth- but not eighteenth-century scientists including Boyle, Descartes, Borelli, and Huygens. He also discusses Musschenbroeck's experiments on cohesion and the pyrometer, and those of von Guericke and Toricelli regarding the air pump. His most extensive discussion, however, is concerned with a full elaboration of Newton's

---

[7] Cited from Barnett, "Dr. Jacob de Castro Sarmento," p. 94.

[8] See chapters 3 and 4, and my previous work cited in note 3 from which this summary is drawn. See also the appendix.

physics, especially his three laws of motion. Levison finally concludes with a conventional peroration on how the new sciences reveal God's glory and demonstrate the knowledge of the rabbis. How an explanation of the learning of Newton and other "gentiles" fortifies the rabbis' position is never well explained nor does Levison explore in this volume the possible theological implications of Newtonianism. Nevertheless, Levison deserves the distinction of being the first author to offer his readers a serious distillation of Newton's ideas in a Hebrew book.

II

Eliakim ben Abraham (1756–1814),[9] alias Jacob Hart, was a contemporary of Levison, and a fellow member of the ashkenazic community in London. Besides a few passing references to him and his writings in the histories of Anglo-Jewry, only one scholar, Arthur Barnett (with the help of Samuel Brodetsky), attempted in 1938 to reconstruct the bare outlines of his life, expanding on the few details already uncovered by Cecil Roth several years earlier.[10] Hart earned a respectable living as a jeweler living on the Strand. His economic circumstances allowed him the privilege of offering generous donations to the synagogue he helped to establish, the Denmark Court Synagogue. One indicator of his social and financial position in the community was that at his death, three coaches were sent to the synagogue for his funeral at double the usual cost.[11] As we have mentioned, he was also a member of the Hiram's Lodge, Swan St., of the modern Freemasons. In 1801, he is listed with his age (forty-five) and profession (silversmith).

Barnett surmised that Hart traveled to Germany for some four years; on his return, he adopted the title *moreinu ha-rav*, indicating his rabbinic ordination probably attained in Germany. If this indeed was the case, Hart wore two distinct faces in his professional career and personal life represented by his English and Hebrew names: the secular businessman and synagogue benefactor, on the one hand, and the rabbi, Hebrew author, and "defender" of the faith, on the other. That he was able to occupy

---

[9] Note that my calculation of Hart's date of birth as 1756 is based on the appearance of his name in a Freemason list in 1801 with a reference to his age as forty-five. This differs from Barnett's calculation in his article listed in the following note.

[10] A. Barnett and S. Brodetsky, "Eliakim ben Abraham (Jacob Hart): An Anglo-Jewish Scholar of the Eighteenth Century," *Transactions of the Jewish Historical Society of England* 14 (1940): 207–23; C. Roth, *Records of the Western Synagogue* (London, 1932); A. Barnett, *The Western Synagogue through Two Centuries* (London, 1961).

[11] Barnett and Brodetsky, "Eliakim ben Abraham," pp. 213–20.

two distinct social and intellectual spheres with little apparent relationship between the two suggests a more complex personality than the few details of Hart's life Barnett was able to track down.

Hart's major intellectual project was a planned series of ten works entitled *Asarah Ma'amarot* (Ten essays), of which only five were printed. The first, *Milḥamot Adonai* (Wars of the Lord), was published in London in 1794 and is clearly his most important book. A year later he published also in London *Binah la-Itim* (Chronology), an explication of the Daniel prophecies in the light of past chronologies and contemporary political events. Some five years later the third installment of the series appeared in his native city, *Zuf Novelot* (Nectar of unripe fruit), a concise summary and commentary of part of Joseph Delmedigo's complex seventeenth-century work *Novelot Ḥokhmah* (The fruit, or leaves of wisdom), primarily discussing the notion of creation as understood by Lurianic kabbalah. That Hart had uniquely chosen to revive the name of this remarkable student of kabbalah and the sciences is interesting in light of the merger of prophecy and science informing the Newtonian world view of his own day.[12] Also of interest is the list of subscribers Hart had successfully cultivated, appended to this volume, including several important Jewish families of London, wardens of the three city synagogues and the western synagogue, the Goldsmid family,[13] Joshua van Oven,[14] and more: "The following having seen the first two parts of the work *Asara Mamoroth* [*sic*] desire to see the other parts and have therefore given their assistance to print them."[15]

Two other works were printed in the projected series, both in Berlin in 1803, his probable domicile at that time: *Ma'ayan Ganim* (Well of gardens), a brief summary of Joseph Gikatilia's kabbalistic work *Ginnat Egoz* (Nut garden), and *Ein Ha-Koreh* (Eye or source of the reader), on the Hebrew vowels advocating the alleged correct pronunciation of ashkenazic Jews. In the same year Hart published in Roedelheim an additional work on Hebrew grammar entitled *Ein ha-Mishpat* (Eye or source of the law) that was not mentioned in the planned series. The other five works apparently were never printed dealing primarily with kabbalah, especially with that of Isaac Luria and on the speculations of the kabbal-

---

[12] On Delmedigo, see I. Barzilay, *Yosef Shlomo Delmedigo (Yashar of Candia): His Life, Works, and Times* (Leiden, 1974); Ruderman, *Jewish Thought and Scientific Discovery in Early Modern Europe*, pp. 118–52.

[13] On them, see P. Emden, "The Brothers Goldsmid and the Financing of the Napoleonic Wars," *Transactions of the Jewish Historical Society of England* 14 (1940): 225–46; Katz, *The Jews in the History of England*, index.

[14] Katz, *The Jews in the History of England*, index.

[15] Eliakim ben Abraham [Jacob Hart], *Zuf Novelot* (London, 1799), end of the book.

ists regarding mathematics and the secrets of numbers.[16] Such a mixture of grammatical, mathematical, scientific, and kabbalistic passions underscore again the cultural links between natural philosophy and mystical theosophy in Hart's mind, reminiscent of a similar integration in the writings of his Jewish predecessor Joseph Delmedigo and his more recent Christian ones, Newton and some of his students.

Hart's relative obscurity as a writer is surely related to the esoteric subjects that he elected to treat and to the relative brevity and unfinished nature of his planned works, but mostly to the fact that he chose to write in Hebrew, essentially excluding any potential readership either among Jews or Christians in England. The fact that the last three volumes he published were printed in Germany, despite his promising lists of English subscribers, might suggest his great disappointment in ever finding a readership for his writings in his native country. That Hart's collaborator and publisher in England, David Levi, composed all of his own work in English and received considerable notoriety for his literary accomplishments both among Jews and Christians alike, as we have seen, strongly suggests that Hart had made the wrong choice if he expected to be read in his own country. Alternatively, it suggests that Hart viewed his primary audience to be those Hebraists living in Germany or eastern Europe and not his highly assimilated coreligionists of London. Levi's wars with deists, atheists, and Christian missionaries were clearly outer-directed, whereas Hart's "wars" were obviously written for internal Jewish consumption, for Jews who were literate, especially in kabbalistic literature, and who struggled with the need to accommodate their traditional values with contemporary concerns. This was not as high a priority for Levi. Nevertheless, he obviously appreciated Hart's enterprise to the extent that he served as a relatively silent partner in its realization, an intriguing relationship to which we shall return.

It is difficult to assess Hart's impact on Hebrew readers outside of England without a thorough search for references to him among his contemporaries. We might safely assume that his impact was limited with one notable exception. He is cited several times by Pinḥas Elijah Hurwitz in his highly popular work Sefer Ha-Berit (Book of the covenant), first published in 1797 and subsequently many times.[17] Hurwitz's interest in Hart is not difficult to understand given their common intellectual interests in the sciences and kabbalah, their disdain for the radical secular enlightenment, and their creative attempts to establish a merger between the study

[16] They include Be'er Mayim Ḥayyim; Ma'ayan Ḥatum; Divrei Emet; Sha'ar ha-Ḥeshbon; and Arẓot ha-Ḥayyim.

[17] I have used the most recent edition of Sefer ha-Berit ha-Shalem (Jerusalem, 1990). The references to Hart are found on pp. 56, 156, 193, and 252.

of nature and prophecy.[18] Hurwitz referred to Hart as a dear friend, a distinguished rabbi, and a perfect scholar whom he met in London. On several occasions, Hurwitz enlists his opinions on scientific matters and cites them. He once quotes a letter of Hart in which the latter praises the first edition of *Sefer Ha-Berit*, which he had read in England. Hart was puzzled by Hurwitz's incapacity to accept the notion that the Earth rises in its revolution around the Sun and Hurwitz answers him sharply.[19] Elsewhere, Hurwitz refers to a popular medical textbook which he had seen in the hands of Hart and which he had consulted.[20] Through Hurwitz's conspicuous esteem for Hart's learning, the Englishman's name was known to several generations of Hebrew readers, especially in eastern Europe.

III

The *Milḥamot Adonai* is ostensibly a polemic against four groups accused of corrupting the beliefs of traditional Jews and impugning the sanctity of their sacred revelation. The first includes ancient pagan chroniclers who unjustly claim that their cultures preceded that of the ancient Hebrews described in the biblical narrative. The second is Aristotle and his followers. The third is Descartes and his followers, and the fourth is Newton and especially some of his students. But the reader who expects a systematic and comprehensive critique of each of "the enemies" Hart enumerates is sure to be disappointed.

Hart, in his chapter on pagan chronologies, is immediately distracted by the subject of idolatry, especially the idolatries of ancient Egypt. He is particularly focused on how the stone or written symbols of the gods are ultimately mistaken for the gods themselves by pagan worshipers. He briefly mentions the pagan practices on the American continent analogous to those of Egypt but then turns his gaze on India and China. This allows him to finally return to his announced subject: that the history of China postdates rather than predates that recorded in the Hebrew Bible. While Mordecai Gumpel Schnaber Levison, Hart's contemporary, had similarly defended the integrity of biblical chronology by citing the Chinese history of the Jesuit Martini Martini, Hart's source for his remark was William

---

[18] On Hurwitz and his work, see N. Rosenblum, "The First Hebrew Encyclopedia: Its Author and Its Development" (Hebrew), *Proceedings of the American Academy for Jewish Research* 55 (1988): 15–65; I. Robinson, "Kabbala and Science in *Sefer ha-Berit*: A Modernization Strategy for Orthodox Jews," *Modern Judaism* 9 (1989): 275–88.

[19] *Sefer ha-Berit ha-Shalem*, p. 156.

[20] Ibid., p. 252.

Whiston's *A New Theory of the Earth*, first published in 1696. I shall return to the significance of this citation and others from Whiston later.[21]

Hart's discussion of Aristotle is superficial and incomplete. His main objection to Aristotelian science is its obsolescence; it has now been superseded by new methods of inquiry ("experiments") and by new technologies of inquiry ("the air pump"). Whereas the Aristotelians relied solely on logical demonstration, the new scientists, through their experiments aided by the microscope and telescope, have actually unveiled the natural world. In so doing, they have disproved such false ideas as spontaneous generation while enhancing the correct notion of a divine purposeful creation. He again momentarily loses focus in his critique of alchemy, citing as his authorities the strange combination of Boerhaave and Delmedigo. He is still comfortable with the Aristotelian discourse of elements and compounds. But he is well aware of the inadequacy of Aristotelian astronomy in the light of the discoveries of Copernicus and Brahe, whom he cites by name.[22]

His treatment of Descartes is similarly incomplete. Although Descartes "absolutely did not write anything against the view of the Torah,"[23] his "atheistic disciples," with their emphasis on the fortuitous and random nature of creation, are worthy of condemnation. Hart excuses himself from elaborating on the deficiencies of Cartesian science by referring the reader to the already well known critiques of Newton himself and the French scholar Mariotte. Although Descartes deserves praise for his own criticism of Aristotle, his views have aligned him with such "atheists" as Locke, Bayle, Spinoza, and Hobbes. Moreover, he is also associated with those contemporary deists who acknowledge God's existence but do not believe in prophecy, such as Voltaire, Hume, and Bolingbroke. Hart interestingly cites Joseph Priestley's refutation of their views and then mentions that he had read in Thomas Paine's *Age of Reason* words reminiscent of Voltaire to the effect that "the people of Israel knew nothing of their Torah other than what they had heard from Moses their teacher."[24] Hart's references to both Priestley and Paine are also significant.

Hart finally turns to Newton but he hardly portrays him as an enemy of the Jewish faith. On the contrary, he presents him in glowing terms: "He had done marvelous experiments and discovered many calculations in the sciences of geometry, algebra, and optics." Most importantly, Hart claimed, Newton "taught people not to destroy even a small part of

---

[21] *Milḥamot Adonai* (London, 1794), pp. 2a–5a. On Levison's discussion of biblical versus Chinese chronology, see Ruderman, *Jewish Thought and Scientific Discovery in Early Modern Europe*, pp. 365–66.

[22] *Milḥamot Adonai*, pp. 5b–9a.

[23] Ibid., p. 9b.

[24] Ibid., pp. 9b–11b. The last quotation is from p. 11b.

prophecy on account of human investigation . . . for the words of the prophets were very precious in his eyes for although he was constantly involved in [human] investigation and experiments, this did not prevent him from composing a commentary on the book of Daniel."[25] That Hart also composed his own commentary on the Daniel prophesies only a year after his discourse on Newton seems more than a fortuitous resemblance. What is important to Hart is his distinction between the pious Newton, the investigator of nature and biblical prophecy, in contrast to many of his students who chose "to despise the words of testimony of the Torah in matters of creation."[26]

Hart offers a cursory description of Newton's principal scientific accomplishments regarding the laws of motion and especially gravitation as well as his optical experiments with the prism.[27] He quickly interrupts this inadequate summary to turn to Newton's critics, "in particular one scholar among his countrymen named Green[e]" who succeeded in contradicting his views concerning the vacuum, that light is emitted from the Sun, and his notion of a monolithic substance of Earth. Green[e], according to Hart, especially criticized Newtonian gravitation, denying that it was equivalent to divine providence, and that Newton's inability to define its cause suggested that gravitation was no more than an innate occult power. And for Hart, the materialist positions of small particles of matter colliding with other particles of Huygens and Descartes were preferred over such a mysterious notion, for "we have no business dealing with mysteries."[28] Hart's main reservation regarding Newtonian gravitation concerns its misinterpretation by Newton's disciples "who attribute to it alone [instead of divine providence] the ability to build and destroy worlds." In this vein, Hart offers Whiston's theory that the biblical flood is attributable to a comet whose movement was engendered by gravitation—a good example of how a secondary force had been identified with divine causation.[29]

Hart concludes his work with a colorful review of the wonders recently discovered in the natural world regarding minerals, plants, and animals, and including the new inventions of the barometer and telescope. He cautions that, despite the adulation modern science has deservingly received,

[25] Ibid., p. 12a. Hart refers to Newton's *Observation upon the Prophecies of Daniel and the Apocalypse of St. John* (London, 1733).

[26] *Milḥamot Adonai*, p. 12b.

[27] Ibid., pp. 12a–14a.

[28] Ibid., pp. 14b-17b. The reference to mysteries is found on p. 17b. On the accusation against Newton that his vocabulary was occultish, see L. Stewart, "Samuel Clarke, Newtonianism, and the Factions of Post-Revolutionary England," *Journal of the History of Ideas* 42 (1981): 71–72.

[29] *Milḥamot Adonai*, p. 17b.

one should not confuse human theoretical knowledge with absolute truth. The latter is known only through revelation and especially through the kabbalistic tradition. When seen in their proper perspective, the new scientific theories enhance the belief in a universe created by God. The book ends with a brief description of Herschel's most recent discoveries of the moons of Uranus in 1790, 1792, and 1794, discoveries also mentioned by several other contemporary Hebrew writers.[30]

Published only a year later, Hart's *Binah la-Itim* hardly appears to be penned by the same author of *Milḥamot Adonai*. Only the aforementioned casual reference to Newton as the interpreter of the prophecies of Daniel betrays an oblique connection between the two works. Unlike his first book, Hart hardly mentions Christian authors.[31] His interpretations rely almost exclusively on Jewish exegetes, especially his favorite, Isaac Abravanel. He also cites the usual commentators, Rashi, Kimḥi, and Ibn Ezra, as well as the less usual—Eliezer Ashkenazi,[32] Samson of Ostropolia,[33] and even Abraham Abulafia, from an unprinted manuscript.[34] He recalls the messianic pretender Solomon Molcho based on the description of Gedaliah ibn Yaḥya[35] and quotes from David Gans's Hebrew astronomical work.[36]

Hart distinguishes two messianic dates: the "end of the years" and the "end of the generations." He hints to the latter as falling in the 1840s, but regarding the former he is quite specific, indicating that it already occurred some twelve years earlier, or in 1783.[37] Moreover, not unlike a growing number of Christian millenarians in his day as well as David Levi himself, as we have seen, he is quick to link the political upheavals of the American and French revolutions with the imminent coming of the messianic age:

And now blessed be Thou O Lord for behold I have alerted you justly in chapter 10 to view God's miracles in every era where novelties and great changes occurred in the governments of the earth. You should know and take notice that today in the year 5543 = 1783, that which is designated as the "end of the years," peace and freedom was then declared for the inhabitants of the land of America and from there the light of freedom gleamed and spread upon the government of France so that the land shined from its honor removing the fe-

[30] Ibid., pp. 18a–33b. Herschel's discoveries are also mentioned in *Sefer ha-Berit*, p. 37, and by Barukh Lindau, *Reshit Limmudim* (Berlin, 1788), p. 5b.

[31] The one exception is *Binah la-Itim* (London, 1795), p. 6b.

[32] Ibid., p. 15b.

[33] Ibid., pp. 18a, 22a.

[34] Ibid., p. 26a, quoting *Sefer Ḥayyei Olam ha-Ba*.

[35] Ibid., pp. 10b–11a.

[36] Ibid., p. 24a.

[37] Ibid., pp. 2a–b, 5a, 10b, 17b, 20b, 23b.

tishes from the land and crushing heads far and wide [cf. Psalm 110:6] (This is the first-born of the religion of the Christian kingdom). And the light still grows stronger ever brightening until noon [Cf. Proverbs 4:18].[38]

Written as a composition for internal Jewish consumption, the book betrays, nevertheless, the millenary enthusiasm of the end of the eighteenth century, a frame of mind commonly shared by Jew and Christian alike.

IV

The most significant clues in understanding the historical context of *Milḥamot Adonai* are Hart's reliance on two authors explicitly cited on several occasions, Robert Greene and William Whiston, and one who is not mentioned by name in the text itself but whose influence is nevertheless apparent throughout it, the ubiquitous David Levi.

At first glance, Robert Greene (1678?–1730) seems a rather bizarre choice of an author from whom Hart learned of the inadequacies of Newtonian physics. Greene, a fellow at Clare College at Cambridge, appeared to many as a fish out of water in attacking Newton within the walls of an institution that had done so much to publicize the *Principia*. Greene's literary career began in earnest in 1711 with the publication of *A Demonstration of the Truth and Divinity of the Christian Religion*. A year later, he initiated his challenge to Newton in his *Principles of Natural Philosophy*. The latter served ultimately as a prelude to his magnum opus, published in 1727 under the title *The Principles of the Philosophy of Expansive and Contractive Forces*, a huge and largely unreadable volume of some 981 folio pages. It is this latter work (and perhaps the earlier *Principles* as well) that Hart suprisingly consulted, at least in part, a work that one author referred to as "a monument of ill-digested and misapplied learning."[39]

More recently, John Gascoigne, in his study of Cambridge in the Enlightenment, has offered a more nuanced and general appraisal of Greene's project. Gascoigne places Greene's efforts in the context of the political struggles between Whigs and Tories that divided Clare college in 1713 during the election of a new master. Greene's *Principles of Natural*

---

[38] Ibid., 26b. On millenarians during the era of the French Revolution, see especially Garrett, *Respectable Folly*, J.F.C. Harrison, *The Second Coming: Popular Millenarianism, 1780–1850* (London and Henley, 1979); and the previous chapter for the views of Priestley and Levi, as well as additional bibliography.

[39] On Greene, see the entry on him in the *Dictionary of National Biography* 8 (London, 1937): 517, where the quotation appears. See also D. Gjersten, *The Newton Handbook*

Philosophy was dedicated to the Tory leader Harley, "one rais'd by the Providence of Almighty God for the Support and Patronage of our most Holy Faith, against the Insults of the Several Atheists, Deists, Socinians, and I may now say, Arrians [Gascoigne suggests that he means Whiston and Clarke] of our Age."[40] Gascoigne proposes that the dedication was meant as a challenge to the chief candidate for master, Richard Laughton, a strong supporter of Newton and the leader of the Whig faction.

Whether or not Hart had any inkling of the political wranglings with which Greene was involved, he clearly grasped and identified with his theological leanings that informed the critique of Newton. Greene was a staunch opponent of the Latitudinarians, who argued that Scripture was only meant to convey "good wholesome Institutions only, for our Conduct and Acting, for our Worship of the Diety, and paying the Natural Homage which is due to Him."[41] On the contrary, Greene claimed, and Hart appears to echo his words, that the doctrines of Scripture transcend the limits of human reason and are "above the highest stretch of our Faculties to find out."[42] Attacking the principles of Locke, Spinoza, and Hobbes, especially those of Locke, which Hart also noticed,[43] Greene underscored the cleavage between human and divine knowledge, arguing that the Latitudinarians had placed too much confidence in reason when so little of nature is comprehensible. He also pointed out the inadequacies of the "corpuscular System, or the Philosophy of Homogenous Matter," an Epicurean view he associated with Newton who claimed that "God in the beginning formed matter in solid, massy, hard, impenetrable, moveable particles."[44]

In the preface to his later work of 1727, he was more respectful of Newton, even claiming that "in many Particulars, rather Justifies, than Contradicts, what I Propose."[45] Nevertheless, he still claimed that Newton's theory of matter undermined Christian belief, that his notions of absolute space and time were flawed, and that action through a vacuum was not possible, for all such ideas implied the finitude of God's power. Greene argued for his own theory of "heterogeneous matter," agreeing

---

(London and New York, 1986), pp. 241–42, and especially Gascoigne, *Cambridge*, pp. 167–74. My thanks to Professor Margaret Jacob for referring me to this book.

[40] Robert Greene, *Principles of Natural Philosophy* (Cambridge, 1712), dedication, and cited in Gascoigne, *Cambridge*, p. 167.

[41] Robert Greene, *Demonstration of the Truth and Divinity of the Christian Religion* (Cambridge, 1711), pp. 139–40, and cited by Gascoigne, *Cambridge*, p. 167.

[42] Greene, *Demonstration*, pp. 139–40; Gascoigne, *Cambridge*, p. 167.

[43] *Milḥamot Adonai*, p. 15b.

[44] As summarized in Gascoigne, *Cambridge*, p. 168.

[45] Robert Greene, *The Principles of the Philosophy of the Expansive and Contractive Forces* (Cambridge, 1727), preface.

with Descartes that action implies a plenum, though an active rather than passive force.[46] Hart succinctly summarized Greene's positions on all these matters as well as his critique of Newton's understanding of light as a composite of seven colors deriving from the sun and his substitution of the motions of contraction and expansion for Newtonian gravitation. Hart also noticed Greene's strong opinions against Locke, who "prefers the reasonings of natural religion to evidence of Revelation and the precepts of the messiah."[47]

Gascoigne considers Greene as an eccentric but hardly an obscurantist who, unlike most high churchmen, had familiarized himself with contemporary natural philosophies and found them wanting. Newtonian philosophy imperiled the Christian faith by allowing nature to be controlled by seemingly random forces rather than the direct providential hand of the Creator. Together with the Hutchinsonians and other critics of the "holy alliance" between Newtonian philosophy and Latitudinarian theology, Greene articulated the uneasiness of high churchman which "left little room for a sacerdotal class."[48] Greene's critique of Locke was also an indirect assault on Newton. Both Newtonians Whiston and Laughton were zealous defenders of the political philosopher; Greene knew exactly his target in devoting a long section of his work of 1712 to "the Metaphysicks and Logicks, or the Systeme of Ideas of Mr. Locke."[49]

In thus selecting Greene as his chief source of criticism of Newtonianism, Hart consciously aligned himself with a carefully chosen political and theological position. It is unclear whether Hart had actually expended the effort to peruse all of Greene's massive tomes. In addition to the preface, he could have culled most of his summaries of Greene's views from the first chapter of book 1 entitled: "Concerning Similar Matter, a Vac-

---

[46] Ibid., pp. 17, 41–47; Gascoigne, *Cambridge*, p. 168.

[47] *Milḥamot Adonai*, pp. 14b–15b, 24b, 26b. The reference to Locke is found in Greene, *Expansive and Contractive Forces*, p. 718, and cited in Gascoigne, *Cambridge*, p. 174.

[48] Gascoigne, *Cambridge*, pp. 169–71. On the fundamentalist opposition to the "Holy Alliance" between Newton and the Latitudinarians, see Stewart, "Samuel Clarke"; A. J. Kuhn, "Glory or Gravity: Hutchinson versus Newton," *Journal of the History of Ideas* 22 (1961): 303–22; C. B. Wilde, "Hutchinsonianism, Natural Philosophy, and Religious Controversy in Eighteenth Century Britain," *History of Science* 18 (1980): 1–24; Katz, "The Hutchinsonians," pp. 237–55. On the Hutchinsonians and their reading of the Hebrew Bible, see chapter 1. On the positive influence of Newton on fundamentalism, see R. Popkin, "Newton and the Rise of Fundamentalism," in *The Scientific Enterprise: The Bar Hillel Colloquium: Studies in History, Philosophy, and Sociology of Science*, ed. E. Ullmann-Margalit, vol. 4 (Dordrecht, 1992), pp. 241–59, and "Newton and Fundamentalism II," in Force and Popkin, *Essays on the Context, Nature, and Influence of Isaac Newton's Theology*, pp. 165–80.

[49] Robert Greene, *Principles of Natural Philosophy*, book 5; See also Gascoigne, *Cambridge*, pp. 171–74.

uum, and the New Theory of Light and Colours, and of Sounds, with a Solution of the Rainbow." And he could have glanced at the long section on Locke. What Greene gave him was an informed battery of arguments against the cozy relationship between Newtonianism and the Jewish faith already forged by such Jewish luminaries as David Nieto and Mordechai Schnaber Levison. It was also a powerful antidote to the negative example of Jacob Sarmento and his ultimate betrayal of Judaism. Like most Christians of his generation, Hart could also be swept up by the gushing enthusiasm of Newton's supporters who triumphantly proclaimed the new merger of science and faith. And he could appreciate Newton's piety as a man committed to prophetic truth like Hart himself. But the Newtonians had empowered human beings and their intellects with an overconfidence that threatened Judaism's beliefs in divine providence and transcendence and in the finite human need to embrace the revelatory truths of Sinai. Greene, the Tory and Christian cleric, offered him the brake on the excesses the Latitudinarian and deist followers of Newton were espousing. Like Greene, Hart could extol Newton's glorious achievements while distancing himself from his more radical interpreters.

Hart's two citations of William Whiston, Newtonian enthusiast and student of ancient Jewish history and prophecy, are interesting because they appear to be the first time Whiston was cited in Hebrew literature, despite his close intellectual and spiritual sympathies for Judaism.[50] They also reveal a certain ambivalence to this complex and prolific thinker on the part of Hart, who seemed to be caught in the tug of war between Tories and Whigs on how to interpret the Bible in the light of the Newtonian cosmos.

Hart first mentions Whiston's *New Theory of the Earth* in most favorable terms, as we have seen, for its defense of the priority of biblical chronology over that of the Chinese.[51] Whiston had hypothesized that the inhabitants of China were the offspring of Noah and that the first king of China, Fohi, was even Noah himself.[52] The assumption thus followed, as Hart put it, that "all their ancient stories had no basis in reality."[53]

Hart was skeptical, however, of Whiston's view, when referring to him a second time, citing one of the major arguments of his book—that the

[50] On Whiston, see J. Force, *William Whiston: Honest Newtonian* (Cambridge and New York, 1985), and M. Farrell, *The Life and Work of William Whiston* (New York, 1981).

[51] *Milḥamot Adonai*, p. 5a.

[52] William Whiston, *A New Theory of the Earth* (London, 1737), pp. 137, 140, 139, 413, and summarized in P. Rossi, *The Dark Abyss of Time: The History of the Earth and the History of Nations from Hooke to Vico*, trans. L. Cochrane (Chicago and London, 1984), pp. 68–69.

[53] *Milḥamot Adonai*, p. 5a.

biblical flood could be explained by the high tides and outpouring of internal waters engendered by the Earth's passage through the tail of a comet. By reducing the supernatural miracle of the deluge to a naturalistic explanation based on Newton's universal law of gravity, Whiston had severely diminished the role of divine providence, implying that the world was subject to random naturalistic forces and not to God alone. Hart adds that Whiston's explanation was at variance with that of Newton himself who believed in all his writing that "everything was created with the intention of the Creator, may He be blessed." Thus it would appear that Hart patently aligned himself in the debate over Newtonianism with the high churchmen like Greene against Clarke and Whiston.[54]

Hart's understanding of Whiston's project differs markedly, however, from a more recent scholarly interpretation of Whiston's actual intentions in composing his best-selling *A New Theory of the Earth*. According to James E. Force, Whiston composed his work against Charles Blount's *Oracles of Reason* and against Thomas Burnet's own *Theory of the Earth*. Both men had diminished God's special providence almost to the vanishing point, conflating special and general providence, while dismissing the Mosaic history of the six days of creation as sheer allegory. This continual emphasis on the mechanical secondary causes of general providence and a disregard for preserving the authenticity of the biblical account were clearly seen by the deists as supporting their own position.

According to Force, Whiston's ingenious explanation of a comet transforming the Earth's history was an attempt to validate Christian revelation against the claims of the deists. As a good Newtonian, there was a way to locate a consensus involving Scripture, reason, and philosophy because a scientific understanding of nature could often demonstrate the literal meaning of the Bible. Whiston's median path between deists and literalists, as Force explains it, was also Newton's path. He too had similarly explained the mechanism of comets and the passive nature of matter, and he too subscribed to a literal nonallegorical interpretation of biblical history and prophecy. Whiston, as Force sees him, was simply carrying out the mandate of his teacher Newton.[55] By distancing student from teacher, Hart sought to place Newton in an even more traditional camp than Whiston's. Despite Whiston's apparent intentions of faithfully following his mentor, Hart saw his effort as a failure and placed him squarely in the camp of the students of Newton "who expected [the force of gravitation] alone [and not God] to build worlds and destroy them."[56]

[54] Ibid., p. 17b.
[55] Force, *William Whiston*, pp. 32–59.
[56] *Milḥamot Adonai*, p. 17b.

Besides Greene and Whiston, David Levi also left his mark on Hart's Hebrew composition as publisher of all three of Hart's Hebrew works appearing in London. He most likely approved of their contents and endorsed their publication. If Levi wrote in English for a public of Christian and Jewish readers while Hart wrote for a Jewish audience who still read Hebrew works primarily outside of England, both Jews, nevertheless, shared a common universe of discourse. Levi never enjoyed the economic stability shared by his colleague Hart, although his fame far surpassed his less audacious friend, as we have seen, as the consummate public intellectual and polemicist ready to defend the honor of Judaism at every turn. Although Levi virtually wrote nothing in Hebrew, he knew the language well and used his knowledge as a sword to bludgeon his Christian opponents and to ridicule their tendentious reading of biblical texts. But Levi reveals little interest in scientific discovery in all of his writings, and in this field he seems to have relegated to his friend Hart the task of articulating a Jewish response in line with Levi's traditionalism. He, of course, knew of Newton's works on prophecy and mentioned them several times to make an exegetical point.[57] He also was acquainted with the nefarious uses of the new science in the hands of radical deists like Voltaire and Paine and in the hands of so-called atheists like Spinoza, Locke, Hume. He walked gingerly and adeptly among the minefields placed by millenary Christians on the right and radical deists on the left. But distinguishing carefully between a Newtonianism in consonance with Jewish traditional beliefs and one that was capable of undermining them was obviously not his strong suit. In this, he would defer to his learned friend to digest the obscure writings of Greene and to fashion them into a fitting Jewish rejoinder to radical Newtonians.

Despite the differences between them in style and substance, and in their addressing different audiences, Hart and Levi shared the same concern for protecting the integrity of the biblical text and the cardinal principles of the Jewish faith, especially the Jewish doctrines of creation and divine providence. Both of them singled out the same pantheon of deist and "atheist" enemies including Voltaire, Spinoza, Hobbes, Bayle, Bolingbrook, and Hume. When Hart alluded to both Priestley and Paine in the same breadth, he most probably thought of his friend's dual assault on these vaunted intellectuals of the Western world. In Hart, Levi thus found a faithful friend and financial supporter of his expensive publishing projects. He also discovered in him an articulate and formidable ideological ally in his struggle to defend the integrity of his religious faith and community.

[57] See, for example, Levi, *Dissertations*, 1:95, 104.

V

In looking beyond the specific impact of the ideas of Newton and his more radical and more conservative followers on Jewish thought, a good starting point is the aforementioned Mordechai Gumpel Schnaber Levison.[58] Of note here is his remarkable indebtedness to Carl Linnaeus and to a theological system commonly known as physicotheology. This tradition became prominent as early as the late sixteenth and early seventeenth centuries through the writing of such well-known figures as Pieter van Musschenbroeck and J. Albert Favricus in Holland and John Ray and William Derham in England. It was based on the assumption that the natural order functioned through a compensatory system of checks and balances whereby God provided just the right number of every creature that inhabited the earth. On the basis of this inference of a natural equilibrium in all creation, Linnaeus developed an elaborate scheme of world ecology that informed an elaborate three-pronged cycle of propagation, preservation, and destruction. Through the divine will, all creatures in all their states have a higher purpose, even stinking carcasses or pesky insects. By promoting their own good in the great chain of being, each promotes the good of other creatures. The study of this intricate system thus verifies God's ultimate goodness and providential design, confirming with overwhelming details his existence and his continual involvement in nature.[59]

Levison enthusiastically adopted the language and ideas of the physicotheologians in several chapters of his *Shelosh-Esre Yesodei ha-Torah*, published in Altona in 1792. In a long excursus "On the Righteousness of the [God's] Administration," Levison produced many examples of how what might appear as negative or evil might ultimately serve a higher plan. He even includes in the great chain of being the higher reaches of the world of intelligences, spirits, and angels, which by analogy function in the spiritual realm like those creatures in the material world. Even the seemingly irrational notion of the revival of the dead is given a Linnaean twist in Levison's natural system of rewards and punishments. Recounting the intricate cyle of the silkworm, Levison insists that even the possibility of resuscitating human life cannot be ruled out of hand.

No Jewish thinker in London approaches Levison in his detailed presentation of the sciences, especially that of mechanics, his careful delineation of Newton, and his exuberant embrace of physicotheology. Even Hart or Nieto did not devote the kind of attention to elucidating these disciplines

---

[58] The following on Levison is essentially drawn from my work cited in note 3. For a more detailed discussion, the reader is referred to that chapter.

[59] For a list of scholarly references to physicotheology, see the notes to my work cited in note 3.

as Levison. The only other Jewish writer in England to even consider such matters, albeit infrequently and unsystematically, was Abraham Tang. Perhaps if Tang had completed *Beḥinat Adam* he might have developed a more expansive treatment of the natural world. As we shall presently see, many of his interests clearly parallel those of Levison, but given the unfinished state in which this material has come down to us, Tang's discussions of nature and science are much less compelling than his views on God, mythology, and ancient history.

Nevertheless, his limited discussions are not without interest entirely. Like Levison, he too is fascinated with the intricacies of nature and is convinced that God created the world in a purposeful way and not accidentally. He finds particularly compelling the study of human anatomy and offers a detailed description of the human eye and an even more authoritative portrayal of the structure of the human ear. In the latter case, he provides his own illustrations of the inner, middle, and outer ears, a description of the outer auricular muscles, the Eustachian tube, and the muscles of the bones of the middle ear.[60] His primary sources are Antomaria Valsava's *De aure humana tractatus*, published first in Bologna in 1704, and Joseph-Gudichard Duverney's *Traite de l'organe de l'ouie, contenant la structure, les usages, et les malades de toutes les parties d' l'oreille*, first published in Paris in 1683 but appearing in English translation in 1737 and 1748.[61] Tang's thoroughness in researching this subject, his intelligent use of reliable scientific works, and especially his impressive ability in drawing detailed illustrations of the ear all suggest that he was a serious student of the sciences, especially the life sciences and medicine.

In one other instance, Tang utilizes his artistic ability to demonstrate the sphericity of the globe through a series of illustrations of sailing ships circumventing the Earth and returning ultimately to their point of departure. In the course of his description, Tang mentions Magellan, Drake, Dampier, and the Englishman George Anson (1697–1762).[62] Though not a groundbreaking insight for an observer living at the end of the eighteenth century, it does display Tang's talents for simple scientific explanation and illustration.

---

[60] The description of the eye is found in *Beḥinat Adam*. MS St. Petersburg RNL Heb.II A 22, fols. 22b–23a. On the ear, fol. 59b, 116a–119a, and in MS Frankfurt 8*59, fols. 91a–93b. The diagram of the ear is on fol. 93b.

[61] On Valsava and Duverney, see the entries by L. Premuda in *Dictionary of Scientific Biography* 13 (New York, 1976), pp. 566–67; and by W. C. Williams in 4 (New York, 1971), pp. 267–68. In the same discussion Tang also cites Fabricius Ab Aquapendente's treatise on the ear. On him, see B. Zanobio in *Dictionary of Scientific Biography*, 4:507–12.

[62] See *Beḥinat Adam*, MS St. Petersburg, fols. 83b–84b; MS Frankfurt, fols. 116b–119b.

Perhaps the most interesting of Tang's musings on the natural world is his thorough description of a beehive, the kinds of bees, their specific functions, their manufacture of honey, their protective systems, their obsession with cleanliness and order, and the generally harmonious way in which thousands of these insects interact with each other. This description, together with another describing the water cycle,[63] is reminiscent of Levison's depictions of the natural equilibrium and the purposefulness of creation, extending even to the most minute of creatures. No doubt Tang was also infatuated with physicotheology and saw the bees as convincing testimony of God's wondrous providence.

But even Tang's enthusiastic narrative on beehives was no more than a popular description of a well-known phenomenon in nature, hardly unconventional for the well-informed community of scientific enthusiasts living in London in his era. More noteworthy, however, is Tang's digression in considering Samson's experience with bees and honey in the fourteenth book of Judges. The Bible explains how Samson stopped to look at the remains of a lion he had previously torn with his bare hands when he passed by the vineyards of Timneh a year later. Finding a swarm of bees and honey in the lion's skeleton, "He scooped it into his palms and ate it as he went along" (Judges 14:9). But Tang cannot take this account too seriously since "nature would not allow bees to inhabit a rotten and smelly carcass. The substance of the matter is that Moses our teacher did not relate this to us [and thus we are not obliged to believe it]." "It is possible," he adds, "that it actually happened since it is related that it took place near the vineyards of Timneh where, because of the nature of the air or the soil, the carcass deteriorated to the point where nothing remained but the bones." But, he concludes: "In the final analysis, if it wasn't for the fact that many people believe the book of Judges was written by an important person, I wouldn't have bothered to write in the first place about Samson and his honey."[64]

Tang's dismissive attitude toward the biblical narrative provides some indication of how seriously he took the authority of science when weighed against the veracity of a mere biblical story, especially one not even ascribed to Moses himself. Beehives were serious subjects of empirical science that could demonstrate God's existence and his magnificent designs so prominently arranged in nature. Their impression in the imagination of an unenlightened biblical author, however, was of little consequence. For Tang, we recall, a faith based on unsubstantiated miracles

[63] Tang's description of the beehive is found in *Beḥinat Adam*, MS Frankfurt, fols. 94b–100b. His description of the water cycle is found in MS St. Petersburg, fols. 92a–96b.

[64] *Beḥinat Adam*, MS Frankfurt, fols. 100a–100b.

that contradicted reason and the senses was unworthy of serious consideration at all.[65]

VI

As in the case of Freemasonry considered in the preceding chapter, the literary and scientific societies of England were important social frameworks for personal advancement and intellectual excitement for Jews who had the talent or the connections to gain entrance to them. Todd Endelman, in his skillful account of the social integration of Anglo-Jewry, has already pointed out that not all assimilated Jews felt the need to renounce completely their links with Judaism and the Jewish community while pursuing their intellectual and social contacts with non-Jews. He singles out especially educated sephardim who found their way into literary and scientific circles, "religiously neutral cultural spheres," as he calls them, where "their secular diversions took them into the non-Jewish world but their occupational concerns brought them back to the Jewish community."[66] Endelman mentions in this regard the remarkable example of Emanuel Mendes da Costa (1717–91), one of the most acclaimed natural historians, conchologists, and mineralogists of his era, clerk and fellow of the Royal Society, fellow of the Society of Antiquarians, author of several important scientific texts and numerous published papers in the "Philosophical Transactions" of the Royal Society, and referred to by one of his Christian admirers as "le grand monarch des fossilistes."[67] His brilliant career was severely handicapped by his dishonesty in handling the society's funds, which led to his dismissal from this body in 1767, his arrest, and his imprisonment in the king's bench prison. Even with his reputation irreparably tarnished by his crimes, he continued to publish in his later years and to enjoy financial and moral support from his loyal academic

---

[65] See chapter 3.

[66] Endelman, *The Jews in Georgian England* (1979), pp. 262–63.

[67] Ibid., p. 262. On Mendes da Costa, see the essay on him in the *Dictionary of National Biography* 4 (London, 1937): 1196–97; P.J.P Whitehead, "Emanuel Mendes da Costa (1717–91) and the *Conchology* or *Natural History of Shells*," *Bulletin of the British Museum of Natural History (Hist. Ser.)* 6 (1977): 1–24 ; in the *Encyclopedia Judaica* 5 (Jerusalem, 1971): 986; E. R. Samuel, "Anglo-Jewish Notaries and Scriviners," *Transactions of the Jewish Historical Society of England* 17 (1951–52): 131–32; and S. J. Gould, "The Anatomy Lesson: The Teachings of Naturalist Mendes da Costa, a Sephardic Jew in King George's Court," *Natural History* (1995): 12–15, 62–63. Charles Singer apparently lectured before the Jewish Historical Society of England on "The Correspondence of Emanuel da Costa." Despite an announcement in 1941 on its forthcoming publication, it does not seem to have appeared. Isaac Romilly of Fleetstreet in MS Add. 28542, f. 27r, British Library, referred to da Costa by the latter title.

colleagues and friends, especially the physicians Dr. John Fothergill and Dr. Richard Pulteney.

Endelman has considered the entire Mendes da Costa family as a prime example of radical assimilation and has also mentioned Emanuel and his close associations with fellow Jews and non-Jews in this context.[68] Emanuel Mendes da Costa can also be considered from a somewhat different perspective, that of Jewish intellectual and cultural history. Mendes da Costa is important not only for his extraordinary scientific achievements and his remarkable intellectual contacts with many of the major scientific figures of England and Europe throughout much of the eighteenth century but also as an intellectual figure. Quite conscious of his Jewish identity, he attempted to navigate the complex byways of intense and intimate contact with non-Jewish scientists, who clearly perceived him to be a Jew and even came to value his Jewish affiliation, while maintaining open and even warm relations with the leadership of the Jewish community and with individual Jews who took pride in his outstanding accomplishments and in the unusual social status he had attained, at least up until 1768, the time of his imprisonment and humiliation.

Mendes da Costa was hardly a systematic Jewish thinker such as Levison or Tang who seriously considered the relations between science and religion. But he did think about his Jewish identity, was knowledgeable in Hebrew and Jewish history, and took a certain pride in displaying that knowledge. David S. Katz has already pointed out how he was perceived as a kind of specialist on Jewish affairs by his colleagues in the Royal Society.[69] To retrieve a deeper sense of his connection to Jewish intellectual life in eighteenth century England, one must start with the mammoth collection of da Costa's correspondence at the British library, comprising 2,487 letters in eleven folio volumes, an additional volume designated as his "common-place book," and one more volume of materials of a specifically Jewish nature.[70] The mere fact that a Jew maintained intellectual and social contact with some of the great scientific luminaries of England and Europe, including a large number of clergymen, visited their

---

[68] T. Endelman, *Radical Assimilation in English Jewish History, 1656–1945* (Bloomington, Ind., 1990), pp. 12–17.

[69] D. Katz, "The Chinese Jews and the Problem of Biblical Authority in Eighteenth- and Nineteenth-Century England," *English Historical Review* 105 (1990): 899–907, especially p. 903, n. 1, and 907, n. 4. My sincere thanks to David S. Katz for sharing with me his notes on the da Costa correspondence and for his helpful comments on this subject.

[70] They are listed in the British Library as Add. MSS 28534–44, and arranged in alphabetical order according to name of correspondent (a selection of these were published by J. Nichols in *Illustration of the Literary History of the Eighteenth Century*, vol. 4 [London, 1817]); Add. MS 29876 (selections were published in *Gentleman's Magazine* 83, pt. 1 [1812]: 205–7, 513–17); and Add. MS 29868 (selections were published in *Gentleman's Magazine*, pt. 2 82 [1812]: 329–31).

homes, conversed with them on both scientific and personal matters in both his official capacity as the society clerk but also unofficially, already defines da Costa's unique position in this era.[71] Within the context of Jewish history, I cannot think of any parallel eighteenth-century figure, including Mendelssohn, with such an international reputation and with so wide a network of associates. He corresponds with scholars in Russia and eastern Europe, France, Germany, Italy, Spain, and America, as well as those from England in English, French, German, Italian, Spanish, Portuguese, and Latin. He did not write in Hebrew but used Hebrew words frequently. Admittedly, much of the correspondence deals with fossils, but for the perceptive observer, there are also nuggets for Jewish cultural history to be gleaned from this massive written record.

Katz has already described how, thanks to da Costa, the Royal Society became involved in a search for unidentified Chinese Jews. Da Costa agreed to write in 1760 to an unnamed correspondent familiar with Chinese matters and to pass on to him the official Hebrew letter of the Jewish community signed by Ḥakham Isaac Nieto in search of Chinese of Jewish extraction. Katz also lists several other occasions where Jewish subjects are raised in his letters which might be considered more closely.[72] Note, for example, the erudite exchange in 1757 between da Costa and William Stuckeley, the well-known antiquarian and Freemason on the origin of an alleged Hebrew word, with citations from *Targum Yonatan*, the Talmud, Rashi, Buxtorf, and Bochart.[73] His letter of 1758 to Lord Hugh Willoughy, the president of the Society of Antiquaries, represents a paper written together with a foreign clergyman [a rabbi?] on the derivation of the words "Ammaea Dea," recently discovered on a Roman altar in England. Da Costa's erudite presentation to show the ultimate Hebraic origin of the term is not only an impressive demonstration of his mastery of Hebrew and classical sources; it is also a subtle, or perhaps transparent attempt to assert the priority of the Hebraic element of Western civilization and to underscore the enduring legacy of Jewish culture in both Roman and English history.[74] Da Costa's translation in 1753 of three ancient Jewish bonds from Hebrew originating in the thirteenth century is similarly intended to indicate the longevity and pride of ancestry of Jews living on English soil. Da Costa's message is clear: we Jews are not newcomers; we derive from a culturally sophisticated legal culture of long

[71] Da Costa is presently the subject of a forthcoming doctoral dissertation by Stefan Siemer of the University of Bonn on his role as a disseminator of scientific knowledge in the eighteenth century.

[72] See note 69.

[73] Nichols, *Illustrations*, 4:505. On Stuckeley, see M. Spurr, "William Stuckeley: Antiquarian and Freemason," *Ars Quatuor Coronatorum* 100 (1987): 113–30.

[74] Nichols, *Illustrations*, 4:794–97.

duration; and, despite our medieval departure from England, our roots extend back to the formative period of English civilization.[75]

The letter of James Ducarel to da Costa in 1752 raises the potentially awkward question of whether it is appropriate to ask a Jew a question pertaining to his cultural background. Thus Ducarel timidly asks: "I hope you will not take it amiss if I desire your assistance," to which da Costa graciously responds: "I shall at all times with great pleasure be very ready to solve any questions you may put to me relating to our religious ceremonies, customs, etc. as far as I am capable of doing." Ducaral's query concerns the unusual subject of the dress and arms of a Jewish soldier, whether he was attired in the same manner as Roman soldiers. That Ducaral would propose the subject of a Jewish military man is interesting in its own right. Da Costa's response is also revealing. Da Costa checks all the books he knows but proves inadequate to the task: "And not being wise, greatly conversant in Rabbinical learning, I desired a very learned and curious student of our nation to carefully peruse all the Rabbinical authors about it." He turns to the sephardic rabbi Isaac Mendes Belisario,[76] who definitively concludes that they wore no special dress. He finally cites several Christian authorities of ancient Jewish history, some of whom he had not been able to consult. Far removed from da Costa's scholarly expertise on fossils, his Christian interlocutor deems him an expert on ancient Jewish dress and rabbinic sources. He plays out this role to the extent that he is capable and turns to his more knowledgeable contact within the traditional Jewish community, who willingly accepts the task of being his research assistant.[77]

Despite the proper and even friendly tone with which da Costa relates to his non-Jewish correspondents, neither he nor they can completely ignore his Jewish origin. Todd Endelman has already quoted from the fascinating letter of Martin Folkes inviting da Costa to the home of the duke of Richmond to see his fossil garden in 1747.[78] Folkes raises, on more than one occasion, the issue of Jewish dietary laws and whether da Costa will be able to dine "without breach of the Law of Moses." It is hard to imagine that da Costa observed kashrut at all, being married to a non-Jewish wife, and conducting his affairs, at least in one case, even on a Saturday morning.[79] Nevertheless, Folkes assumes this food might present an obstacle to da Costa's visit. At the same time, one cannot miss a subtle

[75] *Gentleman's Magazine* 82, pt. 2 (1812): 329–31.

[76] I have referred to him twice earlier, in regard to his acquaintance with Anselm Bayly, discussed in chapters 1 and 4; and in regard to his political flattery in chapter 4.

[77] Nichols, *Illustrations*, 4:604–8.

[78] Endelman, *Jews of Georgian England*, p. 262.

[79] In Add. MS 28542, fol. 220r, da Costa mentions an appointment at ten on Saturday morning to view fossils.

note of disrespect in tempting da Costa with the nonkosher delicacies of the duke's table: "unless the lobsters of Chichester should be a temptation, by which a weaker man might be seduced." And one might sense even a touch of arrogant superiority when after one more reference to barbecued shols "and other abominations to your nation," Folkes concludes: "But we are all citizens of the world, and see different customs and different tastes without dislike or prejudice, as we do different names and colours." Da Costa, apparently because of the approaching high holy days, declined the invitation.[80]

To James West, da Costa insinuates his Jewish identity with the following line, written in 1765: "Wretch as I am for the sake of literature, I have even invaded the Holy Decalogue by not having a seventh day of rest, so strictly ordered by the Law of Moses."[81] To Isaac Romilly of Fleetstreet he writes: "I wish you and yours many and happy festivals and other worldly joys and when our human race is run may we meet in the glories of Heaven through the mercy of our great Creator."[82] And to Anthony Tilsington of Swenwick in Derbyshire, he launches still another subtle reminder of his particular identity: "Well at last my head is a little settled and I have entirely rid myself of the maggots in my brain of the gadding fit which possessed me all the summer so that with propriety I might have been called a wandering Jew."[83]

There are several instances where da Costa or his interlocutor readily acknowledge that his Jewish identity is clearly a liability. Endelman has already referred to the letter from Thomas Birch who admits that "your religious profession may possibly be a prejudice to you with some persons," but, nevertheless, encourages him to present his candidacy for the librarianship of the Royal Society in 1763.[84] On the same matter da Costa writes to Dr. George Lavington, the bishop of Exeter, and to Thomas Knowlton, where he laments the fact that he was passed over for someone less qualified as a natural historian since "alas not being of the established Religion of the country it was concluded I could not have a place."[85] On yet another occasion in 1766, he is reminded by Edward Hasted that his desire to inspect a Hebrew inscription on the old walls of the Castle of Canterbury might be thwarted since the authorities "would make great objections to admit a Stranger and a Jew to search for it."[86]

---

[80] Nichols, *Illustrations*, 4:635–37.
[81] Ibid., 4:792.
[82] Add. MS 28542, fol. 6r.
[83] Add. MS 28543, fol. 243r.
[84] Endelman, *Jews of Georgian England*, p. 264 (see Nichols, *Illustrations*, 4:540).
[85] Add. MS 28540, fol. 46v.
[86] Nichols, *Illustrations*, 4:645.

A good number of da Costa's letters are written to and from fellow Jews, especially sephardic Jews in Amsterdam and elsewhere, such as his cousin Joseph Salvador, David da Fonseca, Mordecai Aboab, David Abenatar Pimentel, Isaac Belisario, Isaac de Pinto, Ives [sic] Rebello, and more. There is clearly a different tone, a greater intimacy, and a playful exchange of Jewishly coded messages, suggesting the relative absence of social barriers and cautious formality between correspondents. I conclude this discussion with two rich examples.

Emanuel's exchange of letters with Dr. Ralph Schomberg in 1761 have been mentioned at least twice previously by modern scholars.[87] Schomberg is certainly a interesting figure in his own right, both because of the upbringing he received from his talented but contentious father, Dr. Meyer Schomberg, and because of his own literary career and cultural interests. In many respects, his intellectual world and attenuated but still persisting Jewish loyalties are analogous to those of Mendes da Costa and suggest why the two friends could fully appreciate each other. Meyer's path from Judaism, his Hebrew articulation of his deistic philosophy, and his complaints about the organized Jewish community have been briefly discussed in a previous chapter. His contest with the College of Physicians over his credentials to practice medicine, his remarkably successful practice, his affiliation with Freemasonry, and the English private education he offered his sons—Ralph and Isaac—to attend the Merchant Taylor's school have previously been noted.[88] Ralph's development as an intellectual and apparently as an unconverted Jew, despite his Christian wife and baptized children, remains unstudied. Ralph was trained as a physician and received his medical degree from Aberdeen. Like Emanuel, he was a fellow of the Society of Antiquaries and also, like him, received notarial faculty. John Nichols appears to be the only scholar who bothered to examine his assorted writings on political, medical, and classical subjects. He paints a most unflattering portrait of his work on Pindar and Horace, which appears to be completely plagiarized from a contemporary work in French. It would appear that Emanuel and Ralph had something else in common besides their intellectual interests, parallel careers, and Christian families—a fatal proclivity for dishonest and deceitful behavior (fig. 14).[89]

---

[87] By Samuel in "Anglo-Jewish Notaries," p. 119, and by Endelman, *Jews of Georgian England*, p. 125.

[88] See especially Samuel, "Dr. Meyer Schomberg's Attack on the Jews of London, 1746," pp. 83–111, and see my discussion of Meyer Schomberg in chapter 3, and Ralph Schomberg, in chapter 4.

[89] J. Nichols, *Literary Anecdotes of the Eighteenth Century*, vol. 3 (London, 1812), pp. 26–30. On Ralph, see also Samuel, "Anglo-Jewish Notaries," pp. 118–19; A. Hyamson, "The Jewish Obituaries in the Gentleman's Magazine," *Miscellanies of the Jewish Historical*

14. Portrait of Ralph Schomberg, based on the original
painted by Gainsborough.

Be that as it may, Schomberg began to correspond with Mendes da
Costa regarding his nomination of an old friend John Stephen Bernard of
Amsterdam for fellowship in the Society of Antiquaries. Schomberg had
also written to James Ducarel, da Costa's colleague in the society, on the
same matter. In that letter, he offered several comments and corrections
to a journal he had seen, curiously indicating his interest in Hebrew and

Aramaic words and revealing his expertise in both languages.[90] Over the course of many months, the correspondence between Emanuel, the sephardic Jew of London, and Ralph, the ashkenazic one of Bath, is preserved. Their initial formality eventually gives way to a warm intimacy; "Dear Sir" soon becomes "Dear Manny" and "Dear Ralph." Emanuel speaks of an "esteem and friendship . . . inculcated in our tender years, and though we have been distant from each other for a long series of time, yet my heart ever wished you well, and joyed in your welfare," and Ralph returns the gushing affection. "Manny" sends regards to the family in one instance, requests that he be sent a small pot (of about three or four pounds) of "sour crout," while Manny returns the warm regards from his wife and children, adding his own with the Hebrew words *amen ve-amen*. The oft-quoted line of Schomberg then follows: "Bath is at present very full and brilliant. . . . I am not idle. We have a good many *bnai yisrael* here." The Hebrew references, of course, express more than personal friendship; they suggest a distinct sense of Jewish self-awareness. In the relatively Christian space that both intellectuals inhabit, they still continue to see themselves as Jews. This is all the more remarkable when Manny asks his dear Ralph in the following letter to "tell your Lady from me, with my sincere respects, that I wish her a merry Christmas and happy new year," and immediately following is a phrase strangely omitted from the version of the letter printed by John Nichols but equally fascinating: "My compliments attend Ms. Schomberg [apparently Ralph's recently engaged or married daughter] and the young gentleman and wish them the same and you my dear Ralph a good Rosasana." The last sentence provides ample proof that Ralph remained a Jew until the year of his death in 1761. But even more interesting is the matter-of-fact way in which both Jews acknowledge their complicated fate as spouses of Christian women with Christian offspring while at the same time, being bound in their special bonds of "Jew-talk"—the Hebrew words and the Rosh Ha-shanah greetings—that define, no matter how faintly, who they are and what unites them as friends.[91]

My second and last example of da Costa's correspondence is of a different sort and allows us to consider the rare encounter between a well-known enlightened Jewish physician from Germany and a prominent English scientist who happened to be Jewish. In 1759, writing from Paris, and then again in 1767, writing from Hamburg, Aron S. Gumpertz, MD, as he signs his name, penned two letters to Mendes da Costa.[92] Gompertz,

[90] Nichols, *Illustrations*, 4:763.
[91] Ibid., 4:764–69. The additional line is found in Add. MS 28542, fol. 162r.
[92] Add. MS 28537, fols. 434r–436r.

of course, is none other than one of Mendelssohn's primary Jewish teachers. In 1751 he had received his medical degree from the University of Frankfurt an der Oder. For ten years he practiced medicine in Berlin but eventually took up residence in Hamburg where he died in 1769. In addition to the critical impact he had on Mendelssohn, he is known for his Hebrew commentary on Abraham ibn Ezra and a short Hebrew treatise appended to the latter work called *Ma'amar Ha-Maddah*.[93]

Rather remarkably, Gompertz wrote both letters in an adequate but somewhat unintelligible English to his scientific colleague. He might have written in German, the language of several other letters to da Costa, and he might have also written in Hebrew to a coreligionist who certainly understood the language. That he wrote in English suggests a lack of familiarity with his associate—in striking contrast to the Schomberg correspondence—despite the friendly tone and the fondness expressed for England and his English addressee. In fact, what is most strange about the letters is the distinct impression they convey that Gompertz does not consider his interlocutor a Jew or, at the very least, was uncertain about his Jewish loyalties. At several points in his letter Gompertz openly acknowledges his own Jewish identity. In a sentence not fully comprehensible to me, he refers to "a newspaper of a witty member of my fraternity," most likely meaning his Jewish community or possibly his medical community. Later on, he again displays his Jewish affiliation when describing his meanderings in the Low Countries and the Netherlands: "But to the purpose, dear sir, I have rambled about, not unlike the everlasting Jew, through the low clammy countries and through the milky Dutch dominion." In an ingratiating gesture to his English correspondent, he expresses his dislike for those countries in comparison to England "because of the nauseous abundance of milk and the scarcity of roast beast."[94] Whether the roast beast he relished was kosher or not he does not say, but what seems oddly unexplainable about these benign pleasantries is that they could have easily been addressed to a non-Jew. It was Gompertz, as da Costa had done on numerous other occasions, who was "testing the waters," so to speak, with his faint signals of Jewish identification, seemingly unsure how the clerk of the Royal Society and renowned English scientist might react. There are unfortunately no responses preserved from the pen of da Costa by which one might examine this conjecture further. A potential forum

[93] On Gompertz, see Ruderman, *Jewish Thought and Scientific Discovery in Early Modern Europe*, pp. 334–35; A. Altmann, *Moses Mendelssohn: A Biographical Study* (University, Ala., 1973), pp. 23–25; D. Kaufmann and M. Freudenthal, *Die Familie Gumperz* (Frankfurt am Main, 1907), pp. 164–200; and Sorkin, *The Berlin Haskatah and German Religious Thought*, pp. 56–62.

[94] Add. MS 78537, fol. 436r.

for a significant exchange of views between a distinguished Anglo-Jewish intellectual and his German counterpart never materializes. In the end, we are left with a rather stiff and unsuccessful attempt on the part of the German Jewish doctor to establish any meaningful dialogue with his colleague at all.

It would be useful to explore further Mendes da Costa's other intellectual contacts with Jews more fully identified with the organized Jewish community, such as the rabbis Belisario and Isaac Nieto. One assumes that he would have had much in common with Tang or Levison. But these are speculations with no substantial evidence to confirm them. It is a fact worth pondering that one of the most prolific letter writers of the eighteenth century had relatively little to write about on matters pertaining to his faith and cultural identity, suggesting at least in his case, in contrast to those of Levison and Tang, that the professional path of the scientist and naturalist and that of the religious thinker were generally distinct from each other. This does not mean that issues pertaining to Judaism were unimportant to other contemporaries who reflected seriously on natural history and medicine. Certainly, the evidence of this chapter suggests the contrary. But this kind of thinking seems to have been more readily pursued by nonscientists like Hart or Tang or by physicians with rabbinic knowledge like Nieto or Levison who were still following well-trodden paths of fusing their medical and theological interests.[95]

Nevertheless, as his correspondence clearly demonstrates, his Jewish identity was never totally invisible and it continued to insinuate itself into his professional and personal relations. In fact, his pride of Jewish ancestry not only failed to disappear; it was enhanced by the general civility extended to him within the neutral space in which he and his scientific associates worked and by a general openness and intellectual curiosity about his cultural heritage that seemed to mark their social and intellectual fellowship. And unlike Dr. Jacob de Castro Sarmento, who had left the synagogue because he firmly dissented from the opinions and sentiments of its members, da Costa remained a member throughout, apparently because the Jewish contacts he continued to maintain with family and friends were precious to him, and because he was genuinely interested in the intellectual and cultural history of his community.

From the time of his imprisonment in 1768 until his death in 1791, his scientific career became a mere shadow of what it had previously been and his remarkable social and intellectual contacts were severely diminished,

---

[95] On these well-trodden paths of early modern Jewish thinkers, see Ruderman, *Jewish Thought and Scientific Discovery.*

although he continued to lecture, publish, buy and sell shells, and maintain the support of several close associates. Evidence of his Jewish contacts is scanty in this later period, although he corresponded with his cousin Joseph Salvador as late as 1785–86, complaining bitterly about his declining health. On his death five years later, he was given a Jewish burial in the old cemetery of the Spanish and Portuguese congregation.[96]

[96] Whitehead, "Emanuel Mendes da Costa," pp. 11–16, well describes his later years until his death. His exchange of letters with Salvador is found in Add. MS 28542, fols. 82–93. See also M. Woolf, "Joseph Salvador, 1716–1786," *Transactions Jewish Historical Society of* England 21 (1962–67): 104–37, where Salvador's letter is printed.

Six

Translation and Transformation: The Englishing of Jewish Culture

AT THE CENTER of David Levi's controversies with the Christian clergy was the issue of translating the Hebrew Bible, as we have seen. Levi felt the acute need of defending the time-honored Jewish prerogative of preserving the integrity of the Masoretic version as well as safeguarding its English translation from the unwarranted intrusion of Christian theological contamination. Levi never found the time and energy to offer a thoroughly original translation of the Old Testament, but the necessity of the project was constantly on his mind. Abraham Tang, in contrast, focused his energies on writing in Hebrew, although he too expressed his dissatisfaction with Christian translations of Scripture and felt obliged to translate the primary compendium of rabbinic moral sayings into English. But translation for both intellectuals, as well as for their other colleagues, played an even more critical role in their self-understanding of Jewish culture and in its presentation to Jews and Christians alike. It was always obvious to Levi, and increasingly apparent to other Jewish thinkers and educators as time went on, that Judaism could not survive on English soil unless they translated its classic texts into the language of their new homeland.

The goal of this final chapter is to consider the legacy of Anglo-Jewish thought beyond the small coterie of intellectuals examined thus far. I wish to begin to study the process of how the articulations of this group were presented and disseminated as a pedagogic and publishing program among a larger public of nonintellectuals. In this process, translation became the primary mechanism for educating simultaneously an indifferent Jewish community and an occasionally hostile Christian one. With the steady decline of bilingualism or multilingualism among English Jews—that is, the condition where immigrant Jews knew not only Hebrew but often Spanish, Portuguese, or Yiddish, along with a rising tide of Jewish assimilation and cultural illiteracy—the "Englishing" of Judaism became an unavoidable necessity. By the end of the eighteenth century, a younger generation of English Jews increasingly required Jewish educational texts in English. Levi and his colleagues responded by flooding the market with biblical translations partially correcting Christian "mistranslations," extensive translations of Jewish liturgy, new English statements of the essence of Jewish faith, and new "hands-on" English manuals for the observance of Jewish ritual in the home and in the community. In short, within the course of some sixty years, roughly from 1770 to 1830, they rendered into English a radical reformulation and distillation of Judaism to be studied and scrutinized by a laity almost fully removed from the original sources upon which the translations were based.

An examination of this new literature in English opens the even larger question of the role of translation in restructuring Jewish culture and society in the modern age. Translation, in the language of J. Hillis Miller, is a kind of "border crossing" where one culture passes over into another, whether to inform it, to enhance its development, to capture and stifle its growth, or merely to open a space between the original text and itself. When a work is translated, it is displaced, transported, and alienated from its original context.[1] Translation, as André Lefevere and Susan Bassnett remind us, is always a rewriting of the original text. And all rewritings, whatever their intention, reflect a certain ideology. They manipulate literature to function in a given society in a certain way. Translations as rewritings often signal the vibrancy and continued vitality of a culture. They inject new energy, concepts, and understandings into the original foundational texts. They also introduce these texts to new audiences and readerships, who in turn open up novel ways of responding and engaging the primary texts. But translations can also serve to repress innovation, distort the original, and even contain and arrest its potential appeal. Translations, along with commentaries, summaries, and anthologies of cultural texts, ultimately construct images of the prototype, profoundly distancing them from the original pattern on which the image was molded. Translation then is never a simple technical activity or an innocent process of rendering a text from one language to another.[2] Translation in this larger sense is a major shaping force in the development of modern Jewish societies and cultures, although its manifestations have generally been taken for granted.

In a stimulating essay on the notion of cultural translation in the ancient world, Jan Assmann posits three types of possible translations: assimila-

---

[1] J. Hillis Miller, "Border Crossings, Translating Theory: Ruth," in *The Translatability of Cultures: Figurations of the Space Between*, ed. S. Budick and W. Iser (Stanford, Calif., 1996), pp. 207–23, especially p. 207; see also in the same volume, S. Budick, "Crises of Alterity: Cultural Untranslatability and the Experience of Secondary Otherness," pp. 7–8, 11.

[2] A. Lefevere and S. Bassnett, "Introduction: Proust's Grandmother and the Thousand and One Nights: The 'Cultural Turn' in Translation Studies," in *Translation, History and Culture*, ed. S. Bassnett and A. Lefevere (London and New York, 1990), pp. 1–13. See also in the same volume, A. Lefevere, "Translation: Its Genealogy in the West," pp. 14–28; and A. Lefevere, *Translation/History/Culture: A Sourcebook* (London and New York, 1992).

tory translation of a distinct minority group into a dominating language or culture; mutual translation where the majority restrains from imposing its hegemony over its minority cultures; and syncretism, or translation into a third language. The first two modes seem relatively straightforward; the third is not. To illustrate the latter, Assmann uses the insight of G. W. Bowersock regarding Hellenism, which he understands as "a flexible medium of both cultural and religious expressions." Hellenism, generally synomous with paganism, provided a common language for local traditions and religions to express themselves in a voice more eloquent, articulate, and flexible than their own. It served as a common semiotic system that allowed the borders between different traditions to remain intact but, at the same time, to become more permeable. Hellenism not only provided a common language that transcended the original language barriers but helped to create a cosmopolitan consciousness. Assmann labels this example as syncretism, a kind of merging of two languages or cultures that coexist with the original distinct entities. Native beliefs and practices preserve their original meaning but when translated into the third language of Hellenism assume "a new kind of transparency which smoothes down idiosyncratic differences, offering double membership in native as well as general culture." Assmann goes on to suggest that only this last option might present a realistic and desirable model of cultural translatability in our own day.[3]

Could Assmann's notion of syncretism help to explain the process of the Englishing of Jewish culture? Did English culture for Jews living in the modern West ultimately function as the Hellenistic culture of late antiquity? When Hebrew prayers and the biblical text could now be understood in English, was not their essential character preserved albeit in a medium that now enhanced their universal and humanly shared message? For the architects of the massive project of translation of Jewish texts into English, their intention was always syncretistic, always seeking the status of double membership, always aspiring to preserve their own voice in the voice of the other. English to them was merely a neutral medium meant to provide direct access to the essential meaning of a tradition in jeopardy of cultural extinction. English was only meant as the path by which Judaism's cultural alienation would be diminished and the universal relevance of its human message would be enhanced. But was this ideal actually realizable? Was English indeed a neutral medium or did it tacitly condi-

---

[3] J. Assmann, "Translating Gods: Religion as a Factor of Cultural (Un)Translatability," in Budick and Iser, *The Translatability of Cultures*, pp. 25–36. He refers to G. W. Bowersock's *Hellenism in Late Antiquity* (Cambridge, 1990), p. 5. The citation of Assmann is found on p. 34.

tion the subject matter of the translations?[4] Did the medium ultimately create a new message? And, therefore, did the process of Englishing Judaism ultimately become a form of assimilatory translation whereby the distinct identity of the original eventually succumbed to the weight of the hegemonic Protestant culture, notwithstanding the best intentions of the translators?

The subjects of Yiddish and Hebrew as semiotic systems and their transformations in modern Jewish culture have previously been treated by modern scholars.[5] Others have examined the German Jewish paradigm of cultural symbiosis, and the well-publicized projects of translating the Bible into German, first by Mendelssohn in the eighteenth and later by Buber and Rosenzweig in the twentieth century.[6] To my knowledge, the project of Jewish translation into English, the lingua franca of Western civilization and even the world in our own day, has not been seriously considered. The Anglo-Jewish experience in the late eighteenth and early nineteenth centuries is the obvious starting point of this process, radically altering Judaism as a semiotic system, and transforming its own self-perceptions and self-definitions. In fact, through translation the presentation of Judaism to self and to other apparently coalesced; the image of Judaism Jews projected to the other virtually became indistinguishable from their own self-image.

My examination of translation projects of the Bible and liturgy, of manuals and anthologies is admittedly preliminary and hardly exhaustive. It is meant only to point to an important subject in understanding the evolution of modern Jewish culture in general, and in the English and eventually American orbits, in particular.[7] In these endeavors, the striking figure of David Levi again rises to the surface. He, more than any of his contemporaries, foresaw intuitively the significance of English translation for the future survival of Judaism. While he was capable of expressing himself in Hebrew, he consciously devoted his entire literary career to creating from scratch a virtual library of Jewish knowledge in English translation. Accordingly, he assumes a prominent place in this chapter as well.

[4] This is Karlheinz Stierle's question in his "Translatio Studii and Renaissance: From Vertical to Horizontal Translation," in Budick and Iser, *The Translatability of Cultures* p. 55.

[5] See especially B. Harshav, *The Meaning of Yiddish* (Berkeley, 1990), and his *Language in Time of Revolution* (Berkeley, 1993).

[6] On Mendelssohn's project, see Breuer, *The Limits of Enlightenment* (and the earlier studies he cites. On the Buber-Rosenzweig project, see K. Reichert, " 'It is Time': The Buber-Rosezweig Bible Translation in Context," in Budick and Iser, *The Translatability of Cultures*, pp. 169–85.

[7] I would like to note the valuable bibliographical references generously offered to me by Arthur Kiron, especially in helping me to appreciate the close connections between the process I am tracing in England and that in America. See also the afterword.

One final word about the chronological spread of this chapter is in order. One of the primary arguments of this book, as I have indicated, is that Jewish thought in England emerged independently of German developments, shaped indigenously by English society and culture. Whether foreign or native-born, English Jews, who articulated their own sense of cultural identity, were primarily affected by their formative exposure to the religious and cultural life of the Protestant majority. Only belatedly, in the early decades of the nineteenth century, did English Jews become cognizant of the image of Mendelssohn and the powerful intellectual currents emanating from the continent.[8] While the previous chapters of this book have essentially focused on the eighteenth century, this chapter extends my examination into the first three decades of the next century. This extension is warranted, I believe, by the subject at hand. It charts a process of dissemination and translation of knowledge that actually began in the 1770s, at about the time that Tang, Levi, Hart, Levison, and the others, began their literary careers, but became more visible only in the course of the next half century. By the late 1820s, German ideological and educational trends were finally leaving their mark on Anglo-Jewish culture and were fully absorbed by the latter. Nevertheless, I would still contend that the initial thrust of these developments is to be located long before the invasion of German Jewish culture. By the end of this period, a new generation of Jewish intellectuals in England was emerging, such as Solomon Bennett and Hyman Hurwitz. But the latter wrote prior to the era of full political emancipation and religious reform, and they still expressed themselves in the shadows of their predecessors. In many ways, the first decades of nineteenth-century Jewish cultural life in England had already been stamped by the themes and concerns of Levi, Tang, and their contemporaries. Bennett and Hurwitz were very much of their intellectual mold. Thus my foray into the nineteenth century is merely to glimpse at the flowering of a process initiated decades earlier when English Jewry marched to the beat of its own internal drummer still relatively oblivious to any rhythms emanating beyond its borders.

I

To any English person living in the eighteenth century, reading the Bible, the literal rendering of divine revelation, meant always the English authorized version. Given the long history of this translation and the ubiquitous role it played in the religious, cultural, and political life of English society for centuries, its familiar phraseology and cadences were understandably

---

[8] On this, see the appendix.

conceived as identical with the way God actually spoke.[9] For the vast majority of English Jews with diminished capacity to comprehend fully the Hebrew original, the English translation gradually began to function as their major entry point into the biblical narrative as well. It is difficult to chart this process precisely except to observe its final results confirmed by the candid observations of rabbis and educators that Hebrew literacy, except for a small elite, was hardly the norm by the end of the eighteenth century, either among sephardic or ashkenazic Jews. Hyman Hurwitz, writing in 1807, offered as reliable an estimate as any in claiming that only a fifth of the young students graduating Jewish schools could read Hebrew with any accuracy and even less could read the Bible without consulting the English version.[10]

As we have seen, Levi and his Jewish colleagues had much to say about the inadequacies of the standard English translation and its "metrical" successors, but they were in no position to dislodge their usage among Christians and even among Jews. When Anselm Bayly, that self-proclaimed friend of the Jewish people, produced a bilingual edition of the entire Hebrew Bible in 1774, with the Hebrew text on the left side of the page and the authorized English version on the right, it was obviously intended for Jewish usage as the Hebrew title page makes clear: "On one side Hebrew [Yehudit] and the other side English [Britanit] to assist the Jews who speak English to understand the Bible and its secrets from their own tongue that was in the past."[11] Even the long-awaited "Jewish" version of the Torah and *haftarot*, published in Hebrew and English by Alexander Alexander in 1785, was hardly an improvement over the Bayly edition. The set of five volumes was obviously intended for synagogue use, but it too provided only the authorized English version. There are supplementary notes, especially to the book of Genesis, but they are hardly a serious encounter with the translation as an essentially Protestant rewriting of the Torah. In fact as Samuel Daiches perceptively pointed out many years ago, in his still useful summary of Anglo-Jewish biblical exegesis and translation, even the notes display a distinctly English Protes-

---

[9] See especially F. F. Bruce, *The History of the Bible in English* (New York, 1973); D. Daiches, *The King James Version: An Account of the Development and Sources of the English Bible of 1611 with Special Reference to the Hebrew Tradition* (Chicago, 1941); C. Hill, *The English Bible and the Seventeenth-Century Revolution* (London, 1994); H. G. Reventlow, *The Authority of the Bible and the Rise of the Modern World* (Philadelphia, 1985).

[10] H. Hurwitz, *Sefer Rishon Le-Mikra'ei Kodesh Or Elements of the Hebrew Language in Two Parts*, pt. 1 (London, 1807), preface, p. ii: "That out of a hundred, scarce twenty can read the Hebrew with any grammatical exactness; and fewer still who understand the Scriptures without the aid of an English translation."

[11] Cited in Daiches, "The Beginnings of Anglo-Jewish Biblical Exegesis and Bible Translation," p. 25. The translation is my own.

tant flavor. Such rubrics as "explanatory, historical, critical and practical" or Alexander's use of "the argument" at the conclusion of each book betray the formidable influence of the English Bible tradition (fig. 15).[12]

When Lion Soesmans offered his own rival edition of the Pentateuch for Jewish usage in 1787, he had apparently outdone his rival in securing the services of David Levi himself. The title page reads ambiguously: "Corrected and translated by David Levi." What this means exactly is that Soesmans again used the authorized version but added the more extensive and scholarly notes of Levi (fig. 16).[13] Even Alexander Alexander's son, Levi, eventually realized that this edition was superior to that of his father and republished it again in 1821. This later version was still essentially the same as the original despite its somewhat exaggerated claims that the "practical, critical, and grammatical" notes of Levi had been "carefully corrected and revised, with various improvements and additions distinguishing also from the six hundred and thirteen precepts . . . as observed by the Jews."[14] Thus over the course of some fifty years, with the broad dissemination of either the Alexander or Soesmans edition within the Jewish community, English Jews inevitably assumed that the authorized version was in fact synonymous with that of the traditional text. They undoubtedly absorbed the mellifluous sounds of the original Hebrew text chanted aloud in the synagogue, although this kind of exotic recital performed by a small elite of expert readers was generally remote from the immediate cultural tastes of most of the congregation. It was more likely that the majority of synagogue worshipers internalized the meaning and embraced the spiritual force of the text solely through its majestic English translation. In this respect, their aesthetic experience with the Bible increasingly mirrored that of their Christian contemporaries in churches throughout London and beyond.

Anglo-Jewish intellectuals surely regretted this sad twist of fate but despite their strong desire to create a Jewish biblical translation, one authentically reflecting the Hebrew original as they understood it, they could not accomplish such an undertaking. Either the task was too difficult for one

---

[12] Ibid., pp. 26–27, 29. On Alexander and his publishing son Levi, see also C. Roth, "The Origin of Hebrew Typography in England," *Journal of Jewish Bibliography* 1 (1938–39): 7.

[13] Daiches, "The Beginnings of Anglo-Jewish Exegesis and Bible Translation," pp. 27–29. In addition to Daiches, see also J. Hertz, *Jewish Translations of the Bible into English* (London, 1920). For the United States, see J. D. Sarna and N. M. Sarna, "Jewish Biblical Scholarship and Translations in the United States," in *The Bible and Bibles in America*, ed. E. S. Frerichs (Atlanta, Ga., 1988), pp. 83–116.

[14] *The Holy Bible in Hebrew Conformable to the Accurate Text of Everado Van der Hoote . . . Printed in Amsterdam, in 1705 and the Musical Accents after the Manner of Pramselo with the English Translation on the Opposite Page . . .*, 5 vols. (London 1821–22), published by L. Alexander.

THE
Firſt Book of *MOSES*,

CALLED

GENESIS, §

IN

HEBREW and ENGLISH,

The Muſical Accents after the Manner of PRAMSELO's.

WITH

Remarks Critical, and Grammatical,

ON

The HEBREW,

By A. ALEXANDER.

---

§ The word *Geneſis* is Greek, and ſignifies the Generation or Formation of things.

LONDON.

Printed by A. ALEXANDER and SON, No. 11, Church-Street Spittal-Fields,

A. M. 5545.

Levy phillips 1822

15a. The title page of the authorized English version of Genesis in the so-called Jewish version of the Torah and *Haftarot* published by Alexander Alexander in 1785.

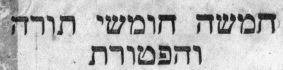

תמשה חומשי תורה
וההפטורת

אורו כמו עיש · וכימה מאורים ·
יהל במלאו ובחסרו · כידלום וספירים ·
עמק תהום רבה · דימשל לעמקו ·
גבה שמי רומה · הידמו לרומו ·
ערוך בשלחן · ועליו מעדנו ·
נורא שמו על כל לפניו בצלמו :

באותיות נקדות וטעמים אותיות נדלות וקטנות ·
מלעיל. ומלרע בלי שגיאות הא לכם זרע קודש
פרי חדש · עשו חושו גושו חזו וראו בנין
מצוין בהדר :

באר היטב
בלשון ענגליש
וטעם המאכל נמצא באכילה

נדפס
בלונדן
בבית ובדפוס
אלכסנדר בר יהודה ליב זצ"ל ·
ובנו יהודה ליב בר אלכסנדר שי' :
בשנת תקמה לפ"ק

15b. The Hebrew version of figure 15a.

16a. The cover page, in Hebrew, of Lion Soesman's rival edition of the Pentateuch, the book of Leviticus, for Jewish usage. London, 1786.

THE

Third Book of

MOSES,

CALLED

•LEVITICUS.

IN HEBREW,

WITH THE

ENGLISH TRANSLATION

ON THE OPPOSITE PAGE;

WITH

N O T E S.

EXPLANATORY, PRACTICAL, CRITICAL, AND

GRAMMATICAL,

By LION SOESMANS,

Corrected, and translated By, DAVID LEVI.

---

* It is called LEVITICUS, because it treats of the tribe of Levi, (in which is included both Priests and Levites,) and the things pertaining to their offices : as the offerings, the examination and cleansing of the leprosy, in both men and houses; the yearly feast of expiation, &c. It affords nothing of Historical matter, except the relation of the young man of the tribe of Dan, who was stoned for blasphemy.

LONDON:

Printed by LION SOESMANS, and Co. No. 9. Duke
Street, Aldgate.

16b. The cover page of figure 16a in English.

person to carry out or the authorized English version was too firmly entrenched in the consciousness of their community. David Levi had announced his hope in producing "a new translation of the Bible, with a copious commentary, on a plan never before attempted; and in which the errors of the present translation will be clearly pointed out, the difficult passages explained, and the seeming contradictions reconciled,"[15] but he clearly failed to fulfill this desire.

One of Levi's contemporaries, an otherwise obscure sephardic Jew named Isaac Delgado, took the unusual step of publishing in 1789 *A New English Translation of the Pentateuch, being a Thorough Correction of the Present Translation, Wherever it Deviates from the Genuine Sense of the Hebrew Expressions, or where, it renders obscure the meaning of the Text; or lastly, when it occasions a seeming Contradiction: proving the Validity of such Emendations by critical Remarks and Illustrations grounded on other Instances in Scripture where the like Words or Phrases Occur.* Delgado, who called himself "a teacher of the Hebrew language," actually accomplished considerably less than his pretentious title seems to indicate. The new English translation was in fact "a specimen of the whole,"[16] that is, a list of corrected translations in one column facing the standard English translation, along with extensive notes that justified the emendations. What was unusual about Delgado's effort was neither the significance of his changes nor the extent of his erudition but the auspices under which he proposed this modest effort. The work was dedicated to the "honourable and Right Reverend Dr. Shute Barrington, the Lord Bishop of Salisbury,"[17] and was meant as an ecumenical project since "we both, my Lord, worship the One True God."[18] Delgado thus writes in the preface:

> Religion is the greatest bulwark that can be introduced in a commonwealth. . . .
> Every man's duty, as much as lies in his power, is to remove every obstacle to
> the reading of the Bible, and to obviate everything that may have the appearance
> of an absurdity in it, it being the source of all the present established religions.
> It is greatly to be lamented, that, in a Christian country, which abounds with
> men eminent for their abilities and learning, a correction of the present translation of the Bible, and a literal explanation of it, so much wanted . . . hath been
> hitherto neglected; For the want of which, people, meeting with several obscure
> passages, which cannot be properly understood, are apt to throw it aside, and

---

[15] Levi, *Lingua Sacra*, III, epilogue, p. 7.

[16] Isaac Delgado, *A New English Translation of the Pentateuch* . . . (London, 1789), preface, p. viii.

[17] On Barrington, see *Dictionary of National Biography* 1 (London, 1908): 1214, and note his relation to Henry Owen mentioned in chapter 1.

[18] Delgado, *A New English Translation*, dedication page, p. iii.

seldom view it again. What most surprises me is, that none of all the publishers of family Bibles, that have come to my knowledge, ever undertook such a task."[19]

Delgado, accordingly, undertook his work as a service to English society in general. Since the English Bible was the common possession of Christians and Jews alike, it followed that if it was deficient, a Jew knowledgeable in the Hebrew text could volunteer, for the common good, to improve the translation. The issue was not to preserve a Jewish version exclusively for Jewish usage but to refine a text to be shared by all religions. To be sure, Delgado could not withhold his stinging barbs regarding the Kennicott project, although he refrains from mentioning Dr. Kennicott by name. He strongly insists that he will never avail himself "of that pernicious method of supposing an error in Scripture, committed by transcribers after the compilation of the Bible by Ezra and his synod, who faithfully handing it down to us as they found it, without venturing to alter a single letter, and was since preserved by the Massorites as pure as they received it."[20] He notes that Jews all over the world preserve the same text and that to pretend to correct the original Hebrew by the different readings found in manuscripts is a profane act, "as it would give us a spurious copy, instead of a divine narrative."[21] Given the scrupulous manner in which Jews throughout the ages protected the text, errors in the Pentateuch are virtually impossible while errors in the rest of the Bible are possible but rare. It is better to explain apparent mistakes as purposeful, pointing to a deeper meaning of the text while explaining them through thoughtful exegesis.

The latter point is reminiscent of Delgado's sephardic coreligionist Raphael Baruh and his defense of the Masoretic reading against Dr. Henry Owen.[22] Indeed, among the long list of subscribers is the same Raphael Baruh, along with other familiar sephardic leaders such as Isaac Mendes Belisario, Isaac Henrique de Castro of Amsterdam, Phineas Netto, and Samuel Vita Montefiore. But even more surprising is another name in the list: Reverend Doctor Henry Owen. He is mentioned more prominently at the end of the preface. Delgado confesses that he had been reluctant to publish the work given "the uncouthness of my language." He consulted friends who encouraged him and advised him "to shew it to the reverend and learned Dr. Owen, rector at St. Olave." Owen encouraged him to publish this specimen as the first step toward a complete translation.[23]

[19] Ibid., p. v.

[20] Ibid., p. vii.

[21] Ibid.

[22] On Baruh and Owen, see chapter 1.

[23] Delgado, *A New English Translation*, p. ix. The list of subscribers is on pp. xi–xiii.

Owen, we recall, had been the recipient of Baruh's polite but firm criticism of the Kennicott system; he had, in turn, responded to Baruh negatively but respectfully. Now, some fourteen years later, he was supporting, together with his former Jewish antagonist, the beginning of a new translation promoted by a Jew who would not countenance so irresponsible an attack on the Masoretic edition as that of Kennicott. It is as if Owen had been disillusioned with his Christian mentor and was ready to put his support behind a colleague of Baruh who, in turn, would willingly join in supporting this enterprise.

In addition to Owen and the lord bishop of Salisbury, several other Christian clergy are listed in the subscriber list: a Reverend Gilbert Gerard (1760–1815), the minister of the English established Church of Amsterdam, a Reverend Edward Parker of Durham, a Reverend Thomas Pierson, another minister of the English Church of Amsterdam, along with other distinguished ashkenazic Jews (Joseph Hart Meyer, Joshua Van Oven) and Christians (Granville Sharpe [1735–1813], the Anglican antislavery reformer Richard Holbert, James Morgan, Joshua Pym).[24] No more convincing testimony of active Jewish collaboration with Christian clergy in improving the English translation of their common Bible could be found than this remarkable ecumenical list of supporters, especially the names of Owen and Baruh. Equally compelling is the evidence this work offers in demonstrating how English Jews understood the English Bible to be the basis for a translation they could accept. Taking into account the probability that Delgado's preface was "politically correct" in seeking not to offend his Christian associates, it nevertheless illustrates how Jews could genuinely embrace a Christian rendering of the Bible as their own and, in the interest of both faiths, offer to improve it.

Some forty-five years passed before another Jewish scholar advanced the idea of a new translation. In 1834, Solomon Bennett, a well-known engraver and critic of the rabbinate, published his *Critical Remarks on the Authorized Version of the Old Testament Containing some Examples of its Errors, with Specimens of an Amended Translation*. His objective was "to promote a pure, correct, and perfect version of the Bible, critically and etymologically demonstrated, which has never been attempted by any one; and to ascertain if it meet the original or not, which has remained for near 1800 years in a state of great indecision."[25] He was motivated to

---

[24] On Gerard, see *Dictionary of National Biography* 7 (New York, 1909): 1099; on Sharpe, 17 (New York, 1909): 1339–45. Among the many affiliations of Sharpe, he was also one of the founders of the Society for the Conversion of the Jews in 1808.

[25] Solomon Bennett, *Critical Remarks on the Authorized Version of the Old Testament* (London, 1834), p. iv. On Bennett, see A. Barnett, "Solomon Bennett, 1761–1828: Artist,

consider so daunting a task by the diatribes of Thomas Paine against the Bible, which arose, in Bennett's view, because of the inaccurate English translation Paine consulted. Bennett had clearly examined a variety of English editions, including the edition of Anselm Bayly, as well as the most recent Oxford Bible of 1824. In a conversation with his friend Thomas Burgess (1756–1837), coincidentally also the bishop of Salisbury,[26] Bennett had occasion to offer his own negative appraisal of the Kennicott project:

> The venerable bishop then asked my opinion with respect to the Hebrew and Samaritan Bible, edited by Dr. Kennicott in reference to the collations he . . . made between the several Ms. copies which he collected from different parts, even from the Asiatic and African dominions, by means of the English ambassadors and consuls residing there (which, as I was informed, cost the government about 24,000 pounds) in which collations Dr. Kennicott thought he had discovered thousands of variations in the bulk of the Mss., which he styled different readings (the term different errors would be more becoming). I then demonstrated to his Lordship the impropriety and the vagueness of the mode of his collations, and the unhallowed consequences resulting from it. "Dr. Kennicott," said I, "would have done better to bestow his learning in behalf of a perfect version, instead of a collation of Mss. which are without authority and correctness." It is to be lamented, that the enormous sums of money devoted by government to that religious, most sacred, and most essential subject, the possession of a perfect version of the Bible, have been all in vain.[27]

Precisely as Delgado had done, Bennett insists that only the Jewish community "is the lifeguard of the original Hebrew language," and therefore is in the best position to serve as "the best judges of the integrity of any version of the Bible."[28] As a full-fledged member of the English nation (he had arrived in London as an immigrant from eastern Europe some thirty-five years earlier), he hopes to make his contribution to knowledge and piety, and to receive in return a receptive following of patrons and subscribers:

> [Having arrived] in a country which is the grand repository of literature of every description—the treasury of arts and sciences, the mother of invention! who nourishes, encourages, and patronizes her intellectual offspring; in which prejudices of every description are banished from her plains, and whose sons are the

---

Hebraist, and Controversialist," *Jewish Historical Society of England Transactions* 17 (1953): 91–111; Endelman, *The Jews of Georgian England* (1979), pp. 142–44, 155–57.

[26] On Burgess, see *Dictionary of National Biography* 3 (New York, 1909): 313–14.

[27] Bennett, *Critical Remarks*, pp. 6–7.

[28] Ibid., p. 22.

co-operators of Divine Nature, who has spread her splendid radiance to the
most remote and desolate parts of our sublunary habitable globe, and said to
her settlers, "be fruitful, and multiply, and replenish the earth, and subdue it,
&c." In a nation like this, I hope that my labours, my sincere and upright views,
will also find their zealous advocates, who will cordially patronize and support
me in my proposed sacred labour.[29]

Two years later Bennett succeeded in publishing a small specimen of
his new translation. In 1841, after his death, two additional sections from
the book of Genesis were published by Francis Barham. Although it is
quite possible Bennett completed this project, the full manuscript has
never been found.[30] The impact he had hoped to have on his adopted
country remained unrealized. Nevertheless, in offering his proposal as an
antidote to the disastrous satire of Paine, he was following the well-trodden path of Levi and Delgado before him. He, as a Jew with a particular
expertise in reading the Hebrew Bible, was offering his service for the
greater good of humanity. It was not "their" problem alone that Paine
exploited in ridiculing the Bible. It was "our" problem, Christian and Jew
alike. Both faith communities considered the authorized English version
as their own Bible, despite its deficiencies. Kennicott has tried to improve
it, only to fail because of the false assumptions regarding Hebrew manuscripts upon which his ridiculously expensive project was based. Only a
Jew with proper training and understanding could accomplish the task of
creating a more perfect translation; and only in so open a society as England, Bennett believed, would such a effort be appreciated.

In the light of this peculiarly Anglo-Jewish perspective—of taking for
granted that the authorized English version was the common property of
both Jews and Christians, and that its revision was in the interest of society as a whole, not Jews alone—the comparison with German Jewry's
own translation projects is instructive. Mendelssohn's ambitious translation and commentary emerged out of the need to offer a Jewish alternative
to the Luther Bible, to present a German text that obliterated the Christian German tradition. Even as late as 1917, Franz Rosenzweig clearly
articulated the challenge: "Meaning depends upon language, and it is a
gross underestimation of the intimacy which Christendom and the German language have been mated since Luther and even before his time, if
one believes to be able to convey Jewish contents in German without the
flavoring of an alien faith."[31] There is no indication of any similar concern
on the part of the Anglo-Jewish translators we have examined. The re-

[29] Ibid., p. 26.
[30] Barnett, "Solomon Bennett," pp. 98–100.
[31] Cited by Reichart, " 'It Is Time': The Buber-Rosenzweig Bible Translation," p. 173.

markable contrast provides one strong indicator of how pervasive the influence of the English Bible on Anglo-Jews actually was, and how critical this one factor was in defining their unique self-identity, one shaped primarily through the medium of the English language.

II

Alexander Alexander was also responsible, with his collaborator B. Myers, for the first complete English translation of the prayer book. In the fourth volume published in London in 1771 entitled *Seder Tefillot Succot: The Tabernacle Service which are publickly read in the Synagogue by the Spanish and Portuguese Jews and Used by all Families*, a work that he translated alone, he offers the following "soliloquy" to the reader:

> That prayers ought to be understood by him that supplicates to the Supreme Being, every person must allow, that the almighty God is our Creator, Saviour and Redeemer; to whom we are to answer at the day of Judgement, for all our misdeeds and transgressions, as the Scripture says . . . "When wisdom entreth unto thy heart knowledge is pleasant unto thy soul" [Proverbs 2:10]. By this word knowledge, is meant to serve God in a language we understand, which gives penetration to the heart; that when thou prayeth and supplicates to the sole God of Heaven and Earth, thy knowledge becomes pleasant to thee, and thou will enjoy the benefit of its futurity. Therefore as the holy language becomes Daily, more to be lost, that it is by many but little understood, and by some not at all; by which reason the soul can receive but little benefit to those that have not the knowledge of the solemn words in the prayers explain'd, for the reception thereof, to the supreme king of kings, and for the redemption of the soul. What is the sole motive of my printing the English opposite the Hebrew; that the Reader may say his prayers in the holy language; and by his having the English on the opposite side, they have the knowledge thereof. For when a person doeth not understand what he is reading, it can convey but little knowledge for the soul's benefit, as the wise kind plainly expresses . . . "Trust in the Lord with all thy heart, and lean not to thine understanding" [Proverbs 3:5]. Which implies reading which is not understood; for he that says prayers, in a language he understands not, must give great offence to the Diety.[32]

Simeon Singer, writing in 1896, could see no value whatsoever in Alexander's accomplishment: "I am sorry to say Alexander translated the whole of the Festival Services of the Portuguese Rite. It was a melancholy

---

[32] Alexander Alexander, *Seder Tefillot Succot: The Tabernacle Service* . . . (London, 1771), a soliloquy by the translator.

performance. Indeed, it almost seems as if the worst literary service ever rendered to the Portuguese was done by an Ashkenazi, and, as an Ashkenazi, I feel inclined to apologize to them." Judged by the high standards of his own generation's English aesthetic and literary senses as well as his personal standards in producing his own prayer book translations, Singer was right to consider Alexander's work a crude and unpolished exercise. But perhaps Singer was too harsh in judging the work in the context of its time. Being the first complete edition of its kind in the English language, it was indeed an ambitious and pioneering act for this "bold, bad bookmaker" to undertake.[33] Alexander was no great intellectual, only an enterprising publisher with minimal literacy in Hebrew and English. Moreover, the task he and his colleagues set for themselves in translating the Hebrew liturgy was considerably more difficult than what they were doing simultaneously with the publication of bilingual Bibles. In the latter case, they merely refined and polished an already established literary masterpiece universally acknowledged by all. In the former case, they began from scratch. Spanish translations preceded their English versions. There were a few seventeenth- and early-eighteenth-century versions they could consult. Indeed, Alexander Alexander and later his son, Levi, did succeed in "borrowing" heavily from others without acknowledgment: Alexander "borrowed" from Isaac Abendana, and Levi Alexander from David Levi, as we shall soon see. Nevertheless, despite these glaring deficiencies, they were trailblazers. They succeeded in the course of one generation to supply English Jewry with its basic religious and pedagogic needs: Hebrew-English Bibles and prayer books and some essential handbooks on how to utilize both. In an era where serving God "in a language we understand" meant only English, their contribution cannot be so easily dismissed.

Singer has provided a relatively complete description of the evolution of Jewish prayer books in English throughout the eighteenth- and early nineteenth-centuries.[34] There is no need to review that history here but only to provide some additional observations on the scope and meaning of the achievements of the Alexanders, the more skillful David Levi, as well as several others Singer omitted. One of the first liturgies to be translated was that of the Passover seder. Isaac Abendana and Gamaliel ben Pedahzur (Abraham Meers) had translated it many years earlier. It was rendered into English again by Alexander Alexander and by David Levi in separate editions. Levi's work was republished several times and, like his other superior translations, became the standard translation for En-

---

[33] Singer, "Early Translations and Translators," p. 53.
[34] Ibid., pp. 36–71.

glish Jews (fig. 17). What is most striking about all of these translations, especially those of Levi, is their critical need not only to translate, but also to explain and justify. Levi's long note explaining the service of the first two nights of Passover, reprinted in the edition of Hyam Barnett of 1833, includes the following rationale for the entire ceremony:

As the Passover was instituted in commemoration of our Redemption from Egypt, this Ceremony is itself a clear evidence, and demonstration of the truth of that event, as related by divine revelation, as a great number of the Precepts contained in the Mosaical dispensations are founded, on the said Redemption: and it would be highly absurd, to imagine it possible, that near four millions of people could suffer themselves to be imposed on in such a barefaced manner, by agreeing to accept of an institution, said to be founded on a miraculous deliverance wrought for them, if in fact no such deliverance had taken place. A Position like this, surely no deist, freethinker, nor sceptic will be hardy enough to advance. Now this institution took place at the very time of their departure from Egypt and hath continued to this day: So that it is impossible to doubt the truth of it. Indeed, the miracles of Moses bear such evident marks of truth being performed in so public a manner, and on their notoriety several festivals and other precepts being instituted, and immediately taking place, that it really is astonishing how any rational person could doubt their authenticity."[35]

So transparent an apology, directed to the apparent multitude of "wicked sons" ready to ridicule the quaint ceremony as an exercise in foolish credulity and blind faith, provides some sense of the challenge Levi and his fellow translators faced in presenting so fundamental a liturgy to an English Jewish public. The historicity and rationality of this ceremony had to be underscored. The translator had to translate in a way that brought to the surface the spiritual value and continuing relevance of the service in general.

Alexander Alexander had earlier felt the need to justify the entire activity of prayer in an Anglo-Jewish context. In his *Seder Petiḥah Le-ha-Tefillot Or a Key to Part of the Hebrew Liturgy Containing Several Remarkable Paragraphs Worth the Reader's Notice, Likewise a Chronological Summary of the Remarkable Things Related Thereto*, published in 1775, he sets out to offer "a brief account of the necessity and excellence of the prayers in general, but especially in public."[36] Singer has categorized this

---

[35] *Service for the First Two Nights of Passover in Hebrew and English According to the Custom of German and Polish Jews Translated by D. Levi, Reprinted from David Levi's Original Copy by Hyam Barnett, Hebrew Bookseller and Publisher* (London, 1833), "Note Explaining the Service of the Two First Nights of Passover."

[36] Alexander Alexander, *Sefer Petiḥah Le-ha-Tefillot . . .* (London, 1775), p. 3.

THE ORDER

OF THE

FORM OF PRAYERS,

FOR THE

NEW YEAR,

IN

HEBREW AND ENGLISH,

According to the Custom of the

𝕾𝖕𝖆𝖓𝖎𝖘𝖍 𝖆𝖓𝖉 𝕻𝖔𝖗𝖙𝖚𝖌𝖚𝖊𝖘𝖊 𝕵𝖊𝖜𝖘;

AS

READ IN THEIR SYNAGOGUES,

AND

USED IN THEIR FAMILIES.

———

Translated and Printed into English from the Hebrew,

By DAVID LEVI.

———

VOL. II.

———

CAREFULLY REVISED AND CORRECTED.

═══════

SECOND EDITION, WITH AMENDMENTS.

═══════

London :

Printed and Sold by E. JUSTINS, at his Hebrew Printing Office, 34, Brick Lane, Spitalfields.

———

A. M. 5570.

1810

17a. One of the many editions of David Levi's prayer books, showing the title page in English of the sephardic prayer book for the New Year. London, 1810.

סדר התפלות

לראש השנה

במנהג ק"ק ספרדים יזי"א ·

כאשר נדפסו ע"י התורני

כהר"ר דוד בר מרדכי הלוי סג"ל ז"ל ·

ועתה הובאו אל הדפוס שנית · בתכלית היופי באותיות יפות על נייר לבן ומהודר ·

והוגה בעיון דק ובשקידה רבה ·

להכינו כדמות ותבנית אשר הכינו · המניח הנאמן הגביר המעלה כהר"ר שמואל רודריגיז
מינדיז זצ"ל ספרדים מ"ל בק"ק באמשטרדם יע"א וקרובו הנטהרו ומצרפו
במטהר ובמצרף כסף כהר"ר יעקב דא סילוא מינדיז זצ"ל אשר כפעו
סדרי תפלותיהם בכל ערי ישראל ליהודים אשר מספרד ה"ו ועל פיהם ינהגו וחזי דוותא משרתי ה"
אשר בק"ק שער השמים יע"א · פה עד המהוללה יע"א :

לונדון :

PRINTED AND SOLD BY E. JUSTINS, 34, BRICK LANE,
SPITALFIELDS.

שנת

וזה שער השמים

לפ"ק

17b. The title page of figure 17a in Hebrew.

work as a crude act of plagiarism, pointing especially to the lifting of large passages from Isaac Abendana's much earlier work, *Discourses on the Ecclesiastical and Civil Policy of the Jews* (Oxford, 1706, 1709).[37] No doubt, Alexander was not gifted enough to provide a fully original excursus on prayer. Nevertheless, his rewriting of Abendana and possibly other sources still to be identified provides a window into his world as much as that of an earlier period. Most obvious is his need to universalize the act of prayer and to legitimate it as appropriate for a rational moral person. He first pleads for the need of religion in a political world as "the sacred anchor, by which the great ship of state is held fast, that she may not be split upon the rocks of sedition: the contents therein consists of Holiness, Peace, and Righteousness, which no man enjoys reward. This is that which embalms your name here, and crowns your soul with true happiness hereafter." If religion is critical to the functioning of society, then prayer has its significant place as well: "When we look upon the confused multitude of Idolaters in the Universe, then we ought not only to honour his name, but to give thanks unto him for his daily benevolence with its due Honour, Glory, Reverence, and Obedience, and render thanks unto Him for creating and giving us knowledge about the beasts in the field, can any man without the Lord's salvation be saved?"[38]

In a long paragraph on the notion that man is by nature a religious being, Alexander implores his reader to recognize his eternal obligations to the Creator. When man uses the bounties of nature, he cannot allow himself to neglect "the necessary return of praise and thanksgiving . . . whatsoever usest the creatures without previous intercessions, and subsequent thanksgiving, is chargeable with theft or rather sacrilege, inasmuch as he invades God's sovereign right and title to the disposal of his creatures, and sets up for propriety, when he is at best but a precarious dependent being."[39]

One is hard pressed to find in this handbook a clear statement about the specific purpose of Jewish prayer and the specific needs of the Jewish worshiper. There are ample citations from the Bible; the prayers recited in 1 Maccabees, Josephus, and Philo are mentioned as well; and, of course, a general description of the rubrics of the daily and sabbath services is provided, based heavily on Abendana. But even when Alexander's focus is on Jewish liturgy, the universal message of this activity is constantly underscored. Josephus, Philo, and the *Ethics of the Fathers* offer testimony

---

[37] Singer, "Early Translations and Translators," p. 53.
[38] Alexander, *Sefer Petiḥah*, pp. 46–48.
[39] Ibid., p. 58.

that Jews pray in support of the government in which they live, for "the entire human race," and "on behalf of the whole world."[40] If this primary concern for humanity seems odd in a prayer book of Jewish worship, Alexander is quick to stress that this specific duty flows "from a consideration of those common principles of nature, in which all mankind agree, however distinguished from one another in their moral and political capacities."[41]

In the final analysis, Alexander's work is not merely a good copying job; it is a remarkable effort to recast the entire Jewish liturgy into a universal language of prayer. Prayer is no longer a specifically Jewish obligation but an essentially human one. By praying, using the ancient formula of Jewish liturgy, Jews participate in the same experience as their Protestant neighbors, demonstrating anew their spiritual and political obligations as full-fledged members of the English nation.

The republication of traditional Jewish prayer books with English translations by the Alexanders and Levi continued well into the first decades of the nineteenth century with few alterations or innovations. In 1817, Levi Alexander experimented with the manner of presentation of the translation, producing an interlinear English version based on his father's work. He called it *Alexander's Interpreting Tephilloth, Or Daily Form of Prayers with the English Translation Affixed under Each Word of the Original According to the Order of the German and Polish Jews Adapted for the Improvement of Youth in Jewish Schools, to Render it Easy, as well to the Master as Scholar.* Despite its innovative technical design for pedagogic purposes, it followed the earlier translation without deviation or additional commentary.[42]

Although Alexander hoped to capture the school market with the unusual format of his prayer book, it still essentially represented the mediocre translation of his father. To other Jewish educators, especially the chief rabbi Solomon Hirschell himself, the liturgical products of Levi Alexander's press were markedly inferior to those based on David Levi's translation. Even when Alexander proposed to publish a new festival prayer book based on Levi's translation, Hirschell supported his competition. This remained a source of constant irritation and frustration to him. He publicly ridiculed the rabbi in anyway possible and was even capable of

---

[40] See, for example ibid., pp. 33–36.

[41] Ibid., p. 36.

[42] Alexander Alexander, *Alexander's Interpreting Tephilloth . . . An Entire New Work and a Useful Family Companion by A. Alexander, Original Translator of the Portuguese Jews' Daily and Festival Service into English, and the German and Polish Jews' Daily Prayers . . . Printed by and for L. Alexander* (London, 1817).

disparaging the good name of Levi as well.[43] Not unexpectedly, Hirschell promoted his own new prayer book for school use, which appeared only five years later in 1822. It was entitled *The Form of Daily Prayers According to the Custom of the German and Polish Jews as Read in their Synagogues and Used in their Families Carefully Translated from the Original Hebrew Published For the Benefit of the Jews' Free School.* Hirshell personally supervised the preparation of the Hebrew text while the translation was primarily based on that of David Levi, although the earlier translations of Gamaliel ben Pedahzur, B. Myers, and A. Alexander (but not Levi Alexander) were also consulted. For the first time, the direct impact of German Jewry is noticeable. The editor indicates that the German translations of liturgy by Euchel and Friedlander were consulted along with the Psalms translations of Mendelssohn as well as the Christian translations of the standard English Bible and that of Alexander Geddes.[44]

The preface to the prayer book was composed by Joshua Van Oven and is clearly written in the same spirit as that of Alexander Alexander with its emphasis on the universal urge to pray. The students of the Jews' Free School are urged "to give praise to the Omnipotent Creator of all things, to solicit his favour, and with a grateful heart to acknowledge his mercy and kindness." Similarly, "the wonderous composition of the Universe, the Immensity, the Grandeur, and the Order of the heavenly bodies, the intricate yet regular construction of the animal and vegetable creations, all excite our admiration of the First Great Cause, and our reverence for the Omnipotent Creator, whom we thus almost intuitively led to fear, to love, to worship, and to adore."[45] Clearly adumbrating the language of his later catechism,[46] Van Oven also stressed the biblical foundations of prayer, and the constancy of the traditional liturgical forms across the centuries. He acknowledges "the neglect and increasing ignorance of the sacred and ancient language," and he offers the naive hope that this translation "may revivify the sparks of religion and piety, and induce God's early selected people to return to the knowledge of their venerable language, whereby they may feel its sacred force and again address the Almighty with true heartfelt devotion, that their prayers may

---

[43] Hirschell's minimal English skills would not have allowed him to offer any serious judgment about translations. His skirmishes with Alexander were clearly of a personal nature and are summarized in Katz, *The Jews in the History of England*, pp. 326–28.

[44] *The Form of Daily Prayers According to the Custom of the German and Polish Jews . . . For the Benefit of the Jews' Free School* (London, 1822), pp. xiv–xv. Alexander Geddes (1737–1802), the Catholic Bible scholar, published his incomplete translation of *The Holy Bible . . .* in 2 volumes between 1792 and 1797.

[45] *The Form of Daily Prayers*, preface, p. v.

[46] On this, see chapter 3 and also my subsequent discussion.

be accepted as in days of yore."[47] To this is added another cautionary statement that "it never was in anyway contemplated that the translated prayer should supersede the use of the sacred original or in any way lead to a disuse of that holy language which, in truth, is the only remnant of inheritance left us from our forefathers."[48]

In a work directly sanctioned by the chief rabbi and directed to students learning the Hebrew language, such an expression regarding the inadequacy of translation is understandable. However, it is the only such statement I have yet to discover that acknowledges so explicitly that prayer in English is less valued than prayer in Hebrew, "the vehicle of divine revelation." It seems, however, to be an exception to the general trend earlier articulated by A. Alexander regarding the universality of prayer with his preference for understanding prayer in translated form over the rote recitation of the incomprehensible Hebrew. But even with this explicit wish that the translation not replace the Hebrew, the theme of the universality of prayer is clearly the primary message imparted. Van Oven, of all people, understood quite well that the translation, not the original, was the channel by which the specificity of Jewish liturgy could be converted into a sentiment shared by all humanity.

Because of its unusual nature, I offer one more example of the universalizing tendency of English translations of Jewish liturgy. This last case is well beyond the time frame I have set for myself but it illustrates quite well the tendencies we have discussed since the first complete prayer books of the early 1770s. In 1837, N. I. Vallentine composed in Hebrew a short booklet entitled *Korban Todah: The Form of Prayer and Thanksgiving to be Said by the Ladies when they go to the Synagogue on the First Time of Leaving Home After their Accouchment*. H. A. Henry, the master of the Jews' Free School, translated the original Hebrew liturgy into English. A quick perusal of the Hebrew introduction and its corresponding English version delineates quite distinctly the license of the translator to universalize the message of the author. In Vallentine's Hebrew version, the author begs the indulgence of his readership in offering this innovative prayer written for the specific needs of women to supplement the generic *birkat ha-gomel* (benediction of deliverance) prayer. Presented in classical rabbinic language with the patina of pious orthodoxy, Valentine explains how several women who had just given birth

pleaded and sought after distinguished God-fearing men to compose a prayer of praise and thanksgiving for child bearing Jewish women to the God of life on saving their souls from the danger of the pangs of birth. I searched in all

---

[47] *The Form of Daily Prayers*, p. xiii.
[48] Ibid., p. xiv.

petitionary prayers composed in our Hebrew language and I found nothing but the *birkat ha-gomel*. However, this prayer alone was not appropriate to calm their spirit since it is directed only to the past cause [of one's affliction] and to the individual, while they seek [a prayer] that focuses on both the past and the future and addresses two souls: the mother and child. For this I satisfied my own wish by carrying out their desire . . . by composing this prayer to the Creator of everything according to the ability of my intelligence and knowledge."[49]

The English version surely conveys the sense of the original but its embellishment underscores the human, not the specific Jewish, need of this liturgy:

> To give praise to the beneficent Creator of mankind, for all favors conferred, is a spontaneous feeling, inherent in the human breast. Delightful as such feeling may be, the mind is not at all times capable of selecting expressions suitable to the nature of the obligation bestowed. Hence the necessity of prescribed forms of prayers and thanksgiving for all seasons, and for all purposes. This subject, and the happy effects resulting therefrom to society at large, excited the serious attention of our rabbins of blessed memory; who, zealous in the cause of religion and morality, composed for us, a set of prayers and supplications for almost every requisite occasion. Among these, however, no specified form of thanksgiving is to be found, for ladies going to synagogue after their acouchment. . . . The necessity of the mother's thanks for past events, and supplications for her future welfare, as well as that of her tender offspring . . . has induced us to publish this short prayer, hoping it will prove acceptable to the Divine Creator.[50]

The divergence between the two versions is slight but, I would argue, not insignificant. It displays quite well the capacity of English to smooth out cultural difference, to homogenize the nature of prayer, and to integrate the distinctive flavor of the Hebrew liturgy into a universalizing form accessible to all humankind. This innocent exercise, hardly the product of more liberalizing reform tendencies, exposes once again the transformative power of English to reshape the primary medium of Jewish self-reflection and self-affirmation.

III

One of the marks of a changing consciousness on the part of Jews and Christians toward "the other" in early modern Europe was the emergence

---

[49] N. I. Vallentine and H. A. Henry, *Korban Todah: The Form of Prayer and Thanksgiving to Be Said by the Ladies* . . . (London 1837), *Hitnazlut ha-meḥabber*.

[50] Ibid., translator's preface.

of both literary and visual depictions of Jewish customs and ceremonies, produced by members of both communities. In the case of the works of Jewish self-portrayal, the authors were clearly interested in presenting a positive image of their community and its faith before a sometimes tolerant but sometimes hostile Christian reading public. For the first time, Jews composed works in foreign languages to influence public opinion, to correct the false impressions of uninformed and biased Christian authors, and to argue for the social and intellectual utility of Jews in Western culture. The first works of this genre were written in Italy by two Venetian rabbis, Leon Modena and Simone Luzzatto, in the middle of the seventeenth century. While each had somewhat different purposes, the two shared a common concern in presenting a positive profile of their community and its religious practices. Modena's work published in Italian in a form revised by the author appeared in 1638 as *Historia de riti hebraici*.[51] An unauthorized French version had appeared a year earlier and served as the basis of a new translation into English by Edmund Chilmead as *History of the rites, customs, and manner of life, of the present Jews, throughout the world*, published in London in 1650. Simon Oakley retranslated the work with additions on the Samaritans and Karaites. His version appeared in London in 1707 and was reissued in 1711. At about the same time, John Toland incorporated significant sections of Luzzatto's apologetic work into his *Reasons for Naturalizing the Jews in Great Britain . . .* that appeared in London in 1714.[52]

Besides these compendia of Jewish culture authored by Jews, a growing number of handbooks of Jewish customs appeared throughout the seventeenth and eighteenth centuries, especially in Holland, Germany, France, and England. They not only included narratives of Jewish life but also incorporated artistic renderings of Jewish rituals and holidays in synagogue and family scenes. The most famous of these works was the collection of magnificent engravings of Bernard Picart first published in Amsterdam in 1723. Picart's entire *Ceremonies and Religious Customs of the Various Nations of the Known World* appeared in English translation in six volumes in London between 1733 and 1737. Its first volume on the Jews included as well the complete narrative of Modena's work. As Richard Cohen has recently shown, this new literature of Picart and many

---

[51] On this work, see M. Cohen, "Leone da Modena's Riti: A Seventeenth-Century Plea for Social Toleration of Jews," *Jewish Social Studies* 34(1972): 287–321, reprinted in D. Ruderman, ed., *Essential Papers on Jewish Culture in Renaissance and Baroque Italy* (New York, 1992), pp. 429–73.

[52] See I. Barzilay, "John Toland's Borrowings from Simone Luzzatto," *Jewish Social Studies* 31 (1969): 75–81. On Luzzatto's apologetic work, see B. Ravid, *Economics and Toleration in Seventeenth Century Venice: The Background and Context of the Discorso of Simone Luzzatto* (Jerusalem, 1978).

others reveals the emergence of a new attitude toward Jews and Judaism, one that was even capable of presenting the internal, religious life of Jews in a relatively objective manner. Although the more conventional medieval stereotypes of Jewish life did not totally disappear, and they would return in new form with alarming ferocity in the nineteenth century, the public image of Jews as constructed by Jews and Christians through the eighteenth century was significantly changing.[53]

In England itself, Christians could learn about Jewish life from translations of such works as those of Modena and Picart but also from English traveler reports, accounts of Christian Hebraists, missionaries, and others. Most of this material has not been adequately studied but even a quick glimpse at the huge inventory of such works compiled by Cecil Roth confirms the initial impression of a significant interest on the part of Christian authors, from as early as the sixteenth century, in depictions of contemporary Jewish life and customs.[54] By the eighteenth century, however, a new phase of this literature emerges, clearly linked to the subject of this chapter. I refer to English depictions of Jewish liturgy, observances and customs written by Jews but primarily directed for internal rather than external usage. No doubt the apologetic dimension of these works is still present. The authors are still concerned with correcting the false and negative image of Jewish life in Christian eyes. But by the eighteenth century, many Jews were in need of such handbooks to orientate themselves about Jewish rituals and holidays. Unlike Modena and Luzzatto, who offered a narration of Jewish life for Christian readers, the authors of the new manuals were cognizant of the alarming need to inform Jews about basic concepts and ritual acts necessary for the preservation of Jewish life in the home and synagogue. And they were also painfully aware that these potential readers could only be addressed in the English language.[55]

The first work of this kind appeared in London in 1738 under the elaborate title *The Book of Religion, Ceremonies, and Prayers of the Jews as Practiced in the Synagogues and Families on all Occasions: On their Sab-*

---

[53] R. I. Cohen, *Jewish Icons: Art and Society in Modern Europe* (Berkeley, 1998), pp. 10–67.

[54] Roth, *Magna Bibliotheca*, "Contemporary Jewish Life and Customs," pp. 390–98.

[55] The only precedent for these manuals are some of the apologetic works composed by former conversos in the seventeenth and eighteenth centuries. Directed to their coreligionists, these works encouraged them to return to the Jewish fold by presenting the basic concepts and customs of Judaism to them in a clear and precise manner. For an introduction to some of this literature, see Y. Yerushalmi, *From Spanish Court to Italian Ghetto* (New York, 1971), chap. 8; Y. Kaplan, "The Portuguese Community in Amsterdam in the Seventeenth Century: Between Tradition and Change" (Hebrew), *Proceedings of the Israel Academy of the Sciences* 7 (1986–87): 161–81.

bath and other Holy-Days Throughout the Year, to which is Added a Preface Shewing the Intent of the Whole, the Contents and an Index, with the Hebrew Title of each Prayer made English; with many Remarkable Observations and Relations of the Rabbies; all of which are what the Modern Jews Religiously Observed. The author called himself Gamaliel ben Pedahzur. On the basis of an article in *Gentleman's Magazine* of 1758, Cecil Roth identified the author as an ashkenazic Jew named Abraham Meers, "a modest good man, who has favoured the Jews as much as he possibly could in this whole book, converted to the Christian religion." Roth, following Singer before him, underscores the numerous errors and distortions of the book, especially the "exaggerated importance [it gives] to the least attractive minutiae of observance and by an undue insistence upon anything of a scrofulous nature."[56] This seems to me an overly harsh assessment in contrast to that of Isidore Harris and Joseph Jacobs who had earlier described it as "an exceedingly quaint compilation, evidently written by a Jew."[57]

Meers is no intellectual giant, and some of his mistaken translations are indeed "howlers," as Cecil Roth called them. He is also fascinated with Jewish folklore, what Roth might have called "superstitions," and offers entertaining descriptions of Jewish dream interpretations, ghosts, evil spirits, the evil eye, witchcraft, a prayer for the willful waste of seed, the stinking breath of a wife, and male urination on the bed.[58] The latter items are obviously what Roth meant by "anything of a scrofulous nature." Meers's inclusion of such materials is reminiscent of similar mixtures of fact and fiction in the Christian inventories of Jewish customs mentioned earlier. Both the focus on these subjects as well as Meers's inaccuracies raise questions about the judgment and competency of its author, not necessarily about his motivation. Even if he did convert, he still viewed Judaism and Jewish ceremonial life in a sympathetic and favorable light. There is no reason to question his sincerity when he insists that Jews should not be ridiculed "on account of their religion." Nor is there reason to question the stated objective of his work:

Wherefore, I hope, no one will peruse this work of their Ceremonies and Prayers with such a thought I have collected their ceremonies, and represented the Difficulties thereof; in order to render those of my Christian readers the more endearing to them. And that the Jews who are fondest of their own, may not be

---

[56] C. Roth, "Gamaliel Ben Pedahzur and His Prayer Book," *Jewish Historical Society of England Miscellanies* 2 (1935): 1–8; Singer, "Early Translators and Translations," pp. 51–53. The reference cited by Roth is taken from *Gentleman's Magazine* 28 (1758): 468.

[57] In *The Jewish Encyclopedia* 5 (1903): 563.

[58] Gamaliel Ben Pedahzur, Gent., *The Book of Religion, Ceremonies and Prayer of the Jews* . . . (London, 1738), pp. 71–88.

less obliged to me for explaining the Meanings of, and citing the Quotations for theirs; to instruct the Illiterate of their nation, in what they are ignorant of at present."[59]

Presenting a positive image of Jewish life to Christians is then only the first of his book's objectives. The second is for Jewish self-edification. For this reason he translates the Hebrew prayers for "beginners in the Hebrew Tongue" and provides an alphabetical index of prayers and also a table of contents of the ceremonies discussed—in short, all the trappings of a "hands-on" manual for Jewish usage. Despite his misgivings, Roth draws attention to the work as a reliable window into the social history of London's ashkenazic community in the early eighteenth century. He points to the peculiar penetration of some sephardic customs into askenazic practice, the custom of selling *mitsvot*, the characteristic Anglo-Jewish pronunciation of Hebrew, particular foods and costumes, and more. Nevertheless, he is noticeably upset that Meers "had the impertinence to imagine that the book might be utilized also by those Jews who could not understand the Service in the original." "The hope was preposterous," Roth adds, as he unmasks his identity, thus affording himself the pleasure "to deprive the apostate of this last shred of interest."[60]

Needless to say, Roth's judgmental posture is out of character with his role as a historian. Indeed, it was not preposterous to assume that the work was consulted by Jews, especially its preliminary translations of prayers. Even so reputable a prayer book as the Jews' Free School version of 1822, as we have seen, openly declared its indebtedness to Meers's preliminary translations composed almost ninety years earlier. And even more startling is Levi Alexander's "borrowing" from Meers in his own Jewish compendium of 1819 (to be considered shortly). Alexander incorporates Meers's "quaint" descriptions of dream interpretations, the evil eye, Jewish ghosts, and more, into his own work without acknowledgment, of course. Irrespective of the crudities of his imperfect composition, Abraham Meers seems to have been the first English author to produce a manual of Jewish life both to satisfy the curiosity of Christian observers and to provide rudimentary instruction for Jews on reading Jewish prayers and performing Jewish rituals. For this reason, his guidebook is still of considerable interest, contrary to Roth's personal estimation.

David Levi's *A Succinct Account of the Duties, Rites, and Ceremonies of the Jews as they are Observed, by the whole Jewish Nation Throughout the World, and the Present Time, also an Account of the Jewish Calendar to which is added a faithful and impartial Account of the Mishna, and*

[59] Pedahzur, *The Book of Religion*, pp. iii–iv.
[60] Roth, "Gamaliel Ben Pedahzur," pp. 6–8. The last citation is from p. 8.

the Teachers Thereof, in their Respective Ages; till the Time of Rabbi Judah Hakadosh, who compiled the Mishna. With a chronological Summary, of several remarkable things relating to the People of the Jews, from the most authentic Records was a vast improvement on Meers's work. As we have mentioned,[61] this was Levi's first publication, printed in London in 1782, and it was clearly meant to fulfill a need not met by previous works written by either Jews or Christians. Levi had no illusions about the low level of Hebraic literacy in his community: "Yet it hath please the Divine Providence, to appoint our Lot, in a Country, where the Hebrew is not used as a common Language, and therefore but imperfectly understood by many, it must certainly be very acceptable to those, who are natives of England, to Receive a Clear, Impartial, and Distinct Account, of their Religious Tenets, in English."[62] He was also quite aware of the inadequacies of earlier works, either uninformed or intended "to throw a ridicule upon the whole Jewish Community."[63]

Levi's exhaustive handbook summarizes the Jewish holiday cycle, beginning with the Sabbath and the calculation of the new moon and then each holiday with its particular ceremonies and rituals. It also includes translations of specific prayers, translations of the marriage ceremony, the *ḥaliẓah* ceremony, a sample writ of divorce, the construction of phylacteries and the *mezuzah* (with illustrations), the service in the house of mourning, and the grace after meals. In addition, in its second half, it provides a chronological survey of all the rabbis until the time of codification of the *mishnah*, a clear summary of the sections of the *mishnah*, and a briefer comment on the *gemarah*. It includes, as we have mentioned, a long digression challenging some historical statements of Dr. Humphrery Prideaux on the Jewish notion of resurrection.[64]

Levi's is a serious work, meant to be accurate, comprehensive, and useful. There are no fanciful digressions regarding Jewish folk customs, only Levi's initial polemic in print against Christian scholarship on Judaism. And outside of this spirited attack, the book is clearly intended as a book of handy instruction for Jews. As a work of translation, it is impressive in its scope, in its readability, and in its matter-of-fact style of presentation. Within the limits of a single volume, Levi includes a dazzling amount of information. The scriptural basis of Judaism is constantly emphasized, with a large array of biblical citations. But Levi makes clear to his readers that Judaism comprises both a written and oral law, and the *mishnah* receives a substantial treatment.

[61] See chapter 2 above.
[62] Levi, *A Succinct Account*, preface.
[63] Ibid., preface.
[64] See chapter 4.

But even such an ambitious agenda must have its limits. With only the last ten pages devoted to the *gemarah*, the reader receives the distinct impression that the oral law is essentially the *mishnah*, to which Levi devotes about ninety pages.[65] Furthermore, most of the description of the *mishnah* is actually a historical account of ancient Judaism until the time of Judah the Prince. The historical thus takes precedence over the prescriptive, halachic part. Levi succeeds more than adequately in providing a guide to essential Jewish practice for those who know no Hebrew, but he fails to provide a summary of Jewish law in general. Synagogue and home worship on sabbaths and holidays becomes the essence of Jewish practice. In this shortcut to the essentials of Jewish living, the scope of the theological and juridical is severely attenuated. Even armed with a copy of Levi's faithful translations of the liturgy, the user of Levi's instruction book is offered no more that a bare skeleton of Jewish civilization, denuded of its intellectual, literary, and aesthetic dimensions. Levi's prodigious effort notwithstanding, his *Succinct Account* reduces the meaning of Judaism to an arid and emotionless instruction manual. It shows the practitioner what to do; but it provides neither the intellectual justification nor the spiritual motivation regarding why it should be done in the first place. In the absence of a nurturing family life, a vibrant communal setting of learning and celebration, and the knowledge of a holy language linking this community across time and space, could a mere English digest serve the purpose for which Levi had hoped? The answer is obvious.

Levi's handbook remained the standard English guide to Jewish practice for almost four decades. Given the high regard the chief rabbi Hirschell had for his work and his uncompromising orthodoxy, it assumed a prominent place in the instruction of uneducated Jews young and old. Levi's chief competitors in the market of Judaic works in England were the Alexanders, as we have seen. When Levi Alexander took over his father's business, he found himself frustrated by both Rabbi Hirschell and his sephardic counterpart Raphael Meldola, who clearly favored the products of David Levi's hands and the republication of his works after his death by others. Alexander published his prayer book in 1814 and 1815 in installments, placing on the wrappers highly insulting remarks about both rabbis.[66] Even earlier, in 1808, he published *The Axe Laid to the Root, or Ignorance and Superstition Evident in the Character of the Rev. Solomon Hirschell Major Rabbi Commonly Called the High Priest of the Jews in England.* . . . Alexander explicitly mentioned the rabbi's support of another edition of the festival prayers rather than his own and complained that he was "not ashamed of its blunders and impieties" while

---

[65] Levi, *A Succinct Account*, pp. 210–300 (on the *mishnah*), 300–310 (on the *gemarah*).
[66] See note 43.

"secretly helping in the vineyard of Mammon." In the course of his long diatribe against the rabbi, he proclaims:

> As a Printer and Publisher of the first translation of our Hebrew Prayers, I find myself hurt by your partiality towards my Antagonists. . . . My father before me had satisfied the public of his capacity to translate our Prayers by the portion he published about forty years ago. We are both highly serviceable to the late David Levi, in all his labours of this sort; For I can say as a fact, that Levi would never have been known as an Author, if my father had not lent him the first assistance in his Account of the Rites and Ceremonies, a book he borrowed mostly from Buxtorf and Wooton's Miscellanies.[67]

Levi Alexander's intemperate criticism of the rabbi inevitably led him to question David Levi's credentials as well. As Alexander saw it, Levi could not have produced his handbook without his father's help and, in any case, the book was unoriginal and "borrowed" from Christian authors. In the light of such a pronouncement, it is truly ironic to consider the publication of Alexander's own manual of Jewish observance published in 1819. He gave it the immodest title: *Alexander's Hebrew Ritual and Doctrinal Explanation of the Whole Ceremonial Law Oral and Tradition of the Jewish Community in England and Foreign Parts Being a Necessary Companion to the Holy Scriptures Together with several remarkable Events relative to the People of the Jews from the Most Ancient Records.* Alexander dedicates the work to the duke of Kent, expecting rather naively that the good duke would be interested in reading a book on Jewish rituals in the first place: "and notwithstanding, your goodness of heart may have placed you at the head of a Society, of seemingly opposite principles; yet I presume, every effort for the general diffusion of knowledge, will not fail at all times to have your Royal Highness's approbation; more especially that knowledge which is calculated to make mankind acquainted with the being and attributes of the omnipotent God."[68]

He tries again to justify himself to a Christian readership in the preface:

> Under the happy form of government which has long fostered our existence in England, and to which, as Israelites, we are anxious to pay the most profound

---

[67] Levi Alexander, *The Axe Laid to the Root, or Ignorance and Superstition Evident in the Character of the Rev. Solomon Hirschell . . .* (London, 1808), pp. 21–23. The last quote is from p. 23. On William Wotton (1666–1726) and his work, see *Dictionary of National Biography* 31 (New York, 1909): 976–78. In 1718 Wotton published his two-volume work entitled *Miscellaneous Discourses Relating to Traditions and Usages of the Scribes and Pharisees.* It consisted of four parts: the first two dealt with the *mishnah*; the third with the *shema* prayer, phylacteries, gates and doorposts (the *mezuzah*); and the fourth with the sabbath.

[68] Levi Alexander, *Alexander's Hebrew Ritual and Doctrinal Explanation of the Whole Ceremonial Law . . .* (London, 1819), p. iii.

respect; in a country where we enjoy laws suited to our station, and where our condition is pre-eminently ameliorated, nothing can require less apology for its appearance than an impartial and correct account of all the rites and ceremonies of the most ancient people in the world. . . . The religious duties enjoined by God to his people, need here neither comment nor detail; but the particular manner of keeping those ordinances in a state of exile, as we are now in, may not be unprofitable to an English reader, as well as many of our Community, who in their youth have neglected their Hebrew learning, are happy to receive instruction from an English version; and certainly there cannot be a more laudable undertaking than that of conveying that species of knowledge to the world, by which man becomes acquainted with his duties, and is enabled to answer the great end of his creation.[69]

Despite the flowery rhetoric, Levi's argument in favor of the universal import of his parochial handbook seems rather unpersuasive in the final analysis. His final lines seem utterly confused and contradictory:

Secluded as we are from the rest of the world, and confined within our own narrow sphere, by a rigid adherence to rules from which we cannot depart; and connected by marriage and diet, we present the world with a spectacle as singular as it is ancient and as remarkable as it is holy: A Faith! supported by long established rites, punctilious, and ceremonies, and which are here laid down for general information . . . a reward if the reader is rewarded [and] if not, [he] must be content with the adage of Pope or Seneca [sic], you can't please everybody.[70]

Such a self-promotion regarding Jewish seclusion, narrowness, and rigidity would hardly sell books, certainly not to Christians! It seems as if Alexander had hardly convinced himself of the need of such a work, let alone the necessity of the rituals and prescriptions the book purported to describe.

Be that as it may, Levi's ambivalence regarding the value of his endeavor was surely heightened by the fact that he had hardly written one original line in the entire book. *Alexander's Hebrew Ritual* was nothing more than a flagrant act of plagiarism. Its major source was none other than Levi's *Succinct Account*. That he could offer unflattering comments about Levi's unoriginality, and then turn around to copy from the same author, was surely an act of remarkable temerity on his part. Levi's copying is so obvious (he includes, for example, Levi's long polemic against Prideaux,[71] copies precisely Levi's long descriptions of the holidays and special religious ceremonies, and even divides his work into the same two parts of

[69] Ibid., p. vi.
[70] Ibid., pp. vi–vii.
[71] Ibid., pp. 244–55.

Levi's composition), that it most likely could be detected by anyone familiar with its source. Alexander also copied heavily from Abraham Meers's book, as we have mentioned, and even includes some lines from Abraham Tang's translation of the *Ethics of the Fathers*, a work he had published many years earlier.[72] The only original lines I have been able to detect, other than the preface, is a short excursus on the synagogues and their cemeteries in London and a brief note on Jewish charity.[73] Alexander's compendium was clearly not a literary and probably not a financial success either. It is not hard to understand why, with such unsavory competition, Rabbi Hirschell gave his unqualified support to the original publications of David Levi.

IV

By the early nineteenth century the Jewish catechism made its first appearance in England. Published as early as 1782 in German translations, Jewish catechisms were produced with growing regularity throughout the next century. One early estimate of the number of these works published throughout Europe is 161 between the years 1782 and 1884. There were probably considerably more. As Jacob Petuchowski and others have shown, the catechism was created in schools where little or no Talmud was taught; it was often associated with the popular confirmation ceremony; and it stressed the universal and moral foundations of Judaism at the expense of the ritualistic and the particular. As a necessary means of promoting Jewish identity with the disintegration of strong communal cohesiveness, the catechism defined Judaism as a confession, stressing the dogmatic content of Judaism, offering a creedal affirmation at the expense of ceremonial law, and providing a cursory textbook as a replacement to any substantial encounter with the original sources of Judaism.[74]

A Jewish catechism had actually appeared in England over a hundred years earlier. It was the English translation of Abraham Yagel's catechism written in Italy as early as the late sixteenth century. The English version was entitled simply *The Jew's Catechism Containing the Thirteen Articles*

---

[72] Ibid., p. 8, is clearly taken from the introduction to Tang's translation of the *Ethics of the Fathers*. On Tang and this work, see chapter 3 and my subsequent discussion.

[73] Alexander, *Alexander's Hebrew Ritual*, pp. 197, 210–11.

[74] J. Petuchowski, "Manuals and Catechisms of the Jewish Religion in the Early Period of Emancipation," in *Studies in Nineteenth-Century Jewish Intellectual History*, ed. A. Altmann (Cambridge, Mass., 1964), pp. 47–64; S. Schreiber, "Catechisms," *Jewish Encyclopedia* 3 (1903): 621–24; M. Eliav, *Ha-Ḥinnukh ha-Yehudi be-Germaniya Bimai ha-Haskalah ve-ha-Emanzipazia* (Jerusalem, 1960), pp. 243–59. According to Eliav, the first modern catechism was that of V. Dessau, *Grundsätze der jüdischen Religion* of 1782.

of the Jewish Religion. It was published in London in 1680 and reprinted
in 1721 with a "prefatory discourse against Atheism."[75] But for all inten-
sive purposes, the heyday of the catechism in England was postponed
until 1815 when Rabbi Solomon Hirschell commissioned S. I. Cohen, a
German Jew, to prepare a Hebrew catechism called *Shorshei Emunah* for
the use of Jewish children in England. It was published with the eloquent
English translation of Joshua Van Oven, which was entitled: *The Elements of the Jewish Faith for the Use of Jewish Youth of Both Sexes.* The
English version without the Hebrew original was subsequently published
in Richmond, Virginia, in 1817 by H. Cohen. Because the catechism was
to a great extent a German Jewish import, I am primarily interested here
in its English version and the extent to which it facilitated the teaching of
Judaism in the English language and reflected the larger trends of Anglici-
zation already noted.

Although Cohen had previously prepared a German edition of this
work, the version he offered Hirschell was longer and written with its
English audience in mind. The preface and subsequent dialogue between
teacher and student are relatively innocuous and unoriginal. Cohen reflects on the universality of belief in one God known through the awe of
his creation. He stresses the moral nature of all religion, singling out the
Noahide laws open to all humanity. For Cohen, their ordinances reflect
three grand principles: the refinement of thought and understanding
"whereby we cling to truth and avoid falsehood and deceit, which com-
prehends the love of intellectual purity, and the negation of the grosser
corporeal speculations"; the love of creation; and "a sacred observance of
the laws of nature and a repugnance to any act that shall tend to derange
them."[76] Although anyone upholding these commandments is considered
a religious person, God treated the Jews with special affection by bestow-
ing on them a special law. Nevertheless, they are instructed never to mis-
sionize and even to dissuade potential converts.

The issue of Christian missionizing of Jews receives special attention in
the author's preface, clearly reflecting the actual concerns of the Anglo-
Jewish leadership in the first decades of the century. Because all religions
lead to morality, Cohen contends

> it follows that man is destined by the circumstances of his birth and education,
> to adhere to the religion of his fathers; and in most cases the apostate . . . is

---

[75] On this work and its Catholic background, see S. Maybaum, *Abraham Jagel's Katchis-
mus Lekah-tob* (Berlin, 1892). On Yagel, see generally Ruderman, *Kabbalah, Magic, and
Science.* On the history of the English catechism, see the massive work of I. Green, *The
Christian's ABC: Catechisms and Catechizing in England, c. 1530–1740* (Oxford, 1996).

[76] S. I. Cohen, *Elements of the Jewish Faith Translated from the Hebrew* (Richmond, Va.,
1817), p. 5 (the text is identical with the English text of the first edition).

generally without any pure intention, and only takes such a step from a sordid interest, or a desire to enjoy some advantages among the partizans of the faith he has joined. . . . It is therefore a strange thing in our eyes, that persons should be found who lay in wait for the members of the Jewish faith . . . to entice them by flattery, lures, and tempting gifts, to abandon the religion wherein they were born and educated, in order to embrace Christianity![77]

Cohen ends his plea for allowing the Jews the dignity of their own faith on a positive note:

Behold the light of truth is now illuminating all Europe; peace and brotherly love is prevailing among nations of various religious persuasions; the sword of persecution has been returned to its sheath, and those dark ages, when nations strove with nations, and made human blood flow in streams, on account of the different modes of worship, have passed away; all nations now acknowledge one universal Father; and virtue, justice, and righteousness are the only tests whereby men are estimated.[78]

The actual catechism itself reflects the universalizing sentiment of the preface. Students are first introduced to religion, the existence of God, and creator and sustainer of all matter, before Judaism as a particular manifestation of religion is presented. Cohen elaborates on the thirteen principles of faith and the decalogue, stresses the civic responsibilities of all Jews to honor the king, and underscores the duty of all Jews to love mankind as a whole.

Except for its denunciation of Christian missionaries, Cohen's catechism with its English translation seemed to be nothing more than an innocent, bland, and highly uncontroversial presentation of the Jewish faith meant for both Jewish and Christian eyes. But one Jewish reader was incensed by its publication and finally opted to publish a most uncomplimentary account of its author, its translator, and, last but not least, its official rabbinic sponsors, primarily Solomon Hirschell and secondarily Raphael Meldola. The reader was the biblical scholar and engraver, Solomon Bennett, who we have already encountered regarding his plans to retranslate the Bible. Bennett first published in Hebrew his *Tene Bikkurim* (A basket of criticism) in 1817, clearly directed to a continental audience of rabbis and educated Hebraists as a blatant effort to embarrass the rabbis before their peers. It immediately incurred the wrath of the two rabbis who apparently sanctioned a vicious attack on Bennett's work as well as his character in another Hebrew pamphlet entitled *Minḥat Kena'ot* (An offering of jealousy/vengeance), written by a certain Meir Rintel and pub-

[77] Ibid., pp. 7–8.
[78] Ibid., p. 8.

18. Self-portrait of Solomon Bennett.

lished in the same year. As if this wasn't sufficient, a Meir Hahn published several Hebrew letters against Bennett in Hamburg, also in 1817, entitled *Shot Lashon* (The whip of the tongue). Finally, Bennett responded the next year in an English work called *The Present Reign of the Synagogue of Duke's Place Displayed*, published in London (fig.18).[79]

Arthur Barnett has previously studied this controversy and has argued persuasively that the primary issue in these polemics was a personality clash between Bennett and Hirschell. The more Bennett attacked, the more Hirschell counterattacked through his representatives. As we have seen in the case of Levi Alexander, Hirschell, although relatively inarticu-

---

[79] For previous accounts of this debate over Cohen's catechism, see Barnett, "Solomon Bennett," pp. 101–6; Katz, *Jews in the History of England*. pp. 328–29; Endelman, *The Jews of Georgian England*, pp. 142–45.

late as an intellectual opponent, had his means of severely punishing his opponents. As a personal clash of interests and as a conflict involving the integrity of the rabbinate in England and beyond, the debate should not detain us here. However, the substance of Bennett's charges, his own understanding and those of his opponents of what a catechism should be, and how this relates to the presentation of Judaism in the English language deserve our attention.

Although Barnett is probably right in seeing Bennett's attack on *The Elements of Faith* as primarily directed against Hirschell rather than the content of the catechism itself, it appears to me too facile to dismiss his intellectual arguments altogether. Both in his Hebrew book and in the expanded English version of his polemic, he makes specific criticisms of Cohen's pamphlet that deserve a closer scrutiny. He begins by acknowledging the positive: "I own conscientiously, that the book, the Elements of Faith . . . contains a good stock of religious and moral principles suitable for the purpose intended; the Hebrew language thereof, is also plain and easy, agreeable to the taste of Jewish youth; God, that they might only practice it." The difficulty arises, however, because Cohen "did not care whether his lessons were agreeable with the text of the Pentateuch or not; if its precepts were of the nature of a general accord with the Hebrew forms, or that of mere private and individual sentiments, if it be consistent with Scripture, with reason, and matters of facts, or only sentimental, and but matters of opinion; proper reference in some of his lessons to the original text, ought also to be have been strictly observed, in a book which is adapted for youth."[80]

Bennett then proceeds to present nine specific criticisms of the text among them, Cohen's imprecise replication of the Noahide laws; his omission of the biblical basis for Sabbath observance; his neglect to mention the biblical name of the holiday of Shevuot; his extension of the commandment to honor parents to include siblings (a "Talmudic ethic," not a biblical one); and his sloppy derivation of the festivals not from the Pentateuch but from a logical inference regarding sabbath worship.[81] There is a clear consistency throughout: the foundation of Judaism for Bennett is biblical. If one is to present an accurate formulation of what Jewish faith is for young people, it needs to link precisely the principles of Judaism with biblical proof texts. Lacking the latter, they represent only the personal opinion of educators or rabbis.

---

[80] Salomon Bennett, *The Present Reign of the Synagogue of Duke's Place Displayed in a Series of Critical, Theological and Rabbinical Discussions on a Hebrew Pamphlet Entitled Minḥat Kena'ot* (London, 1818), p. 20.
[81] Ibid., pp. 22–47.

Rintel's rebuttal focuses more on the character of Bennett, casting aspersions on his orthodoxy. He reviews carefully Bennett's nine points, arguing in each case that Cohen's articulation is fully in line with traditional faith. He substantiates this view by citing regularly the Talmud and medieval codes. At one point, Rintel succinctly captures Bennett's position: "You have demonstrated how you prefer the opinion of the Karaites over the *midrashim* of the rabbis and also what the Men of the Great Assembly [the precursors of the rabbis] established."[82] He concedes only "that some things in the preface of the *Elements of Faith* are of a questionable nature," but since this was written after Rabbi Hirschell had inspected it, the rabbi could not be held responsible for an indiscretion.[83] What he may have had in mind was the unrestrained attack on missionaries. But this concession was surely unnecessary since Bennett never mentioned it.

Hahn's collection of letters opens with a strong endorsement of Cohen and his catechism, singling out especially the remarks on missionaries and the use of the book for Jews and Christians alike. The rest of the work is hardly of great consequence, except for an interesting short letter written by Cohen himself expressing his sense of shock and disappointment over Bennett's attack. He finds little merit in any of Bennett's specific charges and does not consider them worthy of his response. What is most interesting, however, is the general way he characterizes his approach in contrast to that of his opponent. For Cohen, "Most of our Torah consists of laws, testimonies and statutes based on moral authority, especially good for Israel, given from God's love to his people in order that they will be enlightened and prosper in this world and the next. However, according to his [Bennett's] strange opinion, they are only a rod of chastisement to subdue and to sadden the hearts, saying: 'Cease your activity from day to day, and if not, I will chastise your ruthlessly. Do this and this and don't ask why! And don't investigate the reason, and if not, I will blot out your memory from humanity for it is sufficient for you that this is a ruling in the *gemarah* and codes'. . . . He thus was incensed with me for mentioning the reason behind the essential commandments according to reason and morality."[84]

Cohen's understanding of Bennett's position is generally consistent with Rintel's and with Bennett's own words. Bennett was a literalist who saw the catechism as a precise formulation of Jewish articles of faith. As such, each article required a strong scriptural grounding to be considered

---

[82] Meir Rintel, *Minḥat Kena'ot* (London, 1817), p. 14.

[83] Ibid., English appendix, p. ii.

[84] Meir Hahn, *Shot Lashon* (Hamburg, 1817), pp. 4–5. My thanks to Professor Shmuel Feiner for supplying me a copy of this rare pamphlet.

true, what Rintel called a "Karaite" position. The only statement that seems to contradict this position is the statement of Cohen that Bennett demanded blind obedience to the rulings of the *gemarah* and codes. But this observation is obviously a misstatement since Bennett always challenged Cohen on the basis of biblical, not rabbinic statements.

Why then did Bennett assume so strongly the biblicist position he did take? Was it simply a pretext for hammering his hated rabbinic opponent, or can one detect a more ideological position on his part, or, at least, a particular intellectual style? From Bennett's other writings, especially his efforts to defend the integrity of the biblical text against Christian misrepresentations, it is obvious he cared deeply about what Scripture actually said and prided himself on his Hebraic erudition to ascertain its correct meaning. At the same time, as his opponents took pleasure in pointing out, he was not an observant "rabbinical" Jew. He once declared that "love, unity, and justice are the chief points of the universe. The rest, I look upon merely as ceremonial affections, which can make no difference with mankind at large and less to a Supreme Power. In this principle I live, and in this principle I will continue."[85]

One possibility for understanding his strong biblicism is to suggest that it was rooted in the Christian Protestant world he had inhabited since leaving eastern Europe at a young age, especially the religious ambience he encountered in England. He had lived in London for nearly twenty years virtually ostracized from the organized Jewish community whose leadership he had come to despise, while developing meaningful social and intellectual relations with Christians who supported him enthusiastically in his literary studies of the Bible. Rintel's designation of Bennett as a Karaite may not be far off the mark. In Yosef Kaplan's fascinating study of the meaning of "Karaites" in early eighteenth-century Amsterdam, he points to the pervasive influence of the Christian Hebraist Richard Simon's idealization of the Karaites, especially the correlation he made between Karaites and Protestants and Catholics and rabbinic Jews.[86] Si-

---

[85] Cited by Barnett, "Solomon Bennett," p. 92, from *The Constancy of Israel*. In the light of my interpretation of Bennett's understanding of Judaism presented here, I find it altogether unconvincing what Marsha Keith Schuchard suggests about his possible Sabbatean, Masonic, alchemical and kabbalistic interests. See her "Blake's Healing Trio: Magneticism, Medicine, and Mania," *Blake: An Illustrated Quarterly* 23 (1989): 20–31, especially 27–30. His social relations with Christian artists need not suggest at all a spiritual or intellectual compatibility with them.

[86] Y. Kaplan, "'Karaites' in Early Eighteenth-Century Amsterdam," in *Sceptics, Millenarians and Jews*, ed. D. Katz and J. Israel (Leiden, 1990), pp. 221–29, especially pp. 228–29. See also J. van den Berg, "Proto-Protestants? The Image of the Karaites as a Mirror of the Catholic-Protestant Controversy in the Seventeenth Century," in *Jewish-Christian Relations in the Seventeenth Century: Studies and Documents*, ed. J. van den Berg and E.G.E. van der Wall (Dordrecht, 1988), pp. 33–49.

mon's insight fits Bennett and the dispute with his rabbinic adversaries quite well. He was a "Protestant" Jew, affirming a universal notion of the Diety while upholding a deep-seated biblicism reinforced by his textual studies and the conversations he held with his Christian associates. To him the English catechism for Jews was appropriate as long as it faithfully reflected positions clearly articulated in Scripture itself. As a digest of mere opinions of later rabbis loosely supported by the biblical text, it could do untold harm to innocent youth who were not proficient enough to consult the text directly. If my interpretation of Bennett's posture is correct, then both the emergence of the Jewish catechism in England and the ideological debate it engendered were both by-products of the larger religious and cultural setting to which Anglo-Jewry were so intensely exposed.

Cohen's catechism specified that it was written for both sexes. Nevertheless, only a few years later, a catechism addressed specifically to female children appeared, emanating from the special school for girls of the Jews' hospital. The hospital, founded in 1807 by a group of wealthy ashkenazic Jews, was both an old age home and a trade school for the poor. Boys were taught shoemaking, chairmaking, and cabinetmaking, while the girls learned domestic skills so that they could be hired to work in wealthy Jewish homes, generally by the age of fifteen.[87] *The Jewish Preceptress, or, Elementary Lessons, Written Chiefly for the Use of Female Children Educated at the Jews' Hospital by a Daughter of Israel* appeared in 1818, with the stated objective "to aid instruction of Children in an humble station and calculated to impress on their minds sentiments of religion and virtue."[88] Given the specific needs of the school, its relatively uneducated and undisciplined student body, as well as the lack of scholarly pretensions of its author, the manual has its special character. Nevertheless, it still exemplifies the general trend of catachismic instruction in English where general religious and moral instruction seem to have assumed primary importance at the expense of imparting information about particular Jewish beliefs and rituals.

For *The Jewish Preceptress*, the essence of Jewish instruction is the fear of God, who should be addressed constantly in prayer; the strict observance "of the rites of our holy religion"; and the observance of the Sabbath.[89] Besides citing a few biblical quotations (without reference to book or chapter), however, these general concerns are only mentioned without detailed elaboration. What seems more compelling is the obligation to obey parents and superiors for "Esther listened to her uncle Mordecai,

---

[87] See Endelman, *The Jews of Georgian England*, pp. 236–42.

[88] *The Jewish Preceptress, or, Elementary Lessons, Written Chiefly for the Use of Female Children* . . . (London ,1818), p. ix.

[89] Ibid., pp. 13–32.

obeyed him exactly, and thereby became (through Divine Providence) the Saviour of the House of Israel. . . . Ruth obeyed the commands of Naomi and through her obedience became the wife of Boaz, and the grandmother of David, from whose royal house will come the promise of the Messiah."[90] Like Esther and Ruth, it is incumbent on the young girls of Jews' hospital to be submissive to their own elders and to those who care for them, especially the patrons of the institution that supports them:

> Bear always in mind, I conjure you, that you owe the Patrons of this noble institution, the most lively gratitude, and the most implicit submission. It has pleased God . . . to place your parents in a station that will not permit them either to maintain and instruct you in those duties which alone can make you good and happy. Your generous Benefactors have rescued you from this deplorable state of poverty and ignorance! They have placed you in a most desirable asylum, where every care is taken of your health and morals. You are bountifully fed, neatly clothed, and tenderly sheltered from evil: and taught by industry to procure an honest subsistence, when of an age to quit this blessed home. . . . But above all, how earnestly are the principles of religion and piety instilled in your mind: . . . Gratitude, humility, obedience, industry, truth, a teachable spirit: these are the qualities expected from you, these are the duties the performance of them to the best of your power will endear you to your benefactors, make you valuable members of society, and insure to you the divine protection, while a contrary conduct will make you odious to your fellow creatures, and be offensive to God.[91]

Despite its Jewish sponsorship, there is little to distinguish the education of these Jewish children from their counterparts in Christian schools. Critical elements are submissiveness, gratitude to the wealthy patrons, and industry to serve the latter as obedient domestic help. This last quality is not specifically Jewish but English: "The industry of England's sons is as proverbial as their bravery in the field, or their generosity to a conquered enemy; and this industry has raised England to a proud height among surrounding empires."[92] Moreover, it is the consciousness of class and gender not Jewish solidarity, with which these young girls are inculcated. The result is the natural harmony of the classes, where each knows its place: "and it is admirable to observe the regular gradations of industry, by which the three classes of society, the great, the middling,[93] and the

[90] Ibid., p. 34.
[91] Ibid., pp. 39–40.
[92] Ibid., p. 52.
[93] On the appearance of this term in early nineteenth-century England, see A. Briggs, "The Language of Class in Early Nineteenth-Century England," in *Essays in Labour History in Memory of G.D.H. Cole*, ed. A. Briggs and J. Saville (London, 1960), pp. 43–73.

poor are united. The peasant labors for his immediate subsistence . . . the labor of the mechanic and the ingenuity of the artist . . . the Statesman in the Cabinet, the Soldier in the field, the Sailor in the Ocean."[94] And similarly nature differentiates the male from the female: "but the gentle female is more peculiarly formed by nature to be feeling and tender. It is hers to exercise the rites of hospitality, the whispers of benevolence, and the soothing offices of charity. . . . Without these qualities, a female cannot be estimable. But she whose heart is hardened to the voice of sorrow or the cry of distress, is a Monster! a disgrace to her sex, and the curse of her family!"[95]

The manual then extols the virtues of a good house servant—industry, obedience, attentiveness, and truthfulness—that will "endear you to your superiors, and make you most happy in yourselves, and a bright example to others in your station."[96] Instruction in the basic features of the Jewish holidays is offered in the remainder of the book, with some cursory reflections on "a future state," that is, on the rewards of an afterlife.[97] The author closes with an apology for the low level of the handbook ("I am writing to children whose uninformed minds will not admit of more than an outline") and the low level of the author's educational credentials ("the production of an unlettered female")."[98] As a textbook in transmitting class, gender, civic, and institutional obligations and loyalties, the author apparently succeeds in imparting her unambiguous message. As a textbook for teaching Judaism, however, besides a scant review of the Jewish calendar and a general appeal to religion and morality, the catechism has little to impart. It offers a sobering look at the pedagogic priorities the patrons of the Jews' hospital assigned themselves in offering a "Jewish" education to the poor children under their supervision.

One additional catechism published in London is worthy of some attention in this chapter despite its late date (1835). *A Manual of Judaism Detailed in a Conversation Between a Rabbi and His Pupil Being an Introduction into the Knowledge of the Principles of the Jewish Faith for the Use of the Juvenile Members of that Persuasion* was written by the same Joshua Van Oven who has translated S. I. Cohen's manual of 1815. That Van Oven decided to compose his own work some twenty years after the appearance of the earlier handbook suggests, with the passage

---

My thanks to Arthur Kiron for the reference. See now D. Wahrman, *Imagining the Middle Class: The Political Representation of Class in Britain, c. 1780–1840* (Cambridge, 1995).

[94] *The Jewish Preceptress*, pp. 52–53. This passage was previously cited by Endelman, *The Jews of Georgian England*, p. 240.

[95] *The Jewish Preceptress*, pp. 55–56.

[96] Ibid., p. 59.

[97] Ibid., pp. 91–94.

[98] Ibid., p. 95.

19. Joshua Van Oven's grandchildren, Lionel Van Oven and his sister.

of time, a dissatisfaction on his part with the original text. There are clearly noticeable differences between the two works. I have already had occasion to mention Van Oven's composition regarding the deistic positions he and his father adopted (fig. 19).[99] I shall add here only a few remarks about its innovative features as a Jewish catechism.

Like its predecessors, Van Oven's work introduces the notion of religion in general and only later focuses on the specifics of Judaism. In the context of religious education, as we have seen, Van Oven has no compunctions in citing Joseph Priestley and even another "acute Unitarian writer."[100] His manual, like the others, is also heavily based on biblical instruction. At one point, it specifically mentions the importance of translating the Bible as a prerequisite to religious instruction.

Three novel aspects of the work, however, distinguish it from the earlier compositions. In the first place, Van Oven is more self-conscious about the unique challenges of elementary education and the need to develop new educational strategies to overcome the ineffectual methods of the traditional Jewish school:

[99] See chapter 3.
[100] Joshua Van Oven, *A Manual of Judaism Detailed in a Conversation Between a Rabbi and His Pupil* . . . (London, 1835), pp. viii, 25.

By exciting the spirit of inquiry in the young tyro, rousing his feeling, and appealing to his consideration; he is brought to think seriously on the subject, and to exert his utmost powers to comprehend what at first sight may appear very difficult, but which, by a gradual development, becomes more evident as the discourse proceeds. . . . The mind is attempted to be awakened, and the heart made to feel, by which means the inquiry becomes earnest, and the soul acquires a deep interest; a wide field is opened for the scientific and holy exertion of a competent teacher, a beautiful path of delight made permeable for the speculation of a piously disposed and animated scholar.[101]

Van Oven's language of "awakening," "feeling," and "animation" betray an awareness that religiosity cannot be imparted to the young student through conventional means. Surely his citation of Priestley points to the fact that he had consulted the literature of Christian educators in reassessing the needs of the Jewish school. Along with this new emphasis is a second deviation from the earlier catechisms: an emphasis on a more spiritual and romantic notion of religion. In the new formulation of Van Oven, "religion is an inward feeling of awe and veneration," and "true religion . . . may be said to affect the heart and soul, understanding and sensibility: general knowledge is a mere acquaintance with things of the world, but religious knowledge interests the feelings and regulates the actions of life."[102]

Finally, by 1835 the penetration of educational materials from German Jewry into England was obviously in full force and is quite visible in this manual. Already in the preface, Van Oven mentions the paucity of elementary Jewish texts in English, whereas "on the continent of Europe, but most particularly in Germany, much has been done in this line."[103] In the body of the text, Mendelssohnian notions of Judaism are present throughout, including his justification of the ceremonial law. And in addition to the usual inclusion of the Maimonidean principles and the decalogue, Van Oven offers his translation of a list of the 613 commandments, as distilled from the massive work of the reform Jew Moses Creizenach (1789–1842), who had compiled his own German code, informed by the notion that talmudic Judaism was a reform of biblical Judaism.[104] Clearly by 1835, the best ideas Van Oven could articulate in his new recapitulation of Jewish faith and praxis were German imports.

---

[101] Ibid., pp. xii–xiii.

[102] Ibid., p. 19.

[103] Ibid., p. xi.

[104] Moses Creitznach, *Shulchan Aruch, oder encyclopaedishe Darstellung des Mosaischen Gesetzes*, 4 vols. (Frankfort am Main, 1833–40). On this work and author, see M. Meyer, *Response to Modernity: A History of the Reform Movement in Judaism* (Oxford, 1988), pp. 119–21.

V

Having examined the impact of English Bible translations, translations of Hebrew liturgy, handbooks of customs and ceremonies, and catechisms on Anglo-Jewry, I now wish to consider the presentation of rabbinic literature in English and, specifically, the emergence of the anthology of translated samples of rabbinic writing. Recently, several scholars have given considerable attention to the place of the anthology in Jewish culture from antiquity to the present. Particularly in modern times, the essentializing, canonizing role of defining what is worthy of being read and what is not has served as an important vehicle for the reshaping of Judaism across ideological lines. Linked to this objective is the role of the anthology as a medium of transmission, preservation, and creation of tradition.[105]

England is surely the birthplace of the first rabbinic anthology in English, Hyman Hurwitz's *Hebrew Tales Selected and Translated from the Writings of the Ancient Hebrew Sages to which is prefixed an Essay on the Uninspired Literature of the Hebrews*, published in London in 1826. In fact, appearing some seventy-five years or more before the classic anthologies of the rabbis—Bialik's and Rawnitzki's *Sefer ha-Aggadah* (1908), Ginzberg's *Legends of the Jews* (1909), and Berdyczewski's *Me-Ozar ha-Aggadah* (1913)—it might be considered one of the first of its kind in any language.[106] Certainly in the Anglo-American world, it became something of a bestseller for over a hundred years. Isaac Leeser included it in his new Jewish Publication Society list of publications as the second work to be published, and it was reprinted as late as 1911, 1917, and 1927. An edition was printed in Edinburgh in 1863 and the work was even translated into German in 1828, a rare instance of the transmission of Anglo-Jewish culture into Germany in that period.[107]

Before examining more closely Hurwitz's work, it would be useful to speculate on the intellectual roots of his unusual collection. As we have seen, one of the major outcomes of the translation of Judaism on English soil was the preoccupation with the Bible as the primary font of religious inspiration. The handbooks and catechisms quite blatantly display their preference for biblical, not rabbinic, materials. The educational shift is both the result of a diminution in religious practice as well as a lack

---

[105] See most recently the double issue of *Prooftexts* on "The Anthological Imagination in Jewish Literature," 17, nos. 1–2 (1997), ed. D. Stern, especially his introduction, pp. 1–7.

[106] Cf. M. Kiel, "*Sefer ha-'aggadah*: Creating a Classic Anthology for the People by the People," *Prooftexts* 17, no. 2 (1997): 177–97.

[107] See L. Hyman, "Hyman Hurwitz: The First Anglo-Jewish Professor," *Jewish Historical Society of England Transactions* 21 (1962–67): 237. Isaac Leeser, *Jewish Miscellany*, no. 2. (Philadelphia, 1845–49).

of regard for rabbis and their traditional intellectual activity. One of the few exceptions to this tendency is David Levi's emphasis on the *mishnah* and on ancient rabbinic history, but even in his compendium, as we have mentioned, the talmudic legacy is shortchanged and history essentially replaces both the literary and judicial aspects of rabbinic civilization. In his conscious choice to promote rabbinic literature as worthy of translation, Hurwitz was clearly a pioneer, with the exception of one intellectual precursor.

I have in mind Abraham Tang and his translation of the *Ethics of the Fathers*, published more than fifty years earlier in England.[108] Hurwitz, to my knowledge, never mentions Tang, but we may rightfully consider Tang as Hurwitz's intellectual ancestor in at least two respects. As we have seen, Tang was a pioneer in the critical literary study of rabbinic literature. In his Hebrew writing, he examined both the political context of rabbinic activity but also the literary strategies the rabbis employed. In his modest way, he called for a new approach to the study of rabbinic literature, particularly in a comparative context. Despite his disdain for some of the contemporary rabbis of his day, and despite his deistic religious views, he appreciated the value of the rabbinic corpus and attempted to introduce new exegetical and historical methods to study it. Tang also initiated the process of rendering the rabbis into English. By translating the most familiar compendium of rabbinic moral maxims, he hoped to show that Judaism was consonant with a universal moral and rational faith common to all humanity. In the context of England, he was the first Jew to attempt to rehabilitate the image of rabbinic Judaism through English translation.

The general outlines of Hyman Hurwitz's pedagogic and literary career, especially his close relationship with Coleridge, have been studied by others.[109] Through the efforts of his famous friend, he succeeded in receiving the first appointment in Hebraic Studies at any European University. In his emotional inaugural address delivered at University College London in 1828, he seems to have been the first to appreciate not only the significance of university studies in Jewish civilization for Christians, but for Jews as well. Addressing the Jews in his audience, he proclaimed: "Bestow upon your sons those manifold blessings as which flow from a superior education, and prove that you know how to value the sympathy with which the founders of the University have contemplated your priva-

---

[108] On Tang and his work, see chapter 3 and Leperer, "The First Publication of *Pirkei Avot* in English," pp. 41–46. Tang's work is *The Sentences and Proverbs of the Ancient Fathers*.

[109] See Hyman, "Hyman Hurwitz," pp. 232–42; Endelman, *The Jews of Georgian England*, pp. 157–59; S. Stein, *The Beginnings of Hebrew Studies at University College, a Lecture Delivered at University College London 1 August 1951* (London, 1952).

tion."[110] Although lacking students, he designed a curriculum of Jewish studies informed by a rich appreciation of the varieties of Jewish literary creativity and the larger contexts in which they were written (fig. 20).

Prior to assuming his university professorship, Hurwitz served as principal at the Jewish academy of Highgate. During his tenure there he composed an innovative textbook in the Hebrew language, offering an eloquent justification of his new pedagogic approach and severely criticizing the manner in which Hebrew had been taught and neglected in the past. Fully appreciative of the larger English culture to which Jews had to be connected, Hurwitz lamented the archaic methods of translating the Torah not into English but into Yiddish or Spanish, so that a "boy knows no more of what he is repeating than if he were reciting so many sentences from the Zendavesta."[111] Moreover,

> it was considered a sin to learn to read English! . . . Happily for our nation, those times are no more. The condition of our people has been considerably ameliorated in every part of Europe, and no where more so, than in this country, in consequence of which, our whole system of education has experienced a revolution. We look no longer on the acquisition of the English language as a sin; but on the contrary, we look upon it, as a most necessary and indispensable part of education. To this is added, a knowledge of languages in general, such as the German, French, and Latin. Nor are the liberal arts and sciences excluded; we begin to appreciate their value and importance; and consider them as essential parts of education.[112]

Such a revolution in the expansion of the Jewish curriculum also implied a new approach toward the study of Hebrew:

> In proportion, therefore, as the sphere of our instruction has been enlarged, the time formally allotted for the acquisition of the Hebrew becomes abridged. Unless, therefore, we adopt a more judicious and expeditious method of teaching the knowledge of this important language, it must, in the course of another generation, become totally extinct: and with it must perish the very religion, which has stood the test of ages, and for which our ancestors suffered so many persecutions, and shed so many torrents of blood.[113]

While conceding the need for translation, then, Hurwitz championed the cause of Hebrew as the lifeline of Jewish survival. If indeed its disappearance were also to mark the loss of Judaism in general, the grammar he

[110] Hyman Hurwitz, *An Introductory Lecture Delivered in the University of London on Tuesday, November 11, 1828* (London, 1828), p. 31.

[111] Hurwitz, *Sefer Rishon*, pt. 1 (London, 1807), p. vii.

[112] Ibid., pp. xiii–xiv.

[113] Ibid., p. xiv.

צורת החכם מהורר חיים הורוויץ זצ"ל:

מודעי ישבעו את תמונתו.   כי בחכמת אדם תאיר שבעתים.
אוהבי מחקר יהללו עומק בינתו: לדרשי אמת ספריו המה לעינים:

Hyman Hurwitz Esq[re]
Professor of Hebrew University College London
Author of Vindicia Hebraica, Hebrew Grammar, Hymns &c &c

Died July 10th 1844, in his 74th year

London. Published March 6th 1844, by J.W. Johnson, N[o] Great Street Holborn

20. Portrait of Hyman Hurwitz, published at his death in 1844, with Hebrew epitaph.

presented was the primary avenue by which the Jewish student could revivify his attachment to his ancient legacy. Moving from the simple to the more difficult, Hurwitz introduced the novice first to short Hebrew prayers, then to reading "moral sentences" from the rabbis, to the decalogue and the Maimonidean principles of faith. In other words, Hurwitz's objective was both a Hebrew grammar (with a spirited defense of preserving the Hebrew vowel points) and a catechism, or an introduction to Jewish thought and literature, all within the covers of one volume, conveyed in this case through the original Hebrew words themselves.

Hurwitz knew too well, however, that most Jewish students would not avail themselves of his plan for Hebrew instruction. The new reality of England, for good or for bad, depended on deriving a cultural literacy through translation. He once wrote in another work: "It is well known, that by far the greater part of Christians and Jews derive their religious knowledge from the translations of sacred writings. Unable to approach the original fountain of truth, they drink of its invigorating waters by means of aqueducts; entertaining a well-founded confidence, that the translations, however they may differ from each other, or from the original, in difficult passages or in unimportant points, convey substantially, and in the main, the word of God."[114] Hurwitz was referring in this instance to biblical translations but he could also have meant translating the rabbis. While a small number of students still received instruction in the biblical text, there were considerably fewer who could approach rabbinic literature. And for most Christian students, the wisdom of the rabbis was fully unattainable. They sorely required an "aqueduct" to taste "its invigorating waters."

The *Hebrew Tales* anthologizes seventy-one moral tales taken from rabbinic aggadic literature and translates them into an elegant English. Three of the tales were translations of Coleridge himself and had been previously published in *The Friend*. Hurwitz also includes an appendix of rabbinic "aphorisms and apophthegms" and a long introductory essay "on the uninspired literature of the Hebrews." By the adjective "uninspired" Hurwitz may have had two things in mind. On the one hand, he clearly acknowledged that this literature was not part of the canon of divine revelation but assumed a lower spiritual status as postbiblical. Furthermore, "uninspired" connoted the common perception of this literature as intellectually discredited, morally objectionable, and spiritually unedifying. The challenge that Hurwitz assigned himself in this introduction was to present a positive image of the rabbis, their moral leadership, and their

---

[114] Hyman Hurwitz, *Vindiciae Hebraicae or a Defence of the Hebrew Scriptures as a Vehicle of Revealed Religion Occasioned by the Recent Strictures and Innovations of Mr. J. Bellamy* (London, 1820), pp. 12–13.

literary creativity. He could only accomplish this task by approaching this
material in a balanced and objective tone and by presenting it as literature
to be favorably compared with that of other cultures and peoples.

He acknowledges throughout that the Talmud is not "a faultless
work."[115] On the other hand, its merit "has been obscured by adver-
sity."[116] by the obscurity in which this work has languished due to the
constant oppression the "unhappy descendants of Israel" had to face.
Although since the Reformation some Christian scholars have discovered
the riches of Hebrew literature, the greater part of the Jewish people "turn
their back on the wisdom of their ancestors," while "the demon of infidelity is making strong and bold approaches on the precincts of Judaism."[117]
Part of the problem, admits Hurwitz, is the association of this literature
with the narrow parochialism of medieval and modern rabbis and their
excessive preoccupation with talmudic learning: "The unjust depreciation
of those writings may, in part, be explained as a revulsion from the opposite extreme of an undue and excessive veneration."[118]

To read the Talmud correctly, declares Hurwitz, is to read it in context.
The rabbis' dicta need to be compared with those of Aristotle; the rabbinic
notions of the divine blueprint of creation are reminiscent of Plato; a rabbinic parable about the mundane egg should be compared with the comparable Hindu myth; and the rabbi's cosmology is based on the Pythagorean system of the earth's turning on its own axis. Even the rabbinic
interest in witchcraft, demons, and devils needs to be viewed as part of a
mind-set common to the ancient world in general.[119] After interpreting a
rabbinic narrative on spirits, Hurwitz offers the following comment:

> Now, though it is far from my wish to exalt the learning of the Rabbis (and
> indeed they need it not), yet I be allowed to say, that had this beautiful allegory
> appeared in the writings of the Heathens, it would have been fondly admired.
> But because it is found in the works of the Rabbis, it is perverted and distorted,
> and brought as a proof of their belief in witchcraft and devils. But so it is; for
> all our boast of being enlightened, we are still governed by names. When Plato
> says—"that the main object of human pursuits ought to be a resembling God
> as much as possible," . . . we justly regard it as a divine truth; but when the
> Talmud expresses the same sentiments, only in different words, it is passed over
> in silence. When Esop, in answer to the question put to him by Chilo, What

[115] Hyman Hurwitz, *Hebrew Tales Selected and Translated from the Writings of the Ancient Hebrew Sages to Which Is Prefixed an Essay on the Uninspired Literature of the Hebrews* (London, 1826), p. 34.

[116] Ibid., p. 4.

[117] Ibid., pp. 11, 13.

[118] Ibid., p. 14.

[119] Ibid., pp. 22, 26, 28, 30, 33.

God was doing? said, "that he was depressing the proud, and exalting the humble,"—the reply is considered as most admirable.[120] But when a poor Rabbi says the same thing, only differently expressed, then it is treated with ridicule.[121]

Hurwitz vigorously defends rabbinic literature against the charge that its laws "militate against humanity" and are deficient in "universal charity and good will." The problem is one of bad press, of the misplaced attention the rabbis give to "the dictum of unimportant traditional ordinances, and lifeless spiritual ceremonies" instead of impressing on the minds of their students "these pious and charitable precepts." He laments the domination of "the injudicious guides of Israel's unhappy children . . . who intended to transform the whole nation into Rabbis." Instead he yearns for rabbis "like those of ancient days . . . such as Aben-Ezra, Maimonides, Abarbanel . . . who in addition to most extensive biblical and rabbinic knowledge, were well versed in the sciences, and in all the learning of the respective ages in which they lived."[122]

In the end, whatever the blame contemporary rabbis share in this predicament, the Talmud and its authors have been treated unjustly, concludes Hurwitz. He compares the rich narratives of the Talmud to "miniature paintings of the habits, manners, and modes of thinking of an ancient people at a remote period of antiquity."[123] He concludes by citing the sympathetic remark of his friend Coleridge: "I lament with Schelling (in the words of my esteemed friend), 'that the learned should have turned their backs on the Hebrew sources; and that, whilst they hope to find the key of ancient doctrine in the obscure, insolvable riddles of Egyptian hieroglyphics; whilst nothing is heard but the language and wisdom of India; the writings and traditions of the Rabbins are consigned to neglect without examination.' " And even more difficult for Hurwitz is "the general apathy amongst my own brethren."[124]

Hurwitz's project of rehabilitation in the final analysis, despite its relative success and influence, could not stem the tide of neglect and apathy on the part of both Jews and Christians toward rabbinic literature. And rabbinic literature, as Hurwitz had readily admitted, was hardly equivalent to the rewritten moral narratives he had dressed up in English translation. By comparing the rabbis with Plato, Esop, and the Hindus, he had

---

[120] Ibid., p. 81, offers the following note at this point to explain who he means: "Bayle, in his *Dictionary*, admired this answer of Esop, and thought it wonderful. But the same sentiments are to be found in the *Medrash*, though expressed in different words; and conveyed, as was usual with the Jewish writers of ancient days in the form of a story [which he then cites]."

[121] Ibid., pp. 79–81.

[122] Ibid., pp. 50–57. The last quotation is from pp. 56–57.

[123] Ibid., p. 81.

[124] Ibid., p. 82.

attempted to restore their dignity within the literate culture of English society but, in so doing, he had inevitably distorted both their message and the medium in which their reflections were conveyed, by singling out those elements common to all humanity rather than those that differentiated them from the other. In translation, the rabbis could be made to sound like Aristotle and Pythagoras, but could they still sound like rabbis with their unique idiom and cultural perspective? Hurwitz, like other cultural anthologizers in the early nineteenth century, had attempted to bring a lesser known and disregarded culture into the full light of Western civilization, by simply substituting a recreated tradition for a defamed and unappreciated one.[125] In so doing, he joined his colleagues Levi, Tang, Alexander, Van Oven, Bennett, and others, in constructing a radically new image of what they thought Judaism meant to their age. This image was so formidable and pervasive that, to the readers of their prodigious translations, the reality on which their new image was based was virtually displaced.

[125] Hurwitz's project might be profitably compared with literary anthologies of other European nations in the same period seeking to gain legitimacy through translation. See, for example, John Bowring's *Cheshian Anthology*, published in London in 1832. This was followed by Russian, Batavian, and Magyar collections of translated literary works of each culture. See V. Macura, "Culture as Translation," in Lefevere and Bassnett, *Translation, History, and Culture*, pp. 64–70.

Afterword

ONE OF THE most interesting aspects of David Levi's legacy was the trail his own publications and those relating to them left on the American continent.[1] Only seven years after its original publication in London, his exchange of letters with Joseph Priestley was published in New York in 1794 in two separate editions.[2] This appears to be the first time any serious articulation of Jewish thought and exegesis written by a contemporary Jew had appeared in any North American publication. A year later James Bicheno's response to Levi was published in Providence, Rhode Island.[3] In the same year, Richard Brothers's prophecies appeared, first in New London, Connecticut, and then in Philadelphia, together with Nathaniel Halhed's commentary.[4] Two years later, Levi's famous response to Thomas Paine was published simultaneously in London and New York editions.[5] Priestley's later publications about Judaism and the Jews emanated from his new American home in Northumberland, Pennsylvania, in 1799 and 1803.[6] The Levi-Priestley exchange was republished in two separate editions in Albany, New York, in 1824.[7]

Beyond the ubiquitous presence of Mr. Levi and his interlocutors in America, was the larger cultural impact of London's Christian writing on Jews and Judaism through a steady stream of local republications of London imprints. George Horne's commentary on Psalms appeared in Philadelphia in 1792.[8] Richard Cumberland's positive depiction of Jews on the London stage in his play *The Jew* was republished in the course of one year (1795) five times in four different American cities.[9] Even the London Society for Promoting Christianity among the Jews succeeded in printing

---

[1] I want to acknowledge the critical help Arthur Kiron offered me in thinking about the American Jewish context and in offering me bibliographical guidance.

[2] See R. Singerman, *Judaica Americana: A Bibliography of Publications to 1900*, 2 vols. (New York, Westport, Conn., and London, 1990), 1:24–25, nos. 0080, 0082.

[3] Ibid., 1:25, no. 0084.

[4] Ibid., 1:26–28, nos. 0086, 0087, 0095, 0096.

[5] The New York edition is listed in ibid., 1:32, no. 0114.

[6] Ibid., 1:35, 39, nos. 0127, 0146.

[7] Ibid., 1:90, 93, nos. 0401, 0414.

[8] Ibid., 1:22, no. 0073.

[9] Ibid., 1:27, nos. 0089–93.

their propaganda in Brooklyn in 1811;[10] the memoirs of its notorious founder, the former Jew Joseph Frey, followed a few years later and engendered many published responses.[11] Robert Lowth's lectures on Hebrew poetry and Humphrey Prideaux's historical studies also found their way into American publications.[12]

American Jewish educators at the beginning of the nineteenth century were hardly oblivious to the pedagogic and liturgical materials previously prepared for Anglo-Jewish usage. Although the first American Jewish prayer book of Joseph Pinto (1760) seems to have been produced locally,[13] the subsequent impact of David Levi's masterful liturgical translations on later American Jewish prayer books was still significant. In the 1820s a proposal appeared in New York to reprint Levi's sephardic prayer books for American subscribers. The project, however, was never implemented.[14] Isaac Leeser's six-volume edition of the Hebrew prayers, published in Philadelphia in 1837–38, was based for the most part on David Levi's work, even adapting the same six-volume format. Leeser, in his preface, openly acknowledged his great debt to Levi: "I may be asked, why I did not then make [the translation] better? To this I would reply, that our people, particularly those not conversant with the Holy Tongue, have been familiar from their infancy with the translation issued by David Levi; I therefore did not think myself at liberty to altyer it so much as to break up all connexion between the books in common use and those now offered."[15] In the preface to the 1847 edition of his prayerbook, Leeser again acknowledged his indebtedness to David Levi (fig. 21).

The first American edition of the *haggadah* of Passsover was a reprint of Levi's version, published in New York in 1837 and in a second edition in 1850.[16] The controversial catechism of S. I. Cohen that had been commissioned by the London rabbi Solomon Hirschell, translated by Joshua Van Oven, and published in a bilingual London edition in 1815 was republished in English in Richmond, Virginia, two years later.[17] When Isaac Leeser founded the first American Jewish Publication Society and inaugurated his series called *Jewish Miscellany*, he selected Hyman Hurwitz's

[10] Ibid., 1:52, no. 0209.

[11] Ibid., 1:59, no. 0245.

[12] Ibid., 1:60, nos. 0246, 0249.

[13] Ibid., 1:14, nos. 0032, 0035. See A. J. Karp, "America's Pioneer Prayerbooks," *Jewish Book Annual* 34 (1976–77): 15–16.

[14] Singerman, *Judaica Americana* 1:73, no. 0313.

[15] Isaac Lesser, *Sidur Sifte Tzadikim: The Form of Prayers According to the Custom of the Spanish and Portuguese Jews*, 6 vols. (Philadelphia, 1837–38), preface to vol. 1, p. vi. My thanks to Arthur Kiron for this reference.

[16] Singerman, *Judaica Americana* 1:135, nos. 0631 and 1129.

[17] Ibid., 1:64, no. 0271, and 1:82, no. 0364, published in Philadelphia in the 1820s.

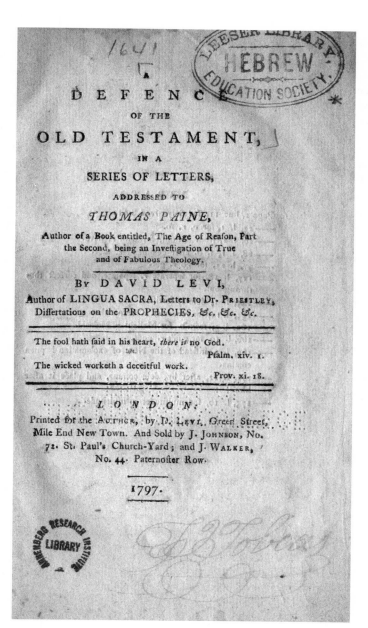

A DEFENCE

OF THE

OLD TESTAMENT,

IN A

SERIES OF LETTERS,

ADDRESSED TO

THOMAS PAINE,

Author of a Book entitled, The Age of Reafon, Part
the Second, being an Inveftigation of True
and of Fabulous Theology.

BY DAVID LEVI,

Author of LINGUA SACRA, Letters to Dr. PRIESTLEY,
Differtations on the PROPHECIES, &c. &c. &c.

The fool hath faid in his heart, *there is* no God.
Pfalm. xiv. 1.
The wicked worketh a deceitful work.
Prov. xi. 18.

LONDON:

Printed for the Author, by D. Levi, Green Street,
Mile End New Town. And Sold by J. JOHNSON, No.
72. St. Paul's Church-Yard; and J. WALKER,
No. 44. Paternofter Row.

1797.

21. Title page of David Levi's *Published Letters Defending the Old Testament Addressed to Thomas Paine,* London, 1797. The library seal indicates that this copy was in the library of Isaac Leeser of Philadelphia, the prominent American Jewish educator.

Hebrew Tales as the second work to be published. Hurwitz's anthology was first issued in Philadelphia in 1845, republished the same year in Boston and again in New York in 1847.[18] In contrast, the influence of Anglo-Jewish scholarship on Leeser's monumental translation of the Hebrew Bible of 1853 was minimal, primarily because Levi and his colleagues aspired to but never succeeded in carrying out what the tireless Leeser finally accomplished.[19]

Undoubtedly, many other examples could be offered to demonstrate the obvious linkages between Anglo-Jewish and American Jewish cultural life from the late eighteenth through the first half of the nineteenth century. One additional dimension of early American Jewry that seems to parallel closely its Anglo-Jewish counterpart is the conspicuous presence of Jews in the early years of American Freemasonry.[20] This topic, as well as the larger relationship between the two communities and their respective cultural profiles, requires a more comprehensive examination than the cursory survey I have offered. But this task is both beyond the scope of this book and beyond my own competence.

Nevertheless, it would be safe to say, based even on this limited sampling, that the Jewish cultural ambience shaped on English soil at the end of the eighteenth century left a significant mark on that of North American Jews as well. Despite the attempt by some rabbis and communal leaders such as David Einhorn or Bernhard Felsenthal to assert a German linguistic hegemony over nineteenth-century American Jewish culture and society, their efforts were doomed to failure as their laity insisted on English usage in Jewish schools and synagogues.[21] In a community where rabbis played a relatively diminished role in shaping Jewish communal priorities, where the intellectual legacy of European Jews (their textual study and theological reflection) was hardly meaningful for most Jews, and where the Jewish laity was asserting its right to adapt the tradition as it saw fit, the American Jewish community looked more and more like its English counterpart than its German one. Hasia Diner's observation

---

[18] Ibid., 1:183, 195, nos. 0896, 0897, 0973. See also S. Grayzel, "The First American Jewish Publication Society," *Jewish Book Annual* 3 (1944): 43–44.

[19] See L. Sussman, "Another Look at Isaac Lesser and the First Jewish Translations of the Bible in the United States," *Modern Judaism* 5 (1985): 159–90, and his *Isaac Lesser and the Making of American Judaism* (Detroit, 1995).

[20] See S. D. Temkin's brief summary in *Encyclopedia Judaica* 7 (Jerusalem, 1971): 124; S. Oppenheim, "The Jews and Masonry in the United States before 1810," *Proceedings of the American Jewish Historical Society* 19 (1910): 1–94, and A. M. Friedenberg, "A List of Jews Who Were Grand Masters of Masons in Various States of This Country," in the same volume, pp. 95–100; H. R. Diner, *A Time for Gathering: The Second Migration, 1820–1880* (Baltimore and London, 1992), pp. 160–62; and Bullock, *Revolutionary Brotherhood.*

[21] Diner, *A Time for Gathering*, pp. 219–23.

on the language of nineteenth-century American Jews equally applies to English Jews as well, as we have seen: "From Europe's linguistic cross-roads, where multiple languages existed side by side, Jewish immigrants came to a nation committed to a single language. In their everyday lives, Jews picked up English, broken though it may have been, out of necessity."[22] This common linguistic predicament in which both English and American Jews found themselves ultimately strengthened the intimacy and kinship between their two cultures.

What I am suggesting, ultimately, is that historians pay more attention to the impact of the Anglo-Jewish paradigm, of being Jewish in an English key, on the fashioning of a an American Jewish culture. With the recent revisionism regarding the inaccurate notion of a definitive German epoch in American Jewish culture, its previously supposed monolithic nature, and its alleged dominance of Jewish communal life,[23] a rethinking of the Anglo-Jewish connection seems called for. I refer not merely to the amount or frequency of Anglo-Jewish materials published in America or the impact of individual thinkers or ideas. I point to a much broader basis for comparing the two communities and weighing the ultimate significance of the Anglo-Jewish experience for English-speaking Jews on both sides of the Atlantic. Topics worth pursuing might include the strategies by which both communities struggled to define and adjust their Jewish identities within an English linguistic field; the means by which they presented and disseminated Jewish information and values to their Jewish constituencies; the ways in which they presented themselves to non-Jews and asserted their place within the larger public spaces of English and American cultures; their common political agendas, aesthetic tastes, and especially their common collective psychology of feeling relatively adjusted and comfortable with their social and political surroundings, less defensive and socially repressed than other European Jews, and ultimately willing to identify more openly with the larger societies in which they lived. If such a reappraisal is indeed undertaken, the ultimate significance for modern Jewish history of the unique English circle of Jewish thinkers, educators, and publicists treated in this book might be more fully appreciated.

---

[22] Ibid., p. 219.

[23] This is a major theme of Diner's work and see the bibliography she cites for earlier treatments of the so-called "German" period of American Jewish history.

Moses Mendelssohn through Anglo-Jewish Eyes

I HAVE ARGUED throughout this study that the literary and intellectual output of Anglo-Jewish thinkers, at least through the eighteenth-century, was the result of their primary encounter with the cultural and religious stimuli of their own English surroundings. While it is easy to point to isolated examples of contacts between English and German Jews, German Jewish cultural influence on Anglo-Jewry was initially sporadic and minimal. Only in the early years of the nineteenth century did the echoes of the German *Haskalah* reach England, and only by the third decade of that century were Anglo-Jewish educators and thinkers fully cognizant of German intellectual trends and utilizing German-authored textbooks with some regularity.

I would like to strengthen my point about the relative autonomy of Anglo-Jewish culture until the turn of the century by considering the image of Moses Mendelssohn in England from about 1780 until 1825. I do not intend to present here a full inventory of Mendelssohnia in England both during and after his lifetime. The basic signposts of the gradual dissemination of his ideas in England have been collected before.[1] One need only recall the most important: the English publication of Lessing's *Nathan the Wise* in 1781; Count Mirabeau's French publication in London of his *Sur Moses Mendelssohn, sur la réforme politique des Juifs* in 1787; the English appearance of the *Phaedon* in 1789; Isaac D'Israeli's "A Biographical Sketch of the Jewish Socrates," published in 1798; Moses Samuel's *Memoirs of Moses Mendelssohn* of 1825; and finally the publication of the English version of *Jerusalem* in two volumes in 1828.

I offer here a brief discussion of a previously unstudied "sighting" of Mendelssohn by a Jewish thinker I consider essentially English-trained and whom I have mentioned several times above. Written around 1780, long before Mendelssohn was well known outside of Berlin, it offers a relatively unflattering portrait of the philosopher and his ideas, reflecting quite accurately, I would argue, the considerable cultural and intellectual distance separating English and German Jewries in this period. By way of contrast, I close with a brief discussion of two more familiar adulatory

---

[1] See the unsigned article, "Moses Mendelssohn, One Hundred-and-Fifty Years Ago: The 'German Socrates' and England," *Jewish Chronicle*, January 10, 1936, p. 24, from which I draw the brief list that follows.

portraits of Mendelssohn some twenty and forty-five years later: the aforementioned "Biographical Sketch" of 1898, written by Isaac D'Israeli, and the ovation of Moses Samuel published in 1825.

Mordechai Gumpel Schnaber Levison (1741–97),[2] strictly speaking, was not solely an English thinker. He was born in Germany and, after a significant sojourn in London and in Sweden, eventually returned to his homeland where he practiced medicine until his death. In fact, Michael Graetz, in his recent treatment of the German *Haskalah*, has identified him as one of its participants.[3] While acknowledging the complexity of Levison's thought and the multiple intellectual environments that nourished him, I would still argue vigorously that his primary intellectual debts were English and that the bulk of his most significant work was produced either during or immediately after his highly stimulating encounter with Great Britain. This is not merely my own subjective impression; it is a sentiment Levison himself acknowledged both through the citation of his sources and in his constant references to this most formative period of his intellectual life.

In an earlier study of Levinson, I sought to understand Levison's thought as reflected in his two major tomes: the *Ma'amar ha-Torah ve-ha-Hokhmah* (Essay on the Torah and wisdom), published in London in 1771, and his later *Shelosh Esrei Yesodei ha-Torah* (The thirteen principles of the Torah), probably published in Altona in 1792 but written much earlier. I neglected to consider a third work by him of equal importance, his commentary on *Kohelet* (Ecclesiastes) entitled *Tokhahat Megillah* (A reproof on the scroll," a play of words based on Proverbs 27:5), published in Hamburg in 1784, but also composed earlier, at least around the time of his departure from England around 1780.

Levison composed his commentary after acquiring Moses Mendelssohn's recent commentary on the same biblical book. Clearly dissatisfied with the German sage's understanding of *Kohelet*, he decided to compose his own. Levison also had read Mendelssohn's *Phaedon*, on the subject of the immortality of the soul, and was more impressed by its execution. In his *Shelosh Esrei Yesodei ha-Torah*, Levison devoted a chapter to immortality in which he drew heavily from Mendelssohn's German work, although not without criticizing it.[4] This chapter too makes its way into Levison's commentary, providing then an extended reaction to both Men-

---

[2] On Levison, see Ruderman, *Jewish Thought and Scientific Discovery*, pp. 332–68, (where earlier studies are mentioned); H. M. Graupe, "Mordechai Shnaber-Levison: The Life, Works, and Thought of a Haskalah Outsider," *Leo Baeck Institute Year Book* 41 (1996): 3–20. Also see chapters 3 and 5.

[3] Graetz, "The Jewish Enlightenment," 303.

[4] Levison, *Shelosh Esrei Yesodei ha-Torah*, pp. 95v–99v.

delssohn's early German and Hebrew writing.[5] Only recently, through the
kindness of Dr. Shlomo Sprecher of Brooklyn, New York, who recently
republished several of Levison's Hebrew writings, I have acquired a copy
of the original text of Mendelsson's commentary owned by Levison with
his extensive handwritten notes from beginning to end.[6] If there still remains any doubt about the critical impact of Levison's English education
on him, these notes, written in Hebrew and in English, including English
translations of several biblical verses, suggest how natural it was for him,
at least in this instance, to think and express himself in English. To my
mind, Levison's animadversions on Mendelssohn's works, especially the
Hebrew commentary, constitute a remarkable example of the early dialogue between the two communities of thinkers, and provide a vantage
point for pointing to some of the idiosyncratic differences between these
two prominent men but, more important, to some of the differences in
the intellectual ambiences that nurtured them in the first place (fig. 22).

Levison's dedication page sets the tone for the entire volume. He writes:
"When I heard when I was in London during the past six years that there
was a scholar in the capital of Berlin who had written a commentary on
this pleasant book [Kohelet], I hurried to acquire it to see what he had
done with it. His words did not sit well with me and I saw the need to
compose a good commentary a second time with God's beneficent assistance." Levison added that he consulted no other commentary other than
that of Mendelssohn (whom he never mentions by name) and that he
wrote it in fleeting moments "when I was traveling from place to place
and from city to city and on a ship at sea." In striking contrast to the
simple manner in which he introduced Mendelssohn, he immodestly presents himself as a member "of the community of physicians and doctor
of the hospital of the Duke of Portland [the position he had attained in
London through the good services of his teacher Dr. John Hunter] and
Professor [so designated by the monarch] to the King of Sweden Gustaf
III," to whom the volume is dedicated.[7]

Before considering what displeased him about Mendelssohn's commentary, it might be useful to compare his more generous presentation of
Mendelssohn in his chapter on immortality. In this case, he acknowledges
his indebtedness to the *Phaedon*, which represents for him an excellent
digest of old and new opinions on the immortality of the soul, "collected
by the renowned sage whose rabbinical name is our teacher and rabbi,

[5] Levison, *Tokhaḥat Megillah*, pp. 22r–27r.

[6] See S. Sprecher, ed., *Mivḥar Kitvei Moreinu ha-Rav Mordechai Gumpel Schnaber Ha-
Levi Levison* (Brooklyn, New York, 1995), who prints the first page of Mendelssohn's commentary with Levison's notes toward the back of the volume (there is no pagination in this
section).

[7] Levison, *Tokhaḥat Megillah*, p. 1r.

קהלת י"ב

בְּמִשְׁפָּט עַל כָּל נֶעְלָם אִם טוֹב וְאִם רָע ׃

סוֹף דָּבָר הַכֹּל נִשְׁמָע אֶת הָאֱלֹהִים יְרָא וְאֶת מִצְוֹתָיו שְׁמוֹר כִּי זֶה כָּל הָאָדָם ׃

בֵּאוּר הַטְּעָמִים

שהאמתיות שנחכמם הזאת תהיינה קשורות בו • זו ב"ע"פ דרכי
ההקש המופתי • וכאדר פרטיו שהמושכלות הראשונות תונקנם
תחלץ • ואחריהן הבנבות התולדות המאתהלעלנת מהן • עז הן
דברי אמת • שלא יוכל אדם לערער עליו כיון שבא מופת מוסף
על כל דבר אמת • אבל לא מצא ספר כזה : רק (יא) דברי
חכמים היו בימין מפוזרים בזה • אפד הכס • ואפד הכנה • כמו
סדרכותבתשאין בכל תלמד הנקרר רק דרכון אחד להישיר בס"ק
לדרך י"לע • ואם ימצא ספר מקבץ אלה ההנכ"ת • הן לכד •
במסמרות נטועים יתד ותד במקום נאמן • ואין להיהדות קשור
זה בזה"פ מופת • לעוד שעהם נטועים כי אם כהעלים
(ותיבת בעלי סוף על משקל עלי זית ועלי עץ שמן וגו' •
נקמי"ח"ט) אשר לאהשונות התכ"תב• כמו בגלה סתריס • כי
באשר מקור חכמת התוזבר כתתא בחכמת הנכם • ולא אבנ החכמים
בימים ההם לגלות חכמת האלהות נהמון • כי כבוד אלהיס הסתר
דבר • ע"כ לא כתבום כי אם לעצמם למזכרת • ומסיים שמבל
מקום כלם כתבנו מרועה (לפורצ"ין) אפד • מהוא השם כ"ה
דיהיב חוכמתא לחכימין • והרי זה מ"פה שהאמתיות האלה כלנס
ואקורדות וקשורות זו כזו • כשם שמקורס אפד פתחי ( )

סוֹף דָּבָר הַכֹּל נִשְׁמָע אֶת הָאֱלֹהִים יְרָא וְגו' ׃

נִשְׁלַם

עַל יְדֵי הַפּוֹעֵל הָעוֹסֵק בִּמְלֶאכֶת הַקּוֹדֶשׁ בָּאֱמוּנָה הוֹעֵצִיר
אלקנה מאיר בן מהו' בצלאל מזאלקווא ולע"ע פה ברלין
ידי הפועל סענוסק במלאכת הקודס באמונה הצעיר הנכמ' יהודה
ליב כן מהו' זאב וואלף זצ"ל מק"ק ברלין ׃

עַל יְדֵי הַפּוֹעֵל הָעוֹסֵק בִּמְלֶאכֶת הַקּוֹדֶשׁ בָּאֱמוּנָה הַדָּרוּקֵר
משה בן מהו' יהודה ליב מזאלקווא • ולע"ע פה ברלין
ידי הפועל סעוסק במלאכת הקוד באמונה הדרוקר קיוון בן
כהד"ר קרדכי זצ"ל מזולקווא • ולע"ע ק"ק ברלין ׃

22a. The last page of Mordechai Schnaber Levison's personal copy of
Moses Mendelssohn's commentary on *Kohelet*, published in Berlin in
1770.

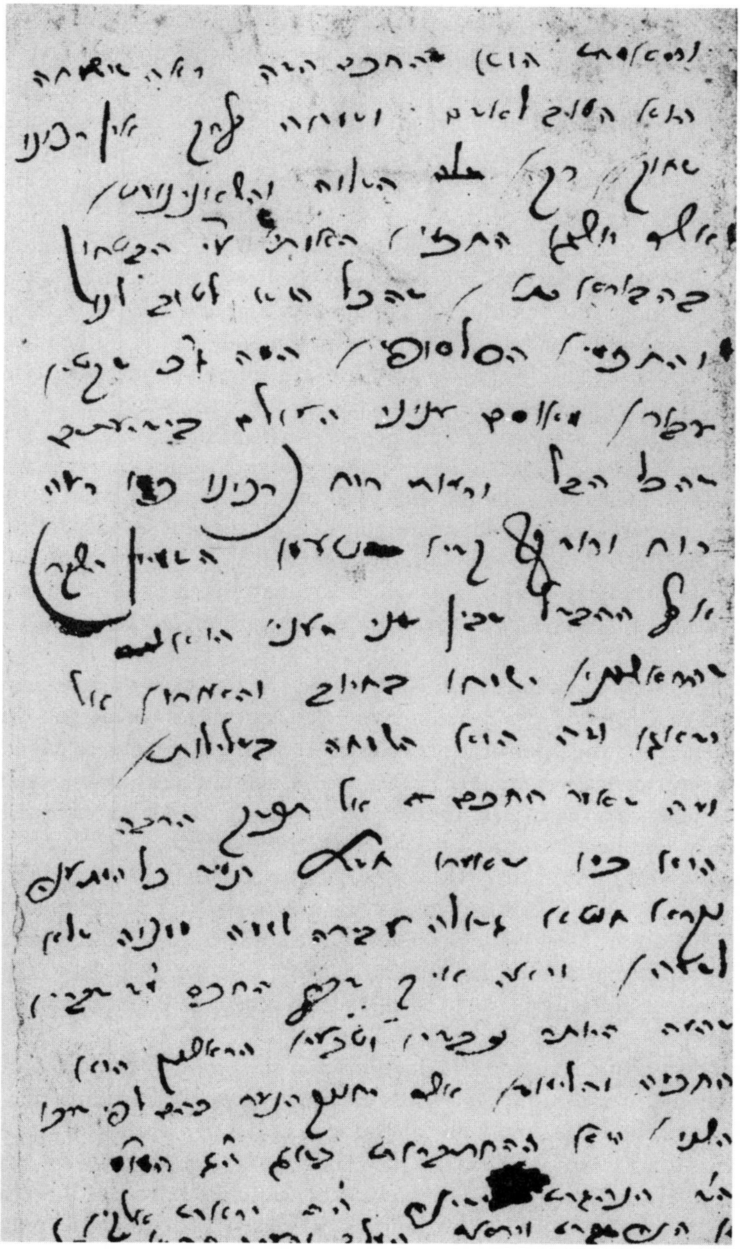

22b. Levison's handwritten notes on the same page.

Rabbi Moses of Dessau in his book on the immortality of the soul called the *Phaedon* which he translated from the Greek into German [*sic*]." Levison claims that his own summary of the first two dialogues amply describe the book, although he has purposely omitted the third dialogue, to which we shall return. The only difference from Mendelssohn's own version of the first two sections and Levison's synopsis is that "you shall find there more expansive words, flowery and pleasant language, eloquence, a pleasant honeycomb [cf. Proverbs 16:24] for his speech is endowed with grace [cf. Psalm 45:3] since this scholar is the head of those who speak in a clear language in German."[8] This second presentation of Mendelssohn is more complimentary than the first, which merely had identified him as a scholar from Berlin. In this instance, the emphasis is on his eloquence and clarity of presentation in the German language. Whether Levison's obvious restraint is motivated by professional jealousy or simply a lack of appreciation for Mendelssohn's heroic image within German Jewry is hard to say. Levison's acquaintance with the philosopher's work came at a relatively early stage of Mendelssohn's career and his impact for a Jew in far off England was clearly limited. Mendelssohn was no more or less than a scholar from Berlin who wrote well in German and summarized (or translated) well; he was therefore not above serious criticism of his work.

Mendelssohn's commentary, as David Sorkin has recently written, was finished in 1768 and published a year later. Its central themes on divine providence and the immortality of the soul are clearly related to Mendelssohn's treatment of them in the *Phaedon*, which had been published two years earlier. The commentary, written to traditional Hebrew readers, generally emphasizes practical rather than theoretical knowledge. For Mendelssohn, immortality was a cardinal principle of Judaism and *Kohelet* was a foundational text in establishing a basis for morality and divine retribution. Mendelssohn believed the soul was a simple, imperishable substance that defines the uniqueness of man, whose quest for perfection could only be realized through a reasoned belief in the soul's eternality.

Mendelssohn attempted to overcome the challenge of *Kohelet*'s many and seemingly contradictory voices on these issues by assuming that the book was actually a philosophical dialogue in which a variety of speakers and viewpoints can be heard. By identifying larger units of speech rather than merely focusing on the meaning of individual words, the reader could consider the conflicting opinions of the speakers before arriving at

[8] Ibid., p. 22r.

the correct view, the authentic voice of *Kohelet* fully endorsing the twin notions of providence and immortality.[9]

As Alexander Altmann and Allan Arkush have emphasized in their separate analyses of the *Phaedon* and its sources, Mendelssohn's overriding concern was to preserve the traditional notion of immortality against the assaults of the French materialists of the eighteenth century. Clearly acknowledging his debt to Leibniz, Wolff, Baumgarten, and Reimarus, among others, Mendelssohn attempted to present a wholly rational proof of immortality, emphasizing especially that the wise fulfillment of God's aims in creating the world requires the need for an afterlife in which rational beings could continue to perfect themselves and carry out fully their Creator's design. As Mendelssohn fully acknowledged, he had put his contemporary argument in the mouth of Socrates because he required a pagan to demonstrate that reason alone without recourse to revelation was sufficient to substantiate these essential notions. As Altmann points out, this exclusive reliance on reason was entirely in the spirit of the Enlightenment and was critical for him in deflecting the arguments of the sophists (read: materialists) of the eighteenth century.[10]

What most irked Levison about Mendelssohn's commentary was precisely this point and the implication that Mendelssohn's rational proofs of immortality were in fact synonymous with the actual position of *Kohelet*. What seems to be at the heart of his passionate attack on Mendelssohn, as I would explain it, is the essential difference between Locke's understanding of the relation between faith and reason, as adopted by Levison, and that of Leibniz and Wolfe, as adopted by Mendelssohn. Levison's discomfort at Mendelssohn's position can best be understood by consulting his carefully constructed chapters on "truth" and "faith" in his *Shelosh Esre Yesodei ha-Torah*. In these chapters, he heavily relies on Locke's *Essay Concerning Human Understanding* in adopting a sensationalist epistemology, rejecting innate ideas, and assuming that all human knowledge rests on probabilities. For Levison, again following Locke, faith is a kind of trust not contradicted by reason that emerges within the human condition, where knowledge of the entire truth is unattainable. We can investigate only what our senses and human experience allow us to know and we should "believe only what is beyond our intelligence and what the angels of God and his prophets have related."[11]

---

[9] See D. Sorkin, *Moses Mendelssohn and the Religious Enlightenment* (Berkeley and Los Angeles, 1996), pp. 33–45.

[10] Altmann, *Moses Mendelssohn*, pp. 147–58; A. Arkush, *Moses Mendelssohn and the Enlightenment* (Albany, N.Y., 1994), pp. 45–64.

[11] The quotation is from *Shelosh Esre Yesodei ha-Torah*, p. 13v. Levison's views on this are explicated in Ruderman, *Jewish Thought and Scientific Discovery*, pp. 353–57.

Levison opens his commentary with a two-pronged critique of Mendelssohn's approach: the first deals with his view of the structure of the book; the second, with the substance of what *Kohelet* was actually saying. On the first point, we recall, Mendelssohn had maintained that the book constituted a conversation between many speakers upholding differing viewpoints until the end, where the correct view was spelled out by *Kohelet* himself. Not so for Levison. *Kohelet* rather "wanders in his examination of the issue, once approving and once disapproving, since the sage will speak according to his opinion as both a scholar and thinker who believes in God." For Levison, the experimental method of the scientific laboratory is that chosen by *Kohelet*. He explores all options, considers one view and then its contradiction, articulates the virtues of each position while also viewing each's limitation. In the end, he is led to the realization that reason alone cannot offer him a definitive answer to the questions of providence and the immortality of the soul. At that point he concludes his investigation, abandons all the theories he has investigated, and accepts on faith the true tradition.[12]

This leads to Levison's second criticism. Commenting on Mendelssohn's understanding of *Kohelet* 4:1, "I saw the tears of the oppressors . . .," both in his handwritten notes in Mendelssohn's book and in the printed introduction to his own work, Levison protests Mendelssohn's understanding of *Kohelet*'s position. He was not saying, contra Mendelssohn, that because the oppressed presently suffer, there should be a reward for them in the next world. On the contrary, *Kohelet* had no intention of proving immortality or complaining about oppression. He understood that this question was beyond the capacity of any human being to know, and the only way one can attain a certain resolution of the issue is through a belief in the Torah view. In other words, what Mendelssohn presumed could be eventually proved by reason is ultimately unprovable. Immortality is only comprehensible through faith.[13]

To be sure, Levison was not fully consistent in his Lockean sensationalism and his convenient fideism. Indeed, by summarizing the first two dialogues of the *Phaedon* he considered directly rational proofs of the soul's existence and its immortality. Moreover, in suppressing the third dialogue, in which he refuted Mendelssohn's so-called argument "from the collision of duties," he appears to have violated his own warning not to argue rationally over matters not susceptible to a rational resolution. In this case, Mendelssohn had offered his own original argument that when the soul is not deemed immortal, the preservation of life becomes the exclusive concern of every person. Anyone would then have the right

[12] Levison, *Tokhahat Megillah*, p. 1r–1v.
[13] Ibid., p. 1v; compare also his statement on p. 40v.

to neglect all moral duties involving the welfare of the community in order to protect his own self. The notion of immorality is thus critical in allowing human beings to worry about a collective good greater than their own self-preservation—that is, the moral obligations of their society as a whole. For Levison, who was not alone in such criticism, the argument was weak on the grounds that even without a notion of immortality, it would still be appropriate, he maintained, to punish murderers in order to protect the public from further crimes. But Levison had already vigorously claimed that such arguments—pro or con—were beside the point. Ultimately they established nothing except their utter futility in establishing the truth, which is unattainable except through faith.[14]

Levison's other disagreements with Mendelssohn are less important but certainly fill out a portrait of a distinct style of rationality each thinker had staked out for himself. As we might expect, Levison took a more open view of the Masoretic text of the Bible, which Mendelssohn maintained was inviolable and not subject to emendations. Despite his familiarity with Raphael Baruh's English work, his sephardic friend from London who, as we have seen, publicly defended the Masoretic text against the variants published by Kennicott, Levison was willing to consider modest emendations of the biblical text.[15] In contrast to Mendelssohn's uncompromising traditionalism, Levison quietly reveals throughout his commentary his less than firm commitment to ritual law and *mizvot* in favor of a universal ethic founded on the knowledge of one God and love of all humankind[16] Levison the physician also inserts periodically his vast medical knowledge (he devotes an entire section to excoriating Jews for their excessive eating on the Sabbath and their overindulgence in meat), as well as his ecological concerns.[17] He is quick to point out Mendelssohn's error in claiming that Solomon discovered the circulation of blood; in fact, he points out, the real discoverers of circulation were Michael Servetus and William Harvey.[18]

In the end, Levison appears to accept, at least tacitly, much of Mendelssohn's conventional interpretations or passes over them without com-

[14] Ibid., p. 22r. On Mendelssohn's argument from "the collision of duties," and the criticism of it especially by Garve, see Altmann, *Moses Mendelssohn*, pp. 155–56; Arkush, *Moses Mendelssohn*, pp. 56–61.

[15] Levison, *Tokhaḥat Megillah*, p. 1b. He mentions his friendship with Raphael Baruh, who published his *Critica Sacra* in London in 1775, on p. 2b.

[16] See, for example, Levison's criticism of Mendelssohn's reading of *Kohelet* 4:17 in *Tokhaḥat Megillah*, p. 1b. Compare also his discussion in 9v–10r, and his final discussion on p. 40b where he criticizes both unbelieving rationalists and silly literalists.

[17] See ibid., pp. 10r–10v, 12v–14a, and see also Ruderman, *Jewish Thought and Scientific Discovery*, pp. 357–65.

[18] Levison, *Tokhaḥat Megillah*, pp. 36v–37v.

ment. His sharp critique is reserved primarily to the issues I have raised. Surely one could find as well a common universe of discourse in the parallel search of these two scholars to reconcile faith and reason, notwithstanding their differing styles of rational discourse. But Levison did pick a fight with the great Mendelssohn, and it emerged in no small measure because of the relative differences in their respective philosophical and scientific backgrounds and in their diverging intellectual journeys: that of Mendelssohn from Dessau to Berlin, and that of Levison from Berlin to London and Stockholm and back to Hamburg.

In July 1798, the *Monthly Magazine and British Register* published "A Biographical Sketch of the Jewish Socrates."[19] Lucian Wolf ascribed this piece to Isaac D'Israeli based on the fact that an anecdote in it reappears precisely in D'Israeli's own writings.[20] Mendelssohn is no longer a mere author who can be criticized and challenged. He has already become a cultural hero fully deserving of unreserved approbation. D'Israeli begins by expressing his esteem for the Jewish literary circle of Berlin in his day, mentioning explicitly Bloch, Herz, Gumpertz, and Maimon. But he reserves his most lavish praise for Mendelssohn: "But a sublime genius; an Israelite, who feels no degradation when associated with a Locke and a Leibnitz, was hardly expected to arise; although a Spinoza had already opened the vast career of philosophy. Such a Jew had appeared, amidst peculiar and controuling accidents of fortune. . . . By the force of his reasoning, Germany calls him the Jewish Socrates, and by the amenity of his diction, the Jewish Plato. Moses Mendelssohn is the name of this illustrious Israelite."[21]

Upon recounting the salient features of Mendelssohn's biography, including his illness and utter poverty, he continues: "Labouring in their mines of lead, it would not then have struck a sagacious observer, than the humbler copier of the reveries of the Talmudist, was one day to open a quarry of platonic marble; and to erect a graceful column of genius, which was to endure with a future age. A Hebrew writer, in his barbarous learning, was to become one of the purest models of composition to a literary nation."[22] In the course of his mentioning the literary influences

---

[19] "A Biographical Sketch of the Jewish Socrates," *Monthly Magazine and British Register* 6 (1798): 38–44 (part 2 for July–December).

[20] Wolf's identification is mentioned in the essay in the *Jewish Chronicle* for January 10, 1936, p. 24. Todd Endelman makes the important point that despite this essay in praise of Mendelssohn, D'israeli was not actually his disciple nor had he actually read the German philosopher firsthand. See Endelman, " 'A Hebrew to the End,' " p. 108. See also my earlier discussion of D'Israeli's deism in chapter 3.

[21] D'Israeli, "A Biographical Sketch," p. 39.

[22] Ibid.

upon Mendelssohn, his associates and opponents, he also inserts the following citation of Rousseau's *Emile*, transparently imparting the message that there could be more Mendelssohns if only the Jews could fully express themselves: "I ever believe that we have heard the arguments of the Jews till they are free, and have schools and universities where they may speak and dispute without risk."[23]

Moses Samuel, who is called by Todd Endelman "the most extreme . . . of Anglo-Jewish *maskilim*,"[24] published his extravagant biography of Mendelssohn in 1825, including generous selections in translation from his books and correspondence. The emphasis is clearly not on an objective close reading of his philosophical ideas, but a popular, unrestrained, and gushing exaltation of a cultural icon. I cite two selections to illustrate Samuel's prose style, one from his opening and one at the end of the work, the inevitable comparison between the German Moses and his biblical precursor. Here is Samuel's initial effort at mythmaking:

> But when we see an individual excel in various sciences, who is the offspring of humble and indigent parents, born in an obscure town, amongst a scanty and poor community;—when we see him soar, eagle-like, to the grand luminary of science and knowledge, nothing appalled, though living in an age that had but just begun to emerge from the mist of bigotry and prejudice, in which so many of its predecessors had been enveloped: when we discover an eloquent writer, a great philosopher, amongst a people deteriorated and paralyzed by ill treatment and oppression; amongst a people cruelly neglected and impolitically excluded from the emporiums of polite learning and useful knowledge:—when we consider that this individual left his native home, a solitary wanderer, unpatronized, unrecommended, without money, decent clothing, or expectation, without anything on earth, indeed, but a firm reliance on Providence: . . . we shall find ample cause for wonder and admiration. And if it appears that this individual had moreover to struggle through life against some of the bitterest opposers of study and meditation, namely, a feeble constitution, pinching want, the bereavement of an only teacher, and the machinations of jealousy, and nevertheless attained to an almost unparalleled degree of perfection in every science he applied himself to, ultimately towering above all his competitors:—we may, without being thought enthusiasts, hail him as the harbinger of better days to a fallen—but not an irreclaimable—people, and of its redemption from the trammals of supineness, and the spell of superstition, in which it had so long previously been lingering; as, indeed, an admirable instrument in the hands of an all-directing Power, to pave the way for the reestablishment of this people

[23] Ibid., p. 42.

[24] Endelman, *The Jews of Georgian England*, p. 156. Having denied the existence of a *Haskalah* in England, Endelman's usage of this term seems inappropriate.

in its natural inheritance of wisdom, knowledge, and individual and national consideration."[25]

Samuel once again returns to the redemptive role of Mendelssohn, heralding the liberation of his people through knowledge, undoubtedly a commonplace in *Haskalah* literature:

> Like his prototype and namesake, Moses Mendelsohn delivered his people from the bondage of their benighted taskmasters; like him, he led them forty years through the desert of ignorance and superstition, during which he sustained them with the manna of his wisdom, bore meekly and patiently with their stubbornness and perversity, and defeated their adversaries; and like him too, he now stood on the summit of Nebo, with the noble prospect before him of the promised land of knowledge and general information, religious and moral improvement, and progressive civil and political restoration.[26]

In the course of one generation then, from the time Levison had voiced his unflattering criticisms of a "Moses of Dessau" to Samuel's overzealous eulogy to a messianic figure larger than life, Anglo-Jewry eventually fell under the spell of the German *Haskalah*. Although it remained highly unlikely that most Anglo-Jews had actually read Mendelssohn's writings or those of his disciples, through the efforts of his English panegyrists his image became firmly enshrined in their cultural consciousness.

---

[25] Moses Samuels, *Memoirs of Moses Mendelsohn the Jewish Philosopher Including the Celebrated Correspondence on the Christian Religion with J. C. Lavater, Minister of Zurich* (London, 1825), pp. vi–vii.

[26] Ibid., p. 112.

Index